PENINSULAR PREPARATION

PENINSULAR PREPARATION

THE REFORM OF THE BRITISH ARMY
1795–1809

BY

RICHARD GLOVER
M.A., Ph.D., F.R.Hist.S.

CAMBRIDGE
AT THE UNIVERSITY PRESS
1963

PUBLISHED BY
THE SYNDICS OF THE CAMBRIDGE UNIVERSITY PRESS

Bentley House, 200 Euston Road, London, N.W. 1
American Branch: 32 East 57th Street, New York 22, N.Y.
West African Office: P.O. Box 33, Ibadan, Nigeria

©

CAMBRIDGE UNIVERSITY PRESS
1963

Printed in Great Britain at the University Press, Cambridge
(Brooke Crutchley, University Printer)

CONTENTS

TO THE MEMORY OF
MY FRIENDS OF ALL RANKS IN THE
STORMONT, DUNDAS AND GLENGARRY HIGHLANDERS,
OF THE NINTH (HIGHLAND) BRIGADE
THIRD CANADIAN INFANTRY DIVISION,
WHO ARE BURIED IN NORTH–WEST EUROPE

PREFACE

THE following pages aim at describing the transformation of the weak and poor British Army of 1793 into the effective force, which could do, and did, solid work toward liberating Europe from Napoleon, when the great opportunity came in the years 1809–14. It covers the army's constitution, which was complicated indeed, equipment, training, discipline, promotion and manpower, with an appendix on the subject of feeding and supplying armies in the field. I have not attempted to tackle the subject of medical services, because I doubt if any layman can. The history of army medicine needs a professional author, who is able to diagnose what real disease is meant by some vague or obsolete name (such as 'sore legs' or 'ophthalmia') and knows both what treatment wounds or disease actually require, and what treatment doctors in the reign of George III supposed them to require. Only a man so equipped can usefully weigh and comment upon the medical arrangements which cured or killed Wellington's invalided soldiers. To such a man I leave this subject.

Nobody can write on the British Army without falling heavily into the debt of the late, and great, Sir John Fortescue. I am aware, of course, that the way Sir John used his considerable powers of invective to assail the reputations of respected statesmen has gained him a name for being biased—'always down on the politicians'. He also took on more work than even he had time and energy to do well, and the partial edition of George III's letters, which he attempted late in life, damaged his own reputation. It will be seen below that I myself differ vigorously enough from some of Fortescue's opinions and judgements. Those who read Fortescue fully, however, will find that he had no special bias against politicians. Rather he had a general, and a violent, bias against the stupid incompetence which lazily or callously causes needless suffering, wastes life and squanders effort. He was not a whit more merciful to incompetent soldiers than to incompetent politicians; witness his handling of the unhappy General John Whitelocke's bungling at Buenos Aires in 1807. He was no less generous to the capable politician than to the capable soldier; witness his esteem for Castlereagh, whom he virtually 'discovered', as a great public servant, years before Sir Charles Webster published his fine study of that statesman's foreign policy; or again his balanced respect for Liverpool, whom Napier had so vigorously attacked. I must own that I have sometimes found documents which Fortescue must have read too, and which certainly influence my judgement as they apparently did not influence his; but here subjective judgement has an inevitable effect, as different men weigh things in different scales. But equally certainly, as far as I have checked his narratives of campaigns, I have found that wherever

Fortescue states a fact there is a document to support it, maddeningly inadequate as his references were. Sometimes, I think, Fortescue accepted other writers' unfavourable judgement on men, such as Sir Henry Bunbury's on Sir John Stuart, who twice held exceedingly difficult commands in the Mediterranean. On these occasions Fortescue was apt to ignore evidence in favour of the men concerned and to err from doing so. At other times he formed his own fearlessly independent judgements of men based on evidence before him. In these latter cases I suspect history may ultimately vindicate Sir John Fortescue; yet it is also these cases which have shocked those who know only, or primarily, the civilian side of the administration of such men as Pitt or Dundas.

I wish to thank Her Majesty the Queen for permission graciously granted to study the Duke of York's letters preserved at Windsor Castle; also the librarians at the Castle for their unfailing kindness and helpfulness. For the same reason my thanks are due to the librarians of the War Office library; and to the librarians of the University of Manitoba, especially those in the inter-library loan department; and not least I must thank the Canadian Social Service Research Council and the Canadian Humanities Research Council for financial assistance, without which it is so hard for a historian on the prairies to study documents that can only be found in England. The Humanities Research Council also assisted the publication of this book with funds provided by the Canada Council. Finally my thanks are due to my friend, Dr Charles Mowat, for permission to reproduce in various places in this book material I once concentrated into an article in *The Journal of Modern History*, when he was that journal's editor.

Since the text of this book was completed Alison Olson has published *The Radical Duke: Career and Correspondence of Charles Lennox, third Duke of Richmond.* As, however, the author is interested only in Richmond as a politician, and not as an administrator, she has nothing to say of the Duke's reforms at the Ordnance. Of greater interest is the announcement that the John Rylands Library has acquired the papers of John, the second Earl of Chatham. It would appear from the description of these papers that Chatham behaved at the Ordnance as he had done at the Admiralty, and had his official papers sent to his own home; and as, when he left the Admiralty, 'many hundred packets' of public correspondence 'carried into the house of the First Lord, were found there unopened,'[1] it is unlikely that the papers now available at the John Rylands Library will do much to raise Chatham's reputation. They should still be very valuable to anyone interested in the work which the Ordnance Department was supposed to do. R. G.

---

[1] William Marsden, *A Brief Memoir of the Life of William Marsden, by himself; with Notes from his Correspondence* (London, 1838), p. 115 n. As Marsden became Second Secretary of the Admiralty in 1795, he speaks with authority.

INTRODUCTION

M Y subject is the reform of the British Army during the long years
when revolutionary France overturned the peace of the world;
years which saw the middle-aged statesmen, who accepted France's
challenge in 1792–3, pass from the scene and leave the conduct of affairs
to younger men; years, too, which saw those younger men become themselves middle-aged, or more, before peace at last returned to an exhausted
Europe in 1815.

Britain was involved in all but the first half dozen months of this well-
nigh continuous strife. Her contribution to the struggle is a large historical
subject, and many aspects of it are familiar. The policies, speeches, and
negotiations of her ministers have been described by not a few hands; some
operations of her fleets have been intensely studied; the campaigns of her
armies have been written for all to read in the great work of Fortescue.
But even Fortescue could not find space for much more than a cursory
sketch of the fabric and nature of British military power. This remains an
unfamiliar topic, yet it does not deserve neglect. It is a key to understanding a good deal of history.

'I have seen the English. They are the finest troops imaginable', Turenne
had written to the minister of a youthful Louis XIV, in days when Cromwell's Britain was France's ally.[1] Just half a century later an aged
Louis XIV, who was now Britain's foe, echoed the opinion of Turenne
when he instructed another of his marshals to 'avoir une attention par-
ticulière à ce qui essuiera le premier choc des troupes anglaises'[2] (but the
advice did not prove very helpful to the marshal, who was Villeroi, setting
out hot-foot for Ramillies). One half century more passed and still
another Frenchman is found writing 'I never thought to see a single line
of infantry break through three lines of cavalry in order of battle, and
tumble them into ruin';[3] but Contades had just seen precisely that done
to his own cavalry, on the field of Minden, by six astonishing English
regiments of foot, with their peers, the three battalions of their King's
Hanoverian Guards. Again in our century the Germans have praised as
'a perfect thing apart' the British Army which opposed them in 1914;[4]

[1] Cited by H. A. L. Fisher, *History of Europe* (London, 1935), II, 657.
[2] G. M. Trevelyan, *England under Queen Anne; Ramillies and the Union with Scotland*
(London, 1934), p. 107, citing 'Pelet, VI, p. 19'.
[3] Cited by J. W. Fortescue, *History of the British Army* (London, 1899–1930), II,
504.
[4] So says Lord Moran, who quotes the phrase several times in his *Anatomy of Courage*
(London, 1945), pp. 36, 164, 195.

and they have equally praised the hardihood, the stoicism, tenacity, and morale of the British troops whom they overpowered in 1940.[1]

So through the centuries a whole succession of witnesses, mainly hostile, have borne testimony to the unsurpassed quality of the British soldier. It should have been a grim hour for revolutionary France when such a formidable fighting man was added to her foes in February 1793.

But it was not. Instead, for the first fifteen years at least of the wars that sprang from the French Revolution, the British Army was the least feared and least respected of all France's principal enemies. Given approximately equal leadership, the Austrian soldier was something more than the mere equal of the French, as he proved time and again, under Clerfait in 1795, under the Archduke Charles in 1796, under Melas in 1799–1800 at the Strura and almost at Marengo; yet again under the Archduke Charles at Caldiero in 1805, and at Aspern in 1809. The great and hard-won reputation of the Prussian remained almost untarnished till the fatal day of Jena. The Russian was dangerous indeed under Suvorov's leadership, and embarrassingly stubborn under any man's leadership. But the low repute into which the British soldier had fallen is made painfully clear by the Frenchman who in 1820 looked back to the days of his youth and wrote retrospectively that then 'To doubt the defeat of an army sent by the British ministry to any part of the continent to contend against our troops would have been imputed to disaffection'.[2]

Nor is there anything surprising about the disrespect with which the British Army was regarded in these years. In an age when the fate of nations was repeatedly decided by battle, the British Army notably failed to influence events. To contemporary British soldiers the causes of that failure were not obscure. Ten years of peace and political interference, of neglect of training, discipline, and the proper selection of officers had gone far toward rotting the British Army's capacity for war. Much of our story will tell how the damage was repaired; for repaired it was. In 1793 the army was also weak in numbers, and the chief methods of recruiting used by the government were themselves an abuse rather than a cure for a weakness. Here too reform was needed, and was in time achieved. Yet again, some military supplies were alarmingly scarce for an alarming number of years. Lastly, no army can ever give effective service to its state without sound strategic direction at the political level; and of that there was little indeed till the year 1807 was more than half gone.

---

[1] For example, General Siegfried Westphal writes of the Dunkirk campaign: 'Hardly any unwounded British allowed themselves to be taken prisoner. On the contrary it was not rare to find in captured positions dead men with two, or even more, shots in the head', *The German Army in the West*, English ed. (London, 1951), p. 83. See also the appreciation of the English soldier given in the report of the German IV Corps, August 1940, and cited by L. P. Ellis, *The War in France and Flanders* (London, 1953), p. 326.

[2] F. P. C. Dupin, *View of the History and actual State of the Military Force of Great Britain*, translated with notes, by an officer (London, 1822), II, 1–2.

So it befell that in the first years of the war the British Army was equal to little more than the task commonly and unflatteringly described as 'filching sugar islands'. In the Flanders campaigns of 1793–5 there were certainly some good British officers, and some regiments that distinguished themselves; indeed, as an example of glory snatched from defeat, by sheer fine conduct in adversity, the battle of Turcoing may perhaps rank with Fontenoy and Dunkirk in British annals. Yet the whole British record in these campaigns is still a shoddy one. On its retreat in the autumn and winter of 1794, so Jomini noted, the British Army's dirty jobs on rearguard and outpost duties were repeatedly given to their hired contingents of German mercenaries; and he charged the command with saving their native troops at the expense of foreigners. But the British did not save their own troops. To their immortal shame, the officers of the British Army lost most of their enlisted men while they saved their personal baggage;[1] and the student of the army is led to suspect that, if the British commanders gave the dirty jobs to hired mercenaries, it was because of all the troops they led these were most likely to perform them competently.

By 1800–1 the worst military defects of the British Army were made good; during those years its victories over the French in Egypt, in Jomini's words, marked 'l'époque de sa régénération'.[2] Yet these successes, in what was regarded rather as a colonial than a European theatre, did little to restore the lost prestige of British arms, even in their own land. And observe here the extraordinary conduct of the British negotiators who were making peace with Bonaparte at this time. They so little believed in the possibility of British victory ashore that they hastened to sign the preliminaries of the Treaty of Amiens without ever waiting for news of the final success in Egypt;[3] yet that success must have strengthened their hand, could they but have acted with a rather less impetuous despair.

This British belief in the incompetence of the British Army died hard. In 1807 no less a personage than an ex-minister for war declared it absurd even to think of sending British troops to fight beside those of Russia and Prussia in the campaign of Friedland.[4] Again, in 1810 a well-informed British writer, Major Charles James, could aver that the military power of Great Britain was good for nothing more damaging than commando raids, or, as he put it, 'a war of mere descent and alarm'.[5] That is a strange statement indeed to find published after Vimeiro had been won; after Soult had been routed from the Douro; after Victor and Jourdan had

---

[1] In February 1795, General Walmoden wrote the Duke of York that the English Army was 'detruite...les officers, les equipages, les trains immense, cela est rest pendant que la misère et les malades ont detruites les individus combattans'; and 33 battalions could not furnish more than 6000 effectives. W.O. Orig. Corresp.: Entry Book No. 11 in the P.R.O.
[2] H. Jomini, *Histoire critique et militaire des Guerres de la Revolution*, Bk. I, Chap. x.
[3] J. Holland Rose, *Life of Napoleon I*, 2nd ed. (London, 1902), I, 313.
[4] William Windham in *Cobbett's Parliamentary Debates*, New Series, IX (1807), 1038.
[5] Charles James, *A New and Enlarged Military Dictionary* (London, 1810), I, xxi.

I-2

been repulsed at Talavera; and when Massena was first to encounter his rebuff at Busaco and then to recoil in disaster from Torres Vedras. Stranger still, its author was a soldier; and if soldiers themselves had so little faith in their own service, it is hardly surprising that some sailors, like the great John Jervis, Lord St Vincent, regarded the army as superfluous and looked hopefully forward to some happy day when it might be abolished. A somewhat enlarged Corps of Marines would provide a very sufficient substitute, so Jervis supposed.[1]

So politician, soldier and sailor alike all viewed the British Army with, at best, a sort of frustrated diffidence, and that is a phenomenon which the military historian cannot overlook. It can hardly demand less attention from the diplomatic historian.

Broadly speaking, Britain's diplomatic history for twenty years after the outbreak of war in 1792–3 is but a dreary, and on occasion shameful, chronicle of failure. The aim of her policy was a secure peace based on the balance of power. Time and again British diplomats laboriously built alliances to win such a peace, but, till 1813, all their alliances crumbled, leaving their country to confront the great power of France single-handed. In part it may be true that these failures were due to the fickleness or incompetence of the allies or to the overwhelming strength of the enemy. Unfortunately it is also true that at least after 1793–4 the allies who abandoned England could all complain that she had in effect abandoned them; that she had never struck a single competent blow toward winning the objects which her diplomats professed to desire; that, secure behind her ocean barrier, she had stood aside, leaving her allies to bear all the toil, the bloodshed and the devastation of the actual fighting.

Unpleasant as this accusation may sound, a continental observer could give plenty of reasons for making it. He could point to the fact that in 1797, when Bonaparte had hammered the Austrians from pillar to post all across north Italy, Britain, far from racing to her ally's aid, even refused her a loan.[2] In 1799 Britain indeed attempted to support the second coalition's great effort against France with an invasion of Holland; but she did so with such a degree of ineptitude and want of preparation as virtually ensured in advance the ignominious failure that resulted in the end. In 1800, when Austria was to be knocked out again, Britain's conduct was first to make, and then most deplorably to break, a promise to assist her in Italy with 15,000 or 20,000 men.[3] In 1805 Britain did prepare

---

[1] Admiral Sir William James, *Old Oak: the Life of John Jervis, Earl of St Vincent* (London, 1950), p. 118.

[2] J. Holland Rose, *William Pitt and the Great War* (London, 1911), p. 305.

[3] I take these figures from the second edition of Holland Rose's *Life of Napoleon I*, I, 244 n. Lord Dunfermline, on the authority of Sir Ralph Abercromby's personal papers, gives merely 10,000 as the number of troops to be sent to Italy, where the Austrian commander, Melas, wished them to be used at Genoa (Dunfermline, *Memoir of Sir Ralph Abercromby: 1793–1801*, Edinburgh, 1861, pp. 219, 220 and 222). Rose, who relied on

4

a promising plan for a powerful invasion of north Germany, but she was still unready to do anything when Austerlitz, followed by the Peace of Pressburg, once more shattered the hopes of her allies. Then the advance party, which was all that had landed, re-embarked at Bremen and sailed home without having fired a shot. Again in 1807 Britain did 'nothing to help the allies in the Polish campaign except to send a few cruisers and 60,000 muskets';[1] and even so the last did not arrive until after Friedland and Tilsit had metamorphosed Russia and Prussia from friends into enemies. Yet again in 1809 Britain pledged herself to assist Austria, but her stroke at the Scheldt, which, if vigorously led, might have thrown the French badly off balance in April, or even in May, was delayed till the end of July; meanwhile Wagram, and hope deferred, had broken the spirit and resistance of the Austrians on the 6th–7th of that month. As for Wellington's victories at the Douro and Talavera, they were too remote from the Danube, as well as too late, to have any diversionary value at all.

At worst such bungles as these gave substance to the legend of 'perfidious Albion'; at best they displayed British diplomats as virtually powerless politicians in an age of nakedly ruthless power politics—men who could contribute nothing but money, and not always that. In practice a nation which could accomplish so little toward winning the aims she shared with her allies had little right to be surprised if those allies ignored and deserted her.

I have not, of course, forgotten the navy as an instrument of British power. Indeed, it might be argued that historically the Royal Navy has been the most important single British institution. Twice over in our own century millions of British landsmen, who knew the ocean only as something in which they paddled at Blackpool or Brighton, have owed the very privilege of eating their rations to a few score thousand seamen serving in the fleet. In the sixteenth century the navy saved English Protestantism by its rout of the Armada. By destroying the French fleet off La Hogue it saved English constitutional liberty in the seventeenth century. In the days of Napoleon the navy secured the island from conquest as surely as in the days of Wilhelm II and Hitler. It would be hard to overrate the value of an institution which conferred such benefits as these on any people.

Yet, when all this has been conceded, the fact remains that in the period under discussion the Royal Navy was essentially a defensive force. Its

Foreign Office papers, would seem the better authority on the number of troops promised, but Dunfermline on the number of troops actually available; and the difference is not creditable to British diplomacy.

[1] So says Rose, *Life of Napoleon I*, II, 127. The British government also dispatched a weak force with a view to garrisoning Stralsund. But it did not leave England till 1 July 1807. Meanwhile Napoleon had won his decisive battle at Friedland on 14 June, had his famous interview with Alexander 1 on 25 June, and secured a definitive treaty on 7 July. Then the British force arrived at Rügen—the wrong port—on 8 July (Fortescue, *History of the British Army*, VI, 56–9).

numerous and splendid victories might keep England unvanquished, but they still did not make France conquerable. It could convoy troops to capture French colonies or to launch invasions of the continent, but the soldiers, not the sailors, did the decisive fighting. If it swept enemy merchantmen from the ocean and preserved the seaborne trade by which England lived, the unfortunate fact remained that the enemy could live—and fight—without overseas trade. The Royal Navy's blockade might deny him colonial luxuries, compelling him to do without American cotton, to make his sugar out of beets and his coffee out of chicory, but the military power of France was not abated. In spite of the blockade, and in spite of all England's naval victories, French armies still marched as conquerors through every capital in Europe, from Naples to Berlin and from Madrid to Moscow. By its very nature mere seapower was impotent to drive those armies back across their own frontiers, to defeat them on their own soil or to occupy Paris—but these were the things that had to be done before the continent could settle down to a secure peace. Because the navy could contribute little toward them, it could add little weight to Britain's arguments in her negotiations with either her allies or her enemy. There was simply no substitute for a powerful and well-directed army.

It was therefore a happy thing that the British Army did steadily improve. Jomini's verdict that the Egyptian campaign of 1800–1 marked its regeneration, in training and discipline, has already been quoted. It became stronger in numbers too. From a mere 38,945 rank and file in 1793, it grew to 124,262 in 1795, dropped to 102,563 in 1798 but stood at 149,865 in 1801, the year of the Peace of Amiens.[1] In 1802 Addington retained a peace establishment of over 132,000 men, including gunners (out of which total 51,000 were for service in the colonies and India).[2] By 1807 the regular army's total strength had risen to 205,000,[3] to which another 22,000 men had been added by the end of January 1808.[4] 'At the end of January 1809 the regular army numbered, as nearly as can be calculated, 200,000 effective rank and file, of whom at the moment rather more than one half were abroad and rather fewer than one half at home.'[5] But in spite of this decline in the numbers of the regulars over twelve months, their striking power was if anything improved by the increased numbers and quality of various auxiliary forces raised for home defence only.

The numbers necessary for a powerful army were thus obtained. Providing it with good strategical direction, however, was another matter. No politician who really understood how to use the army had control of

---

[1] Fortescue, *History of the British Army*, IV, Appendix D, 940. These figures do not include Artillerymen or Engineers.

[2] *Ibid.* v, 168.   [3] *Ibid.* VI, 39.

[4] *Ibid.* VI, 83.   [5] *Ibid.* VII, 33.

it for any sufficient period till Castlereagh returned to the war ministry in 1807. Then it was high time for Britain to have a competent man on the job, for the job was almost desperate. Castlereagh's predecessor left him without the means to influence events before the Treaty of Tilsit marked a new stage in Napoleon's plans for the conquest of Britain.

Formerly the Emperor had placed his hope in the rowboats of the Boulogne flotilla. Now his plan was to use the fleets of all Europe to master the Royal Navy by sheer weight of numbers. In this crisis Castlereagh used the army in the east and in the west to rescue the navy from the new threat by lopping off whole contingents from the confederate armada Napoleon sought to assemble against it. As Sir Archibald Alison put it long ago, 'Within two years after the treaty of Tilsit, which seemed to put the whole naval forces of the continent at his feet, Napoleon had lost a hundred sail of the line, his two wings were completely destroyed, and all this mainly by the operations of LAND FORCES'.[1]

The process was begun in 1807 by the attack on Copenhagen, which secured twenty Danish ships of the line; this capture preserved twelve Swedish ships of the line which, with five English added, sufficed to neutralize Russia's Baltic fleet of seventeen ships of the line which were blockaded in Cronstadt. That action was followed in the next year by the invasion of Portugal, the victory of Vimeiro, and the capture at Lisbon of two Portuguese and twelve Russian ships of the line. Thereafter the British Army's support of the Spanish revolt denied Napoleon the use of twenty-four Spanish ships of the line and robbed him of five French ones which had lain in Cadiz ever since Trafalgar.[2] The keenest partisan of the Royal Navy will recognize that these operations of the army were extremely valuable in cutting down the odds against the navy and so leaving it with a job which it was equal to handling.

Such were the first fruits of the regeneration of the army and its employment by a minister who understood its use. More was to follow. In succeeding years Napoleon continued to spare no pains to develop his naval power, and English seamen still found themselves in the unenviable position of islanders opposed to a continent. In such a conflict, the islanders may outclass their opponents in naval skill, but the island can never overmatch the physical resources of the continent, by which mere skill may at last be overpowered. So Sextus Pompey came to grief in 36 B.C.; so too English statesmen feared they might fall in the second decade of the nineteenth century; and this statement should surprise none but those who are pleased to believe that at Trafalgar Nelson not only defeated a French fleet, but destroyed French capacity to make naval war as well. That belief, of course, is false. R. G. Albion has shown how

[1] *Lives of Lord Castlereagh and Sir Charles Stewart* (Edinburgh and London, 1861), I, 273.

[2] My figures are taken from Alison, *loc. cit.*

desperately hard-pressed Britain was in this period to find materials to build and repair her ships;[1] and the building of frigates of fir, instead of oak, and the misfortunes of those frigates in the War of 1812, is a familiar story. So also is the story of how that war was brought about by the pressing of American sailors to serve on man-starved British ships; nor were Americans by any means the only foreigners who were pressed to serve in the Royal Navy without regard for their nationality.[2] But France was little handicapped by lack of either material or manpower; and the fear of a day when the Royal Navy would be overwhelmed by numbers in a hopelessly one-sided combat was a real one in the best informed quarters in England. Greville has recorded this fear in the following terms:

At Antwerp the French built 19 sail of the line every year, which number they could increase to 25 sail. They had no difficulty in procuring timber which was found (though not of the best sort) in great abundance all down the Rhine. Neither had they any great obstacle to encounter in manning their vessels, although some time must necessarily have elapsed before the crews became good seamen. With such facilities in the course of a few years [Bonaparte] would have sent forth such powerful fleets, that our navy must eventually have been destroyed, since we never could have kept pace with him in building ships or equipped numbers sufficient to cope with the tremendous power he would have brought against us.—Lord Melville's information.[3]

The Lord Melville whom Greville here quotes was, of course, the second of the name, son of Pitt's old colleague, Henry Dundas. Since 1812 this younger Melville had been First Lord of the Admiralty. There it was his duty to study the odds the Royal Navy faced; he did not lack able assistants; he had command of secret service money to buy the information he needed; this report on the French fleet, which Greville picked up from him at dinner at Lord Bathurst's on 13 August 1814 is therefore not to be dismissed as mere diarist's gossip. Rather, it has the weight of a staff appreciation. Recent research supports it.[4]

[1] In chapter X, 'Trafalgar and Dry Rot' of his *Forests and Seapower* (Harvard University Press, 1926).

[2] For example, in 1812 about one-sixth of the complement of the *Warspite*, 74, was made up of foreigners. They included men from Holland, Belgium, Denmark, Sweden, Prussia, Hanover, Italy, the Azores, Minorca, Russia, Bengal, Java, Sumatra and sundry French colonies. Some were pressed; others volunteers from prison ships (Christopher Lloyd, *The Keith Papers*, III, Navy Records Society, 1955, 314, 321–3).

[3] L. Strachey and R. Fulford (eds.) *The Greville Memoirs* (London, 1938), I, p. 14.

[4] Arthur Bryant credits the Royal Navy with possessing rather more than 100 capital ships in 1812, at which date the Imperial French Fleet 'numbered seventy capital ships with fifty more building' (*Age of Elegance*, London, 1950, p. 2). So far as they go, these figures support Melville's appreciation. An apparent flaw in them is Bryant's omission of the number of ships the Royal Navy had building. The omission, however, need perhaps not be taken too seriously, because ships were useless unless they could be manned; a 74-gun line-of-battle ship needed a complement of 600; besides the battle fleet many smaller craft had to be manned, and, though captains often had to make do with less, a 36-gun frigate could use a complement of 200 or more (the number serving with Samuel Hood on the *Vestal* in March 1758 was 210); the merchant marine also, of course, needed crews; and Admiral Sir Herbert Richmond calculates the total British seafaring population in 1793 at

That being the case, it is hard to conceive of anything more dangerous to Britain than a separate peace between Napoleon and the three Eastern powers in 1813. Reason to fear such a peace was not wanting. The jubilation aroused by the winter disasters of Napoleon in 1812–13 faded fast in the early summer of 1813, as the Russians and Prussians were defeated first at Lutzen, then at Bautzen. Hostilities were then suspended by the Armistice of Pleswitz, while Austria clung to her neutrality and continued the work she had already started of seeking to arrange a peace. The situation was beginning to bear an ugly likeness to the aftermath of Friedland—all the more so because the peace proposals made contained scant mention of the interests of England.

But just then the state of affairs was transformed by a novelty unprecedented in the history of previous coalitions—namely, a resounding British victory on land, won at Vittoria on 21 June 1813. In Austria the news of that victory sent Count Stadion to rouse Metternich from his bed at night, and between them they there and then determined to enter the war and pursue it to the decisive defeat of Napoleon.[1] The same news brought the Tsar to his knees in the first Te Deum ever celebrated by the Russian Church for a foreign victory.[2] On the French side, Baron Fain recognized the 'contre-temps bien facheux' of Vittoria as 'la fatale influence' on negotiations.[3] Sixteen years later a British representative at allied headquarters in Germany, who combined the knowledge of the

no more than 'some 118,000' (*Statesmen and Seapower*, p. 173). Even allowing, then, for the use of landsmen and foreigners, one may question whether Britain could have efficiently manned very much more than 100 ships of the line. It is also pertinent to recall that Collingwood's numerical superiority in the Mediterranean, when he had one, was consistently small; and that the Admiralty could spare few or no ships of the line for the American War till the Russians came to its aid in the North Sea. On the French side Lefebvre states that Napoleon built (i.e., presumably, completed) '83 vaisseaux et 65 frégates de 1800 à 1814'; and in the latter year, after losses incurred in the *guerre de course* to which he turned in 1809, he still 'disposait de 103 vaisseaux et de 54 frégates' (*Peuples et Civilisations, XIV, Napoléon*, 4th ed., Paris, 1953, p. 321). The marked increase of 33 ships achieved between 1812 and 1814 again supports Melville's appreciation, and the accuracy of his information, too. Also in 1814, says Lefebvre, the British 'disposaient de 240 vaisseaux, plus 317 frégates et 611 batiments moins importants' (*ibid.*); but a large discount must be made here. Lefebvre's figures are reached by adding to the Royal Navy the Danish fleet, interned since 1807, and the Neapolitan, Portuguese and Turkish fleets, which were of doubtful value, and the immobilized Spanish fleet as well as the Russian fleet, which only changed sides in 1812, and the Dutch fleet which did not become available till the liberation of Holland in 1814. Accordingly, Lefebvre's overall figures for France's enemies in 1814 do not refute Melville's appreciation of the genuine danger England faced in a long-drawn single-handed war against France, though they do tend to obscure its reality. The degree of numerical superiority which French commanders thought necessary to enable them to overcome the superior skill of the British was 25 per cent (Clowes, *History of The Royal Navy*, v, 281).

[1] According to a tale which Metternich later told Wellington and whose truth S. C. B. Buckland hesitates to deny in his *Metternich and the British Government* (London, 1932), p. 525; and Wellington's victory made a perhaps still greater impression on the Austrian commander-in-chief, Schwarzenberg (*ibid.*).

[2] C. K. Webster, *The Foreign Policy of Lord Castlereagh* (London, 1921), I, p. 143.

[3] A. J. F. Fain *Manuscrit de mil huit treize, contenant le précis des événements de cette année, pour servir à l'histoire de l'Empereur Napoléon*, 3rd ed. (Paris, 1829), II, 64.

man on the spot with ample time for reflexion and the cooling of first enthusiasms, wrote: 'It was easy to see that Lord Wellington's great achievement had produced as great a change in the atmosphere of Dresden and the North as it could have effected in southern Europe'; and he added his conviction that it led to the renewal of hostilities in Germany.[1]

This, as contemporaries saw it, was the effect achieved by the reformed British Army when it turned from defence to offence. It was a very valuable service both to Britain and to Europe. The reputation the British soldier regained thereby was a most useful and timely thing too. It gave an almost unprecedented authority to Britain's diplomacy. In the modern phrase, it enabled her to 'negotiate from strength'. The results of this novelty were very possibly the prevention of a new general war in 1815 and certainly the achievement of that 'just equilibrium of power' which was the aim of Britain and on which the long peace of the nineteenth century rested. The evidence for these assertions is found in the critical negotiations carried on in the last days of 1814 and first days of 1815 at Vienna.

There, after France's defeat, the victorious allies found themselves deadlocked over the division of their spoils; Russia was demanding a lion's share of Poland, Prussia was demanding all Saxony, England and Austria were unwilling to yield to either. At a bitter meeting held on 31 December 1814, Prussia bluntly threatened war if her demands were not conceded, and with Russia's support vehemently refused to let France join the powers in the conference.[2] When the meeting was over, the British representative, who was none other than Castlereagh, the former Secretary for War and now Foreign Minister, went straight to his Austrian colleague, Metternich, and to Talleyrand, the excluded French representative. To them he proposed that famous three-power pact, which was to become known as the Secret Treaty of 3 January 1815, and which bound Britain, France and Austria to stand firm against the two intransigent northern powers. Castlereagh's draft 'was accepted without any substantial alterations by both Metternich and Talleyrand';[3] but, just for the moment, none of the three men signed that document.

The next day, the first of the new year, brought most interesting news to Vienna. Britain was no longer at war with her transatlantic enemy, the United States, because peace had been signed at Ghent on Christmas Eve. The consequences of that treaty are described in a lively letter from Edward Cooke, British Under-Secretary for Foreign Affairs, to the Prime Minister, Lord Liverpool. 'The American peace', wrote Cooke on 2 January 1815, 'has made a great sensation.' It had indeed—such a sensation

[1] Lord Londonderry, *Narrative of the War in Germany and France in 1813 and 1814* (London, 1830), pp. 81, 88.

[2] The Prussians were already 'organizing their army for the field and...employed in fortifying Dresden', as Castlereagh reported to Lord Liverpool on 1 January 1815 (C. K. Webster, *British Diplomacy, 1813–1815*, London, 1921, p. 277).

[3] Webster, *Foreign Policy of Lord Castlereagh*, I, 370.

that the Russians who only the day before had been adamant for excluding Talleyrand from the conference, now were suddenly ready to be accommodating. 'The Emperor of Russia,' continued Cooke, 'in congratulating Lord Castlereagh last night at court, said meanly he thought France should be admitted to the Conference.' Yet the admission of France, against which the Tsar had been so firm the day before, was alone enough to ensure that Russia and Prussia would be outvoted on the Saxon issue and thus to unsettle the Russian hopes in Poland. As for the Prussians, Cooke went on, they 'are very low and begin to talk of modification'.[1] Castlereagh spared no pains to bring them lower still. Just the day before he had only protested in general terms against Prussia's threats;[2] now he bluntly informed her representative that 'Great Britain would resist such menaces with her whole power and resources'.[3] He could afford to use such language now; in his own words the result of Britain's peace with America was that 'we have become more European and by Spring can have a very nice army on the Continent'.[4] On 5 January the end of the crisis was definitely announced. Prussia's soldiers had knuckled under, and her diplomats expressed their willingness to make do with less than the whole of Saxony.[5] Meanwhile—on 3 January—Britain, France and Austria had signed their secret pact.

In the resolution of this deadlock there are two things which need to be disentangled—the three-power pact on 3 January 1815 and the Anglo-American Treaty of Ghent of 24 December 1814. Diplomatic historians have made much of the three-power pact, and naturally so. It bulks large in Castlereagh's correspondence; his readiness to commit himself to it without consulting his colleagues in London speaks volumes for his great political and moral courage. News of it *may* also have leaked out to the Emperor of Russia and have been influencing him by 7 January, though his advisers had much more probably guessed at it than heard of it.[6] Yet this pact, which has attracted so much attention, was not the decisive thing. The thing that tipped the balance was the Peace of Ghent. For the

[1] Cooke to Lord Liverpool, 2 January 1815. *Supplementary Despatches, Correspondence and Memoranda of Arthur, Duke of Wellington*, edited by his son, the second Duke of Wellington (London, 1852–72), IX, 521.

[2] When he said of Prussia's stand 'that it should be competent for one power to invade another, and by force to compel a recognition which was founded upon no treaty and where no attempt had been made to disturb the invading Power' was 'a most alarming and unheard of menace' (Webster, *British Diplomacy*, p. 278).

[3] Castlereagh to Lord Liverpool, 2 January 1815 (Webster, *British Diplomacy*, p. 280).

[4] Cited by Webster, *Foreign Policy of Lord Castlereagh*, I, p. 371.

[5] Castlereagh to Lord Liverpool, 5 January 1815 (Webster, *British Diplomacy*, p. 282).

[6] On the morning of 7 January 1815, the Tsar told Castlereagh of 'reports that had reached him of an Alliance between Austria, France, Bavaria and Great Britain' (Webster, *British Diplomacy*, p. 284). But the addition of Bavaria suggests guesswork or 'fishing' rather than actual knowledge of the Secret Treaty of 3 January 1813. Some days earlier Talleyrand had been proposing alliance both to the Bavarian soldier, Marshal Wrede, and to Castlereagh (Webster, *Foreign Policy of Lord Castlereagh*, I, 367–8). The reports reaching Alexander were more probably derived from these proposals than from the real thing.

three-power pact itself remained unsigned till that peace was known; and while the pact was still both secret and void of the signatures required to give force to any contract, the mere announcement of the American peace was enough overnight to bring concession from Russia and to turn Prussia from talk of war to 'talk of modification'. Well might Castlereagh write to his Prime Minister on 5 January 1815: 'It is difficult to describe...the impression produced here by our pacification with America.'[1] Yet this sensational Treaty of Ghent brought only one difference to the long-standing taut situation at Vienna. It made it clear to everyone that the whole of the British Army's power for war could now be employed on German soil in a struggle which the Royal Navy could never have greatly influenced.[2] Once that was understood, peaceful compromise followed fast. It would be hard to find a more potent tribute than this to the value of Britain's newly regained military reputation.

This new reputation was deserved. In 1815 the British Army's discipline was good; its training first-rate; its staff most competent and well instructed; its great leader's reputation unsurpassed; and—an overlooked point of some significance—its excellent equipment included certain weapons whose devastating effects were personally known to the monarchs of Russia and Prussia, while their shortcomings and their secrets were unknown outside British circles.[3] When such an army was set free to take a hand in the division of Poland and Saxony, it was time for intransigence to cease.

Taken all round, then, the regeneration of the British Army is a historical fact of European importance, and that is the justification of the present book. Its aim is to examine the growth and the fabric of British fighting power on land. The period studied will be confined to the years 1795–1809. There are three reasons for choosing the first date. One is that the winter of 1794–5 saw the close of the first phase of Britain's long struggle against France and brutally revealed the inadequacy of her power on land. In that winter her attempt to defend the Low Countries ended in decisive defeat. After two campaigns her army was driven from the continent, and many years were to pass before it could regain a firm foothold there. Secondly, the end of 1794 marks the time at which everything that was rotten in the British Army had reached its worst—the rottenness of which defeat was but a symptom. Thirdly, the period of effective reform began when the Duke of York became Commander-in-Chief in February 1795.

Three more reasons make 1809 a natural point at which to stop. First,

[1] Webster, *British Diplomacy*, p. 283.
[2] My reasons for discounting the Royal Navy are: (*a*) neither Russia nor Prussia possessed colonies or could be crippled by commerce destruction; (*b*) Prussia had no fleet to contribute to war at sea; and (*c*) even if the American war, and Britain's blockade of American ports had continued, the Russian fleet could not have contended alone against France and Britain.
[3] Namely, Congreve's rockets; on which, see p. 73 below.

Wellington's return to Portugal in that year after Moore's eviction from Spain marks Britain's determination to resume a strategic offensive on land. The phase of preparation was thus over, and the phase of effective action had at last begun. The year 1809 is also a landmark because in it there fell from power the two men who had done most to reform the army and start it on its victorious course. Then the Duke of York resigned his command-in-chief in disgrace, and Lord Castlereagh left the war ministry with, unjustly, a better reputation for straight pistol shooting than for competence as a minister.[1]

[1] His skill with a pistol can be overrated. It was only at the second fire that he shot Canning through the thigh in their duel on Putney Heath on the morning of 21 September 1809. His greatness as a war minister has been rivalled only by Haldane's.

CHAPTER I

THE MILITARY MACHINERY OF BRITAIN

I

WHEN Sir Charles Oman told how Wellington's[1] army in Portugal in 1808 lacked transport for its artillery and commissariat, he quipped, with somewhat ponderous humour, 'Such little *contretemps* were common in the days when Frederick, Duke of York, with the occasional assistance of Mrs Mary Ann Clarke, managed the British Army'.[2] But his jest was unfortunate. It brought down upon him the thundering rebuke of Sir John Fortescue, 'Oman has manifestly forgotten that the Commander-in-Chief [i.e. York] had no control over either the Artillery or the Commissariat'.[3]

So Oman was betrayed into historical misjudgement by his failure to examine the constitution of the army whose campaigns he had set out to chronicle. His lapse is a lively warning for his followers. A pitfall which could entrap Oxford's professor of military history is one of which any historian may wisely beware; further, the nature, and the long innocuousness, of Britain's military effort against the French Revolution and Napoleon hardly become comprehensible till the extraordinary constitution of her army is understood.

Perhaps the most striking facts about Britain's military machinery at the end of the eighteenth century were, first, its sins of omission, for the number and importance of the things it failed to provide were truly remarkable; and, secondly, the utterly irrational division of authority which has already been indicated, for in any logically organized army the Commander-in-Chief would certainly have controlled such essential services as the artillery and commissariat, precisely as Oman supposed he did.

II

This same division of authority reveals the first sin of omission—total failure to provide unity of responsibility and direction. The handiest way to make that lack of unity clear is to list the various authorities which did somehow perform some military duties (though a fuller description of their functions is best left till later).

---

[1] I am aware that this man began life in 1769 as Arthur Wesley; took the name Wellesley in 1798; did not become Lord Wellington till 1810 nor a duke till 1814. Wellington, however, is the name by which he is universally known. It is also one which eliminates any possible confusion with his brother, Richard. He will therefore be called Wellington throughout this book, regardless of the date referred to.

[2] C. Oman, *A History of the Peninsular War* (Oxford, 1902–30), I, 225.

[3] *History of the British Army*, VI, p. 190.

The most imposing title connected with the army was that of the Commander-in-Chief (or 'Captain General'), but his office was vacant almost as often as not in the eighteenth century, and, when filled, it gave its holder but a limited authority over the regular cavalry and infantry alone. Soldiers in the artillery and engineers had another head—the Master General of the Ordnance. He, however, could not give his whole attention to these two branches of the nation's land forces, for he had very much more to do. He was also, in effect, a minister of supply, and yet only a partial one. He indeed dispensed weapons and ammunition, but did so to regiments which looked to their colonels for their clothing, and to a civilian Commissary General for their rations. Nor did division of authority stop there. Troop movements at home were all ordered by a civilian, the Secretary-at-War, while the movement of troops to a foreign theatre depended on the separate exertions, or otherwise, of a Transport Board. But yet again the Transport Board was not responsible for all transport. Its job was only to provide ships for moving men and *matériel* at sea. Ashore, transport was the responsibility of the same civilian Commissary General who supplied fodder and rations.

Thus the administration of the British Army was organized (if that word is not too flattering) on a principle of multiple fission. With such cumbrous machinery, and such lavish scope for interdepartmental frictions, it would have been hard to achieve competent strategy, had there been one man whose whole-time job it was to study how the army might be best and most intelligently used. But there never was such a man. For most of the eighteenth century two rival strategists competed for the services of British troops—the Secretary of State for Foreign Affairs, who was supposed to plan campaigns in Europe, and the Colonial Secretary who was supposed to plan them in the colonial areas. At last, in 1794, Pitt outwardly amalgamated these functions by creating a new Secretary of State for War who was supposed to direct all strategy. Unfortunately, however, Pitt did this only to make the new secretaryship a part-time job for the overworked Henry Dundas, and the job's part-time nature was sealed for over half a century in 1798, when it was re-united to the Colonial Office. Nor did Pitt's seemingly definite decision in fact give any real unity to the direction of the nation's war effort by land. The Foreign Minister could never be indifferent to strategy in wartime, the prestige of his office was great, and, if he was a forceful personality, no Secretary for War could resist his demand for troops for particular enterprises. So conflict continued, and was perhaps of a worse kind than before, because though the Foreign Secretary had not lost his power to influence strategy, he was now divested of responsibility for carrying it out successfully. Nor was success likely when, as too often happened, divergent views in the cabinet were resolved, not by a clear-cut choice between alternatives, but by flaccid compromise of the kind that in 1809 denied Wellington enough troops and services to exploit his opportunities in Spain, while it simultaneously provided too few to ensure success upon the Scheldt.[1]

And as if this conflict of two secretaries of state were not enough, yet a third was added to the fray. Nowadays nothing could seem much less martial than the modern Home Secretary, busy improving his gaols, reprieving his murderers, and training probation officers, but in George III's time the Home Secretary was, in a muddled sort of way, a minister for home defence as well. Under him were raised the militia and the volunteers, troops responsible for home defence alone, and, in the absence of reliable police, he also required the assistance of the regular army in maintaining public order. So, though his genius contributed nothing to an effective foreign strategy, his fears could readily hinder it. Any concentration of troops was likely to bring to his office a flood of bleating protests from justices of the peace in every district from which detachments were withdrawn, all of them pleading the difficulties of maintaining order without men; and it was hard indeed to resist a Home Secretary's claims on behalf of his justices. In particular, the training of the army's higher officers in handling large bodies of men was made almost impossible by his demands for troops to be dispersed all over the country in petty police detachments. The size, too, of any expeditionary force was determined by the number of men it was supposed could be spared from what was called 'internal defence'.[2] Likewise, the raising of the militia drained the countryside of precisely those men whom the army might otherwise have recruited to provide a striking force for overseas service.

The boast that the British constitution has a wonderful faculty for modernizing its real efficiency without altering its ancient outward forms is a familiar one. Therefore one may here pause to note how striking an example of the reverse process is found in the army in the eighteenth century. In that period unchanged outward forms covered a deplorable decline in real efficiency. When Queen Anne ruled, Marlborough had been, in effect, Foreign Minister; he had held jointly the offices of both the Commander-in-Chief and the Master General of the Ordnance; he had worked hand-in-glove with Godolphin at the Treasury; in him was centred unity of purpose, direction, and authority. Under the Georges this unity, which had made Queen Anne's England great, was replaced by the multiple fission described above, to the detriment of sound war leadership and hence to the disadvantage of the nation.

The nation's power for war was damaged still further by want of the very means to devise and carry out an intelligent strategy. For sound

[1] The reader will please mark that I say Wellington needed more 'troops *and services*'. Without a stronger commissariat to provide and move rations, he could hardly have used more troops.

[2] The phrase used by Lord Castlereagh in writing the Commander-in-Chief about the organization of an expeditionary force, or, in the language of the day, a 'Disposable Force' (Lord Londonderry, *Letters and Correspondence of Lord Castlereagh*, London, 1851, VIII, 8).

planning and the effective conduct of campaigns require accurate knowledge on a number of very particular subjects of which civilian ministers were normally, and, it is fair to say, very naturally, ignorant. Nor could the need to correct these weaknesses be readily evident to men whose whole theory of war was at once widely and popularly accepted and, in the circumstances of the time, as entirely misconceived as it was popular.

When King William and Queen Anne ruled, Whig ministers had accepted the doctrine that a nation, once committed to a war, should wage it *totis viribus*. So in their Mutiny Acts they had laid the foundation of all subsequent British military law; under that law they had raised great armies; with those armies they had done Europe great service, won themselves great glory, and burdened their nation with a great debt. Reaction to the cost of the service and the glory came with a vengeance in 1711. On 27 November of that year Swift published his brilliant Tory party pamphlet, *The Conduct of the Allies*. As Trevelyan has well said, the effect of this pamphlet 'was prodigious upon...the political world of that day', but even so he does not tell half the story.[1] By the middle of the eighteenth century (that is, after the day of Carteret and Pelham), the doctrine of a war of limited liability, as laid down in *The Conduct of the Allies*, was no longer Tory. It had been swallowed whole by the Whig party and the greatest of Swift's ἐπίγονοι was the elder Pitt, the first Earl of Chatham, himself.

Swift had argued that belligerents were of two kinds, the 'principal', for whom the war was a life-and-death affair, and the 'auxiliary' to whom it was a matter of mere convenience not to let the principal go under.[2] Pitt so fully accepted this doctrine that he sent no British troops to Germany to serve under Ferdinand of Brunswick and help guard the great Frederick's western flank till 1759; then he sent only 10,000 men; and he regarded the whole war in Germany as 'nothing more than a diversion on a grand scale'.[3] For Swift had pointed to the business advantages of colonial conquests;[4] and, true to his master, Pitt made the colonial world the scene of his main efforts. The key to his system was a naval superiority which prevented his enemies from reinforcing their colonial garrisons; Canada, Guadeloupe, Martinique, Goree and India were his prizes; and the brilliance of his success made his, and Swift's, theory of British war seem a classic doctrine from which it was heresy to depart.

The great Pitt's less warlike son was no heretic. Truly 'he had taken for his model, not Marlborough, but his own father, Chatham'.[5] Like his

---

[1] *England under Queen Anne: Peace and the Protestant Succession* (London, 1934), p. 193.
[2] *The Prose Works of Jonathan Swift*, ed. Herbert Davis (Blackwell, Oxford, 1951), VI, 8–9, 15.
[3] Fortescue, *History of the British Army*, II, 486.
[4] *Prose Works of Swift*, VI, 22–4.
[5] G. M. Trevelyan, *England in the Nineteenth Century* (London, 1933), p. 88.

father he upheld the navy and garnered colonies all over the globe, but the whole sum of his conquests failed to gain his object—peace with a France kept within reasonable bounds—for, unlike his father, he was not opposed to Louis XV. And one appreciates something of the measure of Louis XV's failure when one recalls that it did not take a Napoleon, but only a Carnot, to make France as formidable an enemy to all Europe as she had been in the days of Louis XIV and Louvois. By 1801 the English soldier, Cornwallis, had seen the analogy and had realized that, to restore a Europe in which sovereign states could live in freedom and security, Britons of his own day must 'play the game against Bonaparte that our ancestors did against Louis XIV'.[1] But, though pressure of events more than once drove Pitt to attempt desperately improvised European campaigns, no British politician of this age shows any clear sign of grasping the truth Cornwallis expressed until 1805. In that year, at any rate, Castlereagh organized for the first time a mobile and ever-ready 'Disposable Force' (or as we should say, 'Expeditionary Force') of some 40,000 men;[2] yet even in 1808 Moore could still be told, in the very language of Swift, that he was only an 'auxiliary' in the Peninsula and must look to the Spanish generals for orders.[3] So the theory of Swift died hard. While it lingered, the politicians whose minds it ruled had difficulty in regarding the army as anything more than an instrument for police work at home and overpowering the enemy's isolated garrisons abroad; and while the army's recognized offensive purposes were as petty as that, there could be no object in seeking the means for making more effective use of it. So lack of the very means of sound planning lived on too.

The first great defect of means was ignorance of geography, of the roads and canals by which an army travelled, of the resources of the land proposed as a site of operations, its supply of horses for transport, of meat and flour to feed the army's men and of fodder for its animals, of the surface of the land itself, as it affected operations. The British government was so ill equipped with sources of this geographical knowledge that it had no other repository even of maps than one apartment in the Tower of London, known somewhat elegantly as 'the Drawing Room'. There the Ordnance Department stored plans of fortifications, which ordnance troops might one day have to besiege, and not much else. Very useful for that limited tactical purpose charts of this kind might undoubtedly be, but they could afford little help in planning the broader lines of strategy.

[1] Charles Ross, *Correspondence of Charles, First Marquis Cornwallis* (London, 1869), III, p. 496.

[2] The 'Disposable Force' is discussed below, p. 32. Its mobility here mentioned lay in the fleet of transports kept ready provisioned and available to carry it overseas at any time; but, of course, it lacked land transport as British expeditions always did. On which see p. 33 below.

[3] In a memorandum dated 8 November 1808 and signed 'J. H. G.' (Gordon?) in Londonderry, *Correspondence of Castlereagh*, VII, 3.

The difficulties, too, which this geographical ignorance imposed on British commanders in the field, though strangely little noticed, seem to have been extraordinary. For example, it is recorded that on his retreat through Flanders in 1794 the Duke of York sent home an urgent appeal for all maps and military surveys, which the British archives could produce, of the country round Bois-le-duc; and though both Marlborough and Cumberland had campaigned there before him, not one was forthcoming. Again in 1805 what it was hoped would be the advance party of a powerful British invasion was sent to North Germany under General Don; and the best topographical aid the government could give that commander was thus described by Castlereagh: 'I have entrusted the messenger with a map of Hanover copied from a map belonging to His Majesty, which you will preserve with great care and return to this office after the service is over.' The need to get this precious, and apparently solitary, map laboriously hand copied from the King's library, and the direct order that it be carefully returned, are equally eloquent of the resourcelessness of Castlereagh's empty office; and what if Don's operations had required him to overstep the narrow boundaries of the electorate of Hanover? Again in 1808 Wellington earnestly hoped to meet Junot in the neighbourhood of Lisbon itself, for of that part of Portugal he had an excellent military survey (made apparently by General Sir Charles Stuart in 1799); but he had no such survey of the country around Vimeiro, where he was in fact compelled to fight.[1] In the same year—as everyone knows—Sir John Moore was ordered to advance from Portugal into Spain without information, or the means to acquire it, about routes by which artillery could or could not travel. These are sad and remarkable examples enough of want of the very means required to conduct war competently, for it is hard to conceive of any countries in which British troops might more naturally expect to serve than in Portugal, their country's oldest ally, in their own King's German territory of Hanover, or in the Flemish cockpit of Europe.

And yet there should be the less surprise over the British government's remarkable topographical ignorance of foreign lands, because it was almost equally ignorant of its own. It is an astonishing fact that, had Napoleon's army of England landed, it would have been opposed by British troops who fought in geographical blindness on most of their native soil. After all the alarms and anxieties of the invasion scares of

---

[1] My authorities for the foregoing statements are: on the Duke of York's requests for surveys of the Netherlands, Charles James, *A New and Enlarged Military Dictionary* (London, 1810), p. xxxiv n.; on Don's hand-drawn map of Hanover, Londonderry, *Correspondence of Castlereagh*, VI, 48; on the source and deficiencies of Wellington's surveys of Portugal, Lt. Col. Gurwood, *Dispatches of F. M. the Duke of Wellington*, 'new ed.' (London, 1837), IV, p. 179 (Wellington's narrative read to the Court of Inquiry, undated, but in November 1808). An exact inquiry would probably greatly increase this list of commanders handicapped by want of geographical knowledge. I mention here only the few cases on which I have stumbled while pursuing other subjects.

August and September 1779, and of 1797, the new threat of 1803 found British authorities still without any supply of dependable maps of any other counties than Sussex and Kent.[1]

Here, then, was indeed a grievous lack of knowledge, but it did not stand alone. Sound strategy also requires the most intimate possible knowledge of the enemy; of the personal qualities of his commanders in the field; of his order of battle and the capabilities of the formations which compose it; of the location of his troops, the strength of their positions and the time within which one body of men can move to support another; of his intentions and the means by which he proposes to achieve them. These, of course, are points which the enemy will most assiduously labour to cloak in secrecy. To penetrate his secrecy a body of very capable agents is needed; they must work under the direction of regular officers who have the professional knowledge needed to sift, and draw sound deductions from, information of which much may be irrelevant and some that is very relevant may be exceedingly fragmentary. But Britain had no military intelligence service.

What the lack of that service meant is sharply revealed in one stark sentence written by the Duke of York in June 1804. Then all ports on the French side of the Straits of Dover swarmed with flatboats; a splendid and most formidable enemy army was drilling daily on the cliffs of Boulogne; prospects of an invasion of England had rarely looked grimmer; on the Duke's royal shoulders lay the burden of conducting the defence, if the enemy should land. At the height of this crisis he is found writing to the Secretary of War, 'The Knowledge which I have acquired of the Enemy's Preparation being derived from His Majesty's Confidential Servants, any opinion which I offer on this Head must be subject to the correction of their more extended information'.[2] In other words, the Commander-in-Chief knows nothing of the enemy but what civilians see fit to pass on; he supplies no team of military experts, well versed in the French order of battle, to sift and interpret the whole information the cabinet receives; his decisions are based on information that is almost as certainly stale as it is confessedly incomplete; and whatever decisions he may make are liable to revision by inexpert persons. The situation was cruelly Gilbertian, and yet it was a natural enough consequence of the reforming genius of the Marquis of Rockingham and the lack of realism in succeeding ministers.

For Britain's intelligence system was regulated by an act of 1782. This act decreed that 'Sums of Money...for Foreign Secret Service...shall be issued and paid to one of his Majesty's Principal Secretaries of State or to the first Commissioner of the Admiralty'. These officials were to account for their expenditures 'within three Years' by producing 'the receipt of his

---

[1] See below, pp. 75–80.
[2] York to Lord Camden, 14 June 1804, WO/30/76 in the Public Record Office.

Majesty's Minister, Commissioner or Consul in Foreign Posts, or of any Commander in Chief or other Commander of his Majesty's Navy or Land Forces to whom the said Money shall have been sent or given'.[1] Here one marks the words '*any* Commander in Chief'; the act makes no mention of '*the* Commander in Chief'. That is to say, though the head of the navy may issue secret service money, the head of the army cannot; the only soldiers who handled this money were those holding local commands on service which required their direct use of spies. More surprising still, even 'the first Commissioner of the Admiralty' spent none of this money in peacetime; only the two secretaries of state dispensed it, and, according to Professor Cobban, only ambassadors received it. Britain's secret service on the eve of her greatest war was thus a Cyclops, designed to become useless in the moment of greatest need. In the very hour that war began, its one eye was blinded as the ambassador in the enemy country packed his bags, made his farewells, and was escorted to the frontier. One marks too how swiftly this Cyclopean secret service was blinded in one European capital after another, as French revolutionary armies swept forward in their victorious surge. The embassies of England closed in Paris in 1793, in Brussels in 1794, in The Hague by 1795, to be followed shortly by the embassy in Madrid when Spain switched sides in 1796. The shifts to which Britain thereafter turned for military intelligence were both desperate and inadequate. Indeed, British troops were actually sent against the enemy on expeditions planned with no better knowledge of the enemy than could be gained from a sailor's telescope or smugglers' gossip. Thus in 1800 a force of 15,000 men was sent to Spain on the assurance of the admiral blockading Ferrol that that post was weak and could be easily seized by a *coup-de-main*; but the troops landed, and fought an action, only to discover that the landward side of Ferrol was in fact protected by massive regular fortifications. As they had come in full confidence that nothing of the kind existed, they had neither the battering train nor covering force necessary for a siege, and could only return home after an excursion that made the British war effort look ridiculous. Smugglers' information was likely to be better than admirals', because the smuggler did actually go ashore. But smugglers could be double spies,[2] and were not above inventing tall stories which were hard to check.[3]

Such were the consequences of confiding secret service in peacetime to

---

[1] Cited by Alfred Cobban in his valuable article 'The British Secret Service in France, 1784–1792' in *The English Historical Review* (1954), pp. 232–3.

[2] Of smugglers, Sir John Moore is found writing from Sandgate on 17 February 1804, 'There is hardly a family in Folkestone which has not relatives in Flushing, and there is constant intercourse....When an attempt is made against this Country, no doubt as many of these [smugglers] as can be seized will be stopt by the Enemy and the Captains and Crews employed as Pilots', HO/50/396 in the Public Record Office. See also Christopher Lloyd, *The Keith Papers*, III (Navy Records Society, 1955), 168.

[3] Admiral Lord Keith, 10 November 1805 (Londonderry, *Correspondence of Castlereagh*, VI, p. 38).

the secretaries of state and to ambassadors. It is true, as noted, that the secretaries were empowered to depute the spending of the money to 'any Commander in Chief or other Commander of his Majesty's...Land Forces'. They did this too, but generally at a date that made it almost useless. So one finds Castlereagh empowering Lord Chatham to draw secret service money in a letter dated 16 July 1809;[1] just twelve days later Chatham was already on the coast of Holland, desperately needing all the intelligence he could get for his operations on the Scheldt; and to whom was he then to give his secret service money? The money could only begin to be useful when he had found reliable agents to bring information in return for it; and there is no more impossible job than improvising a secret service at short notice.[2]

All told, then, the assertion that Britain had no military intelligence service seems a perfectly fair one. Money aplenty might be voted for the secret service; an infinite variety of reports might flow in; but little good could come in the absence of a professional staff who would sift all reports, cross-check them, draft specific inquiries, and do their best to ensure that the secret service money did not simply enrich British and foreign rogues for inventing idle tales.

Let it be granted, however, that to penetrate a competent enemy's secrets is never easy. On some occasions there may be grounds for pardoning the British government's ignorance of its foe. It is still a true, and an extraordinary, fact that British ministers are found on occasion to have committed themselves to military adventures without knowing even the extent of their own available forces. This at least seems neither necessary nor pardonable. As examples one may cite Pitt's blindly given and never fulfilled pledge to the Austrians that the British force in Flanders in 1794 would be raised to 40,000 men;[3] or his determination to invade Holland in 1799 when he possessed no expeditionary force to launch upon the invasion.[4]

From what has been written so far, it will be clear that there was little likelihood of the British government ever planning and launching effective campaigns. There never can be, when the job is attempted by civilians without singleness of aim, competent knowledge, skilled staffs, or professional advice; and such was in fact the way in which most campaigns of our period were planned. Theoretically, of course, they should not

---

[1] Castlereagh to Lord Chatham, 16 July 1809 (*ibid.* p. 283).

[2] See, for example, the misfortunes in our own time of Field Marshal Earl Wavell. For 'appeasement' reasons he was forbidden in 1939–40 'to set up an intelligence service in Italian territory'. In North Africa he had no agents at all before Italy came into the war and it was not possible till long afterwards to plant them. So the German 5th Light Motorized Division 'was able to land in Tripoli [as late as 20 February 1941] without his knowing anything about it' (Desmond Young, *Rommel*, Fontana Books, London, 1955, pp. 22, 88). The loss of Benghazi and retreat to the Egyptian frontier followed.

[3] Fortescue, *History of the British Army*, IV, 220–1, 225.

[4] See below, p. 25.

have been. Every cabinet had in its own body one high-ranking professional soldier—the Master General of the Ordnance. In constitutional
theory he was supposed to be their military adviser.[1] But the advice of
the Masters General of our period had singularly little influence on
military operations. The Duke of Richmond, who held the office till
February 1795, was a very clear-thinking practical soldier, but he was
never of Pitt's inner circle. He did indeed invite the Premier to Goodwood,
and mount him to follow hounds (Pitt the austere politician we know
well, also Pitt the pillow-fighter, romping with small boys, and Pitt the
gallant drinking wine from a lady's shoe, but Pitt in the role of Nimrod is
surely a new creature). Yet Richmond never gained his leader's intimacy
or confidence. Strong and sound remonstrances from him went apparently unheeded, while the disastrous military policy of Dundas and
Pitt pursued its tragic way. Richmond's successor in 1795 was Lord
Cornwallis, still fairly newly returned from India with the highest reputation of any living British soldier; but Pitt paid no more attention to him
than he had paid to Richmond.

Finally, even if these soldiers had been heard with every attention, they
could not of themselves have provided all that was required for the
competent planning of war. No private individual's library could provide
the necessary maps or reports of supply conditions in various proposed
theatres of operations; nor could fresh, full, and accurate information of
the enemy's intentions and order of battle be expected without first-rate
agents constantly employed under professional military direction.

It was a further, and very grave, defect of Britain's military machine
that the army's mobility in the field was a matter left all unprepared and
virtually consigned to chance. To understand this point it is only necessary
to remember that an army of, say, 20,000 men has as many mouths to feed
as a fair-sized town; that soldiers are as liable to sickness and more liable
to injury than civilians; that soldiers, like civilians, cannot do their job
without the tools of their trade, namely, arms and ammunition. But while
cities spring up only at particular places, where all that they need can be
readily supplied, an army cannot remain static. If it is to accomplish
anything it must move, and if it is to move, it must haul with it all the
food required by its men and horses, also its hospitals, its artillery,
and the whole reserve of ammunition for horse, foot, and guns alike. All
this stuff, the hundreds of pounds of biscuit, the tons of oats and baled
hay, the scores of hospital tents, the quantities of blankets, medicines, and
surgical equipment, and the bulky mass of ammunition of all calibres,
could not travel without such a number of waggons as filled many miles
of road; the waggons needed horses to draw them; and the horses needed
drivers to conduct, groom, and feed them. Without waggons, horses, and

[1] C. M. Clode, *The Military Forces of the Crown; their Administration and Government*
(London, 1869), II, 206, 767.

drivers, an army remained immobile. The point may seem offensively obvious; it was never obvious enough to British ministries to induce them to equip their army with a waggon train fit to make it mobile. Twice, in 1794 and 1799, the Duke of York tried to create such a train. Nothing effective came of either effort. A waggon train was a very expensive item, which, happily for the taxpayers, could be dispensed with at home, and successive ministries had so little concept of the nature of real service abroad that they always presumed that civilian commissaries could hire all the waggons and teams the army needed in the theatre of war itself after the troops had landed. The disastrous waste of time that might occur while the freshly disembarked commissaries, all green to their job, tried to persuade local owners of horses and waggons to rent them to the British; the inefficiency of using hired civilian drivers, who, unlike disciplined soldiers, might very fairly resent being led into danger, and whom no Articles of War constrained to punctual obedience; these, and all other disadvantages due to the lack of a waggon train, were never clear enough to British cabinets and parliaments in our period to induce them to provide the army with the transport it needed. So the present R.A.S.C. remained unborn till 1855;[1] and no history of the Peninsular War tells the whole truth if it fails to acknowledge the debt Wellington owed to the Spanish muleteers who, faithfully and reliably, carried all his army's gear across Spain for a dollar a day that was promised, but too often not paid, to them.

Such, in broad terms, were the weaknesses of Britain's military machine. What this meant in practice becomes clear the moment one examines a concrete example of British war-making. The Helder expedition of 1799 offers as illuminating an example as any. Petty and impotent effort as it may appear in the whole picture of the Second Coalition's great uprising against France, it was still among the British Army's more notable excursions to the continent between 1795 and 1808. The troops employed made good an opposed landing, captured a fleet, fought two battles without actual disaster, and came home relatively intact; there were many expeditions that did less.

The first hint of this expedition occurs in a letter of 18 November 1798, written to George III by the Duke of York, and describing a conversation the Duke had had with Mr Pitt. Information had been received, said Pitt, that the moment was ripe for a sudden invasion of Holland; troops were to be prepared for service and, to confirm the news, 'a confidential person' was being sent over to investigate and report.[2] Here it must occur to the reader, first, that a professional soldier might naturally be the best judge of whether or not a moment was indeed ripe for a successful invasion, but the civilian Premier apparently does not ask the Field Mar-

---

[1] J. W. Fortescue, *The Royal Army Service Corps* (Cambridge, 1930), I, 155.
[2] Duke of York to George III, 18 November 1798: Windsor, 9078–9.

shal's opinion on the subject; instead, he makes an announcement to him. Secondly, a soldier might very fairly want to know what sort of 'a confidential person' was being sent to make a report on the basis of which the lives of British troops were to be hazarded; how trustworthy was he? How good his judgement? How dependable his contacts? Likewise, the soldier might most reasonably wish to put to the agent some very particular questions, and require very explicit answers to them. But it is the civilian who sends the 'confidential person'; the soldier has apparently to take his reliability for granted. Again one marks that the moment is supposed to be ripe for a stroke at Holland in November 1798, but the means for delivering that stroke are simply non-existent. Merely in order to cross the water, the troops will require shipping; but in November no ships are available; they have still to be found, hired, assembled, and provisioned, thereby giving the enemy ample warning that something is in the wind.

Yet the lack of ships to carry troops was a less grievous want than it might seem, for in November 1798 there were no British troops for them to carry. The country had no expeditionary force ready, recruiting was going badly, and so many battalions were under strength, that it was impossible to send a British force across the water till a special act of Parliament had been passed to fill up the regular army—at the very last minute—from the militia. Even so, no operations were thought possible without an arrangement to hire a couple of divisions from the Russian Army. All this took time, and only after a nine months' period of gestation did the operation conceived in November 1798 at last emerge in August 1799. By then the enemy was not surprised—a fact at which we can hardly be surprised either.

But a real surprise does await the reader of Lord Dunfermline's life of Sir Ralph Abercromby, who in due course led the first British landing. Many and long discussions before the expedition sailed took place between Dundas and Pitt on the one side and Abercromby on the other. By these the fact is revealed that the ministers assembled an expeditionary force without any concrete plan for using it. They were indeed determined that a force should sail from Britain, land somewhere and do something in Holland; but where or for what purpose it should land in Holland were questions to which they had no answer. They pressed upon Abercromby a variety of impracticable projects, none of them with any defined long-range object. Amid the confusions of the statesmen, it was at last the soldier who made the decision; and Abercromby finally selected the Helder, because he reckoned the chance of seizing the Dutch fleet an object of sufficient importance to merit the hazarding of British troops on an unlikely enterprise. But even this decision was only made after the ministers had committed themselves to hiring the two Russian divisions whom they engaged without knowing how they would use them; they let Abercromby sail without informing him that the Duke of York would follow him;[1] and by failing to provide the transport without which no army could pursue a beaten enemy, they secured the fact in advance that any victories won would be wasted.[2]

From this story of dilatory and muddled improvisation it is instructive to turn to Napoleon's correspondence for the first five months of 1800, where the preparation of the Marengo campaign is recorded. The contrast is sharp. In Napoleon's planning there are no hesitations and no oversights. It begins in February with a calculation of the number of mules required to carry eight days' rations for 50,000 men.[3] It proceeds in March to establish dumps of every kind of supply the force would need and to secure the transport to move them by the purchase or requisition of mules throughout France.[4] The whole is shrouded in an elaborate cover plan. The troops intended to cross the Alps are assembled at Dijon, where they threaten Germany far more closely than Italy; they are christened the Army of Reserve, a name which does not suggest active operations; to support the fiction embodied in this name, their concentration area is flooded with raw conscripts, wholly unfit for service; and the force assembled is placed under an officer, Berthier, who has never shown talent for command and is known only for his administrative ability. The contrast between British and French planning is matched by the difference in results. The Duke of York's army in Holland subsisted from hand to mouth and was made immobile by want of transport; French administrative arrangements were so perfect that even the unexpectedly vigorous resistance of Fort Bard caused no serious hitch. In Holland the British achieved no strategic surprise; their enemy's reaction was prompt. In Italy the strategic surprise Napoleon sprang upon the Austrians was complete.

In this comparison of French and English war-making some allowance may indeed be made for the consummate genius of Napoleon, but the point must also be marked that the months in which he prepared the Marengo campaign were likewise his first months as Consul. Then he could hardly do other than work with the machinery he had taken over from the Directory; and that machinery was adequate. The staff available provided everything the commander required and provided it in time. Security at every level was so perfect that no leak occurred anywhere to give the enemy a clue as to what was impending.

This need cause the less surprise because France had long had a war office intelligently designed for the making of war. Take the matter of information. From the days of Louvois that office had been replete with

---

[1] Dunfermline, *Memoir of Abercromby*, pp. 139–56.

[2] Fortescue, *Royal Army Service Corps*, I, pp. 55–9.

[3] 'Note pour approvisionnement de la Reserve', 18 February 1800 (*Correspondance de Napoleon I*, Tome VI, Paris, 1860, no. 4605).

[4] Napoleon to Berthier, 1 March 1800 (*Ibid.* no. 4626).

dossiers containing all the data required for setting on foot almost any campaign; indeed, a contemporary has recorded that the French descent on Ireland in 1798 merely put into practice plans prepared in 1689 and safely and conveniently filed thereafter.[1] But it need not be supposed from the venerable antiquity of the plans used on this occasion that French war ministers could only provide their fighting men with antiquated instructions. The information stored in the Depôt de la Guerre was kept up to date, we are told, by sending abroad 'intelligent officers' and 'sagacious individuals on secret and confidential missions' in peacetime.[2] One such 'sagacious individual' was no less a man than that great British-born soldier of fortune and military writer, Henry Lloyd, who in the winter of 1755–6 was sent by Louis XV's war minister to England to make a report on the ways and means of invading his native island.[3] Thanks to the work of such agents in peace, 'a marked superiority in topographical knowledge...seconded every movement of French armies'.[4] As for the French secret service in wartime, some clue to its efficiency is provided by Napoleon's letter to Berthier, 2 May 1800.[5] In that letter Napoleon already is able to describe, from reports received through more than one channel, the Austrians' wholly false appreciation of the quality and purpose of the Army of Reserve.

In all these matters that belong to the backstage of war, so to speak, French competence provides a standard by which to measure British inefficiency. Only against the background of this contrast between amateurishness on the one side and professional assurance on the other can one appreciate what a miracle of luck the Peninsular War was; luck that in Wellington there existed a commander who, to youth, rare experience and a genius that mastered every obstacle, already added in 1808 the political influence necessary to get him a job over the heads of many generals both senior and inferior to himself; luck that before he was superseded he should have time to win the decisive victory of Vimeiro, whose advantages his lately arrived seniors were to squander in a way that threw his own glory into yet more splendid relief; luck that his further victories should uphold in office the only party that would sustain his campaigns. It was also fortunate that the Peninsular revolt provided a theatre in a friendly land where British troops did not have to fight for a beach-head from which to begin their operations; where the preoccupation of the French with native insurgents gave time in which Britain's haphazard transport could be organized; where Spanish enthusiasm gladly provided the intelligence service which in other circumstances might have been so hard to improvise.

---

[1] James, *Military Dictionary* (London, 1810), p. xxxv n.   [2] *Ibid.*

[3] Henry Lloyd, *A Political and Military Rhapsody*, ed. John Drummond (London, 1790), p. xxxiv.

[4] James, *Military Dictionary*, p. xxvi n.

[5] *Correspondance de Napoléon I*, VI, no. 4747.

III

So much for the varied things that the British war machine ought to have done, but left undone; now for its component parts and the men who manipulated them.

First in importance was the Secretary of State for War and Colonies. The nature and the extraordinary difficulty of his tasks have already been indicated. To his desk came the reports and problems of the governors of every British colony—and the number of those colonies grew mightily as the war progressed. Simultaneously with the handling of all these sufficiently diversified problems, he was supposed to plan campaigns, but to do it without having authority over those on whose competence success or failure depended. He could only set a campaign on foot by exciting and co-ordinating the separate exertions of a Master General of the Ordnance, who had an independent seat in the cabinet, of a Transport Board and a Commissary General who were responsible, not to himself, but to the First Lord of the Treasury, and of a Commander-in-Chief who was responsible to the sovereign rather than to Parliament. Almost the one military task which lay solely within the authority of his office was drafting legislation for raising recruits. But even this was often taken out of his hands by the Prime Minister himself; and neither Prime Minister nor Colonial Secretary had direct access to competent knowledge of how this task might best be done. Recruits were actually gathered by regular officers working immediately under an Inspector General of Recruiting and ultimately under the Commander-in-Chief. Accordingly, the Horse Guards, not the colonial ministry, was the department with the experience best calculated to devise successful recruiting policy. It is clear, then, that the office of the Secretary of State for War and Colonies was no easy place in which to win a brilliant reputation.

The first holder of this office, from its creation in the summer of 1794 till Pitt's fall in the spring of 1801, was Henry Dundas, the future Lord Melville. He is a hard man of whom to write; his many failings as a War Minister have been castigated by Fortescue with a vigour that seems sometimes to be attributed to prejudice, and even to have created a reaction in his favour. So now some labour the point that he had an unusually good grasp of naval affairs.[1] That may be true, and the qualification is indeed a valuable one in any British minister, but it has no particular relevance to the management of an army. Others again tell us that if he and Pitt poured a deplorable amount of British blood into the conquest of pestiferous West Indian islands, they did so because they were convinced of the great economic value of those islands and believed the loss of them would ruin France.[2] Again the accuracy of the statement may be conceded; but

---

[1] Holden Furber, *Henry Dundas, First Viscount Melville* (Oxford, 1931), p. 148.

[2] G. M. Trevelyan, *England in the Nineteenth Century* (London, 1933), p. 88; H. J. Rose, *William Pitt and the Great War* (London, 1911), p. 276; Furber, *Henry Dundas*, p. 99.

it surely amounts to little more than an elaboration of the nature of the falsity of a false strategical concept. All France's colonies were in due course taken from her, yet she still went on from strength to strength over the felled bodies of Britain's allies. That Dundas had courage may be a fair deduction from the nature of some of the extraordinary military enterprises for which he was willing to make himself responsible. But he was not clear headed; 'Let me point out to you that the same messenger brought me from you, advice to besiege St Quentin; secondly, an order to keep some troops at Ostend; and thirdly, strong exhortations against division or detachment of our forces', he goaded one unfortunate general into writing him.[1] The first principle of war, 'the Selection and Maintenance of the Aim', was thus beyond his grasp. So was the principle of concentrating effort; witness his reckless dispersal of inadequate British forces on simultaneous operations in Flanders, Brittany, the West Indies, and Toulon in 1794; also his bewildering vacillations and final vagueness on the eve of the Dutch campaign of 1799, as revealed in his correspondence with Abercromby. Like Pitt, he conspicuously lacked the knowledge of the mechanics of war which distinguishes a good leader from a bad.

In Dundas's defence it may be said that he was overworked, and therefore unable to give military affairs the attention they required. Certainly, in addition to the work of the war ministry, he was simultaneously Home Secretary, Treasurer of the Navy, President of the Indian Board of Control, and also Pitt's very successful manager of the vast pocket borough that was Scotland; but it is often a man's own fault if he undertakes more work than he can do, and he may as easily be led to undertake it by greed for power, as by disinterested zeal for public service.

It is true, however, that Dundas's reputation might have easily been better had he served under any other Premier than Pitt, who knew so little of war, yet was still too powerful a personality and too ready a dialectician to be easily diverted from unpractical enterprises on which he had set his heart. For Pitt was strangely incapable of deputing work to others; in fact, one finds him actually demanding returns of levies directly from the Adjutant General in order that he may himself dispose of recruits instead of leaving it to the Commander-in-Chief;[2] or again he is found compiling lists of gunners for the siege of Dunkirk instead of asking Richmond what could be provided;[3] and from Cornwallis, the most distinguished

---

[1] Murray to Dundas, 20 October 1793; cited by Fortescue, *History of the British Army*, IV, 149. Obviously to keep troops at Ostend was to detach them from the main body. It may be less obvious that besieging St Quentin would have involved a further division of the main body into (a) the investing force and (b) the covering force. Dundas's self-contradiction could hardly have been more complete.

[2] 'I am required to communicate [returns of recruits] without delay to Mr Pitt, as they enable him to form his General Plan for the supply of Troops where wanted and for carrying on the Service in every quarter'(Fawcett to Hewett, 31 October 1794, WO/3/12 in the Public Record Office).

[3] Nepean to Richmond, 13 July 1793, HO/50/369 in the Public Record Office.

English soldier of the day and a fellow minister, he wrung the bitter complaint: 'My sentiments have been so little regarded, and I have met so much discouragement on every occasion, that I feel the greatest disinclination to offer any opinions.'[1] It is then clear that Dundas undertook a very hard task indeed when he consented to become Pitt's War Minister. It is likewise to his credit that Cornwallis adds to the complaint quoted above: 'I must, however, in justice to Dundas, say that he is the only man in the Cabinet from whom I have received the smallest attention.'[2] Dundas was also a sound judge of men; if he sent British troops on many ill-conceived and badly planned campaigns, he nearly always found good generals to command them. Nor does he appear ever to have been vindictive toward unsuccessful commanders so long as he failed to provoke them to sarcasm.[3]

On the fall of Pitt's ministry Dundas was succeeded from 1801 to 1804 by Lord Hobart, whose name is firmly planted on the map of Australia and hardly remembered in any other connexion. Great things were done in his years of office; the demobilization that followed the Treaty of Amiens; the incorporation of the Irish Army (and Ordnance) with the British; rearmament to meet renewed war with France; the bold facing of Napoleon's invasion threat and the first steps to oppose it. No discredit for ill-conceived and ill-planned overseas expeditions rests on Hobart's shoulders, a fact which at least suggests a sound, if obvious, appreciation of the situation in which Britain stood alone at war against the greatest military power the world had seen. The Commander-in-Chief seems to have been given a free hand and considerable support in his preparations to meet invasion, a fact which further suggests that Hobart could sensibly realize his own limitations. Yet Hobart remains a shadowy figure. Like Dundas, he seems eclipsed by his Premier, although that Premier was only Addington; for Addington is found dealing directly with the Duke of York on matters of detail as trivial as deciding which regiments should be retained and which disbanded at the peace.[4]

Addington, then, demands some notice here and the first thing to be said of him is that he seems a very underrated man, than whom few Premiers have been less sympathetically treated by historians. No one, for example, would accuse Holland Rose of wilful bias; but his interest in Pitt was so all-absorbing that he was able to write of Pitt's relations with the Addington government with no more than three references to Adding-

---

[1] Ross, *Correspondence of Cornwallis*, II, 173. The particular occasion here quoted refers to Indian affairs; but since Cornwallis received 'discouragement on *every* occasion', his military advice was evidently disregarded too.

[2] *Ibid.*

[3] But Sir James Murray, whom Dundas provoked to the sarcasm quoted above on the proposed siege of St Quentin, lost his appointment in the next campaign.

[4] Duke of York to George III, 7 April 1802, 8 July 1802, 15 July 1802: Windsor 10589, 10659 and 10663–4.

ton's three-volume biography by George Pellew.[1] Such intense concentration on a single object hardly makes for a broad or an impartial view.
Fortescue did his research on this period in days when Lord Roberts was
trying to convince Englishmen that universal military service was one of
the necessary and rational duties of citizenship, an opinion of which
Fortescue very understandably approved. But in the political climate of
1803 universal compulsion for overseas military service was an impossibility (as it remained till the crisis of 1916), and Fortescue's awareness of
this fact appears chiefly in the irritation to which it goads him. Again, his
County Lieutenancies and the Army was written at the instance of the
same Secretary of State for War who abolished the militia which Addington had increased and turned the volunteers into something of which
Addington had never dreamt. In all these ways Fortescue moved in an
atmosphere of ideas ill-calculated to help him see good in Addington. He
had also an intense hatred of human inefficiency which, though a far from
ignoble passion, could not help him to appreciate the extent of the real
difficulties which human beings have sometimes to overcome.

Then again this was a day of oratorical giants and of real cultivation of
the splendid art of rhetoric. Of that art Pitt, Fox, Sheridan, Windham,
and Canning were the masters and none of them was in the cabinet. The
unfortunate Addington himself had not very much more of the graces of
speech than any average member of a modern front bench; his colleagues
were little, if at all, better than himself, and the one eminently great man
in his cabinet, Admiral Lord St Vincent, was appreciated neither as an
administrator nor as a speaker. The mesmerism of brilliant oratory by
men who were all outside this cabinet blinded contemporaries to the
merits of those within it and seems still to exercise at least a portion of its
spell over historians of later generations. All told, then, Addington had a
bad press. Yet his war policy may be judged worthy of no small praise.

He faced Bonaparte with a staunch, undeceived, and level-headed
sanity. He did not, like the rulers of Britain in 1698 and 1919, inconti-
nently disarm to the limit as soon as a peace was signed. So, when the
question of Malta, which he handled firmly and unprovokingly, brought
hostilities on 18 May 1803, Addington led to war a better armed Britain
than any Prime Minister before or after him. The fleet, in spite of unfortunate economies, had 50,000 men in pay and was immediately able to
blockade all the French bases; the army was at thrice its normal peacetime
strength in numbers, and in training and organization was better than ever.
So, while Napoleon was blustering at Boulogne, and hastily selling Louisi-
ana under the counter, Addington was ready to report conquests; for
promptly the lately restored West Indian colonies of France began to fall
once more to British arms. There was indeed nothing showy about
Addington's foreign policy. He made no attempt to build up coalitions,

[1] Rose, *William Pitt and the Great War* (London, 1911), Chap. XXII.

or to hustle other European powers into a war for which they felt unready; therein he did wisely. On 21 February 1803, Bonaparte had declared to his legislature: 'England today cannot strive alone against France'; and now Addington flung his own words back at him. He did stand alone against France, and so confronted the boastful First Consul with a choice of two almost equally unpleasant alternatives—either to risk disaster in an exceedingly unpromising invasion of England, or, by flinching from the attempt, to suffer that loss of face which he had above all else to fear. Napoleon found no escape from this dilemma till Pitt's third coalition gave him the chance to cover his retreat from Boulogne with the glory of defeating Austria and the opportunity to make Europe his empire at Jena and Tilsit. Then he was enabled to institute that method of blockade, called the Continental System, which did press Britain really hard.

In April 1804 Addington fell, and Hobart was succeeded by that wealthy and noble nonentity, the Lord Camden who had been so unequal to the government of Ireland in the admittedly trying years, 1795–8. The real War Minister was the Premier, whose measures Camden defended in the Lords until he was fortunately replaced by Castlereagh in July 1805.

Castlereagh held this office for the seven months between July 1805 and February 1806, and again for twenty-six months from July 1807 to September 1809. He is described by Fortescue as 'the ablest man that ever controlled the War Office',[1] and the praise is just. His first great quality was the unflagging industry and mastery of detail to which his published papers bear impressive witness. His second great quality was the engaging modesty which constantly prompted him to take the unfortunately novel step of seeking professional military advice on military matters.[2] If the advice was not always taken, and if British strategy during his administration continued frequently to be foolish, Castlereagh should not be too harshly blamed; in deciding strategy his numerous amateur assistants, who were in the cabinet, could override his professional advisers who were mostly out of it. Castlereagh's third great quality was foresight. A particular weakness of British strategy in the past had been the haphazard improvisation of 'secret expeditions', which too often took so long to organize that many of their secrets were common knowledge before ever they sailed.[3] It is therefore refreshing to find Castlereagh, in his very first month as War Minister, writing the Duke of York that the

[1] *County Lieutenancies and the Army* (London, 1909), p. 234. But, as noted below, Castlereagh did not 'control the War Office', which was the domain of the Secretary-at-War. He did his military work at the Colonial Office.

[2] See, for example, his memoranda from the Duke of York on strategy in North Germany and Spain; also on the Indian Army (Londonderry, *Correspondence of Castlereagh*, VI, 122 ff., VIII, 179–83, and 189–91); likewise the memoranda on Antwerp requested from all senior officers at the Horse Guards in May–June 1809 (*ibid.* VI, pp. 257–73); and much correspondence with Chatham and Wellington.

[3] See, for example, Napoleon's comments on Pitt's 'secret expedition' of 1806 (*Correspondance de Napoleon I*, x, 8787).

country 'should be prepared... to menace or attack the enemy on their maritime frontier and, by compelling them to continue in force on the coast and in Holland, [to] weaken their efforts proportionately in other areas.' The aim was sound; so were the methods by which Castlereagh pursued it. He proposed to the Duke that he should 'immediately' select regiments to form a 'disposable force' of 30,000–35,000 infantry and 8000–10,000 cavalry; that for convenience of embarkation these troops should be stationed near Cork and Portsmouth, and in East Kent, handily close to the Downs. For his own part, Castlereagh undertook that the government would maintain 'a fleet of transports perfectly equipped and victualled for foreign service' and capable of carrying 'about 10,000 men' in one lift. This fleet should be 'constantly stationed between Cork and Portsmouth'.[1] Here at last was a military policy framed with real foresight and well calculated to give Britain the means of surprise and of holding her foe in perpetual suspense. It was not without its modest effect on the Austerlitz campaign.[2]

In 1807–9 Castlereagh was to make the 'disposable force' continuously effective by devising, for the first time, a successful manpower policy (as will be told in another place); and he at least shares credit for recognizing the genius of the embarrassingly youthful Wellington, and for sending him and the British Army back to Portugal in 1809 in defiance of the opposition's outcry.

Castlereagh also did his best to secure intelligence. He placed, or retained, a number of smugglers on his payroll.[3] He kept in close touch with the naval commanders operating off the enemy's coast (and they sometimes picked up deserters with interesting information).[4] He secured the fairly prompt arrival of the *Moniteur* from Boulogne to London.[5] In short, he did not fail to do the obvious things. Even so, however, he failed to secure competent intelligence, and the failure was serious.[6] Yet,

---

[1] Londonderry, *Correspondence of Castlereagh*, VIII, 6–7.

[2] As early as 28 August 1805, Napoleon was aware both that Britain had made ready a disposable force and that it totalled some 40,000 men—another example of the excellence of his intelligence. He therefore made preparations for coastal defence, which relied heavily on the National Guard but supported them with a mobile reserve of 5000 regulars and 10,000 conscripts in south-west France and with three regular battalions at Rennes. He specially feared an attack on Boulogne. Here, therefore, he left an 'immense quantité d'artillerie' and 30,000 regulars under Marshal Brune, in addition to sailors, who were to receive military training ashore and to act as sappers to strengthen the defences. Antwerp seems to have been guarded by two divisions, while another two divisions garrisoned Holland. At Mainz he left 15,000 men 'ready to march rapidly to the defence of Holland' till 8 November 1805. On that date he set up an Armée du Nord of six divisions (two in Holland, two in Antwerp and two in reserve at Juliers) in addition to the Boulogne garrison. Castlereagh's 'disposable force' did therefore do something 'to weaken [Napoleon's] efforts in other areas' (*Correspondance de Napoleon I*, IX, nos. 9155, 9159, 9164, 9228, 9248, 9252, 9431, 9466).

[3] Londonderry, *Correspondence of Castlereagh*, V, 95, 109, 116, 122, 132; VI, 38, 198.

[4] *Ibid.* V, 102, 141 ff., 154 ff.   [5] *Ibid.* VII, 18, 29.

[6] As noted above, it took Napoleon barely a month to learn the British secret of the 'disposable force' of 40,000 men, which Castlereagh first and most privately broached to

take him all round, it still seems fair to say that in his thirty-three months as War Minister Castlereagh did more to make his country a formidable power than any British statesman since the elder Pitt. It was a sad day for England when he retired from this office, after that exchange of pistol shots with Canning on Putney Heath, at dawn on 21 September 1809, which broke up the Portland ministry.

William Windham replaced Castlereagh as Secretary of War in the year and a half between February 1806 and July 1807. This is the same Windham who had been the friend of Burke and had sat by Samuel Johnson's deathbed, one of the most attractive personalities in English public life, a man of warm heart, high scholarship, and an orator of no mean talent. He might well have been supposed to know something of the army, because from 1794 to 1801 he had held the lesser post of Secretary-at-War under Pitt; and sometimes his ideas on strategy were both sound and cogently expressed. Yet despite all these points in his favour, Windham's appointment as Secretary of State for War still ranks as a national disaster. He was by nickname a 'Weathercock' of unstable opinions; like many scholars he was also an unpractical doctrinaire; and worst of all, he seems to have been amazingly lazy. 'I have called two or three times at the War Office with hope of meeting you there, but have been out of luck', wrote Boswell's friend and literary collaborator, Edmund Malone, to Windham on 21 May 1795.[1] Malone's bad luck can surprise no reader of Windham's diary.[2] That volume describes its author's meals and the excellent company in which he ate them; the numerous improving books he read, both ancient and modern; his enjoyable rides; his visits to Norfolk (where he owned an uncommonly stately home set in a splendid park) and his impressions of Parliament and of cabinet meetings; but it provides astonishingly infrequent evidence of his ever settling down at his desk to do an honest day's work on the routine of his job. His return to office in 1806 in the higher position of Secretary of State for War simply gave Windham larger responsibilities to neglect and a larger stage on which to display his amateurish, theorizing incapacity.

A major problem facing Windham in 1806 was recruiting to fill the ranks of the regular army. How he bungled this, in a manner that probably did more to weaken his country than any military misfortune

the Duke of York on 26 July 1805. It is a painful contrast to find that at the end of May 1809, some six weeks after Napoleon opened his Danube campaigns, the British government 'possessed no datum that' could 'lead to any probable guess at the extent of force which the enemy' had left 'at Antwerp and the strong towns adjacent, or even' (and this seems extraordinary) 'at the extent of the...militia of the neighbouring districts' (*ibid.* vi, 257, 270). Nor was Castlereagh able to secure a description of Antwerp's fortifications of more recent date than 1794—or so it would appear from this volume of his papers. No blame of Chatham is just which ignores the blindness with which he was sent into action.

[1] Lord Rosebery, *The Windham Papers* (London, 1913), I, 297.

[2] Mrs Henry Baring (ed.), *The Diary of the Right Honourable William Windham* (London, 1866).

since the catastrophic retreat through Holland in 1794–5, must be told in another place. Here it is to be remarked that, though Windham followed Castlereagh by instructing the Duke of York to maintain a 'disposable force', he made sure that force would be useless by scrapping most of the fleet of transports which alone made it 'disposable'. The months during which he held office were those of the life-and-death struggle through which Prussia and Russia toiled to defeat by way of Jena and Auerstadt, Eylau and Friedland; their cries for British aid were loud. But the only blows that Windham dealt the foe in these grim months were struck— unsuccessfully—at points as little likely to cripple France as the Dardanelles, Egypt, and Buenos Aires;[1] (small wonder if Alexander I greeted Napoleon on the raft at Tilsit with an outstretched right hand and the words, 'I hate the English as much as you do'). And when Windham was reproached with making his country helpless to aid its allies by dispersing the transports intended for carrying troops to their assistance, his only defence was to declare that the very idea of sending British soldiers to aid Russia and Prussia was 'so absurd it was unnecessary to answer it'.[2] That a man who could make such a statement as this was a disastrous War Minister is much less surprising than the fact that he was ever thought fit to be a War Minister at all.

As stated above, Windham was fortunately replaced by Castlereagh in July 1807. The work of Castlereagh's successor, Lord Liverpool, who took office in October, 1809, hardly lies in our period.

After the Secretary of State for War and Colonies came 'that rather mysterious functionary' (as Fortescue calls him)[3] with the confusingly similar title of Secretary-*at*-War. This minister, unlike the Secretary for War, was not normally in the cabinet; he, and not the Secretary for War, presided over that remarkable rabbit warren of red tape and civilian clerks which was the War Office, and which had in fact very little to do with the actual making of war. He has been well described as Parliament's watchdog over a much suspected army. Economy was ever Parliament's chief concern with the army, so the Secretary-at-War was responsible for authorizing or making every expenditure of money for military purposes. Himself under the eye of the Treasury, he directed the work of the Paymaster General and the Storekeeper; he dealt with the agents through whom colonels clothed their regiments, checked all regimental accounts, and made good claims for losses on active service. But members of Parliament not only regarded the army as a painful expense to the taxpayer; they also feared it as a potential instrument of lawless royal

---

[1] I omit Maida, the handsome little success fought and won near the toe of Italy on 4 July 1806. The Secretary of State can claim no credit for this operation, as it was undertaken on the local initiative of the commander of the British garrison in Sicily (Fortescue, *History of the British Army*, v, 336).

[2] *Parliamentary Debates*, 2nd ser., IX, 1038.

[3] Fortescue, *History of the British Army*, IV, 872.

3-2

tyranny, and, through their watchdog, kept a jealous eye on all troop movements. So the Secretary-at-War issued all the 'routes' that authorized the shifting of troops from one station to another, and, in Fortescue's words, the Commander-in-Chief could not legally march a corporal's guard from London to Windsor without the Secretary's formal authority. The law also was deemed far too sacred a thing to be entrusted to the brutal and licentious soldiery who ruled the purely military side of the Army from the Horse Guards, so much legal business fell into the lap of the Secretary-at-War. He handled such purely disciplinary matters as the arrest and escort of deserters, and piloted the annual Mutiny Bill through the House of Commons; as a financial minister he had naturally to explain and defend the military estimates in every budget debate.

These duties were not of a kind to demand any very transcendent genius in the man who performed them, but they were wide, varied, and intricate enough to call for solid administrative talent. It was therefore unfortunate that from the fall of the scholarly, but incompetent, Windham in 1801 to the accession of Lord Palmerston in October 1809 hardly a man who can fairly be called even a second-rate politician was appointed to be Secretary-at-War. The sort of zeal and ardour with which these intervening ministers flung themselves into their duties is sufficiently indicated by Palmerston's discovery in 1809 that their office was staffed with clerks to the number of 120, who worked often for only a five-day week, and never for more than a five-hour day, while its arrears of unfinished business stretched back in some cases to so remote a date as 1783, and its files were riddled with gaps caused by the absence of lost documents.[1] Such was the administration of the whole pack of watchdogs who preceded Palmerston at the War Office; *quis custodiet ipsos custodes?*

The third office that dealt with war was, at last, a military one, the Ordnance Department. Primarily, indeed, this office was a very sanely conceived ministry of supply. Soldiers and sailors had both to look to the same manufacturers for arms, ammunition of all calibres, and much other equipment needed by them both. The Ordnance prevented them from running up prices with competitive bids by being the one source of military stores for each service. But it was more than that; it had also 'to defray the expense of the Corps of Artillery, the Corps of Engineers and other Military Corps attached to the Ordnance Service; and also the charge of repairing and building Fortifications at home and abroad; excepting Field Works abroad, and excepting also those Fortifications which Commanders-in-Chief [abroad] may deem it expedient to erect without instructions from home.'[2] The last exception is noteworthy. It virtually concedes that the erection of fortifications should have been the job of the commander of the army, not of 'the ministry of supply'; and friction on

[1] H. F. C. Bell, *Lord Palmerston* (London, 1936), pp. 31–2.
[2] *Twenty-First Report of the Select Committee on Finance* (19 July 1797), p. 424.

this matter between the two departments of the army, which was in a hurry, and the Ordnance, which was too often dilatory, was to hinder the defence of Britain in 1803–5. The inconvenience of having the artillery and engineers under the Ordnance and so set apart from other troops is plain enough.

That the Ordnance Department was at times embarrassingly dilatory has just been stated; it was guilty of numerous other inefficiencies too, and the cause of all its shortcomings probably lay in its very curious constitution. It was under a Master General who 'in his military capacity' was Commander-in-Chief of the artillery and engineers and 'in his civil capacity' had 'the entire management of, and control over, the Ordnance Department'.[1] So far, so good; but by a most unusual arrangement, a committee was also provided to run the Department. This was the Board of Ordnance, comprising the Lieutenant General (the Master General's second in command over the artillery and engineers), the Surveyor General, the Clerk of the Ordnance, the Storekeeper and Clerk of Deliveries; and they, it is stated, 'if [the Master General] does not interfere ...are competent of themselves to carry on all the official business'.[2] This curious arrangement is made partially comprehensible by the fact that the Master General was always a high-ranking soldier who might have to be absent on other military duties; thus the Duke of Richmond had a district to command; Lord Cornwallis was employed across St George's Channel in the Irish rebellion; and Lord Chatham was still Master General when he sailed as commander of the Walcheren expedition. Yet the inefficiency of the arrangement is conspicuous; business could readily fall between two stools, with the Master General and the Board each waiting for the other to act. A Master General of Chatham's indolence could find in the Board's powers an excuse for regularly neglecting his duties; yet the Board was still inhibited from action by his right of interposition which enabled him at any time to overrule it. And, finally, the Board was a board, subject to all the weaknesses of any committee. No one member of it could be held personally responsible for inefficient work; it could not take work home at night, as an individual can; it could only do business at all when a quorum of three actually met. When questioned on the frequency of their meetings, their Secretary fell below his usual standard of concise explicitness, replying, 'In summer about twice a week; ordinarily three times a week; seldom or never less frequently than twice'.[3] It is obvious that three men, meeting at most but thrice a week, could not do the wholetime job of one conscientious and responsible individual; and as all, save the Lieutenant General, had their own departments to run within the Ordnance, their time for committee work, when they did meet, was naturally limited.

[1] *Thirteenth Report of the Commissioners of Military Inquiry* (1810–11), p. 4.
[2] *Ibid.*   [3] *Twenty-First Report of the Select Committee on Finance*, p. 437.

The first and the best Master General of the period under study was Charles Lennox, third Duke of Richmond. It may surprise some to find him praised, for his political career was a remarkable succession of violent quarrels; had he lived a generation or so later, he would presumably have been a Chartist, for in 1783 he was advocating annual parliaments, manhood suffrage, and equal electoral districts. No man who believed in so extreme a kind of parliamentary reform could be expected to survive very long in office in the 1790's, and these opinions, added to his cantankerousness, may make his dismissal in 1795 understandable enough.[1] Yet he was not well treated by Pitt, and the real reforms he achieved in the Ordnance were numerous. He reorganized the department's finance; made a logical division of its offices between civil and military personnel; created the Corps of Royal Military Artificers, who were to be amalgamated with the Royal Engineers in 1812; raised Britain's first horse artillery; made the field artillery competently mobile for the first time by organizing the Royal Corps of Artillery Drivers; and founded the Ordnance Survey.

Lord Cornwallis followed Richmond at the Ordnance from 1795 to February 1801. He was a man of whom much might have been expected; his record as Governor-General in India bespeaks high administrative competence; barring his probably pardonable surrender at Yorktown, his record as a soldier in both America and India was one of almost unbroken success. Yet Cornwallis's work at the Ordnance fell far below his reputation. He was perhaps too much the colonial soldier, for he had seen no service in Europe since 1762, and that only as an infantryman; and there is perhaps the reason why he presents the strange spectacle of a Commander-in-Chief of the Royal Artillery who had seemingly no appreciation of the new importance which the artillery he commanded had acquired in European war in the 1790's.[2] Likewise he presents the equally strange spectacle of a Master of Britain's fortifications who objected to building fortifications.[3] A streak of waspish jealousy seems to mar his character; at any rate it is striking to see how often his references to the Duke of York and General Sir David Dundas are derogatory,[4] though no two men worked harder or more effectively than these for the improvement of the British Army. Oddly, for a man of his unquestioned honour and sense of duty, he seems to have regarded the Master-Generalship of the Ordnance as a sinecure, for he continued to hold it throughout the entire period of his

---

[1] To these liabilities may be added the personal hostility of Lord Spencer and his followers (Ross, *Correspondence of Cornwallis*, II, 283); and the rancour of William Windham whose bitter (and ignorant) attack on Richmond, in a private letter to Dundas dated 16 September 1794, is preserved in the Melville Correspondence in the William Clements Library in the University of Michigan.

[2] Ross, *Correspondence of Cornwallis*, II, 335; III, 218, 382, 493.

[3] *Ibid.* II, 337; III, 515.

[4] *Ibid.* II, 286; III, 500, 515.

Lord Lieutenancy in Dublin, when he could give but the scantiest attention to its duties. Few letters of his on Ordnance business are preserved in the published volumes of his papers.

The decline of the Ordnance, which began under Cornwallis, continued unabated under his deplorable successor, John, the second Earl of Chatham. Fortescue has well and truly said that, when he chose, Chatham could both think and write.[1] Unfortunately, however, he very rarely made this exacting choice, and in sheer laziness he eclipsed even Windham. Any reader of Castlereagh's military correspondence must be struck by the frequency with which Chatham is found to be at his country home when he ought to have been in London. Relatively very few documents attributable to him are to be found in the *Chatham Papers*, or elsewhere, in the Public Record Office; and it is surely significant that among them lies a trim little notebook containing lists of garden flowers written in an admirably neat italic printing hand.[2] This suggests where his real interests lay—not for nothing apparently was he the first-born of 'Capability' Brown's most distinguished patron.[3] Yet in spite of his lack of interest in the duties of his office, Chatham did his country the disservice of clinging like a limpet to that office from May 1801 to 1810, with only the break of the eighteen months when the Ministry of all the Talents was in power.

In the interval between Chatham's two terms of office Lord Moira (later the first Marquis of Hastings) was Master General from February 1806 to March 1807. Moira was a very capable soldier, but he held office for too short a time to have much mark on his department, and his record is not clear of a strong suspicion of favouritism.[4]

The next office to demand notice is that of the Commander-in-Chief.[5] It was his task in an emergency to conduct the defence of Britain against an invader; and though this emergency has never occurred since 1688, preparations for defence occupied much of the Commander-in-Chief's time and energy in our period. His regular duties were to uphold discipline, to supervise promotion, and to be the director and inspector-general of training in the cavalry and infantry. These were the critical jobs on which the fighting efficiency of any army absolutely depended, and it is typical of the carelessness of the British people in matters military that for

---

[1] *County Lieutenancies and the Army*, p. 162.

[2] It lies in the box of Chatham Papers catalogued as 30/8/370.

[3] Lancelot Brown, the famous landscape gardener, had a 'long and cordial acquaintance' with the great Chatham with whom he discussed politics as well as horticulture (Dorothy Stroud, *Capability Brown*, London, 1950, p. 187).

[4] At any rate, his treatment of Major Charles James, the military lexicographer, was curious (*Seventeenth Report of the Commission of Military Inquiry*, 3 July 1811, appendix no. 10).

[5] The title of this officer varied much. He was called successively Captain General; later General or Field Marshal on the Staff; then Captain General again; and finally Commander-in-Chief.

half the eighteenth century there was no one at all in charge of them. The office of Commander-in-Chief was vacant for twenty-three years from the death of Marlborough in 1722 to the appointment of Cumberland in 1745; vacant again for nine years from 1769 to 1778; and finally for ten years from February 1783 to February 1793. These vacancies were bad. The absence of a Commander-in-Chief meant that promotion became the plaything of politics; that discipline, at least among officers, was let slide; and that training was left unsupervised. On every point the consequences were disastrous (as will be shown in suitable places).

Obviously the Commander-in-Chief's duties could no longer be neglected when the nation found itself at war again with France in 1793; and then Lord Amherst was recalled to the long-vacant post. He was a soldier whose service on the field, if not brilliant, had at least been marked by solid competence and by success; he had also held the command-in-chief before, from 1778 to 1782. His was therefore an appointment that might well seem obvious and natural. Unfortunately, it was also an appointment that would have been better unmade. In February 1793 Amherst was already seventy-six years old. It is perhaps most true, and certainly most kind, to regard him as a man who had greatly failed in health and strength. The results of his reappointment as Commander-in-Chief at this date were succinctly and sufficiently summarized by Henry Dundas (before breakfast, of all times) on 21 July 1798 when he wrote to Lord Grenville: 'Lord Amherst was a worthy and respectable old man, and nobody shall ever hear me say a disrespectful thing of him; but the mischief he did [to the army] in a few years will not be repaired but by the unremitting attention of many.'[1]

The deliverance of the army from the effects of long neglect and of Amherst's wretched muddles began in February 1795 with the appointment of George III's second son, Frederick, Duke of York, to the command-in-chief. No one man in this period did more to improve the army than York, yet there are few of whom historical misjudgement has been more gross.

Some, like Oman, remember him mainly or solely for an unprecedented scandal into which an intrigued House of Commons delved for seven full weeks in 1809, almost to the exclusion of other business, and which drove him temporarily from office. Another scandal, lately revived, is that he neglected his duties as a commander in the field in Flanders (1793–4) in favour of wenching and drinking. For such is the import of one of Gillray's cartoons, reprinted in a recent (and an interesting) book over the caption, 'The Duke of York when Commander-in-Chief in Flanders'.[2] It portrays the Duke at table, with a glass flourished in his hand, and a

---

[1] Historical Manuscripts Commission, *Report on the MSS of J. B. Fortescue preserved at Dropmore* (London, 1906), IV, 264.

[2] Godfrey Davies, *Wellington and his Army* (Oxford, 1954), opposite p. 22.

bloated Belgian harlot on his knee, while three files of emaciated batmen troop in behind him with fresh supplies of bottles.

A third accusation, levelled at the Duke by the same author as the last, is that he nursed a bitter prejudice against Wellington, whom, it is supposed, he endeavoured to thwart by ignoring his recommendations for promotion and by inflicting incompetent subordinate generals on him in the Peninsula.[1]

The scandal of 1809 concerned the Duke's relations with his ex-mistress, Mrs Mary Ann Clarke, who accused him of using her as a channel for receiving bribes for promotion. To the grief of the saintly Wilberforce, the House of Commons turned a lenient enough eye on the Duke's undoubted adultery, but they still looked very narrowly at the charge that he had made corrupt profit out of the sale of commissions.[2] They ended by concluding that the Duke, though immoral (like so many others in most ages), was uncorrupt. No doubt the lady used her position to make money by claiming the power to aid promotions; but there is neither evidence nor likelihood either that any of this money reached the Duke, or that he knew Mrs Clarke was receiving it; and when she tried to blackmail him, he defied her. Such, in effect, was the conclusion of the House of Commons in the Duke's day; it is also the conclusion of two students who in our time have waded through the printed evidence: Sir John Fortescue and Lt. Col. Alfred Burne.[3] Away, then, with Oman's canard that the Duke of York 'managed the British army' with the 'assistance of Mrs Mary Ann Clarke', and was commonly guilty of mismanagement in so doing.

As for the charge that the Duke of York neglected his duty for lewd pleasure in Flanders, it should be enough to say that an 'infamous caricature',[4] even though contemporary, is not historical evidence; that the Duke himself was a man credited with waging vigorous and successful war on the vice of drunkenness in officers; and finally that it is hard to see how this imputation could ever have been revived after the publication of Alfred Burne's biography of the Duke. For Burne shows that in Flanders York applied himself with great energy and no mean ability to a task whose difficulties might well have overwhelmed the genius of a Marlborough.[5]

As for the third accusation—that York was prejudiced against Wellington and endeavoured to thwart him in the Peninsula—few reading the

---

[1] *Ibid.* pp. 43 ff.

[2] 'No apparent sense in the House of the guilt of adultery, only of political offence' (Wilberforce's diary for 23 January 1809, in *The Life of William Wilberforce*, by his sons, London, 1839, III, 402).

[3] Fortescue, *History of the British Army*, VII, 28–31; Burne, *The Noble Duke of York* (London, 1949), pp. 309–13.

[4] Burne's description of the cartoon, *Duke of York*, p. 221.

[5] *Ibid.* chapters IV and VIII.

quotation on which it is based would realize that the words Greville there ascribed to York were not spoken till as long after the Peninsular War as 1821;[1] fewer still would guess that Wellington in earlier days had been treated with 'the greatest kindness' by York with whom his conversations were sometimes 'long';[2] or that York's own military secretary wrote Wellington after Vittoria: 'I never saw the Duke of York forward any measure with so much eagerness and self-satisfaction as your promotion' to the rank of Field Marshal[3] (although this distinction was usually reserved for soldiers who were either royal or senile). It is also to be remarked that this last writer, who became York's military secretary in 1811, was the same Henry Torrens who had been Wellington's military secretary in the Vimeiro campaign and to whom he wrote with such intimately blunt frankness throughout the Peninsular War; and that York would hardly have taken as secretary in 1811 a man who was so closely associated with Wellington if he had then been Wellington's enemy. There is further no hint in this accusation of the fact that there was real difficulty in finding good subordinate commanders to serve under Wellington simply because of what Castlereagh had described as 'the inconvenience of Sir Arthur Wellesley being so young a lieutenant general';[4] in other words, the field of choice was much limited because so many of the better generals were Wellington's seniors.[5] Lastly, no one reading this accusation would ever guess that, if York ultimately came to dislike Wellington, we have Wellington's own admission that he himself gave York the strongest and most public reason for thinking him 'false and ungrateful';[6] yet such is the case.[7] In short, this accusation is too defective in fact and loose in chronology to be taken seriously.

So much for the various criticisms by which the Duke of York has been misrepresented; now for the real man.

---

[1] Davies, *Wellington and his Army*, p. 43, citing the page reference, but not the date, of Greville's diary for 24 June 1821.

[2] Wellington, *Supplementary Dispatches*, V, 177, 411, 387.

[3] *Ibid.* VIII, 50–1.

[4] Londonderry, *Correspondence of Castlereagh*, VIII, 43.

[5] For example, Sir John Hope, who had served under Moore in 1808–9 was debarred by his own seniority from serving under Wellington from 1809–13, but volunteered to do so as soon as he was made Wellington's junior by the latter's promotion to Field Marshal after Vittoria. I ignore here Davies's accusation that York ignored Wellington's recommendations for promotion as this subject belongs in chap. 8 below.

[6] Lytton Strachey and Roger Fulford, *The Greville Memoirs* (London, 1938), I, 120.

[7] I doubt if York can have been piqued by reports of Wellington's criticisms of his campaign in Flanders in 1794, as Davies suggests. Wellington's recorded criticisms, to Croker and Stanhope, were only made after York's death; and it was hardly in his character to be loose-mouthed. But, apparently about 1809, he carelessly permitted 'a person named Tucker to dedicate to him a book of whose contents he was uninformed'. On its publication the book was found to contain 'a most virulent libel of the Duke of York' (Lord Stanhope, *Conversations with Wellington*, Oxford, 1947, p. 128). This publication coming at the time of York's disgrace, and after he had treated Wellington with 'the greatest kindness' wore every appearance of falseness and ingratitude.

York had a very good, and a far from uncultivated, mind. He expressed himself well in French,[1] could make a rousing *extempore* speech in German,[2] and won praise for the excellence of even the first of his few performances in the House of Lords.[3] His 'habits of Business, great Quickness of Perception, great facility in disposing of subjects and an excellent Memory were Advantages that forcibly struck all those who communicated with H.R.H.', wrote a contemporary who had known him well.[4] His letters and memoranda to cabinet ministers are first rate. They are well organized, generally clearly and sometimes forcefully expressed; firm-based in fact, they lead directly to conclusions marked by sound and luminous common sense. A good judge of men, he knew both how to choose an able staff and how to trust them to do for themselves the tasks he assigned them; yet he was never the mere creature of his subordinates in his office. 'Everything was directed and superintended by himself, but no opinion or suggestion conveyed by others was disregarded or impatiently received.'[5] His sense of justice was keen: 'no Application, no Representation, however humble the Quarter, was disregarded or neglected, none ever remained unanswered, and the care of the private soldier was as much the Subject of Enquiry as that of the Officer'.[6] His patience was great; his labours for the reform of the Army 'were uniform, consistent and progressive...he did not hastily proceed to destroy all that existed, but...gradually substituted improvements for defects, checks for abuses'.[7] Fortescue justly and concisely summarized his work when he wrote that in 1795 York 'took over a number of undisciplined and disorganized regiments, filled for the most part with the worst stamp of man and officer, and...in less than seven years he converted these unpromising elements into an army'.[8] And, in the eyes of Heaven at least, the noblest of York's many titles was surely the nickname given him by the lowest ranks under his command; they called him 'the Soldier's Friend'.

No description of the Duke's work would be complete which failed to mention the staff through whom he worked. The first of these was the Adjutant General. He dealt with all matters which related to discipline, the arming and clothing of troops, all military regulations and applications for leave of absence. In 1795 this post was filled by a grand old soldier, Sir William Fawcett, whom the Duke retained till age and failing eyesight caused his retirement in 1799, fifty-one years after he had first seen service.

[1] J. Watkins, *Memoir of H.R.H. the Duke of York* (London, 1827), p. 77.

[2] Burne, *Duke of York*, pp. 44–6.

[3] 'The Duke of York's speech was remarkably good, not only in matter, but in manner, and part of it was in reply' (Lord Sheffield to Eden, 17 December 1788, *The Journals and Correspondence of Lord Auckland*, ed. the Bishop of Bath and Wells, London, 1861, II, 257–8).

[4] 'Memorandum on the Duke of York', by Herbert Taylor, British Museum Addit. MSS. Peel Papers, 40,391, f. 288.

[5] *Ibid.*   [6] *Ibid.*

[7] *Ibid.*   [8] Fortescue, *History of the British Army*, IV, 929.

Fawcett was an accomplished linguist, whose fluent German had won him the favour of George II, and who had translated into English Marshal Saxe's *Reveries* and the King of Prussia's *Regulations for the Prussian Cavalry* and *Regulations for the Prussian Infantry*. Fawcett's successor was one of the Duke's staff officers from Flanders, Sir Harry Calvert. As Calvert had been made Assistant Adjutant General to Fawcett in 1795, he was a very natural successor; he served long and ably.

Second in the Horse Guards organization was the Quarter Master General. He was responsible for the marches and quartering of troops—a tedious but hardly a very responsible job in ordinary times; and when the Commissioners of Military Inquiry, appointed by Parliament to examine defence costs in 1805, came to examine his office, they found no records of earlier date than 1803. In that year, however, two things gave a new importance to the Quarter Master General's office; the first was the appointment to it of a new man, Major General Robert Brownrigg; the second was the renewed and more than ever serious threat of invasion, which caused all the detail of defence planning and all defence construction of a temporary nature to be made the Quarter Master General's responsibility.

The Duke's third staff officer was his military secretary. This appointment was a new creation made by York. Amherst had employed as secretary a civilian clerk at a salary of £182 a year (and that may help explain why Amherst left all business relating to promotion in 'a complete jumble'). To straighten matters out, York took as secretary a field officer whose salary had risen to £2,500 a year by 1813; and such a man was needed for the job. The military secretary handled confidential correspondence, all matters concerned with the very delicate business of appointments and promotions, and much correspondence with other government departments, including the East India Company. One can sympathize with, if not entirely believe, the claim of a weary Henry Torrens that no subordinate office under the Crown involved so much 'labour, importance, variety of matter and incessant confinement'.

Lower down the scale were the generals commanding districts—in effect, subordinate local commanders-in-chief. The most responsible post of this kind was the chief command in Ireland, after the Union of 1801.

These four—the Secretary of State for War and Colonies, the Secretary-at-War, the Master General of the Ordnance, and the Commander-in-Chief—were the principal military officials. Others may be dismissed more briefly. Of the Home Secretary one need only repeat that he required the services of the regular army for the police duties termed 'internal defence' and presided over the militia and volunteers. The Treasury, as stated, kept in its own hands control over the Secretary-at-War, who paid the army; over the Commissary General who fed it; and over the Transport Board which moved it across the sea. The Barrack

Master General was a new creation of 1793; as Sir John Fortescue suggested, he is primarily to be regarded as a builder of police stations. For the unrest created by the French Revolution, by Thomas Paine, and the British Jacobins greatly increased magistrates' demands for troops for police duties; fear that troops would be disaffected if allowed to mix too much with the *habitués* of the alehouses where they were normally billeted, added to the claims of magistrates, created a demand for barracks. The Ordnance Department, which had hitherto built barracks, could not keep pace with the demand. Hence the creation of the new office. The thorough-going bad management of the Barrack Master General, one Oliver De Lancey, has caused the history of this office to be uncommonly well documented, up to a point; for the Commissioners of Military Inquiry uncovered much foolish expenditure, much bad building, and many bad contracts. But the establishment of barracks, although done piecemeal and without plan, did give troops a home of their own, of a sort; and it did make discipline easier and better. Therefore it has real importance.

CHAPTER 2

THE ORDNANCE DEPARTMENT: SUPPLY

THE tasks of the Ordnance Department were too varied to be dealt with in one chapter. Here its services to the army as a ministry of supply will be discussed; other chapters must deal with its scientific research and with the equipment, training, and duties of its troops, the gunners and engineers. The recruiting of those troops will be covered in the general chapter on manpower; and the subject of fortification, another Ordnance duty, lies outside the scope of this study.

Even the subject of supply is so large that much connected with it may be very wholesomely omitted. Fifes and drums, haversacks, camp kettles, and such stuff, all have their place in a soldier's life, but it is his weapons that make him a soldier; on the supply of arms, therefore, this chapter will concentrate.

It is a subject that has already entered our histories. Fortescue found a target for his splendid powers of invective in the conduct of Henry Dundas, who sent unarmed reinforcements to the continent in 1793–4 with the hope that 'discipline, arms, ammunition, clothing, victuals, medical stores and medical treatment would descend upon them from Heaven';[1] Holden Furber has come to Dundas's defence with the suggestion that he was let down by 'an inefficient bureaucracy'.[2] Neither author has really understood the problem. At least while the Duke of Richmond presided over it, the Ordnance Department was not, as Furber supposes, inefficiently run; nor, on this occasion, does Dundas deserve the blame Fortescue heaped upon him, for the arms he failed to supply for the most part did not exist, and in any case it was not his duty to supply them. Yet again, neither author seems to appreciate the scale of the problem England faced in her attempts to arm her troops for war against revolutionary France, a problem which challenges comparison with that of 1939–40.

When the war, which Pitt in April 1792 had thought impossible for fifteen years, broke out in February 1793, the army's nominal strength was only 50,000 men, and thanks to long poor success in recruiting, its real strength was much less. The actual force in being was more than adequately armed, for every regiment, whatever its real numbers, had muskets, bayonets, carbines, pistols, and swords enough for its full nominal strength on paper. Besides the weapons of these first line troops, there was a reserve of a further 47,000 muskets in the Tower of London and

---

[1] Fortescue, *History of the British Army*, IV, 300.
[2] Furber, *Henry Dundas*, p. 97.

13,000 in the armouries of its various outports;[1] the total number of spare weapons on hand was thus more than sufficient to meet the doubling of the army overnight. Such a proportion in reserve would seem fair enough by all ordinary calculations.

But then came the wholly unlooked-for war and with it the expansion of the forces on an equally unexpected scale. The army estimates for 1794 called not for a doubling but for a more than fivefold multiplication of the troops to a total of 265,000 regulars, fencibles, militia, and new raised foreign regiments.[2]

It might still be thought that a nation like Britain would have little trouble in providing arms even for such a total as this. The rise of the industrial revolution, with its immense increase of manufacturing power, is commonly dated in the third decade of the eighteenth century; economists enlarge on the enormous increase in the pig iron produced in Britain during the 1790's and through the first decade of the new century;[3] and because this increase outstripped French production it might be inferred that England could easily outrun France in any armaments race.

The facts stated about English and French iron production need provoke no argument, but the inference is not correct. In the event France alone, without counting the production of her satellites, was to produce substantially more small arms than Britain between 1803 and the fall of Napoleon;[4] and as for heavier weapons, it is hard to point to a battle prior to Vittoria in which English troops were not outgunned by the more numerous artillery of the French. Britain's weakness in artillery was due rather to want of men than to any shortage of material, but production of small arms was limited by the nature of the industry that made them.

'There is no such trade as a gunmaker, properly so called', wrote an English author some thirty years after Waterloo; the varied parts of a musket were then made in separate establishments, and 'the only person who could consistently be called a gunmaker is he who has the gun finished by putting the several pieces together'.[5] So it was also with the gun-making industry in our period. The making of gun barrels was one job; making the locks—composed of triggers, springs, seres, and hammers (or flint-holders)—was another; the 'knapping' of the flints was yet another; so were the making of stocks, ramrods, and bayonets. Even the

---

[1] A return sent to Dundas by Richmond on 2 March 1793 shows 39,000 serviceable British arms in store, 2000 Dutch arms in the Tower with 5000 stands kept as 'Expedition Stores at Portsmouth', for a total of 46,000; and a further 16,500 'ordered but not yet delivered by the Contractors' (HO/50/368).

[2] Fortescue, *History of the British Army*, IV, 218.

[3] John U. Nef, *War and Human Progress* (Harvard, 1950), p. 291.

[4] F. C. R. Dupin, *Military Force of Great Britain*, translated with notes, by an officer (London, 1822), II, 175. The total French production of muskets, carbines, rifles and pairs of pistols = 3,956,257½; total British production = 3,143,366; French advantage = 812,991½.

[5] George Dodd, *British Manufactures* (London, 1845), I, 103.

assembly of the parts seems to have been subdivided, 'rough-stocking' and finishing being apparently done by different persons. Every one of these many tasks was mainly hand-done till the 1820's, when the introduction of a new machine to hasten the making of barrels nearly caused riots in Birmingham.[1] For Birmingham was already the headquarters of the industry, though London still had some share of it, and in 1801 it was a London gunsmith, Ezekiel Baker, who provided the British Army with its first rifle.

At the top of the industry were wealthy merchant-manufacturers, well established in the trade, who could undertake very large contracts for arms for British and foreign governments. They would fill them by employing masters and journeymen to make the separate parts which they might have put together in their own assembly plants. Some at least of these big contractors owned their own proving houses, where musket barrels underwent proof (that is, were fired with an overcharge of powder large enough to ensure that any crack or weakness would be revealed before the weapon was finished and issued).[2]

There could be no rapid expansion of such an industry as this. Skill cannot be improvised, and the number of musket parts produced in any given time depended on the number of skilled workmen available to make them. So in July 1794, the Ordnance minutes record that one Mr Hayward, who had received a contract to supply flints, 'would take nearly Six Years to complete them according to the Rate at which Mr Hayward would engage to furnish that article'.[3] Yet again the skilled workmen employed in the industry were no 'wage slaves', and in April 1795, Mr Thomas Gill, a Birmingham contractor, 'represented that he was unable to complete his order for 2000 Pairs of 9-inch Pistols, although he had a considerable Number of Locks and Barrels ready, on account of the large Orders for Store Pistols, which the Workmen preferred to rough Stock and set up rather than Pistols of the Tower Pattern'.[4] This report illustrates the real difficulty the government faced in trying to get arms. Great care had to be taken in placing orders, for orders injudiciously placed might prevent one contractor from living up to his promises by enabling a rival to draw the workmen away from him.

It was therefore peculiarly unfortunate that the Ordnance Board of Great Britain faced much competition for the manufacturers' favour. Portugal had no arms industry and looked to Britain for very considerable supplies of weapons. So too did the new independent government of Ireland; and the East India Company was another old and valued customer of the Birmingham gunsmiths.

[1] Conrad Gill, *History of Birmingham* (London, 1952), i, 88.
[2] *Ibid.*
[3] Extract from Ordnance Minutes, 8 July 1794, WO/47/2365 in the Public Record Office.
[4] Extract from Ordnance Minutes, 17 April 1795, *ibid.*

The manufacturers were often glad to fill the orders of these rival buyers first, while leaving the British Board of Ordnance unsatisfied. There were understandable reasons for this. The workmanship the British Board required was 'more nice'; that done for Ireland and India 'did not require the same precision' and therefore engaged 'the least expert and most numerous body of workmen'.[1] The manufacturers were also very poorly paid by the Board of Ordnance; or rather, they were not paid at all by that body. Instead of money, the Board gave 'debentures' to be presented to the Treasury for payment; long delays in making payment on Ordnance debentures evidently caused the Treasury no inconvenience, and not all manufacturers could afford to wait. 'My circumstances will not admit my waiting the usual Credit of the Office, which I understand is sometimes nearly six Months', wrote one gunsmith in 1794,[2] but he did not know the worst. On 13 May 1797, the assistant clerk of the Ordnance wrote a note of protest to the Treasury over their slow payment. His annexed list of unpaid debts shows thirteen-month-old debts to the tune of £3897. 1s. 5d. still outstanding from the month of April of the preceding year;[3] and similar or larger bills were due for work supplied in every one of the twelve months between. Plainly the British gunsmith had a considerable incentive not to work for the British government when he could work for anyone else.

But this was not all. Besides its old competitors and old dilatoriness at the Treasury, the Board of Ordnance, as soon as war broke out, encountered new competitors born of the surprisingly unbusinesslike methods of Pitt's cabinet. In the early years of the struggle with the French Republic, both the Treasury and the Secretary of State for War rushed into the market to buy muskets on their own without regard to the Ordnance Department. They were tempted to do so by the fact that France, when her hostilities with Austria and Prussia began, had placed large orders for muskets in Birmingham. The outbreak of war between Britain and France left the gunsmiths with both contracts in hand and large stocks of finished weapons which they could not now dispose of to their lost customer. The arms already made were duly offered to the Ordnance and unhesitatingly rejected; of a different calibre from British arms they could use no British ammunition and their workmanship was 'so bad that they would have caused great complaints had we received and issued them'.[4] But the merchants would not take the Ordnance's 'No' for an answer; instead they sought customers in other ministries and, in defiance of all rational administration, found them. In the autumn of 1793 Lord Moira was appointed to command an expeditionary force

[1] Richmond to Dundas, 11 October 1793, HO/50/369 in the Public Record Office.
[2] Ezekiel Baker to the Board of Ordnance, June (?) 1794, WO/47/2365 in the Public Record Office.
[3] Nettleship to Rose, 13 May 1797, WO/46/25 in the Public Record Office.
[4] Richmond to Dundas, 24 August 1793, HO/50/369 in the Public Record Office.

intended to aid the insurgent royalists of La Vendée; and then the Treasury purchased 12,000 stands of British-made French arms for the expedition (which never reached Brittany) to carry with it.[1] In May 1793, Henry Dundas not only bought no fewer than 145 cases containing 3000 French muskets from Alexander Davison of Birmingham, but scored the remarkable achievement of actually losing his bulky purchase.[2] (Six months passed before 'Badger the Carrier' reported to the Ordnance officer at Portsmouth that 'there were a great many cases of Arms marked A.D.; that he had had them some time without knowing who sent them or where they were to go'.) These purchases encouraged manufacturers to continue working on their old contracts for shoddy, and therefore easily made, French muskets in preference to undertaking the new work for which the Ordnance was desperately clamouring; and irregular purchases seem to have continued. So in February 1794 a Mr Parry is found writing Evan Nepean, Dundas's aide, about French arms. Nepean had apparently made the very proper suggestion that Parry should do business with the Ordnance; but the insistent merchant replied

With respect to Mr Nepean's proposal on account of the Ordnance, we can only say that we wish in the first place to finish our French stock which a necessary attention to the interests of our own concern leads us to take the present opportunity of doing, an opportunity that may not soon occur again nor so suitable; when we are once fairly rid of that encumbrance we shall be less attracted to other engagements and it is our intention, that once accomplished, to exert ourselves in the Service of the Ordnance.[3]

Parry added that his 'concern's' work on French weapons would be finished in a month; Mr Davison does not seem to have stopped producing the enemy's weapons so soon. Late in December 1795 R. H. Crew, the Secretary of the Ordnance, is found writing to Portsmouth for an account by express 'of the number of...the musquets furnished by Mr Davison'; though the exact number was unknown to Crew in London, he correctly understood they exceeded 25,000 stands of arms.[4] This was not the first time Crew had had to make inquiry 'to trace out' purchases of arms 'of the French pattern' made 'by order of the Secretary of State';[5] and confusion was further increased by the fact that Dundas's office did not know that some Birmingham firms had more than one London representative, and so it had to be reported 'that the Same Arms have been offered by different People, which has made the Number appear greater than it really is'.[6]

[1] Richmond to Dundas, 24 January 1794, HO/50/371 in the Public Record Office.
[2] Trigge to Nepean, 11 November 1793, HO/50/374 in the Public Record Office.
[3] Parry to Nepean, 20 February 1794, *ibid*.
[4] Crew to the Respective Officers, Portsmouth, 25 December 1795, WO/46/24 in the Public Record Office.
[5] Crew to the same, 14 November 1794, *ibid*.
[6] G. Berkeley to Dundas, 19 February 1794, HO/50/368.

There, then, was the fourfold problem of the Ordnance Department; inadequate peacetime purchases; a hand-working industry which could not be swiftly expanded; independent competitors able to offer more attractive terms; confusion confounded by the irresponsible conduct of other ministries, which recklessly interfered with the performance of the Ordnance Board's contracts. Nothing could recover the ground lost by the failure to build a bigger reserve in peacetime, but the Board tackled its other difficulties with all possible energy. 'No means have been spared to procure a quicker supply of arms', wrote Richmond to Dundas, on 24 August 1793. 'All the gunsmiths of repute have been applied to,' he continued, 'and as many as have made offers of any consequence are Employed, and no offers have been rejected but such as it evidently appeared would only be drawing workmen away from the Persons we did employ and prevent their keeping their engagements.'[1]

So much was done early in the war and proved too little. 'All we have hitherto been able to get from our workmen is a delivery of from Five Hundred to a Thousand [arms] a week', Richmond reported in October 1793.[2] The next step was to eliminate competition. I find no document recording any direct protest by Richmond against the irregular and damaging purchase of bad weapons by the Treasury or Secretary of State, unless one may thus construe a pointed request, put to Dundas's office in January 1794, for a statement of the number of arms 'which have been purchased for Lord Moira, Sir Charles Grey or any other Service independent of what have been supplied by the Board of Ordnance'.[3] But there is no need to suppose that forcible protest was not made. Richmond, never tolerant of incompetence, would be caustic in writing and still more so in speech; irregular purchases of arms by other ministries seem to have ceased from the time the manufacturers finished those stocks of French arms which had originally been ordered by the enemy.

The next competitor to be tackled was the East India Company. Here Richmond had the advantage that Dundas, who had reason to be on the defensive after throwing the Ordnance's market into chaos with his irregular purchases of arms, was also head of the India Board of Control. In October 1793 Richmond first suggested that the Company might be required both to sell the government all arms it had in Britain and to order no more. Three months later he returned to this subject with another plan; this was that the government should take over all arms in the company's British warehouses, but should also simultaneously instruct it to contract for a further and immediate supply. At first sight this looks like organizing the very competition which Richmond wished to overcome, but it was no such thing. The East India Company was to go on making

---

[1] Richmond to Dundas, 24 August 1794, HO/50/369.
[2] Richmond to Dundas, 11 October 1793, HO/50/368.
[3] Hadden to Nepean, 23 January 1793, HO/50/371.

4-2

purchases (and doubtless to give the manufacturers prompter payment than ever the Treasury made), only in order to surrender its arms to the Ordnance as soon as it received them. For Richmond had decided that, inferior as East India muskets might be, 'they must undoubtedly be serviceable, and such as new raised Corps must put up with in an emergency';[1] also, their very inferiority made them easier to get in quantity for the reason that less skilled workmen could make them. What Richmond now urged, Dundas did, a month late, but still vigorously. In February 1794 he ordered not only that 8680 stands of arms in the Company's London warehouse should be immediately surrendered to the Ordnance, but that 5000 stands, which were already embarked for India and actually at sea aboard vessels in the Downs, should be unloaded and deposited in the Ordnance stores in Portsmouth.[2] (Sir John Shore was then Governor in Bengal; he is accused of timid conduct toward native powers; how many of his critics know this story of his sudden disarmament by the authorities at home?)

This drastic measure, so damaging to the exercise of initiative in Calcutta, was intended only as a stop-gap in a critical emergency; but the emergency did not end and the expedient became permanent. Except for the interval of the Peace of Amiens, the East India musket became the standard weapon of the British Army till 1814. The army did not like it. 'The old, or India, pattern [of musket was] in innumerable instances... soon rendered unfit for service', it was stated in 1817, 'for want of the guards the new [model] is calculated to supply';[3] and the description of the new 1814 model gives a clue to the defects of the East India musket. It was too short, it was too weak in the stock, and its locks were not made accurately enough for the parts of one to be interchangeable with another. These flaws 'occasioned frequently a waste of arms to an extensive amount'.[4] However, an unprepared nation must accept anything it can get in a crisis; as Britain took the stop-gap Sten gun in 1940, so she had to take the India musket in 1794, and for twenty years thereafter British soldiers were sent into battle with an inferior weapon.

The next steps were to eliminate competitive buying by Ireland and Portugal. This was done, in the first case, by amalgamating English and Irish purchases, and it did not wait for the Union of 1801. Dublin made large demands for British weapons in the crisis of 1797, and as a result an informal bargain was struck by which the British Ordnance undertook to do Ireland's buying thereafter.[5] In this year, too, the Portuguese problem was handled in the same way. It was not an easy one, for Portugal could not be refused arms. Apart from the importance of her capital, Lisbon,

---

[1] Richmond to Dundas, 11 October 1793, HO/50/369.
[2] Richmond's acknowledgement of this to Dundas is dated 11 February 1794, HO/50/371.
[3] Appendix no. 1, Third Report of the Select Committee of Finance, 1817.
[4] Ibid.
[5] Crew to Pelham, 14 April 1797, HO/50/373.

with its harbour, to the Royal Navy, she was England's oldest ally; and she suffered for it in 1795, when Spain made peace with France, declared war on England in 1796, and thereupon attacked Portugal. In these circumstances interest and honour alike compelled Great Britain to help Portugal, but, when she could hardly help herself, it hurt to do so. All the same, in August 1796 12,000 muskets and 3000 each of carbines and pairs of pistols were issued to the Portuguese from Ordnance stores, just as they might have been to British troops.[1] But these were not the only British arms Portugal received; in February 1797 Cornwallis complained bitterly to Dundas: 'The Portuguese Minister was permitted to order 1000 [arms] and Lord Grenville employed Mr Davidson [sic] to provide 12,000 Musquets for Portugal, which has been so inconvenient an Interference to the Ordnance in the Provision of Arms that it would have been much less felt if 20,000 had been delivered to the Portuguese from our own stores.'[2] It will be marked that this intrusion of Portugal into the market had been made by permission, and that the Foreign Secretary was the man against whom the complaints of the Ordnance were directed on this occasion. At the Foreign Office, then, this could be solved; the peace of Olivenza between Spain and Portugal made things easier anyway; and when Cornwallis exerted himself he was effective. The interference was not allowed to occur again. In June 1799, the Secretary of the Ordnance is found writing firmly to the Portuguese ambassador that he could not export 2000 stands of muskets 'bespoke of the Manufacturers of this Kingdom'; but, the writer continues, if Portugal would accept 'Arms of any Foreign Manufacture', the Board would not object 'to the Exportation of as large a Number of such Arms as your Excellency may be able to make purchase of in this Country'.[3]

This letter evokes two comments. First, it marks the date at which the Ordnance secured something very close to a monopoly for the purchase of all firearms made in Britain. The only competition left was found in the private demands of sportsmen for personal weapons, which relatively were trivial, and in such enterprises as the Canadian fur trade which required guns in numbers too small and of a quality too poor to cause the government any anxiety. Secondly, it reveals that Britain had by now an unwanted surplus of foreign arms.

This second fact was due only in part to the large purchases of Birmingham-made French muskets (for many of these found their way to Brittany).[4] It was more due to the desperate efforts of the Ordnance in 1793–6 to buy abroad the arms they could not get at home. Richmond

[1] R. H. Crew to the Chevalier d'Almeida, 5 August 1796, WO/46/24.
[2] Cornwallis to Dundas on an unnamed day in February 1797, WO/46/25.
[3] Crew to the Chevalier d'Almeida, 27 June 1799, WO/46/25.
[4] For example, on 26 December 1795, Crew writes Huskisson that preparations are complete for sending 25,000 muskets, with 100 rounds of ammunition for each weapon, to Quiberon Bay, WO/46/24.

had first sought arms in Belgium and placed great hopes in one M. Lassence of Liège.[1] Lassence had come to London in July 1793, and had left with a contract for 10,000 muskets, which he bound himself under a heavy penalty to complete by a fixed date, and with a specimen British musket as an exact pattern to copy. Later he agreed to add a second 10,000 muskets to his first order.

Little good came of the hopes placed on these 20,000 stands of arms from Belgium. Lassence's workmen were so dilatory that he never fulfilled his contract; and it was soon found to be 'utterly impracticable for him to get the Workmen at Liège to make their Arms conformable to the pattern agreed upon....Although the bore is the same, and their Arms may be Serviceable, scarce any two of their Musquets are similar to the Pattern or to each other.'[2] Here the civilian reader may smile, with the common civilian's scorn of the army's affection for uniformity, but M. Lassence's artisans carried individualism to excess. In August 1794 it was reported that in 400 of his muskets, lately received at the Tower, 'the Sockets of the Bayonets' were found not 'to fit the sights', and thus to be unusable; and 882 muskets of the same shipment had no bayonets at all. All these new arms had therefore to go to the workshops before they could be issued; and the cost of putting them right was charged to Lassence's account.[3] The charge can have hurt him little; within a matter of weeks he was relieved of his British contract, for Liège fell into the hands of the French and he no doubt found profitable employment with the city's new masters. The workshops of Liège alone provided France with over 250,000 stands of arms under the Empire, and though the data are not available, they presumably supplied a proportionate number to the Directory. The figures give some idea of the price Britain had to pay for the defeat in Belgium in 1794 to which her own unpreparedness contributed much.

In this winter, when France overran Belgium and Holland, Prussia withdrew from the war by the Treaty of Basel. Loss of the Belgian supply, and hope of securing arms no longer wanted for a demobilized Prussia, then led the Board to seek arms in Hamburg, Gottenburg, and Copenhagen. There is a hint of panic in their search. The disappointing weapons from Belgium were at least of British calibre and could take British ammunition, but in the summer of 1795 even this requirement was no longer demanded. Agents dispatched to buy abroad were told to 'send...to England as soon as possible' any serviceable muskets of any calibre that could be had for 25s. each.[4] When a government can only hope to meet a crisis by thus going shopping, cash in hand, to any market that may provide it with the means of survival, it becomes in its desperation the

---

[1] Rogers to Nepean, 3 July 1793, HO/50/369.
[2] Richmond to Dundas, 24 January 1794, HO/50/371.
[3] Extract from Ordnance Minutes, 2 September 1794, WO/47/2364.
[4] Crew to Miller, 27 July 1795, and to Trotter, 15 August 1795, WO/46/24.

natural prey of the charlatan and the confidence trickster. On this occasion the British government was lucky enough to escape from Gottenburg and Copenhagen with nothing lost and nothing gained. In Hamburg
they were gulled by a rogue called 'Monseiur Harel L'Aigle'. For six
months their agent, Major Trotter, waited in hope that this character
would deliver 30,000 arms he had promised to provide by the end of
August. Finally, on 21 December 1795, Trotter was ordered to break
with L'Aigle as the Board of Ordnance were now 'convinced' that 'his
Motive for coming forward in this Affair [had] not proceeded from the
possession of any means to complete his promised Engagements'. The
same letter ordered Trotter home; but at about this very date he had the
luck to find a reputable firm called 'Monsr. J. Desgournay and Co.' who
undertook to provide '15,000 Stands of new Musquets of the French
calibre [in] under a Month', and afterwards 'to furnish 50,000 at stated
intervals in case such a Number should be required'.[1] Deliveries of these
arms were still being made in August 1796,[2] and the Board were so far
satisfied with them as to decline all fresh offers of foreign weapons after
April 1796.[3]

Indeed, this month of April 1796 seems a notable landmark in the story
of arms production. Then the Ordnance had actually declined to buy any
more arms from British manufacturers, because they had 'asked such
exorbitant prices'.[4] The enormous debt of £234,736. 11s. 3d.,[5] which in
May 1797 the government owed British and foreign merchants for new
weapons received but not paid for, is evidence that great numbers had
flowed into the arsenals; much also had been done to increase the stock
by repairing old arms, or making new ones out of the serviceable parts of
old. As a good new musket was supposed to remain serviceable for
twelve years, the Board had now some grounds to take a strong line against
the manufacturers who were perhaps suspected of combining to keep
prices high. Back in November 1793 the merchant, Thomas Gill, had
been paid a mere 11s. 8d. each for 500 new Land Service muskets of the
British model; and the way prices had risen in three years is indicated by
the fact that in 1796 the Ordnance were prepared to buy serviceable
muskets of any calibre that could be had for 25s. each. Yet the merchants
themselves might fairly plead that the long periods they had to wait for
payment by the Treasury were some excuse for demanding high prices; and
the Board was hardly wise to suspend purchases, for less than a year
passed before, in an anxious letter dated 'February, 1797', Cornwallis
was to express the fear that he would soon be faced with a demand to
provide arms for a *levée en masse* called out to meet invasion. (On the

---

[1] Crew to Trotter, 21 December 1794, *ibid*.
[2] Crew to Bellis, 27 August 1796, *ibid*.
[3] Crew to Trotter, 25 April 1796, *ibid*.
[4] *Ibid*.
[5] Nettleship to Rose, 13 May 1797, WO/46/25.

3rd of that month Mantua had fallen to crown the success of Bonaparte's Italian campaign, and as Austria's ability to resist neared its end, it became increasingly evident that Britain must soon fight alone.) To meet invasion, and a resulting wholesale outcry for arms, Cornwallis could look to an excess of no more than 20,000 muskets (many of poor quality) over all currently known demands.[1] However, the invasion did not come; the crisis caused, as noted, some exertion on the part of the Board to make the Treasury pay its bills; and from this point to the Treaty of Amiens the situation continued to improve.

And here a curious fact. When the acute crisis of want of arms was over, and not till then, it was realized that for years a very large number of weapons had been wasted, and in fact, almost literally thrown away to no purpose at all. Weapons were issued by the Board of Ordnance on the authority of the Secretary-at-War. When this watchdog of economy directed the Ordnance to issue arms to a newly raised regiment, or to replace the worn arms of an old regiment, he informed the Board merely of the total number of men provided for in the paper establishment of the regiment concerned. The Ordnance thereupon issued arms for the regiment's full nominal strength; but throughout these years of crisis the failure of recruiting left dozens of regiments far below their paper strength. Dozens of battalion headquarters were therefore cumbered with arms they had no occasion to issue. Unopened cases of muskets lay piled on top of one another from year's end to year's end; no one cleaned the weapons; their storage places were sometimes damp; at every regimental move they were bumped around from the old site of headquarters to the new; and at the last they were commonly returned to the Ordnance, wholly unused and yet, from want of care, wholly unusable. Meanwhile other battalions might be drilling without weapons, or reinforcements sent unarmed overseas, while these unnumbered quantities of muskets rusted into decay. The abuse continued till in 1799 the Duke of York called Windham's attention to it;[2] only then did the War Office adopt the practice of ordering that regiments receive the number of arms they required in fact, not theory. Yet the War Office, being responsible for the pay of every serving soldier, had never lacked knowledge of the number of effective men in the ranks of every regular unit; Windham's incompetence as an administrator could hardly be more plainly demonstrated by anything than by this long continued over-issue of arms to some units and starvation of others in years of critical shortage.

After all the anxieties and all the exertions over arming Britain in the war with the French Republic, it might be thought that the nation would be found ready with all the arms it wanted to face Napoleon's challenge of invasion in 1803; but it was not. The new outbreak of hostilities precipi-

---

[1] Cornwallis to Dundas, February 1795, *ibid.*
[2] Dupin, *Military Force of Great Britain*, II, 165–6.

tated a still more alarming crisis, in the first nine months of which no fewer than 103,572 pikes were issued to save new-raised volunteers from having to advance quite empty-handed against the invading legions of the French.[1] One must still be fair minded in censuring the much abused Addington ministry over its unreadiness for war. That government deserves every credit for maintaining a peacetime army with the unprecedented total of 132,000 men, thrice the force kept up from 1783 to 1793; of these 81,000 men were in Britain; thanks to the Duke of York this very considerable body of men was better disciplined, trained, and officered than any previous British Army in peacetime since the old Duke of Cumberland's day. The Ordnance Department was also in a far better position to satisfy demands for weapons than it had been in 1793; they retained the monopoly of the whole market for firearms which they had still to win at the outbreak of the earlier war; they had a reserve of some 150,000 arms in store; and (as the life of a musket was reckoned at twelve years) a very large number of the weapons issued to the county militia battalions in the previous war should still have been fit for service; and in fact few demands for new weapons were made by the militia. But once more there came a demand for weapons which far exceeded anything that had been foreseen.

This time the demand was made great at least as much by unreasoning panic as by any sober appreciation of the real danger. To be sure, the threat was formidable. From every port between Brest and the Texel hostile troops looked out across the sea toward Britain; their numbers, and the length of coastline they commanded, had never been surpassed in British war experience; their quality was first rate; their commander a host in himself. But even so, a time of danger is above all others a time for clear thinking; and the Duke of York, who kept his head, expressed a simple truth, applicable to the defence of all beleaguered islands, when he wrote on 1 July 1803, 'The extent of army which an enemy may land depends not upon his numbers at home, but upon his means of transporting them to this country'.[2] It is hard indeed to see where France could have found shipping enough to transport a force capable of overcoming the quarter of a million men whom Britain either possessed already armed or had weapons ready for in the moment that war broke out. It would therefore seem much more important for the defending force to be mobile and efficient than for it to be immensely large. The government, however, preferred numbers to competence, and called into being an enormous army of volunteers who could be made efficient only by some months of training; and the Ordnance, which stood ready to issue new weapons to 150,000 additional men, was called upon to find arms for a host of upwards of 600,000. It was thus confronted with an immediate

[1] Hadden to Pole Carew, 6 April 1804, HO/50/397.
[2] Circular to General Officers commanding Districts, 1 July 1803, WO/30/76.

deficit of some half million arms. Nothing within the power of British industry could make good this deficit in any reasonable time. Hence the government was 'drawn into the most hasty and improvident contracts all over Europe for 500,000 stands [of arms] and to the amount of near £700,000. It afterwards cost the nation much to reduce those contracts', wrote R. H. Crew, Secretary of the Board of Ordnance, as he looked back in after years.[1]

The whole story of the purchase of foreign arms cannot, and need not, now be told. The fact, however, that of the half million contracted for only 293,000 arms were delivered indicates it was not a satisfactory expedient; and the manner in which the business was done is eloquent of what is now sometimes called 'the jitters'.

Most eloquent is the extraordinary story of one M. du Roveray. This man was a spy who had modestly introduced himself to the British government in 1794 with the words, 'you will be surprised at My Courage, My Activity, My Diligence and Perseverance'.[2] One fears he may have been regularly receiving secret service money from that date forward, till on 10 November 1803 he wrote R. H. Crew,

A number of 108 to 120 thousand stands of Arms with their Bayonets and Iron Ramrods, constituting a great part of the whole stock of the Dutch Arsenals, is at this instant in the hands of an eminent Mercantile house in Amsterdam under the firm of Haidkoper, Kobler, and Bicker, who, to prevent any obstacle to the free disposal of those goods, have already begun to send about thirty or forty thousand of them to the neutral port of Embden, and mean to forward the rest immediately to the same destination.[3]

These arms du Roveray offered to the Ordnance, with delivery promised in two months, either in Emden or England, for 17s. a stand. He wanted 9s. 4d. paid in advance and 7s. 8d. paid within twenty days of delivery for each weapon, on the security of Sir Francis Baring and Co.

A question that must provoke curiosity here is how 'a great part of the whole stock' of the arsenals of a French puppet state could get into the hands of even 'an eminent Mercantile House' without the French knowing about it; an equally interesting question is why a great military dictatorship would let any arms be sent abroad, if the arms were any good. The price was also suspiciously low. Nevertheless, the offer was accepted the very day it was made. The Board sent an agent, one Lt. Col. A. du Vernet, to Emden, with du Roveray's (evidently satisfactory) samples and orders to pay the advance of 9s. 4d. on every weapon as good as the models.[4] This did not please du Roveray. Apparently he did not wish his

---

[1] Appendix no. 1, Third Report of Select Committee of Finance, 1817.
[2] Enclosure, Nepean to Chatham, 13 July 1794, PRO/30/8/368.
[3] J. A. du Roveray to R. H. Crew, 10 September 1803, WO/46/25.
[4] Crew to Nepean, 30 November 1803, *ibid.*

advance payment to depend on du Vernet's inspection, and he now sprang on the British government one of those surprises he had promised them. A whole shipload of these weapons, evading Emden, proceeded to sail direct from Amsterdam to London in January 1804. It was du Roveray's first, and apparently his last, shipment. Inspection showed that of the 6640 arms it contained, 2140 were 'totally unfit for Military Service, being of various lengths, descriptions of fabric and different calibres; the remaining 4500 are in a very rusty state, and appear to have been in a damp place for a number of years...[they could not] be applied to any use without passing through the hands of the Gun Makers—added to which four out of Fifty barrels, which were proved with a diminished proportion of powder burst, so that serious Apprehensions are entertained' that the weapons would be unsafe to 'put into the hands of troops'.[1]

Prior to this odd transaction, a London firm of Le Mesurier had undertaken in August to supply from 40,000 to 45,000 Prussian arms; du Vernet was instructed to seek out at Emden a Mr Muller who was offering 100,000 muskets. The Board was now willing to pay '34s. for each Musquet that may be new and a proportionate Sum for those that have been used',[2] though in 1795 they had offered no more than 25s.; and for 34s. they were ready to buy from 2000 to 4000 Hanoverian arms offered to the British consul in Hamburg. Later, in February 1804, a contract for 8000 more Hanoverian muskets was made with a firm called Moisez and Co. in Hamburg.[3]

The Board combed South as well as North Germany. On 15 November 1803, R. H. Crew is found writing to a Viennese banker called J. A. Bienenfeld that the Board understood he could supply 'a considerable Quantity of Musquets of the Austrian Manufacture'. They earnestly desired that he 'would collect and purchase on their account, at as reasonable a Rate and with as much dispatch as may be possible, a proportion of Musquets either of Austrian Manufacture or any other Foreign Fabric not exceeding Fifty Thousand Stands..to be shipped from Trieste or Fiume on or before 15th January next'. This is a remarkable request for any government to make of an unknown foreign businessman; the price of the weapons is left entirely at Bienenfeld's discretion. The only check on the quality was an authority to one John Wood, described as Deputy Commissary General in Vienna, and not an Ordnance official, to make a binding contract if he could 'obtain satisfactory information' that 'the arms...are new and of the regular Austrian pattern and have undergone the Austrian proof'.[4]

The upshot of all these contracts was that the Board acquired weapons

---

[1] Ouvry to du Roveray, 31 January 1804, *ibid.*
[2] Ouvry to the British Consul, Hamburg, 30 December 1803, *ibid.*
[3] Ouvry to J. Moisez and Co., 14 February 1794, WO/46/25.
[4] Crew to John Wood, 30 January 1804, WO/46/25.

originally made for at least four different European armies and possibly of four different calibres. Ammunition was obviously going to be a problem, and one would like to know what use was made of all these foreign arms. The question cannot be fully answered. On 25 February 1804, however, the complaint was reported that the Oldham volunteers 'have received 180 Stand of Arms in very bad condition—they are old Dutch pieces'[1] (so du Roveray's weapons were not left long in store). In March 1804, the Manchester volunteers were complaining that they had only 'Prussian Arms';[2] and in June 1807, the Worcestershire volunteers were complaining of 'Old Prussian Arms'.[3] From these complaints it would appear that the Board of Ordnance judiciously issued its foreign arms to the more remote counties; and those counties were lucky to get them. Complaints of volunteers who had grown weary of drilling without any arms at all are frequent.

The real resource for arming any great power at war must, of course, lie in its own industry. Given its monopoly of purchase, the British government could with time get much from British manufacturers. Yet early in the new war the Ordnance is found breaking down its hard-won monopoly by agreeing 'to allow such Infantry Corps as shall provide their own Arms with the same price that the Ordnance shall pay to the Ordnance Contractors for arms of a similar description'.[4] But this was sheer delirium. It invited an open scramble on the manufacturers' doorstep among individual volunteer corps. The first to come would be the first served, unless indeed some at the end of the queue should offer a price increased over the Ordnance allowance with money raised by local subscription. Arms which units secured privately were just so many arms the Ordnance would never see; and therefore this scramble must damage, if it did not end, any rational plan of arming first the volunteers of those shires that were most nearly threatened. One of the results was that Denbigh, than which there could hardly be a safer county, apparently bought its own weapons[5] while volunteers in the maritime counties of Kent and Norfolk remained unarmed.[6]

It is hard to believe that this folly would have been permitted had any man less inertly casual than Lord Chatham been the responsible minister in charge of the Ordnance department; and fortunately it was not long-lived. On 3 January 1804, the Board is found writing the Home Office that it was 'absolutely necessary to put an end to the practice'; the government were 'employing every gunmaker capable of making a Mili-

[1] Lt. Col. Maxwell to Prince Frederick William, 25 February 1804, HO/50/397.
[2] Crew to Pole Carew, 2 April 1804, HO/50/397.
[3] Wynyard to John Becket, 12 June 1807, HO/50/405.
[4] Ross to Pole Carew, 7 September 1803, HO/50/394.
[5] Griffin to Pole Carew, 3 January 1804, HO/50/396.
[6] Brownrigg to Yorke, December 1803, HO/50/395. Crew to Pole Carew, 18 October 1803, HO/50/394.

tary Musquet; and...purchases of Arms by Individuals have been found materially to intercept the public supplies'.[1]

So the monopoly was regained, and a number of other sensible steps were taken to increase production. In 1804 the Board established, under one Lt. Col. James Miller, an office of its own at Birmingham. Miller's job in Birmingham was to 'increase the supplies of articles from thence'.[2] He was also to see weapons 'proved' on the spot, so that no defective arms would be carried to London before their flaws were discovered. Miller was apparently effective. In the last nine months of 1803 the Ordnance received only 40,609 new muskets into store; in the twelve months of 1804 they received 167,749.[3] (But allowance must be made for deliveries received in 1804 on contracts made in 1803, a point on which evidence is hard, if at all possible to obtain; also for the damage done by competitive purchase on which the full facts cannot possibly be learnt.)

Secondly, the Board itself went into the actual business of manufacturing small arms. This was a step that had been proposed, but not taken, in 1794. The failure of the Board to do then what it did later is probably explained in part by the Duke of Richmond's unwillingness to jeopardize deliveries by drawing artisans away from manufacturers employed by the Board; and in part by the objections of contemporary opinion to the government's going into business. The establishment of a national factory was proposed in 1794, because the Board were 'perfectly convinced that the only method that can be taken to prevent in future the present complaints is to have a Manufactory of Small Arms upon the Establishment of the Ordnance, which besides producing a supply of Arms in Case of Emergency would become a checque upon the proceedings of the Gunmakers and prevent combinations among them against the Government'.[4] In 1804 the twin arguments of price control and supply were judged paramount over all objections, yet a curious hesitancy marks the Board's conduct. Two proposals were laid before it; first, that what would now be called an 'assembly plant' should be established at the Tower; second, that a building the Board already owned at Lewisham should be used as a factory to make parts. The assembly plant at the Tower was immediately started. There barrels, locks, bayonets, and ramrods bought in Birmingham were 'stocked' to make complete muskets. It fulfilled its functions: it gave the Board exact knowledge of the cost of putting the parts of arms together, and thus provided a 'checque' on combinations of gunmakers; it did increase supply; and it added a third advantage too. The Board needed professional armourers on the staffs of its outports where damaged muskets were sent to be repaired locally. Hitherto it had apparently filled

---

[1] Griffin to Pole Carew, 3 January 1804, HO/50/396.
[2] Alsop to the Commissioners of Military Inquiry; Appendix 9 of the Commission's Fifteenth Report.
[3] *Ibid.*   [4] Crew to Hadden, 25 July 1794, WO/46/24.

these positions by selecting little-known or unknown men from among such applicants as happened to present themselves; hereafter it selected men of proven competence from among its regular employees at the Tower. From the Lewisham factory precisely the same advantages were expected as from the Tower assembly plant, yet it did not begin to produce till 1808; for want of evidence to explain the delay, I am inclined to attribute it to the indolence of Lord Chatham, and to give credit for the factory's final opening in 1808 to the initiative of Lord Moira, who was Master General from March 1806 till July 1807. At both Lewisham and the Tower artisans were paid for piecework at the rate of wages prevailing in Birmingham. The result of all these efforts to increase the supply of arms led in time to production of a number of weapons far exceeding the number of British soldiers requiring them. The surplus made Britain the armoury of all peoples who rose against Napoleon; masses of British weapons were to sustain the Spanish revolt in 1808–9, and in 1813 to arm Russia, Prussia, and Sweden.[1]

By the spring of 1794 shortage of artillery as well as muskets had begun to cause lively anxiety, but this, as Richmond wrote to Dundas, was 'not from any want of Guns, or the possibility of getting Ammunition for them, but from want of Artillery Men to make use of a larger Proportion'.[2] Another factor than the difficulty of recruiting came into play here, however. Whereas at this date the Ordnance was entirely dependent on private contractors to furnish small arms, it had its own foundry to cast cannon and its own carriage works to mount them. So in August 1794, when Richmond replied to inquiries from the Duke of Portland about guns for Ireland, he was quite ready to send to Dublin 'twelve Desaguliers 6-Pounders...though it will be taking them from our home Establishment', which had no more than 'just sufficient', because he could 'cast more to make up our Number'. But he declined to mount the guns for Ireland, because that 'would so much retard the great quantity of works going on here' in the British carriage factory.[3]

The Ordnance carriage works were indeed loaded with a very great deal of business at this date, and Richmond had very recently had to reorganize it. The navy as well as the Royal Artillery had its guns mounted in the Ordnance carriage works, and claimed a degree of priority that almost prevented artillery jobs from being done at all. Finally, Richmond, whose patience was perhaps never excessive, exploded with a letter whose

---

[1] The weapons supplied to these powers in 1813 are stated to have been 218 cannon; 124,119 muskets, with bayonets; 18,231,000 rounds of ball cartridge; and 23,000 barrels of powder (Charles, Third Marquis of Londonderry, *Narrative of the War in Germany and France in 1813 and 1814*, London, 1830, Appendix I). I have not encountered any statement of the total number of arms furnished to the Spaniards and Portuguese between 1808 and 1814.

[2] Richmond to Dundas, 27 March 1794, HO/50/371.

[3] Richmond to Portland, 14 August 1794, *ibid.*

curt clarity could hardly be surpassed. He really did 'not understand why the Ship Carriage service is always alleged as an Excuse for delaying the Orders for the Land Service'; a division of 'Artificers, Smiths, Forges, Carpenters &c' was to be made forthwith; the navy might have 'a far larger proportion' of them than 'in any former war', but separate shops were to be established for 'the two Services [which were to be kept] entirely distinct in future'; and Mr Butler, head of the carriage works, was told 'immediately to make me a Return of the Number of Workmen of every description which you allot to each'. Lastly (a hint as to the cause of the trouble), no 'alteration of Plans for Ship carriages' was to be made without the Duke's or the Board's order; and 'if any Captains of the Navy [were to] come to' Butler to ask for changes of any kind, he was to inform them that he had the Duke's 'positive orders not to make any without orders from the Board of Ordnance and that the Board will not make any without the approbation and request of the Navy Board'.[1] It is likely that this was a very valuable reform, both from the point of view of speeding the work for the navy by standardizing its equipment and of enabling the Royal Artillery's work to be done within a predictable time.

Though the Ordnance was thus able to rely on its own establishments to produce field artillery, it does not seem to have cast its own mortars before the war; and when thirty 10-inch mortars were demanded to provide high-angle fire for the proposed siege of Dunkirk in 1793, it could only supply a dozen. This failure Richmond attributed to 'the very extravagant prices [manufacturers had charged] for casting mortars' in peacetime,[2] and a hurried conference with the owners of London foundries in July 1793 did not bring much improvement.[3] 'The greatest supply we can expect will not exceed twenty a month', was the report made to Dundas's office.[4] At the date when this order for mortars was given in London, the Carron Company in Scotland seems to have received an order to make shells for them,[5] but this was unusual. The Ordnance normally preferred to have shells made up at Woolwich by its own skilled employees.

If the government in the early years of the war had, as Richmond indicated, no anxieties about the supply of artillery ammunition, it was certainly because of the lack of gunners to use that ammunition, and for a number of years gunpowder was, in fact, alarmingly scarce.

Britain had long relied on the East India Company for deliveries of 'good, clean, merchantable saltpetre',[6] out of which, with brimstone and charcoal, the powder of the day was made. For years the Company had

---

[1] Richmond to Butler, 27 July 1794, WO/46/23.
[2] Richmond to Nepean, 18 July 1794, HO/50/369.
[3] Rogers to Richmond, 19 July 1793, WO/46/24.
[4] Rogers to Nepean, 5 August 1793, HO/50/369.
[5] *Ibid.*
[6] 1 Queen Anne, c. 6, §137.

been required to import a given annual tonnage of saltpetre, which the government reserved the right to buy, to the exclusion of other purchasers. Long reliance on one trusted source prevented the government from looking for other markets; in the years before 1793 economy and the hope of continued peace caused the government not to use its right of compulsory purchase; and so here again war found the nation with short supplies. In March 1793, before the war was a month old, Richmond was asking Dundas to forbid the East India Company holding a saltpetre sale.[1] In August the Board were interested in the offer of a Swedish merchant to supply manufactured powder, and were inquiring what quantities he would undertake to deliver by what dates. In the next summer there came a catastrophe so damaging as to suggest sabotage. It is announced in a letter written to the Board for Richmond by Lt. Col. Hadden. 'The Duke', wrote Hadden on 25 July 1794, 'has just read an account in the News Papers by which it appears that the East India Company's Salt Petre Warehouse in London has just been destroyed with a great quantity of Petre by fire. This intelligence has disturbed His Grace exceedingly'; and therefore the Duke desired that order be given forthwith 'to prevent a Waste of Powder by stopping all Salutes being Fired at the present Moment and during the War, when it is so much wanted for more serious purposes'.[2]

What cause the Duke had to be 'exceedingly disturbed' is indicated by the facts that he had wished to stop the firing of salutes before this;[3] that six months earlier the shortage of powder had been sufficiently acute for the Board to approve of Sunday labour in the government-owned powder factory at Waltham;[4] and also by the probability that the East India Company's warehouse contained nearly all the saltpetre available in Britain. In September 1794, it was recorded that the Company was in arrears with deliveries of 3000 tons of saltpetre due in 1789, 1790, 1791, 1792, and 1793.[5] No fresh supplies could be expected till the next East India convoy arrived safe in London—till then at least the workmen at Waltham could presumably count on having their weekends to themselves; and even then one East India fleet's required consignment of saltpetre in ballast could hardly make good the lost arrears of five years. Meanwhile August brought a pressing demand for a thousand barrels of powder from the Irish government in Dublin; and Ireland had to be disappointed. 'I fear we cannot spare the whole of the Small Grained sort, which is fittest for Musquets', wrote Richmond, and the demand was filled in part with 'the Large Grained sort',[6] which at this date was usually regarded as obsolete for small arms ammunition.

[1] Richmond to Dundas, 4 March 1793, HO/50/368.
[2] Hadden to Sargent, 25 August 1794, WO/46/23.   [3] *Ibid.*
[4] Extract of Ordnance Minutes, 23 January 1794, WO/47/2365.
[5] Extract of Ordnance Minutes, 16 September 1794, *ibid.*
[6] Richmond to Portland, 27 August 1794, HO/50/371.

In September the East India ships at last bore up the Channel, turned the corner of the Kentish coast, and came to their dock up the London river;[1] but evidently their stocks of saltpetre were as inadequate as might have been expected. The only resource was more Swedish powder. In October an Ordnance officer, Captain Miller, was dispatched to Gottenburg, with a technical man from the Faversham powder mill, to prove and buy powder. I have found no record of his purchases, but they were probably considerable, for he was still in Gottenburg in the next July, when Crew wrote to ask him to buy muskets there; and he did not return till September 1795 after a stay of some eleven months.[2] During this period of shortage, the British troops occupying Corsica (in uneasy co-operation with Boswell's friend, Paoli) had needed stocks of powder which Britain could not supply; and again foreign purchase had been the only resource. A Major William Collier, R.A., is reported in January 1795 as having 'lately been sent to Italy to purchase Gunpowder and other stores immediately [sic] wanted for service' in Corsica; and he was given elaborate instructions for 'proving' the strength of the powder by measuring the ranges to which exact weights of it would throw a mortar bomb.[3]

Recovery from this alarming shortage was slow. The Board did indeed secure very large stocks of powder. A letter written by R. H. Crew in June 1796 is very illuminating; it reveals both how well supplied British fortresses were and how well Crew knew his business. General O'Hara, Governor of Gibraltar, had written nervously to complain of a supposed shortage of powder at that stronghold. Crew was unimpressed.

It appeared [he wrote] that there were on the 22nd of April last Nine Thousand whole Barrels of Gunpowder remaining in the Magazine at Gibraltar, which is a quantity considerably greater than the whole consumption of that article during the late three years' siege of that place [i.e. the great siege of 1779–82]; that One thousand eight hundred and thirty-five Barrels of Powder for Gibraltar and four thousand for Corsica, being the supply for the Fleets upon those Stations, are embarked in the River Thames...that when the Naval Supply of Powder for Gibraltar shall arrive ...it will be found the Magazines are nearly full, as they are calculated to hold seven thousand six hundred and seventy-two Barrels, and They cannot contain a greater Number than Thirteen Thousand Barrels even when all the Passages of the Magazine are filled.[4]

There should then be no immediate worry about Gibraltar. But powder supplies were a matter in which the Board of Ordnance had to look rather specially far ahead. East India fleets returned to their homeland only twice a year. The loss of one fleet would mean no new saltpetre within a year of the arrival of the last supplies received; the only guard against

---

[1] Extract of Ordnance Minutes, 16 September 1794, WO/47/2365.
[2] Crew to Miller, 4 September 1795, WO/40/26.
[3] Hadden to Crew, 25 January 1795, WO/47/2365.
[4] Crew to Charles Greville, 16 June 1796, HO/50/372.

possible disaster was therefore to keep very large stocks on hand—as had not been done in the years of peace.

Here again Portugal was a recurrent problem and a revealing one. In July 1798 Lord Grenville was asking the Board to release powder for Portugal, and another power dependent on Britain, the U.S.A. Crew replied: 'General Ross [states] that the Quantity of Gunpowder at present in the Ordnance Magazines is upon a moderate Estimate barely sufficient for a year and a half of our own Consumption, and that, exclusive of the Saltpetre lately arrived from India, the quantity of that at present in possession of the Ordnance and the Company is not quite enough to satisfy our Demand for one Year.'[1] It is interesting that with these stocks on hand, the Board would not take the responsibility of offering any at all of either made powder or saltpetre to either Portugal or the U.S.A. In the light of their statement, Crew proceeded, Lord Grenville 'will be very well able to judge how much Gunpowder and Saltpetre it would be prudent to send out of this country'.[2] A month later Crew was writing another letter. Grenville had apparently decided he could prudently send 'considerable' quantities of powder out of the country, and Crew was now inquiring

whether there are not in H.M.'s Magazines some Sorts of Powder, which, altho' they are not brought into Use for the Services carrying on here, yet are considered in a serviceable state and might perhaps be delivered for the Service of any Foreign State...you will transmit to me for the Board's Information a Return of the Descriptions and Quantities of Powder which remain in H.M.'s Magazines that will answer the Purposes I have described.[3]

This letter, like the last, was written on General Ross's orders; it is eloquent of the anxieties of a man whose fears are not quieted by shifting the responsibility for a decision on to someone else's shoulders. Again in March 1801, the Portuguese demands provoked an inquiry from Crew as to whether the East India Company could produce before 'September next a Supply of 300 Tons of Saltpetre in addition to the Quantity they shall want for the King's Service between this time and that Period'.[4] From this inquiry it would seem fair to conclude that the Board never felt really happy about their reserve of powder till the Peace of Amiens. It does not seem to have caused anxiety when war broke out again in 1803.

Saltpetre was made up into gunpowder partly by private manufacturers and partly at the two government-owned powder mills, at Faversham and Waltham Abbey. Of these the latter was very new, for it was founded only in 1788. It would be a great (if a natural) mistake to regard these government-owned factories of the eighteenth century as forerunners

---

[1] Crew to Hammond, 20 June 1798, WO/46/25.
[2] *Ibid.*
[3] Crew to Congreve, 29 August 1798, WO/46/25.
[4] Crew to W. Ramsay, 23 April 1801, WO/47/2367.

of the nationalized industries of the twentieth century. The government's arms factories of the Napoleonic period were relatively small, operating in competition with private enterprise and run by a handful of enthusiasts. The last point accounts for their efficiency; and, with no shareholders requiring dividends, they produced their goods at a lower price than private manufacturers.

Allsop, the Ordnance officer who had pressed for the establishment of national small arms factories, may perhaps be fairly termed an enthusiast; and there can be no question about giving that name to the Comptroller of the powder mills at Faversham and Waltham Abbey. This was William Congreve, later the first baronet of that name, who died in 1814 and was the father of a more famous son, the second Sir William Congreve (1772–1828). He was made Deputy-Comptroller of Faversham in 1783, and full Comptroller of both factories in 1789. Under his management the government powder mills greatly increased the strength of the powder they produced, and private manufacturers had to produce powder that could meet the same tests as that made by the government.[1] In 1809 about three-fifths of the nation's powder was made in the government mills, namely, 36,623¾ barrels containing 90 pounds of powder each; and 24,433⅓ barrels were purchased from private manufacturers.[2] The last received saltpetre from the government, and provided only their own brimstone and charcoal, but they never made powder as cheaply as it was made under Congreve's management in the national factories. By 1809 it was reckoned that in twenty years the Waltham Abbey mill had paid for itself nearly twice over out of the difference between the cost of the powder it made and the cost of an equal amount of powder bought of manufacturers.[3]

The powder thus acquired was made up into ammunition at government-owned laboratories. It seems to have been rare for private manufacturers to make ammunition under contract. The job was a specialist one, calling for great care and close supervision. The workers in the Woolwich laboratory were paid by time, not by piecework, because that method 'would be running a great risk of having the ammunition imperfectly made up'.[4] The Woolwich laboratory had been established in 1747; branch laboratories for making up small arms ammunition only were started at Plymouth and Portsmouth in 1804.

[1] Twenty-First Report of the Select Committee of Finance, 1797, Appendix B.
[2] Sixteenth Report of the Commission of Military Inquiry, 1810, Appendix 9.
[3] *Ibid.*   [4] *Ibid.*

CHAPTER 3

THE ORDNANCE DEPARTMENT: RESEARCH

THERE is a very natural transition from gunpowder supplies to research because (as indicated above) gunpowder was itself a thing vastly improved in Britain between the American and French revolutions by the application of scientific research to its manufacture; and here it is pleasant to record a notable contribution from one of those older English universities which are often supposed to have been at this period remarkably innocent of scientific knowledge, as well as most other forms of usefulness. In his search for ways of improving powder the Duke of Richmond sought the advice of Cambridge's Professor of Divinity, that redoubtable (and generally absentee) Bishop of Llandaff, Richard Watson; and the Duke did not seek in vain, for his inquiry was by no means so surprising as it might seem. During the five years preceding his election to the divinity professorship, Watson had held the professorship of chemistry, for which, indeed, he had originally applied, not because he knew any chemistry whatever, but because he wished to learn some;[1] and evidently he learnt much. He now suggested to the government that they make the charcoal used in the manufacture of powder

by distilling the wood in close vessels. The suggestion was put into execution at Hythe, in 1787 [records the bishop] and the improvement has exceeded my utmost expectation. Major General Congreve delivered to me a paper containing an account of the experiments, which had been made with the cylinder powder (so called from the wood being distilled in iron cylinders), in all of which its superiority over every other species of powder was sufficiently established. In particular a given quantity of gunpowder, made with this kind of charcoal, threw a ball of 68 pounds weight [to a distance of] 273 feet; while the same mortar, at an equal elevation, and charged with an equal weight of gunpowder made with charcoal [produced] in the best of ordinary ways, threw an equal ball only 172 feet. In this experiment the strength of the cylinder powder, estimated by horizontal range, is to the best sort of other powder, as 100 to 63. By experiments with the Eprouvette, the proportion of strength of the cylinder to other powder was that of 100:54. In round numbers it may perhaps be near the truth to say, that the strength of the cylinder powder is to that of other powder as 100:60; or 5:3.[2]

This invention, which enabled three pounds of gunpowder to achieve as great an effect as had formerly been achieved with five, was later declared by an Ordnance official to have saved the country £100,000 a

---

[1] At the time of his election he had 'never read a syllable of the subject nor seen a single experiment in it' (R. Watson, *Anecdotes of the Life of Richard Watson, Bishop of Llandaff*, London, 1817, pp. 28–9).

[2] *Ibid.* p. 149.

year.[1] Watson must surely rank as a man of greater practical usefulness than any other who ever sat on the English bench of bishops. Nor (though I have failed to uncover further details) did the Ordnance Department's attempt to improve powder end with this achievement; in 1804 Ralph Adye, the gunner, is found writing of improved powder that fresh 'experiments are daily making at Woolwich and elsewhere'.[2]

The next piece of Ordnance research that may be mentioned attracted more attention than Watson's improvement of gunpowder, but was not necessarily more useful. It consisted of the famous rockets invented by the younger William Congreve.

Congreve's own story of his invention begins, 'In 1804 it first occurred to me that...the projectile force of the rocket...might be successfully employed, both afloat and ashore, as a military engine, in many cases where the recoil of exploding gunpowder' made the use of artillery impossible.[3] He began by buying the best rockets on the London market, but found their greatest range was only 600 yards. He knew that Indian princes had equipped their armies with rockets which would travel much farther than this. After spending 'several hundred pounds' of his own money on experiments he was able to make a rocket that would travel 1500 yards.[4] He now 'applied to Lord Chatham for permission to have some large rockets made at Woolwich'.[5] Permission was granted and 'several six-pounder rockets' made 'on principles I had previously ascertained' achieved a range of 'full two thousand yards'.[6] In range at least Congreve's new weapon now began to challenge fair comparison with artillery, and in the spring of 1806 he was producing 32-pounder rockets ranging 3000 yards. By 1810 he had added a 12-pound rocket carrying case shot, which is described as 'so portable that it may be used with the facility of musquetry', but had 'a range nearly *double* that of field artillery', and 'carrying as many bullets as the six-pounder spherical case' shot.[7] And there indeed was the grand advantage of Congreve's invention; he had created a weapon possessing many of the qualities of artillery but free from the encumbrance of guns; roads made no difference to its mobility; wherever a packhorse or an infantryman could go, the rocket would go and there be used. Far less than the hundreds of horses (and the tons of oats and hay they ate), without which no artillery train could move, were needed in a rocket brigade; and the weight of its bombardment was terrific. 'Of rocket case shot', says Major James (speaking of the 12-pounder type), '100 infantry soldiers will carry into action, in any situation where musquetry can act, 300 rounds and 10 frames; four rounds may be fired in a minute' from each frame.[8]

---

[1] *Ibid.* pp. 149–50.
[2] *The Bombardier and Pocket Gunner* (London, 1804), p. iv.
[3] W. Congreve, *A Treatise of the Congreve Rocket System* (London, 1827), p. 15.
[4] *Ibid.* p. 16.   [5] *Ibid.*   [6] *Ibid.*
[7] James, *Military Dictionary, sub* 'Rockets'.   [8] *Ibid.*

The first service trial of Congreve's new weapons took place at sea on the night of 7–8 October 1806. Eighteen boats with rockets, and frames for discharging them, were rowed into the bay at Boulogne to destroy the invasion barges lying in the basin there. Two hundred rounds were fired in thirty minutes; within ten minutes fires were observed ashore. Unfortunately 'the basin escaped injury, the rockets being thrown too much to the left'. But the fire in the town 'lasted from two o'clock in the morning till the next evening'. The ruins of eight buildings '...supposed to be barracks or storehouses...' were distinctly to be counted. That, however, seems a minimum estimate of the damage done. The next day, when Lord Lauderdale passed through Boulogne (on his way back to England after his unsuccessful attempt to negotiate the peace Charles James Fox had so long desired with France), great pains were taken to ensure that he saw nothing of the destruction around him; except when passing through the streets in a closed coach, with blinds drawn, he was confined to his hotel.[1] Shortly after this Napoleon offered a reward to any French inventor who could reproduce Congreve's weapon; and none could.[2] In 1807 rockets played their part in the bombardment under which Copenhagen surrendered. In the bombardment of Flushing in 1809 they wrought such havoc that 'General Monnet, the French commandant, made a formal protest to Lord Chatham' against their use.[3] But their supreme triumph was won at the battle of Leipzig in October 1813, and by the 2nd British Rocket Troop which was attached to the Swedish forces commanded by the Prince Royal (known a few years earlier as Napoleon's Marshal Bernadotte). 'Their effect', says an eye-witness, '[was] truly astonishing; and produced an impression upon the enemy of something supernatural ...a solid square of infantry...after our fire delivered themselves up as if panic struck.'[4] The rocketeers' commander, though only a lieutenant, was honoured on the field by the Tsar Alexander I himself, who removed from his own breast the Order of St Anne to pin it on the tunic of T. Fox Strangeways.

Thus told, the tale of the Congreve rocket is an extraordinary success story; and it has surprised many to find no mention of its use in Napier's pages till the passage of the Adour in February 1814. Then, after Leipzig, Wellington could no longer refuse to have rockets sent him. Earlier he had written: 'I can assure you that I am no partisan of Congreve's rockets of which I entertain but a bad opinion.'[5] In 1815 when a rocket troop under one Capt. Whinyates was sent him for the Waterloo campaign, he insisted that they be re-equipped as regular artillery. Seeing he

---

[1] Congreve, *Rocket System*, pp. 17–18.
[2] James, *Military Dictionary*, *sub* 'Rockets'.
[3] *Ibid.*
[4] Londonderry, *War in Germany and France in 1813 and 1814*, p. 172.
[5] Wellington to Admiral Berkeley, 6 November 1810, Gurwood, *Wellington's Dispatches*, VI.

appeared in a good humour Lt. Col. the Hon. George Wood (the commander of the Royal Artillery) pleaded: 'It will break Whinyates' heart to lose his rockets.' 'Damn his heart; let my order be obeyed', came Wellington's brief but decisive repartee; and only under great pressure did he consent to let Whinyates carry 800 rounds of 12-pounder rockets along with his guns.[1]

The two quotations just cited from Wellington have attracted much attention, and are sometimes used to bolster the legend of Wellington the encrusted Tory, who rejected all new ideas on no other ground than their mere loathsome novelty. Whatever Wellington's true character may have been, his bad opinion of the rocket cannot contribute to that picture. It was based on a very sound appreciation of the weapon's flaws. Ever since artillery began, gunners have striven for more and more accuracy; to that end infinite labour has been expended on finding improved methods of boring, rifling, range-finding, and sighting. Great progress had been made by 1800. In 1809 French gunners were able repeatedly to cut down the Portuguese flag from a British-held fort at Cadiz; in disgust at repeatedly having to haul up a foreign ensign, the troops at last (improperly) ran up the Union Jack. At Dresden Napoleon himself, laying an artillery piece with a sniper's accuracy, is credited with killing his old rival, Moreau, with his first shot. The gun of our period was thus a weapon of precision; the rocket, on the other hand, was wildly erratic. While Congreve had only heard of Tippoo's use of rockets in Mysore, Wellington had served in the campaigns in which they were used. His bad opinion of Congreve's was founded on 'what I recollect of the rockets in the East Indies.... It is but fair, however,' he continued, 'to give everything a trial';[2] and in November 1810, he did give rockets a trial. He sent a troop of them, under Major General Fane, to destroy the French boats at Santarem on the Tagus.[3] The trial evidently failed. 'I hope [your cannonade] will have had a much better effect than you suppose' was the best consolation Wellington could write in reply to Fane's disappointing report.[4] At Quatre Bras Lieutenant Mercer was at least equally disappointed when he tried some of those 800 rockets which Wellington had grudgingly permitted Whinyates to carry. A French battery, drawn up across a road, was causing trouble. Though warned by Strangeways (of Leipzig fame) that the range was long, Mercer could not refrain from trying to silence them with rockets. The first rocket sped down the chaussée, struck one gun, and strewed its crew right and left, dead or wounded all; the other French guncrews fled from their pieces. Excellent, so far, and Mercer would have done well had he stopped there; but his rocketeers continued

---

[1] A. C. Mercer, *Journal of the Waterloo Campaign* (Edinburgh, 1870), p. 166.
[2] Wellington to Berkeley, 6 November 1810, Gurwood, *Wellington's Dispatches*, VI.
[3] Wellington to Fane, 8 November 1810, *ibid.*
[4] Wellington to Fane, 14 November 1810, *ibid.*

laying and firing their weapons; and every other rocket, on reaching the peak of its trajectory, curved over backwards and returned more or less whence it came, the last nearly liquidating Mercer himself. Meanwhile the French gunners, losing all fear of these quaint British fireworks, remanned their pieces, and their havoc continued.[1]

There were, therefore, grounds for Wellington's poor opinion of the rocket, and he was not alone in that opinion. The best that Lt. Gen. Sir John Hope would say of rockets, even after their success at the Adour, was: 'It appears to me that where the object is near, and the ground not intersected by fences, and upon water, they may be useful, but when they have an elevation given them, they appear a most uncertain weapon.'[2] 'Projectiles, which, like the elephants in ancient war, often turn upon their own side' was Napier's comment on Congreve's rockets.[3]

And here, I think, must be recognized one of the unfortunate results of the deplorable subdivision of the British Army. The Ordnance Department invented the rocket, therefore it naturally became the arm of some Ordnance troops; but the Ordnance troops were the gunners of an army wretchedly weak in artillery, and the gun was a reliable weapon; so Wellington, who had been starved of artillery all through the Peninsular war, had not trained gunners enough to spare any for an erratic new weapon; he wanted every effective gun he could find men to serve. Hence the British slighting of the rocket in 1809–15, which may perhaps be likened to French misunderstanding of the new and marvellous *mitrailleuse* of 1870. In each case the new weapon was regarded as an artillery arm; too often the French in 1870 tried to assign an artillery role to the *mitrailleuse*; almost always, under these conditions, the *mitrailleuse* failed. It failed because its range was essentially that of a small arms weapon. Similarly, the rocket also lacked the effective range of gunnery, however far an individual rocket might carry under ideal conditions. At the same time its portability might have made it an ideal supporting arm for the infantry battalion commander to have under his own control. Had a dozen men in each infantry battalion been trained to use rockets, and equipped with no more rounds than one packhorse could carry, they might have made a very different battle of Waterloo.

A wasted opportunity may then be the verdict on Congreve's rockets. But his invention was by no means wholly thrown away. Leipzig had made a tremendous impression on the Tsar; that impression was reinforced by a splendid display Congreve arranged at Woolwich for the visiting sovereigns, Alexander I and Frederick William III of Prussia, on 13 June 1814.[4] The years immediately following the peace saw the in-

---

[1] Mercer, *Waterloo Campaign*, p. 280.
[2] *Wellington's Supplementary Dispatches*, VI, 592.
[3] W. Napier, *History of the Peninsular War* (London, 1853), VI, 91.
[4] *Gentleman's Magazine* (1814), p. 615.

congruous spectacle of continental powers labouring earnestly to equip themselves with that British invention, the rocket, which the great British commander refused to have in his army in 1815. This overrated weapon remained a British monopoly through the hard winter of notoriously bitter bargaining, 1814–15; and when the historian observes Russia and Prussia yielding, under threat of force, a reluctant consent to the survival of Saxony, let him remember, among significant other things, the enthralling fireworks display the sovereigns of those countries had enjoyed at Woolwich in the preceding June.

Yet a third invention of the British Ordnance Department in these years created perhaps less sensation at the time than Congreve's rockets, but has had a much more effective life in the service. Its official name was 'Spherical Case Shot', but soldiers ignored officialdom and, then as now, simply called it 'shrapnel' after its inventor, Henry Shrapnell of the Royal Artillery.[1]

Here it is necessary to enter a little into the technicalities of artillery projectiles, and Major Charles James is the most informative guide. In 1800 two already old types of artillery projectiles were grapeshot and case shot. 'Grapeshot...is a combination of small shot, put into a thick canvas bag and corded strongly together, so as to form a kind of cylinder whose diameter is equal to that of the ball which is adapted to the cannon', writes James of one of these weapons.[2] 'Case-Shot', he writes of the other, 'is so termed from the whole charge of the gun being contained in a tin case. The tin case is cylindric, in diameter a little less than the calibre of the gun or howitzer. It is filled with iron balls so as to make up the weight of the shot.'[3]

The function of both these types of ammunition was to enable a field gun to be used as a sort of much magnified shot-gun, rather than a rifle. The rifle was a sniper's weapon, used to hit a particular mark with precision, a job that could be done by artillery with round shot. The purpose of case and grape, on the other hand, was not to hit one mark with precision, but to shower a whole area with a lethal spray of bullets. The great weakness of these two weapons was that 'little effect is to be expected from firing [them] beyond 300 yards', because of what James calls 'the very great divergency of the balls'.[4] And for that reason guns and gunners had to be deployed in line with the infantry; otherwise they could not use these weapons with effect.

Henry Shrapnell's invention was designed to overcome this lack of range. His spherical case shot was not burst by actual propellant charge, and its balls were not scattered from the very muzzle of the gun. Instead

---

[1] The inventor signed his name with two L's, though long-standing practice dictates the use of one in referring to his invention.
[2] James, *Military Dictionary*, sub 'Shot'.
[3] *Ibid.*   [4] *Ibid.*

it was exploded by a fuse, or rather one of several fuses, each made to burn for a different particular time while the projectile was in flight, thus giving the gunner some control over the distance at which the discharge of the balls from the canister took place.

The advantages of this weapon were listed by James as being that it enabled case shot to 'be fired with an effect equally close and connected to any distance within the range of the piece; and artillery need not advance within musket shot of the enemy to make use of this kind of fire with its full effect, and are not so subject to have their guns charged either by cavalry or infantry'. It also required 'less precision and exactness to point a piece of ordnance charged with spherical case shot than with round shot, because case shot is a wide and dispersed fire'. The destruction done by shrapnel as against round shot 'will be generally as the number of the shot within the shell to one; that is to say, a 3-pounder, 22 to 1 in its favour; a 6-pounder, 50 to 1, etc., in which calculation is not enumerated any effect from the splinters of the shell'. The explosion of the shell made 'no change in the direction of the shot within it; they consequently complete the shell's track, or curve, which has been observed to be 400 yards'. Finally, unevenness of the ground, 'such as hillocks, banks, fallow fields, etc.', provided enemy troops with shelter from round shot, but by using shrapnel 'the whole charge will be carried over these irregularities and reach the object with its full contents of balls'.[1]

At one stage Wellington was inclined to belittle this seemingly excellent weapon.

I have reason to believe [*he wrote on 12 March 1812*, that the effect of shrapnel shells] is confined to wounds of a very trifling description; and they kill nobody. I saw General Simon who was wounded by the balls from Shrapnell's shells, of which he had several in his face and head; but they were picked out of his face as duckshot would be out of the face of a person who had been hit by an accident while out shooting, and he was not much more materially injured. Secondly [*continued Wellington*] from the difficulty of judging of correct distances, and in knowing whether the shell has burst in the air in the proper place, I suggest that an original error of range in throwing these shells is seldom corrected; and that if the shell is not effectual first shot, the continuance of the fire of these shells seldom becomes more effectual.[2]

But a wider inquiry removed Wellington's doubts. Several of the French prisoners found in hospital after the capture of Badajoz 'declared they were wounded by shrapnel balls; and Wellington learned from a person who was in the town during the siege, and had opportunities of hearing French officers talk, that this description of shot had great effect, and that it was quite impossible to keep the men at their guns or at work when they were fired'.[3] So in the next month Wellington is found writing

---

[1] James, *Military Dictionary*, *sub* 'Shot'.
[2] Wellington to Lord Liverpool, 12 March 1812, Gurwood, *Wellington's Dispatches*, VIII.
[3] Wellington to Lord Liverpool, 16 April 1812, *ibid.* IX.

to Alexander Dickson from Fuente Guinaldo: 'We *must* have in this part of the country immediately the 6 howitzers, and as many spherical case (principally) as you can carry.'[1]

The secret of making shrapnel was long and well kept. As late as 1828 an author is found writing as follows: 'SHRAPNEL-SHELLS.—I have been restricted from saying anything on the subject of these shells, or spherical case-shot as to the prejudice of their ingenious inventor...[they are] now most unaccountably termed. This prohibition has arisen from a very proper desire to retain in our own hands the secret of this destructive missile'; and the author thereupon proceeds to cite the statements of one Captain Decker of the Prussian Army and of his French translators as evidence that no foreigner as yet understood either the effect or the manufacture of Henry Shrapnell's invention.[2]

'Accurate surveys of a country are universally admitted to be works of great public utility, as affording the surest foundation of almost every kind of internal improvement in time of peace, and the best means of forming judicious plans for defence against the invasion of an enemy in time of war.'[3] This too typical sample of the cumbrous prose of William Mudge may introduce the next great research job of the Ordnance Board. That was the Trigonometrical Survey which, continuing with us as the Ordnance Survey, preserves the name of the vanished department that founded it. Mudge was its second and its greatest chief.

Today, when reliable maps are taken for granted, it is hard to realize how inadequate was the information on which the defence of England had to be planned between 1795 and, at least, 1805. The best available collection of maps when war broke out was Cary's *New and Correct English Atlas.* Published in 1787 it was still relatively new in 1793, but it was never correct. For example, Cary's map of Cambridgeshire marks not one wood or plantation in the whole county; it gives the Isle of Ely an excessively drunken-looking tilt to the westward; it presents as a body of water existing in 1787 a considerable lake, Stretham Mere, which seems likely to have been drained by this date.[4] No blame can attach to John Cary for these blunders. He had to rely for his information on such county maps as he could find. For some years the Society of Arts had tried to encourage surveying by offering prizes of £100 for good county maps; but, as Sir George Fordham says, the reward was only a nominal one, and he cites one R. Gough as a mapmaker who spent £2400 on

---

[1] Wellington to Dickson, 31 May 1812, *ibid.*

[2] Captain J. Morton Spearman, *The British Gunner* (Woolwich, 1828), p. xi.

[3] W. Mudge and Isaac Dalby, *An Account of Operations...for accomplishing a Trigonometrical Survey of England and Wales from the commencement in the year 1784 to the end of the year 1796* (London, 1799), p. 1.

[4] I can find no exacter date than the statement that it was drained some years before Soham Mere was drained in 1795.

making a mere survey of Sussex, which he apparently never managed to engrave and publish as a map.[1] The making of a map was therefore a profitable enterprise only when the county landowners subscribed heavily and 'it resulted from this system that counties deficient in resident gentry were not surveyed'.[2] By this standard Cambridgeshire would seem very deficient in gentry, but even in much better supplied counties the warmest support of landowners could not ensure accuracy on the part of the surveyors. So 'on Mr Taylor's map of Dorsetshire' Mudge found 'an error of nearly three miles...in a distance of eighteen', between Dorchester Church and Ninebarrow Down;[3] and though this was the worst error he found he describes the best available maps of Devonshire and Kent 'as similar specimens of imperfect topography'.[4] Add that the county maps then on the market normally showed no detail across the county boundary; that their scales varied; that while orientation to true north was usual, one of the best of them, Rocque's Surrey, gives an example of orientation to Magnetic North, which was 18° off true;[5] and it will then be seen how hard a job any staff officer employed on defence planning must have had. An error of three miles in eighteen would upset the timing of any march table; when no two county maps were designed to dovetail together, the difficulty of visualizing and describing any defence position that stretched across a county boundary was great; and the existence of an unmarked wood, or the non-existence of a marked lake, could result in the best laid plans looking singularly foolish when the ground was reconnoitred.

It was no new discovery, suddenly made, that when Britain went to war in 1793 she did so without the topographical information required to defend herself on her own soil. A great Scotsman, General William Roy, had been agitating for a survey through many years. He had been stationed in the Highlands in the years following 1747 when British troops garrisoning that newly pacified district found they knew hardly more of its geography than they might have known of the North American wilderness. Roy was the chief of a team of officers (and David Dundas, of whom more will be heard, was another) who now mapped this *terra incognita*. He was not very proud of the job done. The available instruments were poor, and Roy himself described the result 'rather...as a magnificent military sketch than a very accurate map of a country'.[6] How Roy learnt to do mapping at all seems a mystery. He had had no professional training

<hr/>

[1] H. G. Fordham, *Some Notable Surveyors and Map-Makers of the Sixteenth, Seventeenth and Eighteenth Centuries and their Work* (Cambridge, 1929), p. 73.
[2] *Ibid.*
[3] Mudge and Dalby, *Operations...for accomplishing a Trigonometrical Survey*, p. xi.
[4] *Ibid.*
[5] Sir Charles Frederick Close, *The Map of England; or about England with an Ordnance Map* (London, 1932), p. 31.
[6] Cited from *Philosophical Transactions*, 1785, by Close, *ibid.* p. 19.

and entered the Royal Engineers by the odd method of transfer from an infantry battalion, yet he became and remained a mapping enthusiast. He pressed for a national survey during the years of peace before the Seven Years War and in the twelve-year interim between that struggle and the American and Bourbon Wars of 1775–83. All he achieved was a considerable personal reputation as a soldier-scientist. He developed his own studies, showing a keen interest in Roman antiquities (on which he published a useful book); and he read the Royal Society an important paper on 'Rules for measuring Heights with a Barometer'. Some idea of the man's soundness and accuracy may be gained from his estimate of the height of Snowdon as 3568 feet, differing only by eight feet from the present official height, calculated with the best modern aids, of 3560 feet.[1]

At last his opportunity came. In 1783 M. Cassini de Thury, Director of l'Observatoire Royal in Paris, startled British scientists by suggesting that the longitude of Greenwich was wrongly calculated and proposing that it should be ascertained by triangulation operations carried out in Britain to link up over the Straits of Dover with the triangulation of France. Roy had long since made himself the obvious man to be employed on such a job. The government, officially, were not interested; but the King was; so too, in his private capacity, was the Duke of Richmond; and the Royal Society undertook the operation. Gifts of money from George III made possible the construction of the first great theodolite; the measurement of a triangulation base on Hounslow Heath; and a correction base on Romney Marsh; and the development of a series of triangles from Hounslow to Dover, where British and French scientists could link up the French and the new British system across the Straits. The details are hardly important; it is enough to quote Col. Sir Charles Close's verdict that Roy's work 'provided for the first time a thoroughly reliable framework for map-making' in Britain.[2]

That done, Roy died suddenly on 1 July 1790, an appropriately timed death which caught him in the midst of correcting the proof sheets of the paper that describes his last great work in *Philosophical Transactions*.[3] He had not, however, succeeded in persuading the government to survey its own country. This last undertaking had 'only, for its immediate object, the ascertaining of *data*, by which the difference in longitude between the observations of Greenwich and Paris might be ascertained', as Mudge records;[4] that the very idea of a national survey would die with Roy was apparently Mudge's fear.[5] But the Duke of Richmond was determined that the idea should not die; instead he made it the job of his own department. In 1791 he bought for the nation a second theodolite made, like

---

[1] Sir Charles F. Close, 'Notes on the early Years of the Ordnance Survey', *Royal Engineers' Journal* (1924), p. 9.
[2] *Ibid.* p. 222.
[3] *Ibid.* p. 223.
[4] Mudge and Dalby, *op. cit.* p. v.
[5] *Ibid.* p. 204.

the first, by that great but dilatory craftsman, Ramsden; and he bought measuring chains too. In July he appointed two officers to take charge of the Trigonometrical Survey; in doing so he very reasonably sought the advice of Dr Hutton, professor of mathematics at the Royal Military Academy, Woolwich. No doubt the good doctor was careful to consider well what men had been his brightest mathematical pupils, but unfortunately he gave less thought to character. The senior of his nominees was a sad appointment: a man who 'never made an observation or a calculation nor did he write a line of any of the printed accounts; in fact he proved a deadweight...and the only time he benefited the service was when he took his departure to the next world'.[1] Such is the description of Colonel Williams, R.A., first chief of the Trigonometrical Survey. But his second-in-command and, in 1798, his successor was the indomitable William Mudge. A dull man was Mudge, dreary with the inescapable dullness of any one-track-minded fanatic with a tedious subject; there is not a trace of lightness, brightness, or wit in the numerous and heavy pages of his published accounts of the survey work; but he was unbeatable at his job. The survey is, more than any other man's, his monument.

The survey was work done against heavy odds. It began by being that rather unusual thing in British history, a far-sighted and progressive military innovation begun in a time of profound peace. For it is hard to believe with Sir Charles Close that any fear of war with revolutionary France could have disturbed the Duke of Richmond's mind in July 1791.[2] Indeed, months later Pitt was to introduce his budget of 1792 with his remarkable (if guarded) prophecy of fifteen years of peace. The Duke was simply and wisely seizing the opportunity, created by public interest in General Roy's recent work, to undertake a job whose importance had long since been recognized by a few (and only a very few) keen men. He did this in the teeth of Pitt's economy policy, and therefore the Survey started life on a shoe-string; and when war came, so much money was needed for so many urgent expenditures that the Survey continued to be financially starved, and the work went on with the most time-consuming slowness. By the Duke's orders, Sussex was the first county mapped;[3] it was natural that that county should stand first in the interest of the lord of Goodwood Park, but Sussex also had many good landing beaches, and once an enemy was ashore, it offered him 'a shorter Line of Operation upon the Capital' than even Kent.[4] National was not excluded by local patriotism when the Duke ordered that Sussex should be done first, and in due course, when the slow work of survey was done, the map came out. It had one defect of all its predecessors: it was a map of one county only, on which detail stopped at the county boundary; but it was accurate, and

[1] Cited by Close, *Map of England*, p. 36. [2] *Ibid.* p. 35.
[3] Mudge and Dalby, *op. cit.* pp. xi–xii.
[4] York to Lord Hobart, 25 August 1803, WO/30/76.

it was beautiful—a really splendid piece of engraving. Its scale was the one we still use—an inch to a mile; and hills appeared in a neater and more precise hachuring than had been shown on most of its predecessors.

But the map was not printed till 1795, and then the government was not its publisher. The nation had no engravers to transfer the drawing of roads, hills, rivers, woods, parks and towns to a copper plate, and the first work of the Ordnance Survey was finished by private enterprise. Sussex was published by William Faden, the great map printer and seller of Charing Cross. It was perhaps the discovery of the government's inability to finish its own work that induced the Treasury to approve a new establishment for the staff of 'the Drawing Room' at the Tower in 1794. But 'the Drawing Room' and the Survey were two different things. The work of the first seems to have been, literally, drawing; there one John Wright describes himself as employed from 12 October to 3 November 1795, 'drawing Plans for the Leeward Island Expedition';[1] the Survey men were engaged in gathering the data from which competent 'plans' could be made. The two departments were united at last by a warrant of 1801 which, however, remained a dead letter till 1804. Meanwhile the actual survey went forward with wretched slowness. Under Mudge (and Williams) very few field men were employed in compiling the data within Mudge's triangulations. In 'Kent, Sussex, Surrey and part of Hampshire' a Captain Thomas Vincent Reynolds of the 34th Regiment was employed from December 1793, with 10s. a day staff pay for his pains.[2] In the spring of 1795 a Captain Lewis Hay, R.E., was appointed (perhaps as the last of Richmond's rather than the first of Cornwallis's nominees) to undertake a military survey of the east coast from Essex to Norfolk, but he left this job in October to sail on 'the Leeward Island Expedition' above mentioned;[3] and in May 1796 Reynolds, with no other southern county than Sussex as yet mapped, was directed 'to continue the Military Survey of the Eastern District'[4] (he was a Major now, with an allowance of 20s. a day and 'the assistance of two draughtsmen'[5]). This chopping and changing, the resignation of Hay and switching of Reynolds from one unfinished job to another, may perhaps be diagnosed as ways in which Lt. Col. Williams 'retarded [the Survey's] progress'. The result in any case was that Bonaparte's Italian victories, the peace of Campo-Formio, and the invasion threat of 1797 caught Britain with her south coast still inadequately mapped; and by Cornwallis's order, the Survey was switched back to Kent;[6] and the map of Kent was duly published, at last, in 1801.

---

[1] Wright to the Board of Ordnance, 21 January 1796, WO/47/2367 in the Public Record Office.
[2] Hadden to Rogers, 19 December 1793, WO/47/2365.
[3] Wright to Board of Ordnance, 12 January 1796, WO/47/2367.
[4] Apsley to Crew, 20 April 1796, *ibid.*
[5] Ouvry to Surveyor General's Office, 10 April 1796, *ibid.*
[6] Mudge and Dalby, *op. cit.* p. xiii.

This time the engraving and printing were done by the Ordnance Office's own staff. Next came Essex in 1805—three maps running from Thames mouth to Colchester. And here a curious thing; one would have supposed that these new maps, the first sufficiently accurate and detailed to be reliable for the making of war, would have been regarded as highly secret information, and at first indeed the maps were 'not submitted, for obvious motives of policy, to public inspection'.[1] But unfortunately it was 'expected by the insatiable Public. . . that they should derive the advantage of an improvement in the geography of their country, and possess some general Map published on the same principle as the *Carte de France*'. Faden, the great mapmaker, was eager to have the maps for his own business; and Lord Cornwallis and the Board of Ordnance yielded to public opinion, and permitted 'Mr Faden. . . to engrave, under certain restrictions, this Map of Kent for public use'[2]—a decision in which the Duke of York concurred. A Minute of the Ordnance of 22 May 1805 granted Faden an increase in his commission for 'vending and publishing the new Map of the County of Essex'.[3]

No doubt the public sale of the new maps helped the starved Ordnance Department to pay its own way, yet the profits made on the sale did not hasten the work of producing them. Three maps of the coast of Devon which appeared in 1809 were the first to follow Essex; and the Hampshire coast, which Richmond had wanted Reynolds to map in 1793, did not come out till 1810–11. It was most unfortunate that the removal of Williams's 'deadweight' was so soon followed by the appointment of Chatham who, at a higher level, was perhaps an equal handicap. In any event the whole coastline from the Wash to Land's End was not fully mapped till 1837. But, thanks to Richmond, the work was at least begun, and begun well, in our period.

[1] Mudge and Dalby, *op. cit.* p. xii.   [2] *Ibid.* pp. xii–xiii.   [3] WO/55/574.

CHAPTER 4

ORDNANCE TROOPS: GUNNERS AND ENGINEERS

I

GUNNERS in our period were of four types—garrison, siege, field, and horse artillery. The garrison artillery were intended solely for the defence of fortified places; siege gunners served the battering train in the attack on fortified places; field and horse artillery took part in mobile operations. The garrison artillery was commonly composed of elderly men who were unfit for service in the field and were called Invalids. They play little part in our story; in this period the British Army was not called upon to face any such operation as the great investment of Gibraltar, which ended, on 8 May 1782, as a British victory in the last great action of the American and Bourbon war.

Between gunners of the other three types the distinction was not clearcut; for example, Augustus Simon Frazer served as a field artilleryman in the campaigns of 1793–4; was transferred to Horse Artillery in 1795; rose to the command of all Wellington's Horse Artillery in 1813, and directed it at Vittoria on 21 June; and in July took charge of 24-pounders during the siege of San Sebastian. What mattered, therefore, was the type of weapon with which men were equipped on particular occasions, for this determined their function. As sieges were a very specialized job, the duties of men in the battering train are best discussed alongside those of the engineer under whose direction they worked. Field and horse artillery will therefore be the first subject of this chapter; and if the horse artillery seems slighted in our account, the reason is the scarcity of material especially devoted to this arm.

II

Great changes had come over field guns and their use in the three decades between the Seven Years War and the struggle with revolutionary France. Of old guns had been the dragweight that hindered the march of armies. Early eighteenth-century roads were normally and notoriously execrable; gunteams were frequently oxen and, in Carlyle's phrase, 'the pace of bos is slow'; so for the sake of rapid movement good commanders had often been glad to do with as few guns as possible and to win battles by the musketry of well-drilled infantry. But the great enlightened despots were great road-builders; their work robbed their countries of what Wellington called 'the cheap defence of nations...an unimproved frontier'.[1] As new roads made it easier for guns to move, gunners began to design pieces more capable of movement, and the proportion of artillery in field armies increased greatly. In this development Austria was pre-eminent, and two great soldiers, one well known and one almost unknown, observed her progress. The well-known soldier was Frederick the Great; what he learnt from Austria is demonstrated by his growing reliance on guns in the Seven Years War,[2] his creation of the first horse artillery in 1759, and the very great proportion of guns he had ready for action in the short Bavarian War of 1778. The other man, whose name seems too little known, was the French officer, Jean-Baptiste de Gribeauval. He had served with the Austrians throughout the Seven Years War and then had come home to remodel the French artillery. He met with conservative opposition at first, but under Louis XVI he had his way. When revolutionary France plunged into war against the coalesced kings of Europe, she did so with the advantage of a new-made artillery arm for which she had to thank her own unfortunate king and his appointee, Gribeauval.

Mobility was the grand aim of Gribeauval. His pieces were light, with all parts standardized, and according to the weight of their projectile, they were classed as 4-, 8-, and 12-pounders. Except perhaps in an emergency, oxen were never again to be the artilleryman's draught animals, and guns now accompanied infantry almost wherever they might go.

Changes in tactics were to follow. The old practice had been to allot guns to individual infantry battalions. Infantrymen had been taught to handle them, and these battalion guns (normally a pair) were supposed to deploy on the right of their own battalion, where they served to strengthen its firepower in a manner somewhat akin to the modern infantry battalion's mortar platoon.

For two reasons this was not a good way to use guns. First, infantrymen who had had a short course in gun-handling were never reckoned the equals of real artillerymen who were specialists in their own arm. By their lack of proficiency much of the value of their pieces was wasted. Second, the dispersal of an army's guns by twos, up and down the line on the right of each battalion, conspicuously flouted the principle of 'concentration'. The massing of many guns together was indeed bad, because it drew fire; but the guns needed to be so placed that, under one command, they could 'at any time be united to produce a decided effect against any particular points';[3] that is to say, concentrate all their fire on one chosen target at

---

[1] Lord Stanhope, *Conversations with Wellington* (The World's Classics, Oxford, 1947), p. 116.
[2] Very notably in his operation order of 30 June 1758, for an unfought battle near Prosnitz in Moravia, which remarkably foreshadows the use Napoleon was to make of artillery. It is printed in G. H. Wickham's *Influence of Firearms on Tactics* (London, 1876), pp. 159–60.
[3] Adye, *Bombardier and Pocket Gunner*, p. 26.

a time; and they needed to be free to pick good positions in which to tuck themselves as safely away as possible, for the gunner of 1800 was instructed whenever possible to place his weapons where 'the muzzle only can be seen';[1] in other words, to find what the modern tankman calls a 'hull-down position'. For these reasons progressive soldiers regarded battalion guns as obsolete even before the French Revolution began;[2] yet they lingered on in the French Army till 1800, and in the British till rather later.

The greater number of guns handled as an independent arm introduced a new element into the art of war, a volume of fire unknown to Marlborough and Saxe. In this lies a clue to what stands in many of our textbooks as an incomprehensible military riddle. As is well known, the drill manual of French revolutionary armies was the one issued by the Comte de St Germaine and prepared by J. A. H. de Guibert who had written his famous *Essai général de la Tactique* in 1769. As no less solid a work of reference than the *Cambridge Modern History* states (not incorrectly), Guibert made 'the extended order of Frederick...the drill of the French army';[3] the secret of Frederick the Great's success was the speed and flexibility with which his drill enabled troops to form in *line*; yet, in seeming paradox, many general histories state that French infantry constantly and effectively attacked in *column*. The paradox is unreal. Line was the formation infantry had to use whenever they relied on their own firepower and as long as their weapon was muzzle-loading; necessarily French troops were taught to use it. But, thanks to Gribeauval, French infantry in the revolution needed less than ever before to rely on their own firepower. The new guns of France, which were so readily brought into action in numbers, provided an overwhelming substitute for musketry; every gun loaded with grape had the killing power of many muskets; grape, which was dangerous up to 300 yards, outranged the musket; and good gunners could load and fire faster than musketeers. Now, therefore, the French commander could use his guns, not his infantrymen, to destroy the lines of the enemy infantry in the fire fight; first, his numerous cannon played havoc with the foe; then, when enough damage was done, he could send his infantry forward in column, in a manner Guibert had never foreseen.[4] His long, narrow columns, stretching back from front to rear, did not block the fire of his batteries as troops in line would have done; advancing in the easiest of marching formations, they assaulted

[1] *Ibid.* p. 25.
[2] D. Dundas, *Principles of Military Movements* (London, 1788), p. 6.
[3] *Cambridge Modern History*, VIII, 402.
[4] According to Guibert it was only necessary or advantageous to attack in column 'quand l'ennemie est derrière un retranchement ou dans tel autre poste dont les flancs naturels ou artificiels reduisent nécessaire à attaquer les saillans et à ne pas se presenter sur les faces' (*Essai général sur la tactique*, Paris, 1802 ed., p. 116). Perhaps one of the most interesting things in Guibert's book is his argument in favour of reducing the number of guns attached to mobile armies—a proposal directly contrary to future developments (*ibid.* pp. 243–50).

positions occupied by men of whom many were already mangled or dead and the rest hopelessly disordered by merciless bombardment.

This was the principal tactical change which Gribeauval's reforms created. It is an error to attribute this change to the great development in the numbers and use of light infantry which occurred in this period, although they too did contribute something to the disorganization of the enemy. In 1788 David Dundas, a shrewd and experienced student of war, insisted that light troops 'do not decide';[1] and the gun itself was a major new factor in war which Britain had to face.

Let it be said once and for all that Britain never faced this new factor properly. The true answer to the mobile and massive artillery of France was an equally mobile and more massive British artillery. It was never provided. Until after the day when he captured every gun the French brought into action at Vittoria on 21 June 1813, Wellington consistently had fewer field guns than his opponents; hence, as Oman rightly notes, his preference for positions on reverse slopes which French guns could not command. But his choice of such positions, and his use of line as a defensive formation, was forced upon him by his weakness in artillery, as may appear from his own occasional readiness to attack in column when he had the artillery superiority he needed (as in the attack on the first redoubt at Sare on 10 November 1813).[2] His normal weakness in guns was due to the unfortunate inability of British civilian ministers to grasp the fact, which was not infrequently explained to them, that artillery was a very important arm which could not be hastily improvised. Infantry, of course, could be improvised. Whereas the gunner's training was long and complicated, an infantry recruit could be made an adequate reinforcement for his battalion by a few weeks' instruction,[3] and every war saw the formation of many new infantry battalions of volunteers and militia. These new formations could relieve the regular battalions of much of the garrison duty of protecting England; by doing so, they made infantry available for an expeditionary force to serve overseas, but as a garrison they still needed the support of field artillery, and this could only be provided by keeping regular gunners at home. Hence British expeditionary forces were normally undergunned abroad.

It is indeed true that for all the time it took to train a good artilleryman, some amateur assistance was offered to the regular gunners in the job of defending England, but it was so slight as to be negligible. Because it was easy for an enemy privateer to ravage a coast town, some seaside places

[1] Dundas, *Principles of Military Movements*, p. 12.

[2] J. H. Leslie, *The Dickson MSS* (Woolwich, 1908), p. 1110.

[3] For example, the British force at Waterloo was largely composed 'of recruits from the provinces of the United Kingdom, many of whom had not joined the Army above two months before hostilities began', according to an article on 'The English and Russian Armies' in the *United Services Journal*, II (1836), 296–7. (As was usual in this Journal, the article is unsigned.)

raised volunteer artillery companies to take care of local defence in every war. To such places Richmond was very ready to loan guns, on condition that they were mounted on 'garrison carriages', not 'travelling carriages', and that the locals built their own magazine and found their own ammunition.[1] But such companies could contribute little to the general defence of Britain, though they were scattered from Salcombe to Dunbar, because they naturally sprang up only in those places which the government reckoned too unimportant to merit defence at national expense; and also because their guns on 'garrison carriages' were virtually immobile and could take no part in field operations. When volunteers offered to become field artillery their offer was uncompromisingly rejected, for reasons that the Duke of Richmond expressed bluntly enough when the Bridport Volunteer Company of Artillery asked for field pieces in 1794. Such requests, wrote Richmond, were always refused 'on the Grounds that it would be improper to trust moveable Artillery to Volunteer Corps on the Coast where they would be liable to be taken by the Enemy, and if in his possession would of course prove a great Advantage to him';[2] so much for the professional soldier's confidence in the steadiness of the volunteer!

There was no way, therefore, to increase British artillery except to augment the regular gunners. It was as normal for the gunners as for the regular army to be under strength in peacetime; so the first task in war was to recruit them up to their peace establishment; only when that was done could new increases be attempted; and when peace came again many gunners, like the soldiers of the army, were disbanded, and only such a proportion of them retained as were wanted to make an adequate component in the peacetime army, without reckoning the number of militia and volunteer infantry who might be speedily raised in a new war. And so the vicious circle continued. It may be fair to comment that the need to retain in peace a larger number of gunners than the army required for its own support was a new one; that as long as battalion guns were good enough, the militia at least could receive and man their own pieces; and that the need for a large artillery force in peacetime was therefore a novelty created by Gribeauval's work and its results. It was still unfortunate that recourse had to be had to the practice of issuing battalion guns as late as 1803, although knowledgeable soldiers had regarded this system as obsolete fifteen years earlier, and references to lack of trained gunners and the difficulty of recruiting them indicate that battalion guns were issued only for want of true artillerymen.

The failure to retain enough artillery in peace, both before 1793 and

[1] Hadden to Muncaster, 17 July 1794, WO/46/23 in the Public Record Office. Garrison carriages had small wheels intended merely to permit the gun to run back in its recoil over a short, smooth surface. Travelling carriages had large wheels capable of negotiating the bumps and ruts inevitable in any considerable journey.

[2] Richmond to the Duke of Portland, c. 21 August 1794, HO/50/371 in the Public Record Office.

after 1801, was an error made at the political level, which only Parliament could correct. At the administrative level a number of valuable reforms in the British artillery were made under the Duke of Richmond's eye.

First, there were improvements in *matériel*. In the American and Bourbon War of 1775–83, British gunners had been bedevilled by bad ammunition and bad weapons. The great improvements made in the manufacture of powder under the elder William Congreve have been described. For equal improvement in the quality of her guns, England was indebted to a great public servant of French descent, General Desaguliers. A most important part of any firearm is the bore (i.e. the long hole down the centre of the barrel out of which the bullet is propelled); if this is not truly drilled, the piece cannot be shot accurately. Either by the dishonesty or incompetence of manufacturers, many badly bored guns were delivered to the British government, till General Desaguliers invented his famous 'instrument' for testing them; it was a contrivance of mirrors that threw light into the darkest parts of the hollow of a gun, to reveal precisely what the unskilful contractor most wished hidden. General Desaguliers's instrument remained in use as long as the smooth-bored gun. The general also conducted in England experiments similar to those of Gribeauval in France in the redesigning of guns for greater lightness and mobility.

Beside these technical developments two other progressive steps stand to the Duke of Richmond's credit. One was a long-overdue reform, the creation in 1793 of a horse artillery modelled on Frederick the Great's innovation of 1759. Both the drivers and the gunners of the horse artillery were mounted; their original guns were 4-pounders; their function was to keep pace with cavalry and give them support when they acted independently of infantry; their mobility made them specially useful in the pursuit of a beaten enemy, and, conversely, in supporting rearguards.[1]

The second of Richmond's reforms was the creation of what came to be known as the Royal Corps of Artillery Drivers. For moving artillery the long-standing practice of all armies had been to hire, or to impress, civilian drivers and animals to draw field guns, while the gunners marched alongside their pieces (and hence, after the creation of Horse Artillery, the Field Artillery was sometimes referred to as the Foot Artillery). This practice continued in France until the Consulate. It was then realized that the contractors who undertook to provide drivers and horses were unequal to the job, and one of the earlier acts of Bonaparte was to raise a military body of drivers and make their teams the property of the state.[2] It is worth remarking that though France is regarded as the leader of all

[1] Edward Sabine, *Letters of Colonel Sir Augustus Simon Frazer, K.C.B.* (London, 1857), pp. 158, 161, 544.
[2] I. Favé and L. Bonaparte, *Études sur le passé et l'avenir d'Artillerie*, IV (Paris, 1863), 188–91.

Europe in military developments in this period, Britain under Richmond's guidance anticipated her in this particular reform by six years. For Richmond created the drivers' corps in 1794.[1]

Richmond's reason for doing so was succinctly explained in 1810 by Major James in his *Military Dictionary* as being that 'no reliance could be placed on the service of either men or horses' provided by contractors and therefore 'it was found indispensably necessary to abolish so unmilitary and destructive a system'.[2] So far no one who recalls how the British guns at Fontenoy were hopelessly lost when their hired Flemish drivers fled from the field on their draught horses can disagree with James. But this author then proceeds to launch into eulogies of the Royal Corps of Artillery Drivers, which may be taken with a grain of salt, and which end with the words, 'the corps consists of one colonel commandant, three lieutenant-colonels, one major, nine captains, and fifty-four subalterns' in addition to the rank and file.[3]

Here James does not mention that he himself was the 'one major' in the corps; nor that while drawing the pay and emoluments of that rank, he was busy acting as French secretary to the Earl of Moira and never attended personally to his command;[4] nor again would the reader gather from his description that the few field officers in the corps were apparently not required to go on active service; and from other sources it appears that in spite of what James has to say about 'the high state of excellence on which the brigades are equipped',[5] the driver corps was to prove one of the uglier blemishes on the army in the Peninsula.

Here our witness is that greatest of British gunner officers, the solemnly bespectacled Lt. Col. Alexander Dickson, who in 1813 described the Royal Corps of Artillery Drivers as an 'Augean stable'. 'Many of the officers', reported Dickson, 'are negligent and indifferent to their duty... they are constantly giving their names in sick and in several cases absenting themselves without leave.' A number of extra medical boards recently called to investigate cases where officers reported themselves sick had found no sufficient reason for the report; one board had refused to sit because 'the Chief medical officer felt ashamed to address himself to a man walking about in perfectly good health'. Worse still, Dickson could not 'get the Captains or Officers to feel an interest in paying their men'; as a result some men had apparently been left unpaid since '1810 or 1811'. Worst of all, Dickson observed 'in several instances proof of an improper interest in these payments, which require to be noticed in the most rigorous manner'.[6]

---

[1] Fortescue, *History of the British Army*, IV, 934.
[2] *New and Enlarged Military Dictionary*, *sub* 'Artillery'.
[3] *Ibid.*
[4] *Seventeenth Report of the Commission of Military Inquiry*, Appendix no. 10.
[5] James, *Military Dictionary*, *loc. cit.*
[6] Leslie, *Dickson MSS*, p. 1099.

All this was written home to Major General J. Macleod, R.A., on 13 November 1813, to explain why Dickson felt it necessary to make an example of one Lt. White of the drivers and have him tried by Court Martial. Macleod's reply is instructive: 'I am very glad you are endeavouring to inquire into the interior concerns of the drivers. They want from the nature of their duty, dispersed in fractional parts, more superintendence than any corps, and yet with 8000 [men] they have not a field officer or superintending power belonging to them.'[1]

When all this criticism is recorded, there can be no surprise at finding that the drivers were notorious above other corps for their misconduct in the peninsula; or that, when it was necessary to placate Wellington's wrath against an unfortunate gunner officer, it was apparently enough to explain that the offender had been let down by his drivers.[2] It is also evident that the creation of this corps was an imperfect reform. The real answer to making artillery mobile was not to create a separate body of drivers for the guns, but to amalgamate drivers and gunners both into one corps under one discipline. This step was to be taken some years after the peace. All the same, the foundation of the drivers was a valuable move in the right direction. Richmond, who took that step, can hardly be blamed for the defects of his creation, as it was barely six months old when he left the department; rather, those defects are to be classed with other evidence of the inadequacy of Chatham for the job he held so long at the head of the Ordnance; they also suggest that Chatham's successor, Lord Mulgrave, was not much more alert.

After these remarks on the general nature of the artillery problem and particular reforms in the service, it is time to say something about the guns themselves, their numbers, and their handling. Any historian who deals with a technical subject like this is apt to be handicapped by the nature of his sources. On such subjects experts commonly deal with experts, and their letters tend to leave much unexplained because, to themselves, so little needs explaining. Therefore a letter on the Irish artillery in 1794, written by the Duke of Richmond, who was an expert, in reply to the Duke of Portland, who was as lay as any other civilian, is especially interesting; it gives an unusually clear picture of what was considered suitable or necessary at the time.

The Irish Army then numbered 20,000 horse and foot. For such a force Richmond approved an establishment of 80 battalion guns; in addition he recommended two 'parks' of corps artillery, and one 'park' for a reserve. Each park should consist of twelve weapons—four medium 12-pounders, four long 6-pounders, and four 5½-inch howitzers. Parks and battalion guns together thus give a total of 116 guns to 20,000 men. This is in accord with French practice of the period,[3] which in turn echoes

---

[1] Leslie, *Dickson MSS*, p. 1150.   [2] *Ibid.* p. 1107.
[3] Favé and Bonaparte, *Études...sur l'Artillerie*, IV, 179.

Austrian practice of the 1760's.[1] No horse artillery is mentioned—an omission which, like the inclusion of battalion guns, indicates that the Irish Army was not quite up to date, and this point should be borne in mind.

To Portland's request for 18-pounders of brass or iron for the Irish Army, Richmond replied that there were no such guns in British parks, 'it being now the opinion of all Artillery Officers here that no Guns of a heavier nature than 12-pounders should be taken onto the field'. Here the new stress on mobility appears, as it does also in the following. 'It is supposed', continued Richmond, 'that the long 6-pounders, which are in Ireland, are 8 feet long and weigh 18 cwt.' He could supply more of these guns, but, he went on, 'I must observe that long 6-pounders of 18 cwt. are considered here as rather too heavy for a 6-pounder gun, and we use in our Parks 6-pounders of General Desaguliers' pattern [which are] seven feet long and weigh only 12 cwt.'.[2] As for the 18-pounders, Richmond described them as useful for a battering train, but only if they were made of iron, not brass; as will be seen later, Richmond was entirely correct in declaring brass guns useless for a battering train, and indeed was rather optimistic in calling any 18-pounder useful for this purpose.[3]

Two things any soldier wants to know about his weapons are their effective range and their rate of fire. Little more can be said of the ranges of these pieces than that it depended on the ammunition used. Grape and case shot had little effect at ranges of over 300 yards; round shot travelled much farther, but precisely how far is a riddle on which little light is shed by Ralph Willett Adye, author of that gunner's bible, which ran through so many editions, *The Bombardier and Pocket Gunner*. 'Gunpowder', wrote Adye in 1804, 'has been so much improved of late years that experiments made with the old powder are now of little use [for determining ranges].... As experiments are daily making at Woolwich and elsewhere', he advised his readers to bind a blank leaf in his book 'after each nature of Ordnance in order to insert an abstract' of the ranges they might expect to reach with particular charges of the new powder, as indicated by current experiments.[4]

Not much could be expected in the way of high rates of fire with weapons as cumbrous as guns of this period. For the job of loading and firing was complicated; after each shot the bore had first to be sponged out; secondly, the new charge of powder had to be rammed home;

---

[1] *Ibid.* p. 244.

[2] Richmond to Portland, 14 August 1794, HO/50/371.

[3] 'The difference of effect produced by...a 24-pounder or an 18-pounder shot striking a wall, particularly at a distance of four or five hundred yards, is far greater than would be conceived by those who have not watched the practice of the two natures of Ordnance at the same time. No engineer should ever be satisfied with 18-pounder guns for breaching when he can by any possibility procure 24-pounders' (Major General Sir John T. Jones, Bart., *Journal of the Sieges carried on by the Army under the Duke of Wellington in Spain between the Years 1811 and 1814*, 3rd ed., London, 1846, I, 145).

[4] *Bombardier and Pocket Gunner*, p. iv.

thirdly, the projectile had to be rammed after the powder; fourthly, the piece had to be relaid after its last recoil; only then was the gun ready to fire again. The handling of sponges, rammers, propellants and projectiles required a meticulous drill and great dexterity on the part of the guncrew, if many rounds were to be fired in a short time. The rate of fire also depended on the number of hands available to do these jobs, for there was no fixed number of men in a guncrew. In Belgium in 1793 British guns were manned by crews of fifteen men each; in England at the same date the Duke of Richmond had only ten men to serve each gun retained for home defence;[1] and later editions of Adye prescribe a variety of different gundrills for guncrews of different sizes. In a short crisis a very well served piece of field artillery might get off as many as six or seven rounds in a minute, but much lower rates had to be accepted for the sustained firing of larger pieces with more ponderous ammunition. Siege gunners who maintained an average of some 23 rounds per hour for $15\frac{1}{2}$ hours per day against San Sebastian were reckoned to have done almost unbelievably well;[2] and any modern reader who has tried handling 24-pounder shot may share the scarcely credulous admiration of the gunners' contemporaries.

These figures bespeak so creditable a standard of training in British gunners that it might be supposed that some Master General of our period had been at pains to review training methods and to produce a very effective training manual. In fact nothing of the kind had been done by any of them. The army had its official drill-books for both cavalry and infantry of the line, and it had two official manuals for the training of light infantry and riflemen. The more lethargic Ordnance Department left its troops to be instructed by private enterprise. Very significantly, private enterprise was equal to the task; and there lies one explanation of the improvement of British troops in this period. There were many keen, thoughtful men among the officer corps. The production of unofficial training directives is one symptom of that keenness. It was a very healthy sign that among Britain's few gunner officers there were some who were keen enough to write, and many who were keen enough to buy what was written.

This claim need not be considered as damaged when we confess that we have found only two writers who ventured to instruct their fellow gunners. One of those writers, Ralph Willett Adye, did so thorough a job in his *Bombardier and Pocket Gunner* (already referred to) as to make other attempts unnecessary; and the succession of re-issues of this book is evidence of the eagerness with which it was bought.[3] The other writer,

[1] Richmond to Dundas, 27 March 1794, HO/50/371.

[2] Leslie, *Dickson MSS*, pp. 969, 1029.

[3] The copy I have used is the fourth edition, published by T. Egerton in 1804. This is in the War Office Library and is the earliest I have found. The only copy listed in the *British Museum Catalogue of Printed Books, 1881–1900* (Ann Arbor, 1946) is the eighth, revised by W. G. Eliot and published in 1827.

an anonymous contributor to a rather new periodical (itself a portent), called *The British Military Library*, did not attempt to cover Adye's general topic; instead, he tackled a special problem with a paper entitled 'Practical Observations on the Most Advantageous Use of Artillery in Hilly Situations'.[1] What these two writers offered their fellow gunners was undoubtedly useful to them; and it is equally useful to anyone else who would understand the nature and conduct of war in this period.

Adye first comments on the lack of any guidance for handling battalion guns 'in the established regulations for the movements of Infantry in the British service'.[2] As David Dundas, the author of those regulations, had long subscribed to the opinion that battalion guns were obsolete,[3] the omission is hardly surprising, but it was still unfortunate in view of the shortage of artillerymen which compelled battalion guns to be issued to British infantry even as late as 1803. Therefore Adye himself gives a number of rules, of which the gist is comprised in one general rule: 'with very few variations the guns should attend in all the movements of the Battalion...they should never be so placed as to obstruct the view of the pivots and thereby the just formation of the line; but should always seek those positions from which the enemy may be most annoyed, and the troops, to which they are attached, protected.'[4]

In their directions for handling artillery of the 'park' in its independent 'brigades',[5] both authors agree rather closely; as Adye owns his rules 'are mostly translated from the *Aide Memoire*, a new military work',[6] their agreement may stem from a common source.

Adye is quite modern in what he says about the artillery commander's need of information:

He should of course be acquainted with the effect to be produced; with the troops that are to be supported; and with the points that are to be attacked; that he may place his artillery so as to support and not to incommode the infantry; nor take up such positions with his guns as would be more advantageously occupied by the line. That he may not place his batteries too soon, nor too much exposed; that he may cover his front and his flanks, by taking advantage of the ground; and that he may not venture too far out of the protection of the troops, unless some very decided effect is to be obtained thereby.[7]

Both authors stress the importance of what the Bren gunner of 1939–45 was taught to call 'enfilade fire'. In Adye's words, 'the guns must be so

---

[1] *The British Military Library*, II (published by S. Carpenter and Company, Booksellers to the Duke of York, Old Bond Street, 1801), 364–8. I have found this only in the War Office Library.
[2] Adye, *Pocket Gunner*, p. 21.
[3] *Principles of Military Movements*, p. 6.
[4] Adye, *Pocket Gunner*, p. 24.
[5] A 'park' normally consisted of twelve guns which were 'generally divided into brigades of 4 or 6 pieces, and a reserve...composed of about one-sixth of the park' (Adye, *ibid.*).
[6] *Ibid.*   [7] *Ibid.* pp. 25–6.

placed as to produce a crossfire upon the enemy and upon all the ground he must pass over in an attack';[1] and the anonymous writer explains the importance of 'crossfire' by saying, 'Shots fired in a perpendicular direction to the enemy's front cannot possibly kill above three men, but those which are fired in an oblique direction frequently kill four, five or more men according to the acuteness of the angle at which they take the enemy's line'.[2] Equally both authors emphasize the value of using guns to cover such places as defiles and bridges, which the enemy must pass in close formation and would take some time in passing: 'the fire will...have much greater effect, as the guns will continue pointed in the same direction for a considerable time and as the shots will strike into a greater depth of files', explains the anonymous writer.[3] The importance of concealing batteries till the last moment is another point stressed; and the anonymous author enlarges on the psychological effect on the enemy of a sudden and crushing fire from an unsuspected battery—'it will be dreadful and, the less he expected it, the greater will be his confusion'.[4] A common way of masking batteries was to deploy troops in front of them, and cavalry were preferred because of the speed with which they could be withdrawn; it is also recommended that guns use ditches and fences for concealment.

Yet with all this care for concealment the gunner was still much closer to hand-to-hand conflict than he has often been in more modern times. He had to allow the enemy infantry to approach to a distance of 400 yards or less before he could open on them with grape; it was thought wrong to place guns 'in the rear of the line...because they alarm the troops and offer a double object to the fire of the enemy', according to Adye,[5] so the gunner was commonly as close to the front as the infantry, and as vulnerable as they, both to musketry and to bayonet charges. Moreover, the enemy infantry, says the anonymous writer, 'can advance 100, nay, 120 paces a minute without running; if therefore a battalion advances from 200 to 250 paces in line against cannon, it will not receive more than 12 or 15 rounds out of each piece, and most of them will miss their aim, because, the line being in continual motion, it becomes necessary to change the direction of the gun with each shot'.[6] Here too Adye offers the somewhat grim exhortation: 'Never abandon your guns till the last extremity. The last discharges are the most destructive: they may perhaps be your salvation and crown you with glory',[7] and rarely can the word 'perhaps' have been used more justifiably than Adye seems to use it here!

---

[1] Adye, *Pocket Gunner*, p. 26.

[2] *British Military Library*, II, 367. When he says that fire 'perpendicular...to the enemy's front cannot possibly kill more than three men', he speaks, of course, of an enemy advancing in line in the normal depth of three ranks.

[3] *Ibid.*   [4] *Ibid.* p. 368.

[5] *Pocket Gunner*, p. 27.

[6] *British Military Library*, II, 367.

[7] *Pocket Gunner*, p. 27.

The two writers differ very interestingly in what they say about counter-battery fire.[1] Adye condemns it simply and shortly, saying, 'Artillery should never fire against artillery, unless the enemy's troops are covered and his artillery exposed; or unless your troops suffer more from the fire of his guns than his troops do from yours'.[2] The anonymous author, on the other hand, argues strongly in favour of counter-battery fire.

When it is considered [he writes] that the effect of artillery is much more striking than that of small arms, that it terrifies the troops in a more forcible manner, and that victory is decided not merely by the number of the killed, it appears that it is of much more service to dismount a cannon than to kill 100 or 200 men. Moreover the shots fired against batteries serve two purposes, viz., of dismounting guns and killing the artillerymen. If they miss the former they generally kill the latter, which in fact is of considerable importance, as good artillerymen are extremely valuable, and not easily replaced in a campaign. An army may be able to keep the field though it has sustained very heavy losses, both in cavalry and infantry. The commanding general may reinforce his army by drawing troops from garrisons which can spare them, or calling in detached corps; he may also take up an advantageous position where he may continue long enough to receive troops from the depots, or other places, and train them. Recruits in general, when delivered to each battalion, may be sufficiently trained in four weeks, but artillerymen require a much longer time. They must acquire a certain degree of dexterity and readiness in the active part of the business, which, although but a bodily exertion, yet demands great practice and even then is not within the compass of every man. There is an art to the mere handling of the lever, in which dexterity effects more than strength, and one man, who understands it well, will do more than three who do not. Add to this the fact that an artilleryman ought to have a just and well exercised eye, and be able to reflect with judgement upon what he is doing; it therefore takes much time and attention to form him properly. From these considerations it appears to us evident that it is more advisable to direct the fire of the artillery against the enemy's batteries than against his men.[3]

This is an interesting and informative argument from the pen of the anonymous writer. It does not follow that Adye was wrong. Destruction of an enemy's artillery would no doubt handicap him much in a campaign, but, if the object was to win a battle, it might best be accomplished by overthrowing his infantry. It is perhaps relevant that Benedek, the unfortunate Austrian commander of 1866, agreed with Adye; at Sadowa he ordered his gunners to eschew counter-battery fire in order to concentrate on the Prussian infantry; to the gunners' disobedience of his order has in part been attributed von Moltke's success in this most pregnant of nineteenth-century battles.

[1] That is, of course, the use of one's own guns against those of the enemy.
[2] *Pocket Gunner*, p. 27.
[3] *British Military Library*, II, 368.

III

The use of field artillery in support of infantry in the fashion just described was relatively simple. Sieges were another matter. No branch of war was more exactly scientific, and there was none in which the British Army had less experience. Between the last of Marlborough's great sieges and the first of Wellington's, British troops successfully undertook less than half-a-dozen sieges, and none was of a major fortress. Louisbourg in 1758, Belle Isle in 1761, and Havana in 1762 about exhaust the list; for the siege of Valenciennes in 1793 was mainly an Austrian operation, and Scylla, on the toe of Italy, which fell to British arms in 1805, cannot be classed as a competent fortress; Copenhagen in 1807 surrendered to a mere three-day bombardment; Flushing in 1809 had, contrary to expectation, to be regularly besieged, but it surrendered before an assault could be made, and was in any case a fairly petty stronghold. The criticism is often heard of Wellington that he was bad at sieges; in fact the Ordnance Department's lack of experience in this very specialized branch of its work had much to do with the excessive price in blood that Wellington is judged to have paid for his fortresses.

That said, one can go no farther without some description of the type of work a siege involved.

First of all it was teamwork. Here, more than anywhere else, three arms, infantry, artillery, and engineers, had to co-operate. The chief of these was the engineer, under whose direction the others worked; and therefore this subject forms a natural transition from the topic of the Royal Artillery to that of the Royal Engineers.

The first task of the besieger of a fortress, when he got on to the ground of his proposed operation, was, of course, reconnaissance; he must ride out and inspect his intended quarry.

As he approached it, the first thing likely to meet his eye was an innocent-seeming grassy slope. This was the 'glacis', which Captain Boothby, a favourite young engineer on Sir John Moore's staff, describes as a 'smoothly sloping mound, which conceals and covers the rampart to its very chin...while its own gradual slope is swept by a rain and hail of cannon-balls, grapeshot and musketry'.[1] Behind the glacis lay the 'ditch', an unscalable pit encircling the fortress. The sides of this pit were revetted, 'that is, made strong with sheer masonry walls'; the inner of these two walls was the 'scarp', the outer the 'counterscarp'. At the crest of the counterscarp, immediately in the rear of the glacis, was the 'covered way'; somewhat akin to a firing trench in the First World War, the covered way might be lined with infantry, who, secure in its shelter, could pour

[1] M. S. and C. E. Boothby, *Under England's Flag from 1804 to 1809: the Memoirs, Diary and Correspondence of Charles Boothby, Captain of Royal Engineers* (London, 1900), p. 86.

musketry upon their assailants; from it too sallies could be made against the attackers. Above the scarp, on the inner face of the ditch, rose the 'rampart', and the rampart consisted of two things; one was the 'curtain wall' which enclosed the area the fortress protected; the other was the fort's array of 'bastions'. A bastion was a roughly triangular, or pentagonal, section of the curtain wall thrown forward;[1] the purpose of the bastions was to provide crossfire over all approaches to the fortifications; and, most deadly of all, a flanking fire to sweep the foot of the curtain where men might stumble and flounder as they strove to mount a breach. Conversely, the guns in the curtain wall provided a flanking fire along the face of the bastions, and a direct fire over the approaches.

Such was the general nature of any respectable fortress from the days of Louis XIV, and earlier, till well into the nineteenth century. The task of the besieger was somehow to get his troops over or through the physical obstacles presented by the glacis, ditch, and rampart, and once past these obstacles, to compel the surrender of the troops sheltered behind them. This might be done in a night 'escalade' with scaling ladders, but rarely if the defenders were either numerous or alert. Ordinarily it was necessary to 'breach' the rampart by cutting a gap through it with gunfire. A breach was judged 'practicable' when it was wide enough for men to enter on a fairly broad front, and when the fallen rubble of the shattered wall made a ramp up which they could clamber from the ditch; and few things were more irritating to an attacker than to have the defenders slip out into the ditch under cover of darkness and carry away the rubble over which he intended his assaulting troops to mount the breach at first light.

Once his reconnaissance was made, the attacker's next job was to complete his 'investment'; that is, to encircle the fortress so as to prevent useless mouths from leaving it or aid from reaching it; but the troops he used for his investment could only be a part of his army. He had to have enough men left over to provide a formidable covering force to thwart any attempt of the enemy to make him raise the siege.

His third task was to get his breaching batteries into position. At this point (if not earlier) the chief engineer became the most important man in the attacking force. It was his job to advise the commander on where the fortress might best be breached, and to decide, in conjunction with the chief gunner, where the breaching batteries could best be placed.

These were the first jobs to be done on the scene of the operation, but neither could be attempted without much previous work behind the scenes, nor until the attacker was assured of abundant transport. The investing troops could not stand out in the open, exposed to the defenders' guns. They had to be dug in, and so had the breaching batteries. Many mule- or waggon-loads of picks and shovels were needed here; so was

---

[1] It seems needless to draw here the distinction between a 'bastion' and a 'redan' which served a similar purpose on a smaller scale.

much solid plank to make the emplacements for the guns; also wicker baskets to fill with earth, called 'gabions', and bundles of faggots called 'fascines' to shelter the troops as they dug; and sandbags by the thousand to revet the trenches once they were made. Meanwhile more transport had to be hauling up the battering train, and more still was needed to keep its voracious guns fed. Here some figures may be both enlightening and surprising. As Alexander Dickson noted in his diary, eight rounds of 24-pounder shot was all one mule could carry;[1] at Ciudad Rodrigo 2754 rounds of this calibre were fired in two days and a half—a load for nearly 360 mules.[2] The siege of Badajoz used up a total of 2523 whole barrels of powder of 90 pounds weight each—a good load for 1200 mules; at Badajoz too the total consumption of solid shot was 18,832 rounds for 24-pounders and 13,029 rounds for 18-pounders, some 3590 mule loads of these articles alone, without counting grape and case shot, or $5\frac{1}{2}$ howitzer shells;[3] add that every working mule needs a daily ration of from 7 to 13 pounds of hay, 9 to 16 pounds of oats, and some 8 pounds of straw,[4] and that transport was required for these supplies too; it may then be seen how vast a job the conduct of a siege was and how much planning and foresight were needed to undertake one at all.

Once all this dead weight of ammunition had been brought to the scene of operations, the next problem was to deliver it to the guns of the breaching batteries which were to use it. Though cannon balls in this period might carry well over 3000 yards against targets in the open, it was not really practicable to breach a rampart at a greater range than 700 yards;[5] and the closer the battering guns were to their target the better. Obviously, therefore, any ammunition brought to them had to pass within easy range of the enemy's round shot, and that made necessary the tedious job of 'sapping'. This meant, in the first place, making covered approaches all the way up to the guns by digging 'saps', or trenches, wide enough for a roadway on which two waggons could pass as they shuttled to and fro delivering ammunition. The saps could not follow a direct route, for any such route would almost certainly be commanded by some of the guns of the fortress; so, before fire could open, hundreds of men, working largely by night at first, must dig their saps in zigzags (called 'parallels') up to the batteries.

Nor was that the end of sapping. When the breach was made at last, it might have to be assaulted; as assaulting columns should not be required to expose themselves to fire before they arrived at the breach, the zigzag parallels ought properly to be carried forward to the glacis, and on

[1] Leslie, *Dickson MSS*, p. 592.
[2] Jones, *Journals of Sieges in Spain, etc.*, I, 121.
[3] *Ibid.* pp. 209–10.
[4] From the War Office manual, *Animal Management, 1933* (London, H.M. Stationery Office, 1938), p. 282.
[5] Jones, *op. cit.* I, 379.

through it, till engineers could blow in the counterscarp. Then an assault might be launched, though it was desirable first to silence all guns in the fortress, thus compelling the enemy to defend himself by musket and bayonet alone, if he could.

At this stage it was normal to send a summons to the besieged commander and invite him to surrender. In the eighteenth century it had been conventionally thought honourable for a commander to accept the summons, provided the breach was practicable. A stubborn man might at any time refuse, and under Napoleon's standing orders, at least, the first summons of any fortress was to be rejected. Then there was nothing for it but an assault. First into the breach was sent a wistfully named band of volunteers who, after a custom at least as old as Cromwell's days, were called 'the forlorn hope'. Their task was to rush in as silently and secretly as they might, preferably under cover of darkness, to clear obstacles and to secure a bridgehead, as it were, within the enemy's defences (the point of their name appears to be that, provided all went well, some of them had some hope of living to tell the tale of their daring). Next came the main assaulting force, long columns of men winding their way through the sap, to mount the breach with a charge, to swarm along the ramparts and overwhelm the last defences of the doomed fortress. First light was the ideal time for the main assault to mount a breach,[1] and now there was no longer hope of maintaining the secrecy in which the forlorn hope had attempted to make their entrance. Once the main assault went forward, every musketeer the enemy could still dispose would be thrown against the head of the column at any point within the breach where it might be checked, while simultaneously every unsilenced gun opened up; and grape-shot never reaped a deadlier harvest than when it tore into masses of men, tripping and stumbling as they tried to clamber in the half-light over the jumbled piles of rubble that filled the ditch beneath the wreck of the breached rampart. Yet the success of the attacker should still be certain, if only he had done all things right. He should make practicable breaches; he should blow in the counterscarp and carry his saps right to the foot of each breach; he should silence the enemy's guns; and he should hurl upon the beleaguered fortress such a mass of men as must overpower the defenders by sheer weight of numbers.

Such, in brief, were the tasks involved in any fairly straightforward siege.

The tools the artilleryman required for his part of the job were, first, the 24-pounder gun for battering; secondly, the 18-pounder gun, which, though surprisingly less effective for breaching ramparts than the 24-pounder, was excellent for firing at parapets to dismount the enemy's guns; thirdly, mortars and howitzers to lob shells in a high arc through the air and drop them behind parapets to destroy the enemy's guncrews and so play a further part in silencing the fire of the fortress. It was

[1] *Ibid.* I, 400.

essential that the gunners' breaching fire should be accurate. The rampart ought to be, literally, 'cut through'; that meant cannon ball after cannon ball must strike the same mark time and again. The ideal was, if possible, to get the guns forward on to the glacis itself, at a range where one round after another could strike unerringly in one straight line, till a whole strip of undermined wall tottered and keeled over in a single piece, like a felled factory chimney. Failing that, it was possible, as has been said, to make breaches at ranges of 600 yards, or even more, but this was a slower job done in a different manner. At longer ranges it was necessary to use, so to speak, the woodpecker's method and to chip the wall away in little pieces instead of cutting out a whole section; the gunners must start by striking the foot of the wall and proceed to disintegrate the masonry bit by bit from the bottom up. High shooting at the start simply made a mound of rubble that protected the foot of the wall from later fire, and, if any breach were made, it was unlikely to be practicable.[1]

The first occasion after 1762 on which any demand to undertake a regular siege operation was made upon the Ordnance and its troops came in the summer of 1793, when the cabinet wished to capture Dunkirk and realized they would not have the expected aid of the Austrians. The resources of the British were found unequal to the attempt. First, they lacked men. On 13 July Pitt passed to Richmond a list of artillerymen in England with an inquiry whether 50 of them, with two companies of 100 Irish artillerymen each, could not be spared for the job.[2] Richmond's reply was devastating; the list of artillerymen in England told Mr Pitt nothing, because it was the paper establishment only, giving no clue as to their real numbers or state of training, and the efficiency of the Irish was doubtful; 'not knowing', continued Richmond, 'from whence Mr Pitt has his intelligence that 250 Artillery Men will be sufficient for the Siege... I have no remark to make as to the sufficiency of the number', but, if there were to be no Austrians, 'it would appear to me that triple, if not four times, that number of Men would be required'.[3]

After that, one might fairly expect the siege of Dunkirk to be given up, but it was not, and further deficiencies were revealed. A day or so later Pitt was asking for eighty 24-pounder guns and thirty 10-inch iron mortars. Richmond answered that the guns were in store but not ready; forty would be ready in one week, and another twenty in two weeks, but the last twenty were on the 'Garrison Carriages' used on gun platforms in permanent fortresses; for transport to Dunkirk such carriages would presumably not do and it would 'require a month to mount the last twenty on Travelling Carriages'. As for the thirty mortars, 'we have only 12 with beds of iron', replied Richmond, because the manufacturers

---

[1] Jones, *Journal of Sieges in Spain, etc.*, I, 379.
[2] Nepean (?) to Richmond, 13 July 1793, HO/50/369.
[3] Richmond to Nepean, 14 July 1793, *ibid.*

charged 'very extravagant prices for casting Iron Mortars', so no considerable contract had been given till war broke out; no deliveries on that contract would be ready in time; worse still, continued Richmond, 'we have not even a sufficient number of 10-inch Brass Mortars to make up the Thirty' weapons required; and, finally, asked Richmond, did Mr Pitt and Mr Dundas really wish to send out of the country all the heavy Mortars the nation owned?[1]

Barring a hint that the Carron Company may have been behind-hand with contracted deliveries of mortar shells,[2] there seems to have been no immediate shortage of ammunition; but there was a wretched dearth of transport for hauling it from Nieuport, where it was to be landed, to Dunkirk, where it was needed;[3] and that was yet another factor making for delay and inefficiency.

The results of all this dismal unreadiness are known to everyone who has read the story of the 1793 campaign. The army began its investment of Dunkirk by land on 24 August and for upwards of two weeks remained in its trenches under bombardment from the enemy's gunboats, which operated freely because the cabinet had failed to arrange for a promised naval blockade by sea. Only about 29 August did the battering train and its stores at last begin to arrive at Ostend and Nieuport, while the army waited idle in its trenches, unable to take effective action till it received its equipment. No pains were spared at the ports. Once deliveries there began, 'every Exertion' was made 'for twelve Days in transporting' to Dunkirk 'the Necessary Articles for carrying on the Siege', wrote George Williamson, Ordance commissary at Nieuport, to Richmond;[4] but when he wrote, on 11 September, the 'Necessary Articles' were already lost. On the 6th, near Cassel, and on the 8th, near Hondschoote, the French had successively and successfully attacked the Duke of York's Hanoverian and Austrian covering forces. The second French victory left York and his investing force in a critical situation from which he could only extricate himself by retreat. That retreat saved his men; it could not save his guns, because, though more than a month had passed since Pitt inquired about them, they had still *not* been mounted on 'travelling carriages.'[5]

Of this unfortunate operation it only remains to be said that everything

---

[1] Richmond to Nepean, 18 July 1793, *ibid.* [2] Rogers to Nepean, 5 August 1793, *ibid.*
[3] Richmond to Dundas, 25 July 1793, *ibid.*
[4] Williamson to Richmond, 11 September 1793, HO/50/370.
[5] This is stated in a 'Memoir of the Duke of York' in the *Naval and Military Magazine* (March 1827), p. 13. It is added that the guns had been transported from Nieuport and Ostend to Dunkirk by barge, not by road. Even so, the Duke hoped to save his guns, but, according to Fortescue, was thwarted by the French, apparently in Dunkirk, who controlled the sluices and were able to empty the canals (*History of the British Army*, IV, 132). Why none of the guns had been mounted is a riddle to which I can suggest only two answers. One is that Pitt, out of his depth in business he did not understand, never followed up his inquiry of 18 July by giving an order for the work to be done; the other that want of sufficient artillery horses and drivers made the work pointless.

required of the commander in the field was brilliantly performed. York had been promised that his battering train would reach Nieuport on 20 August, on which day he might fairly assume that unloading would begin.[1] Bearing that date in mind, his advance on Dunkirk seems admirably timed. Its suddenness certainly won him complete surprise. His investment of the town on 24 August caught the French so badly off balance that they attempted no counter-move till 6 September, nor did that move become dangerous till the 8th. Finally, his withdrawal on the night of 8–9 September was so deftly conducted that the enemy, attributing his escape to treachery, actually guillotined their own unfortunate commander, Houchard, the victor of Hondschoote. Between these dates York won a period of fifteen days for the siege of a weak fortress, which, observers judged, 'could only hold out for five or six days' under bombardment.[2] Yet all the fruits of the commander's skill were thrown away, because the nation had not ready a battering train sufficient to attack one second-rate stronghold at one time. Such was the nature of British unpreparedness in 1793, and such the price paid for it.[3]

This was the last occasion on which the British attempted a serious siege till Wellington broke ground before Badajoz in April 1811. In the intervening years a dangerous delusion took hold upon the nation. Many people came to argue that siege operations, with all the science, toil, and time they took, were needless; in the view of these people it was only necessary to make a general bombardment of a town in order to compel its surrender.

That was never the view of competent professionals; to them the very notion was made repugnant by its futile cruelty. 'To bombard a town', says Jones the besieger, 'is merely to shower down upon it shells, carcasses, rockets, hot-shot and other incendiary missiles.'[4] Under bombardment shops, houses, schools, churches, places of work and business were tumbled into ruin; fires grew widespread; the bedridden died miserably in burning homes, and children were slain by falling masonry as they played, or ran in panic through the streets; in a word, bombardment reproduced many of the horrors of a modern air raid. Civilians of every age and sex were mercilessly slaughtered while the investing army denied them that escape which evacuation offered in 1939–45. It was simply an attempt to compel surrender by terror; 'the cruelty of it is inconceivable to those who have not witnessed its effects, which fall chiefly on the aged, the infirm, and the helpless', wrote Jones.[5] By this 'frightfulness' the British indeed forced the surrender of Copenhagen

[1] J. W. Fortescue, *Historical and Military Essays* (London, 1928), p. 125.

[2] Burne, *Duke of York*, p. 71.

[3] In my above estimate of York's performance at Dunkirk, I do not overlook the defeats of his covering forces on 6 and 8 September. But York was, of course, not personally commanding these forces and cannot be held responsible for the conduct of the officers who were—the more so as one of them, the Hanoverian Field Marshal Freytag, had failed to conform to his orders.

[4] *Journal of Sieges in Spain*, II, 373.   [5] *Ibid.* p. 374.

in 1807, to gain possession of the fleet, and the hatred, of the Danes; that success unfortunately gave a false *éclat* to the method of bombardment. By the same means they tried to secure Flushing in 1809. But Flushing was commanded by a conscientious French governor with high regard for his military duty and little sympathy for the agony of Dutch civilians. He would not surrender the post entrusted to him till a regular siege was undertaken, in the best manner that could be improvised, and breaching was imminent. Yet because Flushing was bombarded, and thereafter fell, Chatham's success there was deemed a vindication of bombardment by all men of that class to which *post hoc* is the same as *propter hoc*. What it really proved was the futility of the whole tragic business. The slaughter of civilians, amid the ruins of their homes, did no damage to curtain, bastion, or ditch; while women and children died, soldiers were safe in their casemates and behind their parapets; when the smoke cleared from the rubble of shattered streets, nearly everything that made the unhappy town a place of military strength was revealed as efficient and intact.[1]

Yet this faith in bombardment was important, even if it was a delusion. It gives the most nearly rational explanation possible of the extraordinary fact that Wellington, when sent to a peninsula where the French held most of the fortresses, was equipped with no efficient means of reducing them. It also goes far to explain the long neglect to make the Royal Engineers an efficient corps; in Jones's phrase, belief in bombardment 'threatened to prevent the country from ever attaining due siege establishments'.[2]

Wellington himself never considered bombarding Badajoz, Ciudad Rodrigo, or anywhere else. He had been at Copenhagen, and knew that the people who would suffer most would be his Spanish allies, not his French enemies; for this reason he even prevented his gunners from making proper use of the high-arcked fire of mortars lest it wander from purely military targets[3] (a mistake undoubtedly, but one which his critics seem to have missed). Also, he can hardly have failed to realize one point which enthusiasts for bombardment overlooked; this was that to bombard a town required far more ammunition than to besiege it and would throw a still greater strain on his exiguous transport.[4]

So, with a wisdom surpassing that of many men of his day, he settled down to regular siege operations. His first was against Olivenza in April

---

[1] *Ibid.* p. 373. After Flushing surrendered, 'the left bastion' was indeed found 'almost in ruins, and the sea defences on that side were a good deal injured; but the works on the land front generally were in a perfect state' (*ibid.* II, 273–4). The left bastion, however, had been the direct target of breaching batteries numbers 8 and 9; and the sea defences had been pounded by the broadsides of seven ships of the line, independently of the general bombardment. 'The loss of the garrison' was not great, 'but 335 civilians were killed and a still greater number wounded. The Stadt house, 2 churches and 247 houses were utterly destroyed and the whole of the left of the town more or less injured' (*ibid.*). [2] *Ibid.* II, 376.
[3] Wellington to Lord William Bentinck, 24 March 1812, in Gurwood, *Wellington's Dispatches*, vol. IX. [4] On which point, see Jones, *Journal of Sieges in Spain*, II, 374.

1811; it was weak and gave no particular trouble. His second and third sieges were two attempts against Badajoz in the spring and early summer of 1811, remembered now, so far as they are remembered at all, only because the battle of Albuera ended the first and was the prelude to the second. Both were failures, and in neither did he have any British guns at all. For want of them he used a strange battering train unearthed by Alexander Dickson from the historic Portuguese arsenal of Elvas, and a notable collection of museum pieces it was—thirty brass 24-pounders dating from the reigns of Philip II (1598–1621), Philip III (1621–40), and John IV (1640–56).[1] The attempt to master Badajoz with these simply proved the wisdom of the Duke of Richmond when he warned Portland against including any brass 24-pounders in the Irish artillery. Wellington's brass guns now proved less able than their target to stand the strain of the bombardment; 'seventeen or eighteen' of them, wrote Dickson, 'were rendered *hors de combat*, two of which only were by the enemy's fire and the remainder by drooping or unbushing'.[2] Wellington's fourth siege, that of Ciudad Rodrigo, was conducted in a relatively competent manner, so far as artillery went, with a battering train of thirty-four iron 24-pounders sent specially from England; eight pairs of bullocks dragged up each gun, and ox-carts enough were available to haul up the ammunition. The final siege of Badajoz was a success in spite of incompetent *matériel*; for here Wellington had had to appeal to the navy for more 24-pounder guns, but he had received only 18-pounders, of Russian design, which his ammunition did not fit.[3] For Burgos, whose siege he attempted at the extremity of a very long-drawn supply line, he had only three 18-pounder guns and five howitzers; and the howitzer was a very poor battering weapon.[4] For the second, but not the first, siege of San Sebastian he had 'a force of artillery sufficiently great for all purposes of destruction and annoyance'.[5] If, then, the capture of the feeble Olivenza may be included among Wellington's sieges, the Royal Artillery served him adequately on only three occasions out of eight.[6]

---

[1] Jones, *Journal of Sieges in Spain*, I, 352. Philip II of Portugal was, of course, Philip III of Spain and likewise Philip III of Portugal was Philip IV of Spain. The dates I have given are Portuguese, but if Jones, who calls them Kings of Spain, really intended their Spanish numbers and titles, then the guns were, of course, still more venerable antiques than I have ventured to indicate.

[2] Leslie, *Dickson MSS*, p. 405. 'Drooping at the muzzle' was an injury incurred when a brass gun became overheated from repeated firing. In this case 120 rounds per day proved excessive (Jones, *op. cit.* I, 352). 'Unbushing' means the blowing out of the vent, or touchhole, through which the propellant charge within the gun was fired.

[3] Jones, *op. cit.* II, 403.

[4] Its 'inefficiency' was 'utter', says Jones (*ibid.* I, 342, 403).

[5] *Ibid.* p. 92.

[6] I omit Hill's capture of the French works at Almaraz, because these were carried by escalade, not besieged; also the capture of the fortified posts at Salamanca, because these, though skilfully improvised, were not regular fortifications; and the Retiro at Madrid, which surrendered without being attacked.

IV

He was even worse served by the engineers. The long and tedious job of 'sapping' has been mentioned. This was one duty of the engineers and Jones's description of how it was done cannot be bettered; he writes:

The formation of the covered road is attended with different degrees of difficulty in proportion as it advances.

At its commencement, being at the distance of 600 yards from the fortifications, and not straitened for space, the work can readily be performed by soldiers of the army. The second period is, when the road arrives within a fair range of musketry, or 300 yards from the place; it then requires particular precautions, which, however, are not so difficult but that the work may be executed by soldiers who have had a little previous training. The third period is, when it approaches close to the place—when every bullet takes effect—when to be seen is to be killed—when mine after mine blows up at the head of the road, and with it every officer and man on the spot; when the space becomes so restricted that little or no front of defense can be obtained, and the enemy's grenadiers sally forth every moment to attack the workmen and deal out destruction to all less courageous or weaker than themselves.

Then the work becomes truly hazardous, and can only be performed by selected brave men who have acquired a difficult and most dangerous art called sapping, from which they are themselves styled sappers.

An indispensable auxiliary to the sapper is the miner, the exercise of whose art requires even a greater degree of skill, courage and conduct than that of his principal. The duty of a miner at a siege is to accompany the sapper, to listen for and discover the enemy's miner at work under ground, and prevent his blowing up the head of the road either by sinking down and meeting him, when a subterraneous conflict ensues, or by running a gallery close to that of his opponent, and forcing him to quit his work by means of suffocating compositions, and a thousand arts of chicanery....Sappers would be unable of themselves, without the aid of skilful miners, to execute that part of the covered road forming the descent into the ditch; and in various other portions of the road, the assistance of the miner is indispensable to the sapper; indeed, without their joint labours and steady cooperation, no besiegers' approaches ever reached the walls of a fortress.[1]

Such were the duties of sapping and mining which a commander expected his engineers to perform, and they were duties to which the Royal Engineers of Britain were wholly unequal.

One is tempted to say that the chief defect of the British engineers was that there were none, and indeed such a statement would not be very far wrong. There was, of course, a corps of men, well trained and able, and recently rechristened the Royal Engineers by a warrant of 1787; but these men were all officers, and their peacetime strength in 1783 had been no more than 75. The nation thus had no regular body of enlisted soldiers trained for the conduct of sieges.

That fertile author of improvement, the Duke of Richmond, had indeed come near to providing his country with such a force. He had been much

---

[1] Jones, *op. cit.* I, xiv–xv.

and properly impressed by the great crisis of the American and Bourbon War when, in the months of August and September 1779, the French and Spanish fleets had ruled the Channel, and when nothing but the enemy's own dissensions and hesitations had prevented the landing of 40,000 French troops in England (a force which in the circumstances of that time might not impossibly have dictated peace in London before Christmas). One of the ugliest things about that crisis had been the defenceless condition of Britain's naval bases, for had the French risked an attack on Plymouth 'the dockyard would have been in their possession in less than six hours'.[1] Richmond therefore wished to fortify both Plymouth and Portsmouth. When the House of Commons, in a debate unusually distinguished for fatuity,[2] rejected his proposals and his appropriations for a system of forts, he hit on another scheme. The fortifications of Gibraltar were largely built and wholly repaired by a body of military workmen enlisted for the purpose; following that example, Richmond created in 1787 a new corps of Royal Military Artificers.[3] Primarily the men of this corps were intended to build the fortifications Parliament would not permit to be built by contract, but Richmond was determined that they should be fit for field service too. In August 1792 he actually had them in camp in peacetime practising bridging and mining on Bagshot Heath.[4] In the next year he was able to supply 153 of them to assist the Duke of York at Dunkirk;[5] and had he remained in office, he would probably have developed his new creation into a very effective force of field engineers. When he fell, however, the Royal Military Artificers withered. Their numbers, to be sure, grew; they were distributed all over the world, wherever Britain had fortifications to maintain; but they degenerated into mere patchers and menders of fortresses and nothing more. They were all the worse because they were commonly recruited by 'receiving volunteers from regiments of the line', a system described as enabling commanding officers to get 'rid of their worst men'.[6]

So it happened that when the Duke of York required engineers for field service on the expedition to North Holland in 1799, the Ordnance could provide none. Thereupon the Duke attempted to raise a corps of engineers of his own, who would be under the control of the army, not

[1] Report of Sir David Lindsay, military governor of Plymouth, cited by Herbert Butterfield, *George III, Lord North and the People* (London, 1949), p. 61.

[2] This is surely a fair description of a debate in which the House rejected the carefully argued advice on naval defence of so able an officer as Samuel Hood or in which it listened to an M.P. who could aver that defensive fortifications were a menace to the country because they were 'seminaries for soldiers and universities for Praetorian bands' (*Parl. Debates*, xxv, 1117 and 1114). It is, however, but justice to half the House to record that Richmond's proposals were only defeated on the casting vote of the Speaker.

[3] T. W. J. Connolly, *The History of the Royal Corps of Sappers and Miners* (London, 1855), I, 55.

[4] So Connolly, citing the *Public Advertiser* for 9 July and 7 and 10 August 1792.

[5] Connolly, *Royal Sappers and Miners*, I, 80.

[6] C. W. Pasley, *Course of Military Instruction* (London, 1817), II, iv.

the Ordnance, and so was born the Royal Staff Corps.[1] In due course this corps received a number of very well-trained officers from the Royal Military College, which the Duke was to found in 1801. Its men were mostly volunteers 'from the different regiments and battalions of Foot Guards and Infantry in Great Britain', and a general order calling for such volunteers in 1804 indicates what sort of men they had to be. 'They must be strong active Men...having regularly served an Apprenticeship and possessing a complete knowledge of one of the following trades, Vizt. Carpenters, Wheelers, Sawyers, Shipwrights or Boatbuilders, Masons, Bricklayers, Miners.' The miners must be the real thing, not mere colliers or quarrymen. It was essential that the volunteers 'should be men of merit and good character'; and none was to be accepted till they had been 'examined in their Trades and...approved at Chatham Barracks'. Their function was to construct 'Field Works' and to do 'other Military Duties, of whatsoever nature, in the Quarter Master General's Department'.[2]

In the invasion years 1803–5 the Royal Staff Corps did do some really valuable construction work for the defence of the threatened coasts. Its best achievement and most lasting monument was the Royal Military Canal, which still runs from Shorncliffe westward to Rye and beyond, and makes the Dungeness peninsula and the Pett Level into islands.[3] Personnel of the Staff Corps were also attached to some overseas expeditions, but their numbers were never very great; they contributed little to the Peninsular War and were finally absorbed by the Royal Engineers.

That is about all there is to be said of the Royal Staff Corps. Still less is to be said of yet a third corps of the same type. This was the Barrack Artificer Corps. It was called into being as a result of the Barrack Office being separated from the Ordnance Department, after which the Royal Military Artificers could no longer be required to repair barracks. The men the Barrack Artificer Corps recruited were 'Carpenters and Joiners, Sawyers, Bricklayers, Rough Stone Masons, Plaisterers, Miners, Lime Burners, Smiths, White Smiths, Plumbers, Glaziers and Painters, Wheelwrights, Coopers', according to a General Order of 16 April 1805 which invited such men to volunteer from the ranks of the regular army.[4]

So here was the extraordinary situation of a great power, involved in a war two decades long, with three parallel and competitive corps of quasi-engineers, all recruiting artisans of much the same trades from the same source, but without any body of men capable of performing the duties required of real engineers in the field.

The results of this wretched situation were only brought to light by the

[1] Fortescue, *History of the British Army*, IV, 881.
[2] General Order of 1 February 1804 (in the War Office Library).
[3] R. Glover, 'The Royal Military Canal', in *The Army Quarterly* (October 1953), pp. 97–107.
[4] War Office Library.

casualty lists from Wellington's sieges. He indeed knew his want of sappers and miners, and did his best to supply them. One hundred and eighty rank and file from the Third Division received some training in sapping before the siege of Ciudad Rodrigo;[1] 120 of them 'remained effective' to attempt the same duties at the siege of Badajoz.[2] At Burgos miners of a sort were found by calling upon men who had been coal miners in civil life to volunteer from the ranks, and some came forward. But these shifts did not answer. Neither the peacetime miner nor the infantryman part-trained as a sapper had the skill required for military operations; their instructors were too few and their numbers were insufficient, their morale too often, and perhaps too naturally, poor.[3] Wellington has been severely enough criticized for writing on 28 May 1812: 'I trust...that future armies will be equipped for sieges, with the people necessary to carry them on as they ought to be [carried on]; and that our engineers will learn how to put their batteries on the crest of the glacis and to blow in the counterscarp, instead of placing [the batteries] wherever the wall can be seen, [and] leaving the poor officers and men to get into and across the ditch as best they can';[4] but all criticism of this letter is misconceived. It is no unjust diatribe against his own engineers, against Fletcher, Burgoyne, and John Thomas Jones who served him long and well. It is a simple statement of what needed to be done at any siege, and what no troops of the British Ordnance Department could do for him. No gun of his had ever been placed on an enemy's glacis; no petard had ever blown in a counterscarp for his troops; and no sap had ever been run through a blasted counterscarp to give his men a covered way right to the foot of the breach. There lies the cause of the high price in blood that Wellington paid for his fortresses. Always his assaulting columns had had to go over the top of the sap at a great and dangerous distance from the glacis; they had had to charge for the breach and cross the glacis through 'a tempest of grape from the ramparts' at Rodrigo[5] and 'through a blaze of light and rattle of musketry' at Badajoz;[6] somehow they had to lower themselves down the counterscarp into the ditch before they could begin to clamber up the breach. Hideous casualties were to be expected in these conditions, and the casualties suffered were hideous indeed. 'Three thousand five hundred men were stricken in the assault' on Badajoz, as Napier tells, adding, 'let it

---

[1] Jones, *Journals of Sieges in Spain*, II, 103.

[2] *Ibid.* p. 155.

[3] So John Fox Burgoyne reports that British soldiers refused to work at the saps at Burgos, even after he had laid out gabions and fascines for them to work behind (G. Wrottesley, *Life and Correspondence of John Fox Burgoyne*, London, 1873, I, 232). Yet these men were drawn from the gallant army which had so recently triumphed at Salamanca.

[4] To Major General George Murray, Gurwood, *Wellington's Dispatches*, vol. IX.

[5] Napier, *The War in the Peninsula*, Book XVI, chapter 3.

[6] *Ibid.* book XVI, chapter 5. The 'blaze of light' may be attributed to 'light balls', which, says Jones, were 'of excellent use for discovering working parties' (*Journals of Sieges in Spain*, I, 368).

be remembered that this frightful carnage took place in a space of less than one hundred yards square.'[1]

Where Britain won her fortresses by such lavish expenditure of blood and courage, the French won theirs cheaply by dint of foresight, skill, and training; and French standards provide a clue to what Britain needed. One hundred properly trained miners had worked with 483 trained sappers in the French capture of Badajoz in 1811. They were available because 'no French *corps d'armée* lacked a battalion of sappers and a company of miners'.[2] These men were ready provided with '1700 pickaxes, 170 miners' picks, 1700 shovels, 1700 long-handled shovels, total 5270 intrenching tools; 680 felling axes, 1020 bill-hooks, total 1700 cutting tools; 1802 artificers' tools, 253 miners' tools, and 8318 kil. weight of machinery and stores'. All this very necessary equipment was carried in a total of 35 waggons. Another 10 waggons carried the French engineers' bridging equipment, and what with forge carts and waggons for demolition stores the French engineer battalion was made mobile by some 230 draught horses.[3]

Even now the full tale of Wellington's disadvantages is still untold. British Ordnance officers in every generation tend to have an undue affection for indestructibly robust equipment. In this period French entrenching tools were designed for portability, while the British were designed for durability. As a result French tools were 'so much lighter than the English, that in the Peninsula, wherever French tools were found, they were eagerly seized for the field-depot equipment, and an equivalent weight of English tools abandoned, by which exchange one-fourth was sometimes added to the number of tools carried by the mules'.[4]

Here too it will be noted that the pack mule was the British means of transport. Given waggons, far more tools could have been moved by fewer animals, but even in 1813 Wellington's engineer transport consisted of but 120 pack mules, against the 230 draught horses in each French *corps d'armée*; and the Spanish muleteers, who were hired with their mules, were of course not subject to military discipline. Wellington, however, was still lucky to have them, for no thought was ordinarily given in Britain to the movement of engineers' stores, though very odd results had flowed from this neglect in the past. Thus, Sir James Craig, when he was sent to Naples in December 1805, had bought on landing 'ample numbers of horses...and allotted [them] to the engineers; but although the stores were laden on carts, they never could start for want of drivers';[5] and Jones, who records this fact, adds, 'no one can possibly doubt the superior confidence to be reposed in a disciplined soldier over a foreign peasant, when acting as a driver for the first time under fire'.[6] Yet even in the

[1] Napier, *ibid.*
[2] Wellington to Lord Liverpool, 11 February 1812, in Gurwood, *Wellington's Dispatches*, vol. VIII.
[3] Jones, *Journals of Sieges in Spain*, II, 386.
[4] *Ibid.* p. 193 n.   [5] *Ibid.* p. 385.   [6] *Ibid.* p. 387.

Waterloo campaign the British engineers had no regular transport. They had to make do with Flemish waggons and with drivers who were hired in 'the neighbourhood of Antwerp and Brussels, were generally ignorant of their duties, and many of them men of bad character, so that frequent desertions took place'.[1]

Another engineering duty, indicated in the description of the French engineer battalion given above, was to supply the commander with bridging. The needs of a European army in this line were minutely described by Wellington in India in 1803, when he explained what he expected to want for his pursuit of the Mahrattas in his next campaign.

Military bridges were made of boats, or pontoons, moored head to current across the river, at equal distances from one another, and all made fast to one or more cables stretching from bank to bank; they had also to be lashed together and individually anchored. Once the boats were in position, baulks were laid across them, writes Wellington, and were 'keyed together, their numbers proportioned to the strength required in the bridge'.[2] Then planks were nailed across the baulks to make a roadway. The ideal pontoon measured 21 feet over its greatest length, with a width of 3 feet 11 inches and a depth of 2 feet 1 inch. 'The common mode of carrying pontoons in Europe', continues Wellington, 'is on a two wheeled carriage, on which is placed the pontoon, and within it all its stores....The common calculation of the weight of a pontoon with its equipment is 1200 pounds.'[3]

An army properly supplied with this equipment was not held up by the presence of unbridged rivers in its path, or by the enemy's destruction of existing bridges; but here again Wellington was let down by the Ordnance Department.

The pontoons sent out with our expeditions [writes C. W. Pasley] were merely consigned by order of the Board of Ordnance to the commanding Engineer, like other articles of store, without any provision of properly trained men for manœuvring them and without any establishment of horses and drivers for transporting them. Consequently, in cases of emergency, either country drivers...were to be hired, and horses bought at a disadvantage; or men were to be borrowed from the infantry and means of transport from the Artillery or Commissariat. These temporary expedients created the greatest confusion, and generally tended...to paralyze other important branches of the service.[4]

At times the sheer ingenuity of Wellington's officers did overcome the deficiencies of his bridging equipment. As examples there spring to mind Major Sturgeon's invention of a mobile suspension bridge, made of a network of rope overlaid by planking and used in 1812 to span the broken

[1] Pasley, *Course of Military Instruction*, II, xii.
[2] 'Memorandum respecting Boats etc. for Bridges' enclosed to Lt. Col. Close, 11 April 1803, Gurwood, *Wellington's Dispatches*, vol. I.
[3] *Ibid.*
[4] Pasley, *Course of Military Instruction*, II, xi.

arch of the bridge at Alcantara.[1] Wellington's engineers also became adept at using Spanish wine casks in place of pontoons. But the price Britain paid for lack of complete and mobile bridging equipment was still high. It is thus estimated by J. T. Jones in the first (and rare) single-volume edition of his *Journals of the Sieges undertaken by the Allies in Spain in the years 1811 and 1813*.[2] He concedes that the service of 'a corps of pontoneers' may be rarely

required; but when such occasions occur, they are generally of extreme importance, and no one can tell the moment they may offer; it frequently arrives when least expected. To take a case in point: Suppose in the winter of 1810 and 1811, when the army was in the lines covering Lisbon, it had been proposed that the engineers should be furnished with a due proportion of draught horses, waggons, artificers, miners, sappers, pontoons, and pontoneers, etc., it would have been deemed an extravagance out of reason: but mark how far otherwise; in such case Marshal Beresford might have crossed the Guidiana on the 26th March; Badajos, with the breach open, the trenches not filled in, and without provisions, would have offered little or no resistance;[3] the battle of Albuera would have been avoided, and also the loss at the subsequent sieges. Such a due equipment would therefore in this one instance have preserved the lives of 8 or 10,000 men, and the expenditure of enormous sums of money; sums so great, that to have been used on this one occasion only, economy would have been consulted, if such establishments had been kept on foot the whole war.

V

At the close of this account of the Ordnance two comments suggest themselves. The first is that when Richmond fell his country suffered a loss that has never been appreciated. His abilities and his services have not yet received their due, even in the long-forgotten words pronounced twenty-two years after his fall and ten after his death by a subordinate on whom he had made an indelible impression. This man was R. H. Crew, still Secretary to the Ordnance in 1817 when he referred to his former chief as 'the Duke of Richmond whom no man went before in knowledge of the details of his department'. Any administrator whose subordinates remember him in such terms for so long must be a man of uncommon quality, but this epitaph tells barely half the story. Beside knowledge of the details of his department, Richmond also possessed a mind uncommonly alert to opportunities for reform, and was the author of probably more valuable innovations than any two other Masters General since James II's reorganization of the Ordnance Department. He gives the lie direct to that claptrap maxim: 'No man is irreplaceable'. None of the men who subsequently occupied his office in our period came near to replacing Richmond either as an able administrator or as a clear-sighted reformer.

[1] Napier, *War in the Peninsula*, book XVIII, chapter 1.
[2] (London, 1814), pp. 360–1.
[3] At this date, of course, Badajoz had only just fallen to the French; the still open breaches and unfilled trenches were those that they had made.

The second comment is that no just estimate of the greatness of Wellington can be made except by those who have studied the duties and deficiencies of the Ordnance Corps, for they alone can have some practical idea of the difficulties he had to master. On sheer ignorance of these matters rests the supposition that Wellington was bad at sieges, an ignorance that marks the length of his casualty lists, but does not examine their causes. Any criticism that is to be accepted here must weigh the value of the fortresses attacked; must review the information available to Wellington at the time of the attack;[1] must look narrowly to the means available, not asserting that they should have been increased without showing by what methods they could have been increased.[2] Criticism must heed too the fact that in this very specialized branch of war any commander who ignored or overruled his chief engineer took a very heavy responsibility upon himself.

Some criticisms certainly may be valid. One such possibly acceptable criticism has already been noted, namely, Wellington's failure to use the high-angle fire of mortars and howitzers to silence the enemy's guns at Ciudad Rodrigo and Badajoz. Another criticism, first voiced by John Fox Burgoyne, is that Wellington made the wrong choice when he preferred small forlorn hopes to large ones on the ground that casualties were likely to be less when a small, than when a large, forlorn hope failed. Neither point, however, has bulked very large in modern criticism of Wellington. A third criticism, also voiced by Burgoyne, is that the attack on Badajoz was directed at the wrong places. Here, however, the senior engineer was not Burgoyne, but Richard Fletcher; and he died in the assault on San Sebastian before he could publish his opinions, without which the merits of both sides of this case can hardly be argued. All told, the most sensible line for the modern student to adopt is to consider seriously only those criticisms which are upheld by the few of Wellington's contemporaries who possessed the knowledge necessary for making a valid judgement.[3] These seem petty enough when weighed against the admiration which both Napier and Jones express for the ability of Wellington as a besieger.

[1] As, for example, the report of the deserter, recorded by Burgoyne, that Burgos had not enough provisions to hold out beyond 15 October 1812. It was, as time proved, mistaken, but the notice Burgoyne gives it shows it received serious consideration, as indeed such information must (Wrottesley, *Correspondence of Burgoyne*, I, 222). Undoubtedly it goes far to explain what Davies described as Wellington's 'tenacity in continuing the operation, when success appeared so doubtful' (*Wellington and his Army*, p. 33). The retreat from Burgos began on the night of 21–22 October.

[2] Thus if he is to be criticized for besieging Burgos with too little artillery, it is the critic's task to show either (a) where he could have got more guns from, and (b) where he was to find the transport to keep them fed with ammunition, or (c) that some more promising and more profitable operation was open to him.

[3] For example, there is little point in quoting the opinion of such a person as the author of *The Personal Narrative of a Private Soldier in the Forty-Second Highlanders* (cited by Davies, *Wellington and His Army*, p. 33).

CHAPTER 5

TRAINING: INFANTRY AND CAVALRY

I

THE purpose of training is to prepare troops for battle; and the training they receive must, therefore, fit the sort of battle they are expected to fight. Nothing in the normal modern soldiering, with which most of us are familiar, so much resembles at least the beginning of an eighteenth-century battle as a very large and very formal outdoor church parade.

First on such ceremonial occasions today the ground is duly reconnoitred; next, with drums beating, bugles pealing, and pipes skirling, troops are marched up in column till at the appropriate spot the command is given 'At the halt on the Left form Line'; the pivot man of each column then halts, the rear files make their half-turn to the left and swing forward till, after taking their dressing by the right, they find themselves standing in a three-deep line and facing the padre on his stand with his public address system before him. By the same stately evolutions eighteenth-century soldiery formed line to face, not one lonely and innocent padre, but the serried ranks of their enemy drawn up for battle. They continued to do this into the nineteenth century, through the campaigns of 1848–9 and the American Civil War, till the breech-loading rifle drove the infantryman to become what he is today, a cross between a hunter and a hunted animal, alternately running forward and hiding, as he advances by 'fire and movement' from one patch of cover to the next.

How, in such astonishing contrast to modern practice, men in the days of Napoleon could use as battle drill the formal drill, now reserved for the recruits' barrack square and the church parade, becomes apparent only when one empties one's mind of all that one knows about modern weapons and concentrates on the characteristics of the weapons of those bygone days. Indeed, any discussion of the tactics of any period is about as meaningless to those who do not know the characteristics of the weapons of that period as is the discussion of a chess problem to those who do not know the moves of the pieces. The nature of the weapons of our period is therefore a subject of prime importance in this chapter. Here too it will be proper to ignore the usual order of precedence and to treat cavalry last. In the eighteenth century infantry had already long been the proverbial 'Queen of Battles', and theirs was still the dominant weapon of the age (at least in an army so weak in artillery as the British). The cavalryman had little to do in the normal battle till the moment (or moments) of crisis. Then he would have a shaken enemy to rout or to pursue—unless it were his task to prevent the enemy cavalry from doing these very things by covering the retreat of his own side. I shall therefore deal first with the tactical training of the three classes of infantry. These were infantry of the line, on whose shoulders the solid work of winning battles mainly fell; light infantry who scouted and skirmished; riflemen who blended the light infantryman's job with that of the modern sniper. A short section on weapon training may suitably close this chapter.

II. INFANTRY OF THE LINE

Infantry of the line (and also light infantry) were armed with a 'Brown Bess' musket and ring bayonet. Like a modern shot-gun, the musket had a smooth bore, with none of the spiral grooves that make a weapon a rifle, and, as every amateur in ballistics knows, a smoothbore does not throw a bullet very far with accuracy. Two hundred yards was almost the outside range at which the musket could really be physically effective in killing or wounding an enemy.[1] Frederick the Great had indeed ordered fire to be opened at six hundred yards from the enemy, but that was for moral effect—'to familiarize soldiers to the fire and blind them with regard to danger'[2]—and there were few who agreed with his practice. Guibert, the French tactician, stigmatized Prussian firing as the most innocuous in Europe;[3] he preferred troops to hold their fire till they were within eighty 'toises', or 160 paces, of the enemy. The effect of a musket's fire at any range depended on the care and correctness with which the weapon had been loaded, and, as men loaded best when cool and collected, unhurried by the fear they were entitled to feel in the presence of their foe, the first volley of an engagement was the most deadly of all.[4] And that is why good commanders sometimes made men hold their fire till they were close enough to their enemy to see the proverbial 'whites of their eyes'; at such a range no man should miss, and the first, best volley should have its full effect. Often, too, commanders preferred to have the enemy fire first, and that for a psychological reason which will be plain enough to any one who knows small boys. Watch two youngsters having a snowball fight; as long as each is 'armed' with a well-made snowball, they face each other on an equality, but the moment one throws his snowball, he is disarmed; then he is at his opponent's mercy while he stoops to grab more snow for another, and he very commonly runs away while he pats his next 'round' into shape. So was it with the cumbrous procedure of recharging a muzzle-loading musket; men were never so

[1] Adye, *Bombardier and Pocket Gunner*, p. 126.
[2] 'The common Order of Battle...ordered by the King of Prussia', in T. Simes, *The Military Guide for Young Officers* (London, 1781), pp. 93–4.
[3] 'Ces bataillons Prussiens...sont ceux dont le feu est le moins meurtrier', in *Essai générale de la Tactique* (Paris, 1802), I, 77.
[4] *Ibid.*

likely to break as when they received a shattering volley from the enemy while they fumbled in haste to reload empty weapons they had themselves just fired; in that moment they felt helpless, and the havoc of their own volley was, of course, hidden from them by the clouds of smoke their own crude powder had created in the instant of firing.[1] For this reason good, practical sense underlies the familiar story, which sounds so ridiculous, of French and British officers at Fontenoy each politely inviting the other side to fire first.[2]

Frederick the Great drilled his troops to load and fire as many as five rounds a minute, but again, the advantage, if any, of this rate of fire was psychological; it did not make for good shooting. The more general view was that three times per minute was as often as a man could load and fire satisfactorily. Since the varied tasks of loading and firing—withdrawing and biting the cartridge, opening, priming, and closing the pan, pouring in the propellant charge, withdrawing the ramrod, ramming home the bullet, replacing the ramrod, raising the weapon again to the shoulder, etc.— involved exactly twenty drill movements as taught to the recruit, one can readily believe that three rounds per minute was indeed the highest practical rate of fire for good troops who did all things properly and well. Contemptible as this rate of fire may seem when compared with that of modern weapons, it was still the reason why troops were armed with a smoothbore and not a rifle. The same spiral-grooved bore, which gave the rifle bullet the spin that held it on its course far beyond the accurate range of the musket, made it far slower work to ram a well-fitted bullet down a rifle than down the smooth bore of a musket; and once a minute was as often as even an expert found it possible to load and fire a muzzle-loading rifle.[3] For that reason riflemen had no place in the regular line of battle; were they thus opposed to musketeers, riflemen could indeed begin to shoot with effect from a distance at which they need feel little fear of retaliation; but in a very short time, during which they would receive very few volleys, the musketeers could march up to a range at which they could effectively outshoot the riflemen by three rounds to one. No troops could face such a superiority of fire.

Here the objection may be made that even in the eighteenth century there were breechloading rifles which were being made in England at least as early as 1747;[4] their breech blocks opened and closed on a screw; they could be reloaded and fired up to seven times a minute; they were accurate up to three hundred yards; and one Captain Patrick Ferguson did raise

[1] As the afternoon of Waterloo wore on, 'the smoke hung so thick about us, that, although not more than 80 yards asunder, we could only distinguish each other by the flashes of the pieces'. J. Kincaid, *Adventures in the Rifle Brigade*, ed. Sir John Fortescue (London, 1929), p. 254.
[2] Voltaire, *Siécle de Louis XV*, chapter xv.
[3] Ezekiel Baker, *Remarks on Rifle Guns*, 9th ed. (London, 1829), p. 69.
[4] J. N. George, *English Guns and Rifles* (Plantersville, S.C., 1947), p. 133.

a company of men armed with what are, perhaps mistakenly, called 'Ferguson rifles' of this type in the American and Bourbon War. That is all true. But this innovation was a fleeting and unsatisfactory one; the 'Ferguson rifle' was a delicate sportsman's weapon, short-lived and unsuited to hard usage and the lack of care inevitable under service conditions.[1] No other power even tried using them.

So the regular infantryman continued to be armed with the smoothbore musket, a weapon unlikely to do harm beyond two hundred yards, best used at 160 yards or less, and capable of only some three good shots a minute. The problem of the eighteenth-century tactician was to find the way of handling men that would enable them with this primitive weapon to pour the deadliest possible fire upon their enemy. With such a weapon only a close formation of men could produce a heavy concentration of fire, and, from the days of Marlborough on, the ideal answer was found in the three-deep line of battle of which Frederick the Great was the classic exponent. In any deeper formation the men of any rank behind the third were unable to use their weapons properly; Napoleon sometimes, and Wellington regularly, were to use a two-deep line; but many sound tacticians feared that a two-deep line might fail to keep its front rank filled when fire was hot and men fell fast; and Guibert writes as if the doctrine of the three-deep line were as irrefutable to him as the doctrine of the Trinity to an orthodox theologian.[2] It is always to be remembered that these men were thinking of the enemy's cavalry too, and of the need to present a bristling and unbroken front of bayonets to charging squadrons of mounted swordsmen. Against such a front no horse would charge home. Let the infantry stand firm enough, and, on reaching them, the mounts of hostile cavalry, 'refusing', as a sluggish horse refuses a jump, would either swerve aside or come to a halt that left the swordsmen on their backs sitting still and innocuous within spitting distance of the troops they had intended to attack. But once infantry were broken and disordered, cavalry could crash into them like mounted police charging a riotous mob; right and left, the shock of charging horses bowled over those who tried to stand, while sabres reaped a bloody harvest among those who tried to flee. So (except briefly in America) the three-deep line was standard till Wellington successfully employed the two-deep formation in the Peninsula.

Ground permitting, the line should be continuous and it should be straight. A break in the line made a gap where cavalry might swoop in to take troops in the flank and roll them up. (Flanks were always anxious

---

[1] 'I have tried various ways of loading rifles at the breech, by means of screws placed in different positions; but after a few rounds firing, the screws have become so clogged by the filth of the powder working round them as to be very difficult to move, and will in time be eaten away with rust, which will render them dangerous to use' (Baker, *Remarks on Rifle Guns*, p. 9).

[2] *Essai générale*, I, 32–3.

spots, and therefore the artilleryman was directed to secure them with guns of 'the largest calibre'.)[1] A bulge saw men thrown forward, exposed to fire from either side and deprived of the security of comrades close beside them.[2] Precision of drill was therefore vital, and, while these conditions lasted, the art of drill was no small part of the whole art of war. Likewise, the great offensive action could be fought most advantageously only where ground permitted precise drill on a great scale. Marlborough never bought victory so dearly as when he sent troops to attack through woods at Malplaquet; in somewhat similar conditions the price Cornwallis paid for his Pyrrhic tactical triumph at Guilford Courthouse cost him a campaign. In woods, hedged fields, and villages men might indeed skirmish for petty advantages, but most great and decisive battles were fought in wide and open country, the wider the better; 'Marlborough's battles were all fought on fronts of four or five miles';[3] the Austrian position at Leuthen was nearly seven miles long; Wellington's at Waterloo was three.

These distances may give some idea of the degree of precision in drill that troops required if they were to be good. Those who have done but little drill know that the march-past of a battalion in line is not an easy manœuvre to perform creditably; so much the harder was it to attack when twenty battalions formed the line of battle. Frederick the Great had sometimes at least required his troops to form line at a distance of three miles from the enemy before advancing to attack[4] (that is, to form line before they could come under fire from the round shot of the enemy's artillery). A better method was for an army to advance much nearer in an alignment of separate battalions in column, and then to form line of battle, in the church-parade style, by having each battalion deploy when a little outside the range of grapeshot; but again, to do this well, troops must be precise indeed in their drill. The heads of the columns must keep their alignment straight; distances must be exact; commands perfectly timed; troops prompt and correct in executing their movements.

Such was the battle drill in which troops had to be trained, and such the standard of training they needed to acquire. It was also a drill which the British Army, on the eve of its great war with revolutionary France, was helplessly incapable of performing.

The British Army's incompetence in battle drill was due partly to its recent campaigns in America. It may sound an odd suggestion that experience in war should thus make an army unfit for war, but the American campaigns were fought under exceptional conditions. In that country generally there was much more bush than in most European

---

[1] Adye, *Bombardier and Pocket Gunner*, p. 25.
[2] Compare Guibert's forceful reference to 'l'instinct machinal et moutonnier qui port tout l'homme à se jeter sur son voison, parce qu'il crois par-là se mettre a l'abri du danger' (*Essai générale*, I, 117).
[3] Winston Churchill, *Marlborough: his Life and Times* (London, 1934), II, 111.
[4] Sime, *Military Guide for Young Officers*, p. 92.

theatres; and even where the land was cultivated, wide open fields were few, enclosures and snake fences many. These conditions gave what would in Europe have been an exaggerated importance to the skirmishing activities of light infantry, whose 'service was conspicuous and [whose] gallantry and exertions...met with merited applause'.[1] Likewise by European standards both sides were often uncommonly weak in guns and so, without realizing it, officers acquired the habit of 'every instant scattering and throwing forward light infantry' in a way that would 'often prevent the use of artillery' had there been any to use.[2] The result was that the 'showy exercise, the airy dress, the independent modes [of light infantry] ...caught the minds of young officers and made them imagine that these ought to be independent and exclusive';[3] infantry of the line almost forgot 'that on their steadiness and efforts the decision of events depends; and that light infantry: yagers, marksmen, riflemen, etc., etc., vanish before the solid movements of the line.'[4]

Nor was this all that infantry officers forgot. The numbers of British troops engaged in quite important battles in the late stages of the war were petty. Cornwallis had only some 1900 men to oppose Greene's 4300 at Guilford Courthouse; Moira led but 800 when he worsted Greene's 1200 at Hobkirk's Hill, and Stuart had only 1800 when he beat that general yet again at Eutaw Springs. As such small numbers could be manœuvred far more handily than large masses, speedy movement came to be over-stressed at the expense of the regularity and precision of movement necessary to maintain order and coherence in great bodies of men. Equally, the desire to make the most of small numbers against larger numbers created a temptation to occupy too much ground too thinly, and, as cavalry were few and shock action rare, this was done with an impunity it could never have enjoyed against a regular European foe. So because officers had not 'seen and been accustomed to the rapid movements of a good cavalry' they did not see 'the necessity of a more substantial order ...of being at every instant in a situation to form and repel a vigorous attack'.[5] Instead they became addicted to a 'very thin and extended order to make more show', to 'an affected extreme of quickness of movement', to a two-deep line with 'files so open' and 'such intervals between companies of the same battalion when in line, that all idea of solidity' seemed lost.[6] In other words, many of the 'lessons of America' were lessons that would have been lethal for anyone who tried to apply them on most European battlefields.

The sort of drill British battalions practised after the American War was therefore a bad one. Worse still, they did not even practise it in one common and universally understood and accepted way. No official drill

---

[1] Dundas, *Principles of Military Movements*, p. 13.
[2] *Ibid.* p. 14.   [3] *Ibid.* p. 13.   [4] *Ibid.*
[5] *Ibid.* p. 12.   [6] *Ibid.* p. 11.

manual seems to have been issued to the army since the Seven Years War.[1] In the course of some thirty years all kinds of deviations of drill grew up in different battalions, and by 1790 'every commanding officer manœuvred his regiment after his own fashion; and if a brigade of troops were brought together, it was very doubtful whether they could execute any one combined movement and almost certain they could not execute the various parts of it on the same principle'.[2] Small wonder that it should then be written: 'The situation of a General Officer in our service is at present particularly embarrassing. Let his talents be ever so eminent, with such jarring materials as our battalions now present, it is absolutely impossible for him to attempt the most simple manœuvres before an enemy, much less such complicated ones as the circumstances of his situation may point out and require.'[3]

Here is a situation which it would seem hard to make worse; yet worse it was made by the wretched negligence, lack of discipline, and ignorance of officers who gained commissions and promotions, not by military talent or good service, but by political favour, by money, and by intrigue. Discipline (or the lack of it) and promotion are subjects that require separate chapters; here it may merely be noted that want of any strong military authority to control either bred up a generation of officers of whom many knew not even the particular foibles and system of drill their own regiment was supposed to practise. Says a satirical writer of 1782 to young officers: 'Dry books of tactics are beneath the notice of a man of genius'; if, therefore, 'the major or the adjutant advises you to learn the manual, the salute or other parts of the exercise...you may answer, that you do not want to be a Drill-sergeant or corporal—or that you purchased your commission and did not come into the army to be made a machine of.'[4] To majors the same author writes: 'Whenever you are to exercise the regiment, get the adjutant or sergeant-major to write out on a small card the words of command in the proper order; and if you cannot retain the manœuvres in your head, you may at least keep them in your hat, which will answer the same purpose.'[5] This writer's tone may seem too mocking to be taken seriously; in fact, his jests are made bitter by their literal truth. Years later a perfectly sober witness wrote retrospectively of parades in the army in the 1780's, 'An intelligent sergeant whispered from time to time the word of command which his captain would have been ashamed to have known without prompting'.[6]

[1] Major General J. F. C. Fuller lists only three such manuals issued in the eighteenth century (*British Light Infantry in the Eighteenth Century*, London, 1925, p. 191).

[2] 'Memoir of the Duke of York' by 'the Author of Waverly' [sic] in *The Naval and Military Magazine* (1827), p. 6.

[3] Dundas, *Principles of Military Movements*, p. 17.

[4] Anonymous, *Advice to Officers of the British Army*, new edition ed. Bernard Ferguson (London, 1946), pp. 59–60.

[5] *Ibid.* p. 32.   [6] 'Memoir of the Duke of York', by 'the Author of Waverly' [sic].

So three great ills that afflicted the British Army at the beginning of our period were a false tactical doctrine, an incoherent diversity of manœuvre, and a deplorable number of officers who neither knew nor cared what their duties were so long as they drew their pay. Let it be granted that there were still some good commanding officers; and that, wherever there was a good commanding officer, there was a good battalion; it may still be questioned whether taxpayers ever supported a more useless body of men than the British Army in the early days of the younger Pitt. What would have happened if that very belligerent minister had had his way, when he desired war with Catherine II in 1791, and if this army had then been sent to the shores of the Black Sea to oppose Suvorov's veterans, is not pleasant to contemplate.[1]

A cure for these tactical ills was provided by a Scot, Colonel (later Field Marshal Sir) David Dundas, who, in 1788, published a book, *Principles of Military Movements*, which has already been freely quoted. A very important and much misrepresented man is this Dundas. It has, for example, been alleged that he based his book merely on 'the invaluable work of General von Saldern' and his own experiences at the Prussian manœuvres of 1785.[2] In fact, he states that he based his book on his own 'service of many years in varied situations, of much regimental experience and of five campaigns in the war of 1760';[3] also that the bulk of his work was written before 'the opportunities he had in 1785 of attending the Prussian manœuvres', after which he merely revised 'what he had long before more imperfectly arranged'.[4] One may add that if his first draft was written long before 1785, the debt he acknowledges to General von Saldern can easily be overrated, for that 'completest general of infantry'[5] only turned author in 1784.[6] As a still more baseless criticism, Dundas has been called a 'peace theorist',[7] a statement that can only leave its amazed reader wondering through how many ages of bloodshed a man must toil before he can claim to speak with the authority of experience if the commando raids on the French coast, German campaigns under such a leader as Prince Ferdinand, and tropical warfare in the West Indies through five years of the Seven Years War still leave Dundas a 'peace theorist'. Yet again the 'wisecrack' of Sir Henry Bunbury that Dundas

---

[1] How has the notion prevailed that Pitt was above all a lover of peace? Peace was certainly, and rightly, his aim as long as his country was isolated and nearly bankrupt. But once its finances were restored and Prussia had become its ally, Pitt was ready enough to risk war with France over Holland in 1788, with Spain over Nootka in 1790 and with Russia over Oczakov in 1791.

[2] Fuller, *British Light Infantrymen*, pp. 189–90.

[3] Dundas, *Principles of Military Movements*, p. iii.

[4] *Ibid.*

[5] T. Carlyle, *Frederick the Great*, book xx, chapter vi.

[6] When he published in Dresden his *Taktik der Infanterie*, to be followed by his *Taktische Grundsätze* in 1786.

[7] Fuller, *British Light Infantrymen*, p. 190.

'made the fatal mistake of distributing the whole science of war into eighteen manœuvres which were a sad stumbling block to dull-witted officers'[1] has been repeated *ad nauseam*, for all the world as if Bunbury were an infallible critic and as if any book must be bad when persons of sufficient stupidity are found capable of misunderstanding it. Dundas is further accused of making 'a radical mistake' when he re-introduced the three-deep line and 'opposed the two-deep formation' so widely adopted by British regiments in America;[2] but if this was 'a radical mistake' he certainly made it in good company. The three-deep formation was, and long remained, standard on the continent; what the supposed folly of Dundas restored in England was there retained by the wisdom of the Archduke Charles in Austria,[3] of Blucher, Gneisenau, and Scharnhorst in Prussia,[4] and of Napoleon in France.[5] Of all great commanders of that day only Wellington regularly trusted the two-deep formation, which no less an authority than Fortescue diagnoses as the cause of British disaster in America, when Morgan overthrew Tarleton at Cowpens on 17 January 1781.[6]

However, nearly all these criticisms of Dundas date from the twentieth century, and so, for obvious reasons of chronology, they had no effect on the judgement of George III. In 1792 he decreed that an abridgement of Dundas's book, entitled *Rules and Regulations for the Movements of His Majesty's Infantry*, should be the standard drill manual of all infantry battalions in the British Army. It was well that he did so. The severest of Dundas's latter-day critics candidly concedes 'his influence on the British army...was an exceedingly beneficial one',[7] and the comment is just. More interesting, too, than any modern comment is the criticism of 'a Field Officer' in a series of articles in *The United Service Journal* in 1845–6. This field officer served in days when infantry weapons were still muzzle-loading, and conditions were accordingly little changed from Dundas's time; he was also able to compare Dundas's manual with the two successive revisions that had superseded it, one in 1824, the other in 1833. He is therefore a critic who claims a serious hearing.

He is not in full agreement with Dundas. As a regular British officer he preferred his own army's contemporary practice to alternatives used upon the continent and therefore, like later critics, regretted that Dundas had restored the three-deep order,[8] and approved the manual of 1824 which rejected this in favour of the two-deep line. He further regrets that the

---

[1] H. Bunbury, *Narrative of some Passages in the Great War with France from 1799–1810* (London, 1854), p. 46, cited by Fuller, *British Light Infantrymen*, p. 195, and Carola Oman (Lenanton), *Sir John Moore* (London, 1953), p. 74.

[2] Fuller, *op. cit.* p. 195.

[3] A. Suasso, *The Theory of Infantry Movements* (London, 1825), p. 41.

[4] *Ibid.* p. 38.   [5] *Ibid.* p. 30.

[6] Fortescue, *History of the British Army*, III, 537.

[7] Fuller, *op. cit.* p. 190.

[8] *United Service Journal* (hereafter cited as *U.S.J.*) (1845), p. 243.

revised abridgement of Dundas's book which was issued as a manual in 1792 omitted the explanations given in the original version of 1788; these omissions, he continues, left the young officer to make 'his own uncertain guesses' as to the reason for making particular movements in particular ways[1] (and there no doubt may be found the cause of some of the mis-understandings which Bunbury has made so familiar).

Yet it is still interesting to see how often the 'field officer' finds Dundas superior to his successors, and the number of cases in which his methods had been discarded in the manual of 1824 only to be revived in 1833. He mentions the minor, but interesting, point that Dundas drew his diagrams with his own hand and they were 'sufficiently clear and explanatory'.[2] He praises Dundas's wisdom in stressing that 'the most important exercise that troops can attend to is the march in column of route', for this is the basis of all manœuvring.[3] He declares 'to find a person so fit for the task [of preparing a training manual] as Sir David Dundas would be a matter of much difficulty. He had the advantage not only of a sufficient know-ledge of mathematics, but of opportunities well improved for observations and having for some years made tactics his particular study, practically and theoretically.'[4] Above all, he recognizes the value of Dundas's work in establishing 'uniformity of practice', for want of which newly assembled British brigades had previously been 'of but little value for service' till their brigadier had spent 'much time and trouble' in re-instructing them in his own methods.[5] He gives no hint of the modern suggestion that Dundas oversimplified things when he 'distributed the whole art of war into eighteen manœuvres', and therein the 'field officer' shows himself a practical soldier; for this latter-day interpretation of Bunbury's quip is sufficiently answered by Field Marshal von Hindenburg's dictum: 'In war only what is simple can succeed'.[6] Indeed, Cornwallis wished that Dundas's manœuvres could be made simpler still.[7]

Finally, the 'field officer' declares that the proof of the excellency of Dundas's drill lay in 'its having so long stood the test of experience. The system...after the lapse of half a century, still' remained 'in use almost unchanged' in 1845.[8]

The field officer's statement is therefore a criticism out of which Dundas comes very well, and much credit is indeed due to him for the restored efficiency of British infantry. Yet not the whole credit; much is also due to a far more august soldier than Dundas. Fondness for innovation is a very fundamental instinct in men; so is affection for regimental 'quiffs' among soldiers; against these forces the mere publication, in General

[1] *U.S.J.* (1845), p. 98.   [2] *Ibid.* (1846), II, 235.   [3] *Ibid.* p. 243.
[4] *Ibid.* p. 244.   [5] *Ibid.* (1845), III, 100.
[6] H. Guderian, *Panzer Leader*, translated by C. Fitzgibbon with a foreword by B. H. Liddell Hart (London, 1952), p. 29.
[7] Ross, *Correspondence of Cornwallis*, III, 168.
[8] *U.S.J.* (1845), III, 100.

Orders, of Dundas's *Regulations* in June 1792 could do little to restore uniformity of manœuvre to the very individualistic battalions of Britain's disjointed army. As Dundas truly wrote, any 'system, when introduced, should be enforced and upheld by the strong hand of authority'.[1] Not the least fault of the aged Amherst as Commander-in-Chief was the inability of his puffy hand to uphold anything; and the proof of that assertion lies in the situation the Duke of York found when he succeeded Amherst. Already in 1795 the General Order imposing Dundas's *Regulations* in 1792 was a dead letter.

The Duke, thirty-one years old, fresh from experience in the field and abounding in energy, began his command-in-chief by impressing his personality on the army by travelling fast and far on rapid tours of inspection; and when he could not go himself he directed others to inspect.[2] These inspections taught him much. The first fruit of them appears in a circular letter of 16 May 1795 to certain generals commanding districts. The Duke began by ordering that the 'Rules and Regulations for the Formations, Field Exercises and Movements of H.M. Forces' published '. . . in June 1792 shall be strictly followed . . . without any deviation whatever'. At training camps held in the various districts that summer, he ordered 'Monday and Friday in every week' to be devoted to the exercise of separate battalions, each 'under the Personal Direction of its own Commanding Officer', on every Tuesday and Saturday the exercising of troops was 'to be performed by Brigades, under the immediate conduct and command of their respective Major Generals'. On each Wednesday, continues the order, 'the Commanding General will take out the whole Line, and make them perform such Movements, Manœuvres or other Exercises as he may think proper'. After these stringent commands comes an inducement which reveals the Duke's knowledge of men: 'Thursday is to be set apart as a day of Repose for the whole; such Corps only excepted as may have been negligent or irregular in their Exercises on the preceding Days; or which are otherwise defective or behindhand in their Discipline.'[3] Anyone reading this precise training programme might fairly guess that British battalions did not know their *Regulations for the Formations, Field Exercises, etc.,* very well; that his guess would be right is made very clear by the express statement that 'the essential purpose' of the programme was 'promoting Uniformity in the Discipline of the Troops'.[4]

Nor is this all the evidence of the degree to which the General Order

[1] *Principles of Military Movements*, p. 17.
[2] Adjutant General to Major General White, 12 March 1795, WO/3/28 in the Public Record Office.
[3] Is this the origin of the Army's Thursday privilege which Lord Benira Trig so mistakenly attempted to override in Kipling's 'The Three Musketeers'?
[4] Adjutant General's Circular Letter to Generals the Marquis Townsend, the Duke of Richmond, Sir William Pitt, K.B., Lord A. Gordon, Lord George Lennox, Marquis Cornwallis and Major General Musgrave, 16 May 1795, WO/3/28.

imposing Dundas's system on the army had been ignored. In July 1795 Sir William Fawcett, the Adjutant General, is found writing one Major General Ainslie (who had proved a sad 'croaker' in the Flanders campaigns)[1] warning him that the Duke of York had received a report that he was not enforcing Dundas's system in his camps; and that if, in his tour, H.R.H. should find this information true, he would be much displeased; and accordingly Fawcett offered to send Ainslie a copy of the manual.[2] Finally, in spite of all these instructions issued in the spring and summer, the Duke in August of this year still found some commanding officers who regarded the General Order on drill as nothing to be taken seriously. On 1 September, after a series of inspections between Newcastle and Whitby, he is found writing his father, the King, that all but one of the regiments of infantry he had just inspected were 'drawn up two-deep instead of three-deep'.[3] These instances give some idea of the disparity, inefficiency, and negligence of British troops in so vital a matter as the actual battle drill to be used in the face of the enemy. This was one of the abuses which the Duke of York had to make good, and by steady, firm persistence he did overcome it; thanks to him, British officers did all learn one common method of handling their troops in action. It is likely that no one reform of our whole period did more to make the British Army an effective force than this steadily applied system of training.

III. LIGHT INFANTRY

Light infantry are less easily discussed than infantry of the line. Their duty, according to Guibert, should be purely 'à harceler...à être ce soir sur un point, demain sur un autre',[4] but Dundas gives them a larger role; 'their great province', he writes, 'is to form advanced and rear guards, to gain intelligence, to occupy the outposts, to keep up communications, and by their vigilance and activity to cover a front'. The clash between these two opinions is due to Guibert's very sound view that troops of the line should be taught to do most of these things for themselves; nevertheless, Dundas states correctly enough the common uses made of light troops, and adds that in action 'their skirmishers and dispersed men are loose, detached and numerous according to the circumstances; but a firm reserve always remains to rally upon and to give support as may be wanted—their attacks are connected and their movements the same as the rest of the line'.[5] There, then, were the functions of light troops—protection, reconnaissance, skirmishing—and in addition to doing all these

---

[1] Burne, *Duke of York*, p. 95.
[2] Adjutant General to Ainslie, 24 July 1795, WO/3/13.
[3] Duke of York to George III, 1 September 1795, Windsor, 7955.
[4] *Essai générale*, I, 227.
[5] *Principles of Military Movements*, pp. 13–14.

things they ought also to be capable of the close-ordered manœuvres of the line. So far all is simple, but less easy questions follow.

Before the French Revolution Lloyd, Guibert, and Dundas, experienced soldiers all, are found agreed that the proportion of light troops in contemporary armies was excessive, and ought to be reduced. Yet almost as soon as the revolutionary wars broke out French light infantry proved to be some of the most effective troops in the field. There were swarms of them, and they were a rare thorn in the flesh of their enemies. Why were fact and expert opinion thus in conflict? How did the French come to possess such a mass of such expert skirmishers? And why were they so valuable? It is in the light of the answers to these questions that the adequacy of British light infantry must be judged.

First, it has been suggested that these numerous and deadly light infantrymen of France were the offspring of chance; that French revolutionary commanders, lacking time to train new, raw levies in the formal movements of the line, simply flung them out, untrained, to skirmish, and that the natural genius of their race made them, all untutored, into born experts in this highly intricate art.[1] But this story is impossible to swallow. From Marshal Saxe on, a succession of military writers insist that, to be worth their salt, light infantry needed not less, but more training than infantry of the line. Further, the sober French soldier and historian, Colin, marks that the early campaigns of the French revolutionary wars were not fought with raw levies; they were fought with the old regulars of Louis XVI, and with 'the volunteers of 1791', who had been 'well officered and trained for nearly a year';[2] also, that both rival schools of military thought in France under Louis XVI (for there were two) were at one in ignoring Guibert's opinions on light infantry and in setting a high value on capable skirmishers.[3] The excellence of French light infantry therefore rested on good, hard training, not untutored natural genius; and right excellent they were—in fact 'extremely effectual, in *taking off* or wounding officers, and in producing confusion among columns deploying or manœuvring';[4] they were a 'Waspish soldiery...perfectly trained... clothed in grass-coloured uniforms', who would either 'lie on the ground or cover themselves behind any object offering itself and bring down their mark with unerring certainty'.[5] Equally skilled and no less highly trained troops were needed to meet such light infantry as these.

[1] Fuller, *British Light Infantrymen*, pp. 161–3.
[2] J. Colin, *The Transformations of War*, translated by L. H. R. Pope-Hennessy (London, 1912), p. 23 n.   [3] *Ibid.* p. 22.
[4] John Macdonald, *Instructions for the Conduct of Infantry on Actual Service*, translated from the French with explanatory notes (London, 1807), II, 205.
[5] *Ibid.* pp. xxxix–xl. I cited this passage because, though it was not published till 1807, it is still a vivid description of what good light troops actually did; nothing in the preceding dozen years had altered the nature of their duties; and in 1794 French troops already performed those duties so well as to win Wellington's praise as 'capital soldiers' (J. W. Croker, *Correspondence and Diaries* (London, 1885), I, 12–13).

Yet allow them every virtue, and it is still surprising that their value should not have been foreseen by such practical men as Lloyd, Guibert, and Dundas. This, indeed, is a riddle that may perhaps be best answered by the economic historian, and the suggestion made here is that changes in farming since 1763 had done more to raise the value of light infantry than any changes in military thought or equipment. Every history text-book tells how in the years before and during the French Revolution England was being transformed from a land of open fields into a land of enclosures, fences, and hedgerows. That the same process had occurred in the Low Countries is indicated by General John Money's observations that the country about Lille, which had been open in Marlborough's day, was no longer so in the 1790's;[1] and that the British retreat of 1794 was through enclosed country all the way from Tournai to Breda.[2] To such country the formal movements of the line did not apply; there everything was suited to the well-trained skirmisher. And not there only; Rhenish or Italian vineyards made a country at least as close as any northern chequerboard of hedgerows; and, had they but made good their landing on a hostile shore, French light infantry could hardly have found a country better designed for their special craft than the orchards, paddocks, and hop gardens of Kent.

And here is a point on which Dundas does seem open to a measure of criticism. His own active service had been largely in north-west Germany, where to this day extensive heaths provide much open country; the manœuvres he witnessed in 1785, in Silesia, at Potsdam, and at Magde-burg, were held on ground selected for its suitability to the rigid Frederi-cian drill; in the British Isles no better training area had been available to him than the broad sweep of Phoenix Park at Dublin. With such experience he might well underrate the value of a swarm of well-trained skirmishers; and, right as he undoubtedly was to react against a system of training that overstressed bush warfare, to the near-exclusion of training for other types of terrain, he perhaps failed to appreciate how closely the character of some parts of Europe had come to approximate American conditions.

Yet he was still by no means so blind to those conditions as has been supposed. Students of British military history have perhaps sometimes been misled by one exaggerated sentence of Cornwallis, who wrote (in a private letter to the future Duke of Wellington on 23 February 1798): 'The system of David Dundas and the total want of light infantry sit heavy on my mind.'[3] In actual fact, the 'want of light infantry' was far from total. Dundas's system retained the one light company which there had been in every British battalion at least since the beginning of the American and

---

[1] Cited from p. 35 of Money's 'Open Letter to William Windham' by Fuller, *British Light Infantrymen*, p. 201.
[2] Cited from p. 19 of Money's 'Open Letter' by Fuller, *ibid.* p. 206.
[3] Ross, *Correspondence of Cornwallis*, II, 331.

Bourbon War of 1775–83; one special, though brief, section of Dundas's *Regulations* was devoted to the type of training they should receive. The defect of the system of Dundas was therefore not a complete lack of light infantry; it apparently did fail, however, to provide enough of these troops to cope with the swarms of skirmishers available to French commanders; so, in General John Money's words, the British Army in Flanders had suffered much 'owing to our having only small bodies of irregulars to meet large ones'.[1]

It would certainly be a mistake to suppose that his experience in the Low Countries in 1793–4 failed to teach the Duke of York the value of light infantry, and his efforts to provide his country with this arm were in fact persistent. To accomplish any worthwhile achievement, however, it is necessary to do things in order, to have time, and to have the necessary 'properties' (as theatrical people put it).

As to doing things in order, the first training task confronting the Duke of York, when he became Commander-in-Chief, was to make British infantry of the line capable of manœuvring coherently together; theirs (in the true words of a perhaps overrated writer) was 'the great mechanical power of war'[2] and theirs accordingly was the priority. How the Duke cared for their needs has been described.

Secondly, as to time, it was exceedingly hard to make opportunities for training an army like the British which ministers regarded primarily as a police force and therefore scattered all over the country in penny packets. In these circumstances, it was not even possible to be sure from one week to the next where any particular body of troops might be; at any time a letter from an agitated justice of the peace, who feared riots among the starving proletariat of a nearby city, might cause them to be suddenly moved. Or, again, were a disposable force gathered together, ministers might at any moment demand that it be shipped overseas on some petty, and probably fruitless, expedition. For these reasons it was hard indeed to implement any planned programme of special training.

Thirdly, a special 'property' necessary before there could be any sound training of light infantry was a good manual which devoted much more detail to their specialized duties than Dundas gave. All these are points worth bearing in mind before taking Cornwallis's declamations too seriously as a fair criticism of the reforms proceeding in the British Army in the 1790's.

And now for what the Duke of York had actually done toward providing the light infantry of which Cornwallis declared a 'total want' existed in February 1798. In March 1797 the Duke had sent a circular letter to all generals commanding districts calling for special attention

[1] Cited from p. 19 of Money's 'Open Letter' by Fuller, *British Light Infantrymen*, p. 206.
[2] Robert Jackson, *A View of the Formation, Discipline and Economy of Armies* (London, 1824), p. 267.

to the training of light infantry companies, enclosing a copy of Dundas's light infantry exercise, and promising 'as many more of the same as may be sufficient'.[1] On Christmas Day in the same year he returned to the subject in another circular, requiring 'that Light Infantry Companies in General throughout the whole Army should be diligently trained and perfected, as much as possible, in those movements and manœuvres which are more particularly adapted to them than to heavy infantry'; he accordingly ordered the recipients of his letter that

all the Light Companies...in the district under your command...be frequently taken out in separate bodies, and practised at firing Ball at a mark, and in such different exercises, as they are principally intended for...so that in case circumstances should at any time render it necessary to assemble and form them into distinct Battalions, they may be thoroughly prepared to do their duty in the Field, with that Precision, Skill and Uniformity which will be expected of them.[2]

Evidently the idea of forming special battalions of light infantry was already very much in the Duke's mind as early as 1797. In pursuance of that idea, the Assistant Adjutant General, Sir Harry Calvert, in March 1798 drafted a memorandum on forming a 'Corps of Light Troops', in which may be seen the genesis of the future, and famous, Light Division.[3] Calvert's memorandum was forwarded, with the Duke's blessing, to the War Office, at which august civilian department it was duly filed, but it apparently never occurred to Windham to take any action on it, and the authority the Duke required to carry out this new departure in British military organization was, apparently, not granted. All the same the Duke persisted in his efforts to provide the country with what it needed in the way of light troops. The summer of 1798 saw two light companies from regiments of the line and eleven from regiments of the militia, with two troops of light horse and a brigade of horse artillery all being trained and exercised together in Essex under Sir William Howe. The scale was small, but one need not doubt that the job was well done. This Howe was the same skilful, if too often unenterprising, tactician who had won Long Island from Washington in 1776, and beaten the great American again at Brandywine Creek on 11 September 1777; his special interest in the manœuvres of light troops dates at least from 1759, when he had commanded Wolfe's light infantry.

The Duke of York continued to work on his idea, and at the end of 1799 had 'several arrangements...in their infancy' including the training of 'a Corps of Riflemen by detachments to be returned' to their battalions 'when properly instructed and the exercising of five Regiments together as a Light Corps'.[4] Most of these schemes perished, however, in 1800; then Dundas and Pitt demanded that an expeditionary corps be gathered

---

[1] 17 March 1797, WO/3/31.   [2] 25 December 1797, *ibid.*
[3] 23 March 1798, WO/1/619.
[4] Duke of York to George III, 28 February 1800, Windsor, 9515–9522.

for service in the Mediterranean; overseas therefore most of the troops went, to participate in a fiasco at Cadiz and to fail to aid the Italian Army of the Austrians, as intended, either at the siege of Genoa or in the campaign of Marengo.

At last, however, in 1803 no less a person than the First Consul of France made it possible for the Duke of York to carry out the training programme on which his heart had so long been set. There could be no thought of dissipating troops on distant and fruitless expeditions when Napoleon's great 'Army of England' was massing for invasion on the cliffs of Boulogne; for the time being local police problems had to take care of themselves or be left to new-raised corps of volunteers; circumstances imperiously required the heaviest possible concentration of troops on the south coast; and, as the threatened invasion never came, the troops once concentrated had little to do but train. So, after a five-year period of gestation, the Duke's idea became a fact at last at the famous Shorncliffe Camp. With it was born the almost equally famous legend of 'Sir John Moore's system of training'. And, as with Dundas, so with Moore too, the historian's first task is to clear away misapprehensions that have gathered round his name; but whereas in Dundas's case this task involved the dissipation of a cloud, in Moore's it requires the removal of a halo.

Certainly the British Army, if it never has a finer trainer of men than Moore, will have no cause to complain. He had in rare measure the heaven-sent gift of personality without which no teacher has ever been great, an unrivalled capacity to inspire, to create interest, to arouse enthusiasm; and he had about as much active experience of war as could possibly have been crowded into the forty-two years he had lived when he began his great task at Shorncliffe in 1803. No clearer evidence of the soundness of York's judgement of men could be asked than his selection of Moore for this task. But the idea that Moore originated any system of light infantry training is still a mistake. The system he taught, like the plan of training whole regiments as light infantry, was but one thing more provided by the foresight of the Commander-in-Chief and his staff.

The inadequacy of the light infantry instructions provided by David Dundas is both conspicuous and natural. That officer's book never set out to be more than a drill manual; the nine pages it allots to light infantry accordingly give nothing more than the words of command and movements of the extended order drill used by light troops. But drill was only a very small part of the light infantryman's job; in Dundas's own words (already quoted) 'their great province' was 'to form advanced and rear guards, to gain intelligence, to occupy the outposts, to keep up communications and by their vigilance and activity to cover a front'. Much more than nine pages was needed to instruct officers and men in these varied and intricate duties, and where Dundas left off, another author carried on.

This author was a foreigner in the British service (said to be Austrian), and described in 1816 as 'Maj. Gen. F. Baron De Rottenburg [who] in 1798...submitted to his Royal Highness, the Commander-in-Chief, the rules and regulations for the exercise of riflemen and light infantry, and their conduct in the field; which, having been graciously approved of, was published by authority, and made general for the army'.[1] The book[2] begins with instructions in weapon-handling and marksmanship and proceeds to the extended order drill. It closes with the fifty-seven bugle calls by which alone the widely dispersed movements of light troops would be co-ordinated, for already theirs was necessarily the discipline 'of a well-trained pack of hounds', as Colonel Henderson later wrote of all infantry, and no human voice could effectually control a far-flung chain of skirmishers. De Rottenburg's book also gave much excellent advice on reconnaissance, advanced, flank and rear guards, patrols and pickets. That he wrote it in compliance with a request from the Horse Guards cannot be shown; what is certain is that within a year of its publication in German, his book appeared in an English translation with a foreword by the Adjutant General, Sir William Fawcett, under the title, *Regulations for the Exercise of Riflemen and Light Infantry*. It may not be a very wild guess that Fawcett was responsible for the text of the English version, for he was a notable translator of French and German military works.

On this manual, as Major General Fuller has shown, Moore based his training when, five years after its publication, he undertook the instruction of the 43rd, 52nd, and 95th regiments at Shorncliffe Camp in 1803;[3] and, as has been told, its use had been general in the light companies of the army since 1798. The manual was not, however, thrust upon Moore in the manner in which Dundas's regulations had been imposed on the rest of the army as a manual from which there could be no deviation. On the contrary, Moore was given much freedom, for he speaks of making 'de Rottenburg the groundwork, noting in the margin whatever changes we make from him', but he still seems to have found the manual nearly good enough as it was; 'it only requires to be properly applied', he comments.[4]

De Rottenburg's was not the only officially published manual of light infantry training. It was followed in 1803 by the work of one General Francis Jarry, a French-born soldier of fortune who had migrated to Prussia and long been a trusted staff officer of the great Frederick.[5] The

---

[1] John Philippart, *The Royal Military Calendar*, III (London, 1816), p. 35.

[2] *Regulations for the Exercise of Riflemen and Light Infantry* (London, 1798; 2nd ed. 1803).

[3] For example, on bugle calls Moore wrote on 4 September 1803, 'The sounds at present used by the 52nd and 95th are de Rottenburg's, which are the sounds, I believe, most generally used by the light companies of Regiments' (cited by J. F. C. Fuller, *Sir John Moore's System of Training*, London, 1924, p. 79).

[4] *Ibid.* p. 80.

[5] Francis Jarry, *Instruction concerning the Duties of Light Infantry in the Field* (London, 1803).

Duke of York had recently been glad to secure him as chief instructor at his new Royal Military College. His book was one published with official authority and as such was bound to be called to Moore's attention; and in Napier's pages British light troops are found carrying out drills which Jarry, but not de Rottenburg, prescribes. In general, Jarry covers much the same ground as de Rottenburg, and he does so with the thoroughness to be expected of a man who had formerly been the intimate of Frederick the Great.

Such is the story of British light infantry training as it emerges from the primary sources. The notion that this training was carried out at Shorncliffe because a meekly suggestible Commander-in-Chief followed Moore's advice seems to spring from James Carrick Moore's second-hand recollections of a conversation between his brother and the Duke of York;[1] the fact is that the Duke had been trying for some years to carry out just such a training scheme as he entrusted to Moore in 1803. Likewise, the notion that Moore was an innovator who devised such improvements in drill, discipline, arms, and movements 'as would have placed him...beside the Athenian Iphicrates if he had not had the greater glory of dying like the Spartan Brasidas' is an error sprung from an old man's rosy-tinted reminiscences.[2] The drill and movements he taught to whole battalions had been practised for some five years by light companies; the far happier system of discipline he maintained in his brigade was in large measure made possible by his good fortune in commanding picked officers and men—and for that again he had to thank the Duke of York, without whose authority he could not have done the picking. And the Duke of York it also appears to have been who selected for the 52nd regiment the improved light infantry pattern of musket, which it was their good fortune to carry.

Nor did the training of whole battalions as Light Infantry stop when Moore completed his instruction of the 52nd, 43rd, and 95th regiments at Shorncliffe in 1804.

In May 1808 de Rottenburg himself commanded the exercise and instruction of four battalions of light infantry at the Camp of Instruction, on the Curragh of Kildare in Ireland, under Sir David Baird. In the same year he was transferred from the Irish to the English staff, and stationed at Ashford in Kent, and charged with the formation and instruction of three battalions of light infantry, viz., the 68th, 85th, and 71st regiments assembled at Brabourn Lees barracks.[3]

[1] J. C. Moore, *The Life of Lt. General Sir John Moore, K.B.* (London, 1834), II, 5.
[2] W. Napier, *The Life and Opinions of Sir Charles James Napier, G.C.B.* (London, 1857), I, 58.
[3] Philippart, *Royal Military Calendar*, III, 35.

IV. RIFLEMEN

Except for Captain Ferguson's ill-fated company in the American war, Britain had no native corps of riflemen till 1800. There is a natural explanation for this fact. In the eighteenth century England was already a land where sport consisted mainly of hunting the hare and fox with hounds and of shooting partridge, pheasant, and snipe with a smoothbore. But, then as now, Germany was a big-game-hunter's country, where vast forests sheltered the wild boar, the roe and red deer, and where the greatest of all European great game, the European bison, hung on in East Prussia, under royal protection, till poachers killed the very last one on the eve of the Seven Years War. Germany, then, was a land where men had a very real use for the rifle, and in Germany corps of sportsmen and gamekeepers were raised to use the weapon in wartime; and after their peacetime calling the men of these corps were called 'huntsmen' or 'Jägers'. Such rifle corps could generally be had for the hiring when England went to war, and she hired them so regularly that for a while it looked as if the German word for 'huntsman' would take a permanent place in our military vocabulary in the corrupted form of 'Yagher'. Recruiting Germans for British service, however, was not easy, to say the least, after the treaty of Campo-Formio in 1797, and in the Duke of York Britain had a man who was determined to make the British Army as completely efficient a force as he had the power to do. That in February 1800 he had already in its infancy a scheme for 'the formation of a Corps of Riflemen by detachments to be returned to their Corps when properly instructed' has already been mentioned; now for a little more detail on this corps.

The Duke had begun by wishing to raise a complete and permanent battalion all of riflemen to be commanded by one Lt. Col. Nightingall. Lord Cornwallis apparently persuaded him to do no such thing as raise a whole regiment to be armed with a weapon whose rate of fire was too slow to enable them to stand in line of battle against musketeers; he cited the experience of 'Colonel Wurmb in America who solicited that the rifles should be taken from a great proportion of his Yaghers, and that they should receive [smoothbore] firelocks instead';[1] and accordingly he urged the Duke to raise a corps of which 'only a tenth part' should be armed with rifles and that the others should be armed and trained as light infantry.[2] The Duke evidently accepted Cornwallis's reasoning, but not his conclusion; instead of raising a new corps of light infantry, of whom 10 per cent should be riflemen, he decided to raise no new corps, but to call for detachments of thirty-four men and three officers from each of fifteen regiments of the line to be 'instructed in the use of the Rifle and the

[1] Ross, *Correspondence of Cornwallis*, III, 157.
[2] *Ibid.* p. 177.

system adopted by soldiers so armed'.[1] These detachments, on returning to their regiments, would provide a nucleus of snipers amounting to one-third of the strength of the battalion's light company. It was the Duke's further intention to pursue the system till every regular battalion had its own rifle platoon.[2] Instead of Nightingall, Colonel Coote Manningham was appointed to supervise the training of the first fifteen detachments.

However, this scheme was not carried through in the manner proposed. Contrary to the Duke's first gloomy expectation, it did survive the ministers' demand for troops for service in the Mediterranean in February 1800. The training camp was established in Windsor Forest in the early summer of 1800; under Lt. Col. William Stewart and Colonel Manningham, the 510 men and 45 officers of the selected detachments were instructed in their rifle exercises; then in July the ministers demanded men for a petty and abortive combined operation against Ferrol; Manningham's riflemen being available, they were embarked as a single regiment; and having once seen service as a regiment, a regiment they remained. Their letter of service was issued in 1801, and they became known as the 95th.

As much by accident as intention, it seems, the one battalion of the 95th was to become three battalions within ten years. The original detachments were evidently good men and good officers; they became known as a crack corps; their green uniforms were dashing and distinctive; and when men of the militia were permitted to volunteer for the line, the 95th was found to be almost embarrassingly popular. Its second battalion was thus formed out of militiamen in 1805; its third battalion was virtually thrust upon it during the volunteering permitted in 1810, when 1100 men joined it in three days, and its recruiting was thereupon hastily stopped by the express order of the Horse Guards. After Waterloo, its three battalions 'were taken out of the numbered regiments of the line and styled THE RIFLE BRIGADE', as the *Gazette* of 23 February 1816 put it.

Cornwallis's idea of raising one battalion of mixed riflemen and light musketeers thus went by the board, and the Duke's first scheme of raising a whole unit armed with rifles was carried out three times over; and it was probably best that things happened in this way. Excellent it would no doubt seem for every battalion to have its own leaven of four and thirty snipers; but (as some battalion intelligence officers and mortar platoon commanders of the Second World War may feel), specialists do not always thrive in non-specialist company. Specialized duties are too often ill understood by non-specialists; if the management and training of the rifle platoon in an ordinary battalion went wrong, by no means all commanding officers would know what needed to be put right; opportunities of training with troops of their own kind would be limited; the

---

[1] Adjutant General to Colonel Coote Manningham, 9 January 1800, WO/3/32.
[2] Same to same, 14 May 1800, WO/3/33.

field for selecting good N.C.O.'s would be small. Kincaid, the rifleman, quotes another observer and author as writing of the 95th: 'They were, in fact, as much superior to the French *voltigeurs*, as the latter were to our skirmishers in general.'[1] British 'skirmishers in general' came from the light companies of battalions of the line; their normal inferiority to the *voltigeurs* may perhaps be taken as a sample of the neglect specialists might suffer in a battalion of which they were but a small part. Equally the superiority of the riflemen is a good advertisement for the policy of keeping specialists all together for training and administration. In operations they did not need all to act together; they could be, and were, farmed out in detachments for particular operations. Alternatively, they could act together, and in fact Wellington had all three battalions of the Rifles under his command in 1813–14.

Riflemen differed from other light infantry mainly in that they were almost never used for movements in close order beside infantry of the line. In all their manœuvres they generally kept, as their weapon permitted, at a greater distance from the enemy than other light infantry; for this reason they wore a 'protectively-coloured' green uniform which aided them in finding concealment when dispersed as skirmishers, but was pointless for infantry of the line who operated in masses too great to escape notice. For the latter red was best, because it secured them against being mistaken for the enemy (and indeed there were occasions when the riflemen suffered from the fire of their own side because they were not clad in the distinctive colour of British troops). Among hills and brushwood was found what Kincaid calls 'good rifle country'.[2] 'A rifleman in the rear', he adds, was 'like a fish out of water',[3] and the regiment boasted, generally with justice, of being the troops who fired the first and last shots in every battle; for they were deployed to drive in the enemy's skirmishers, or pick off his officers, at the outset of most actions; in victory they were in the forefront of the pursuit, hanging on the flanks and rear of the enemy; in defeat they, with other light infantry, would form much of the rearguard.

Great pains were taken to see that British riflemen were well armed. 'I conclude that by this time there are at least forty kinds of rifles at the Horse Guards', wrote Cornwallis from Ireland on 4 January 1800,[4] when the scheme for raising the rifle corps was in its infancy; and the fact that they were 'at the Horse Guards' indicates that the Duke of York did not leave the provision of a weapon for riflemen to the judgement of the Board of Ordnance.

These 'forty kinds of rifles', which he gathered at his own headquarters, included weapons submitted by German and American, as well as British,

---

[1] J. Kincaid, *Adventures with the Rifle Brigade*, ed. H. Curling, with an introduction by Sir John Fortescue (London, 1929), p. 215.

[2] *Ibid.* p. 155.   [3] *Ibid.* p. 213.

[4] Ross, *Correspondence of Cornwallis*, III, 157.

manufacturers, and they were one and all taken down to Woolwich to be tested in a practical competition. The winning arm was a rifle submitted by the old London gunsmith, Ezekiel Baker. It was made to a calibre that would 'take the regulation pistol or carbine bullet of twenty to the pound—it being one of [the authorities'] principal objects...that the new weapon should be introduced into the Service without adding to the varieties of ammunition already in use';[1] and J. N. George's description of the weapon cannot be bettered. This rifle, he says, was not

the best that could be devised for target shooting under match conditions—for it was admitted on all sides that by giving the rifling a twist of three-quarters of a turn or more in place of [Baker's] quarter turn and by using a slightly over-sized bullet, far closer shooting might be obtained—but it had the qualities necessary for a military weapon of its type, being comparatively easy to load, carrying a bullet that would stop either man or horse at close quarters....[It might] be reckoned as being deadly up to two hundred yards, and dangerous between two and three hundred, in the sense that a single rifleman, who knew his business, should be sure of his man at the first range, and that it would be rash for an opponent to show himself for more than an instant at anything under full three hundred yards, if more than one man armed with the Baker should be watching the spot—for out of half a dozen shots fired at once, one or other would be almost sure to find its mark at such range. At distances between three and five hundred yards, though useless for firing at single enemies, it still shot close enough to hit a large target, such as a square of infantry, or to be decidedly annoying to troops on the march.[2]

The weapon had in fact enough range and accuracy to be decidedly useful against artillery; at Waterloo Kincaid's riflemen destroyed two French gun crews 'before they could give us a second round'; and similarly George Simmons was able to silence French guns at Badajoz.[3]

Because of the great difficulty usually found in ramming a tightly fitting bullet home down a rifle, British riflemen were at first issued with wooden mallets, to hammer ramrod and ball together down the bore; but these were found quite unnecessary with the Baker rifle. The small ball was placed on a greased 'patch' of leather, and then it was quite readily shoved down the bore, for the grease on the patch made its movement easy; the patch in turn made the ball fit so tightly into the grooves of the rifling that it took from them the spin it needed to give it accuracy; and though it has been asserted that, to reload one of these muzzle-loading weapons, a man must stand up and expose himself, this statement is in fact not true. Rifleman Harris, in a casually matter-of-fact way, describes himself in action as 'loading and firing as I lay'.[4] The Baker rifle was first issued with a triangular bayonet 18 inches long, which was later replaced

---

[1] George, *English Guns and Rifles*, p. 160.
[2] *Ibid.* p. 162.
[3] Kincaid, *Adventures with the Rifle Brigade*, p. 253; and *A British Rifleman; the Journals etc. of Major George Simmons*, ed. Lt. Col. Willoughby Verner (London, 1899), p. 227.
[4] *Recollections of Rifleman Harris*, ed. H. Curling, with an introduction by Sir John Fortescue (London, 1928), p. 23.

with 'a flat single-edged' sword bayonet 24 inches long.[1] The weapon itself was rugged enough to stand up to service in the field, and it continued in use till, after twenty-odd years of peace, it was replaced in 1836–9 by the Brunswick rifle, about which not one kind word seems capable of being said.[2]

V. CAVALRY

The first difficulty in writing about cavalry and their training lies in piercing a terminological fog to discover some real distinction of function amid a welter of varied names—Life Guards, Blues, Horse Guards, heavy cavalry, Dragoon Guards, Heavy Dragoons, Light Dragoons, plain, ordinary Dragoons, Hussars, and Light Horse.

From this confusion one may pick out first the Dragoon as being, in Dr Johnson's mildly malicious *double entendre*, 'a kind of soldier that fights indifferently either on foot or horseback'. They were armed with the sword for mounted shock action, and for dismounted action with the carbine—a short, light, smoothbored musket. Dragoon Guards differed from ordinary Dragoons in neither armament nor function, but only in regimental history, being units converted from horse guards into Dragoons in 1746.

The Blues and the Horse Guards were, of course, one and the same thing, and Life Guards were of the same type. These were the regiments of whom dismounted action was not expected. Their prime function was shock action, and to that end they were composed of big men, mounted on big horses. According to Major James, writing in 1810, their arms were merely sword and pistol,[3] but it appears that they were issued with carbines in 1797, and before that had been cumbered with 'long muskets'.[4] They are all described by the generic name of Heavy Cavalry.

A Heavy Dragoon was a hybrid between the foregoing two distinct types of horsemen.

Hussars, properly so termed, were 'the national cavalry of Hungary and Croatia; their arms [were] sabre, carbine and pistols'; they were originally irregular troops, who were expected to bivouac without tents, and whose only camp equipage was 'a kettle and a hatchet to every six men'.[5] Their special functions were akin to those of light infantry, namely, skirmishing, protection, and reconnaissance; they were therefore called Light Horse. In these roles they served Austria so well that they were imitated in both France and Prussia, and each of these powers sensibly used the name 'Hussar' to describe their own light cavalry of this type.

---

[1] George, *English Guns and Rifles*, p. 163.
[2] *Ibid.* pp. 301–2.
[3] James, *Military Dictionary*, sub 'Horse Guards'.
[4] Count von Bismark (*sic*), *Lectures on the Tactics of Cavalry*, translated by N. Ludlow Beamish (London, 1827), translator's note on p. 140.
[5] James, *Military Dictionary*, sub 'Hussar'.

At last, in 1746, these light horsemen of eastern Europe were imitated in Britain too, but, with the characteristic national talent for confusion, the British imitation was called a 'Light Dragoon', and later still confusion became yet more confounded when 'Hussars' also made their appearance in the British Army. This introduction of a new name, however, meant no real new thing; for the word 'Hussar' was applied merely to 'such regiments of light dragoons in the British service as have been ordered by their respective colonels to wear moustaches, furred cloaks and caps, etc., in imitation of the Germans. The three corps are the 7th, 10th, and 15th.'[1] Hussars and Light Dragoons are jointly described under the generic title of 'Light Horse'.

Such were the interpretations ascribed to these varied names of mounted troops. Whether in 1790 variety of name implied any real distinction of function and training between one regiment and another is a question no man can answer. At that date the drill of the cavalry was in as hopeless a state of chaos as that of the infantry and with consequences yet more depressing. Speed was cavalry's great asset, the charge their great function. The moment in which a charge might be made was fleeting, and was bound to be lost by cavalry who could not promptly and coherently form to make their charge. Cavalry, therefore, more than any other arm, needed to drill and manœuvre with a precision that could only be made possible by a single common system which they, like the infantry, lacked.

Once more it was David Dundas who met that need and provided the single, common system. He found his inspiration partly in the example of Prussia and partly in the work of General Sir James Stewart Denham, who had been in command of all the Irish cavalry when Dundas was serving in that country in 1789. His opportunity he found when the dismal end of the campaign of 1794–5 left him in North Germany, acting as Commander-in-Chief of the relics of the British Army of Flanders and awaiting a passage home from the Weser. He then imposed upon all mounted regiments under his command a system of drill and manœuvre he had previously introduced into the Light Dragoons of which he was himself the Colonel, and on his return the King directed that his system be followed and observed by all cavalry regiments at home till further orders. This much the Adjutant General announced to the Prince of Wales in a letter written on 10 July 1795, in which he added that he hoped 'to carry His Majesty's orders into practice in the course of next week', and to furnish every regiment with two copies of Dundas's *Rules and Regulations for Cavalry*.[2]

Here, again, Dundas was useful in bringing manageable uniformity out of unmanageable chaos, but he was less successful in prescribing for cavalry than for infantry. The major criticism is that he lost sight of the

[1] *Ibid.*
[2] Adjutant General to the Prince of Wales, 10 July 1795.

different functions of the heavy horseman, the dragoon, and the hussar, and that his drill turned them all into one and the same thing. General Sir John Money started a really serious question when he asked what use British cavalry, as trained by Dundas, would be in the event of an invasion of England. All were taught to charge, but when or where they would have an opportunity of doing it were obscure questions. 'Is there', queried Money, 'between London and Harwich, or Ipswich, any ground on which three squadrons of horse can form, without being in reach of musketry from hedgerows on their front and flanks? Of what use, then, in God's name, is Cavalry where they cannot form to charge, for if they cannot form, they cannot charge',[1] and with much vivid language Money urged the need of real light dragoons, trained to fight on foot as light infantry, but provided with horses to make them mobile. Trained as they were, Money saw little use for cavalry for home defence, except to make farmers get away with their horses, before the enemy commandeered them, and to assist in 'driving the country'.

There is a good deal of sense in these criticisms. Not that Dundas's manual failed to teach cavalry to drill and manœuvre on foot; a suitable section covers this subject, but with one significant omission. When cavalrymen went into action on foot in the early days of this century, they always left one-fourth of their number behind to hold the horses of the three-fourths who alone were committed to the firing line; and there is no instruction about horse-holding in at least the earlier editions of Dundas's *Rules and Regulations for Cavalry*. It would then be natural if many commanding officers ignored the foot drill, as something not for use on service but a mere handy means of gathering their men for a pay parade or ration issue; and in any case the *Rules and Regulations* taught only a close-order dismounted drill to cavalry, though it was in the role of light infantry that cavalry might best serve when dismounted.

Flaws in the detail of Dundas's cavalry regulations are revealed in criticisms made in 1827 by a cavalry officer who had never been in action, but was still a serious student of war with nine years' regimental service behind him. This was N. Ludlow Beamish, soldier, historian, German scholar, and student of Norse antiquities. His criticisms of Dundas's cavalry manœuvres occur in his own notes appended to his translation of *Lectures on the Tactics of Cavalry* by Count von Bismark (*sic*), an officer in the Royal Wurtemberg Army.

With what seems good reason Beamish found fault with the position of officers as presented by Dundas's *Regulations*; with the method of 'dressing', that is, correcting irregularities in a line; and, above all, with the practice of forming cavalry in three like the infantry. 'Experience proves', he writes, 'the inevitable extension of files, *in flank, marching by threes*;

---

[1] Cited from pp. 38–9 of Money's 'Open Letter' by Fuller, *British Light Infantrymen*, p. 202.

the repeated destruction of *telling-off* in action; the difficulty of performing the movement *Threes-about*, in deep ground or with tired horses, and the serious inconvenience of manœuvring *with the rear rank in front*'; in all these ways he found drill in threes produced 'complicated manœuvres ...which, like Chinese puzzles, only engross time and labour to the unprofitable end of forming *useless combinations*'.[1] Yet it was most desirable that cavalry drill should be as little complicated as possible, for with the best of systems cavalry took long to train and could not be improvised anything like so easily as infantry.

New raised troops or regiments [wrote Beamish] can be of little service in the field; and if cavalry is so reduced [in peace] as to require...augmentation on the breaking out of a war, its *physical* will be found sadly inferior to its *numerical* force. A battalion of infantry may be augmented without deranging its action; but a few half-formed dragoons, a few unbroke horses, will throw a whole line of cavalry into disorder, and defeat the object of the most talented Commander;[2]

and many other contemporary authorities could be cited in proof of this point.

An added weakness to British cavalry sprang from the difficulty of getting officers who would regard themselves seriously as cavalrymen and devote all their attention to that service. An officer secured promotion by buying his new rank; in a land where all gentlemen could ride it was thought immaterial whether the aspirant for promotion found it in horse or foot, and, as cavalry pay was higher than that of infantry, transfers from one to another were frequent. Thus Wellington had begun his military career as a Highlander in the tartan of the 73rd regiment of foot on 7 March 1787, turned horseman within fifteen months by transferring to the 12th Light Dragoons in June 1788, became an infantryman once more in June 1791, when he bought his company in the 58th regiment of foot, reverted to cavalry for six months when he transferred to the 18th Light Dragoons on 18 October 1792, and at last settled down as an infantryman when he bought his majority in the 33rd foot on 30 April 1793, and acquired the command of that regiment in the following autumn. His career was not untypical, even if his rise was unusually rapid, and few men who expected to follow a similar course would be likely to see much value in learning more of cavalry work than Dundas's manœuvres.

Any officer who did that could acquit himself without disgrace upon the parade ground, but small indeed were his chances of applying the manœuvres anywhere but on the parade ground till he suddenly found himself upon active service. For lack of realistic training in the field was a weakness of all British troops which bore specially hard on cavalry. That this was in part due to the army's use as a police force has been seen; it was also due to want of training grounds. The Dublin garrison did indeed

[1] Bismarck, *Lectures on Cavalry*, Beamish's note, pp. 132–4.
[2] *Ibid.* p. 118.

use Phoenix Park; in London the Foot Guards were sufficiently assiduous in fighting and refighting 'the Battle of Hyde Park'; but cavalry needed more space, and this they were denied by the stolid figure of that thriving farmer 'John Bull [who may] stand at his gate, and not only refuse you admittance, but prosecute and convict you, if you dare to insist upon it'.[1] So, says Beamish, the young officer, after 'galloping through Dundas's manœuvres on Hounslow Heath', would hear 'his elders talk of positions, pickets, attacks, outposts, etc.', but could only 'depend on his imagination for an idea of their nature'.[2] Nor were young officers the only ones whose efficiency suffered for want of realistic training. Few generals knew how to handle large bodies of cavalry, for few had ever had the opportunity of trying.

From all this it will be clear that the reform of British cavalry was incomplete; yet there was still reform. In the words of a hostile critic, Dundas's *Regulations* did establish some general uniformity and concert of manœuvres where previously 'we had none'.[3] Beamish's comment that the young officer had nothing but 'his imagination' to instruct him on the duty of 'pickets, attacks, outposts, etc.', which was made a dozen years after the Napoleonic wars ended, may not be true of the actual period of that struggle. The excellent advice in de Rottenburg's book on outposts, reconnaissance, and on rear, advanced, and flanks was much of it as applicable to light cavalry as to light infantry, and his manual was recommended to both arms. All told, the value and limitations of British cavalry as trained by Dundas and the Duke of York are best summed up in a letter written by Wellington in 1826. He found them useful 'first... upon advanced guards, flanks, etc., as the quickest movers and to enable me to know and see as much as possible in the shortest space of time; secondly, to use them in small bodies to attack small bodies of the enemy's cavalry'. But, because they 'would gallop [and] could not preserve their order', he found them 'so inferior...to the French...[that] although I consider one squadron a match for two French squadrons...I should not have liked to see four British squadrons opposed to four French squadrons; and as numbers increased, and order of course became more necessary, I was more unwilling to risk our cavalry without having a greater superiority of numbers'. He could never use British cavalry as the French cavalry was on occasion used by Napoleon who 'gained some of his battles by the use of courassiers as a sort of accelerated infantry, with which, supported by masses of cannon, he was in the habit of seizing important parts of the centre or flanks of his enemy's position, and occupying such points till his infantry could arrive to relieve them'.[4]

[1] Bismarck, *op. cit.* p. 150 n.
[2] *Ibid.* p. 353 n.
[3] Lord William Russell to Wellington, December 1826, *Supplementary Dispatches*, XIV, 370.
[4] Wellington to Lord William Russell, 31 July 1826, *ibid.* 3rd series, III, 353-4.

VI. WEAPON TRAINING

Finally, there was the business of training troops in the use of their own weapons, and at the outbreak of war this was in no better state than any other kind of training. 'It is absurd', remarked Dr Johnson on a wet Hebridean evening in 1773, 'that our soldiers should have swords and not be taught to use them.' Absurd it was, yet the absurdity was to last till its consequences were discovered in Flanders in 1793–4. Then it was found that the English cavalryman's lack of skill with his sword constantly caused him to be worsted in single combat with the enemy; indeed it frequently disabled him without any intervention from the enemy, for British army surgeons were led to conclude that many of the sword wounds they dressed were self-inflicted; only too often British cavalry horses were horribly gashed about the head and neck by their own riders.[1]

All these things were noticed by a decidedly junior officer, Major John Gaspard LeMarchant of the 2nd Dragoon Guards, the same who was to die as a Major General in the great charge at Salamanca; and LeMarchant was one of those men who cannot see things go wrong without trying to put them right. In a motley allied army there was no want of opportunity of learning, and LeMarchant first put himself under an Austrian cavalry sergeant from whom he learnt all that was taught in that army; next he consulted every individual he met in the allied force who had any reputation for skill in swordsmanship, and from what he learnt he worked out a system of attack and defence, which he taught with marked success in his own regiment. Finally he submitted his system in writing to the Duke of York, who, as it appears from the Commander-in-Chief's letter-books, received it through Lord Cathcart in 1796. In August the Duke ordered the manual to be printed, and early in the next year is found employing LeMarchant to tour the country until he had taught his sword exercise to detachments of every mounted regiment in the kingdom. In April 1797 LeMarchant's new manual, entitled *The Rules and Regulations for the Attainment and Practice of the Sword Exercise*, had to be reprinted and every cavalry officer was ordered to buy a copy (from Egerton's bookshop in Whitehall, and the price was six shillings).

LeMarchant's tour of instruction revealed another reason for the British cavalryman's failure to meet French swordsmen on an equal basis; very few British regiments were armed with an efficient sword, and hardly any two were armed with the same type of sword. To finish his job, therefore, LeMarchant undertook to design a good standard weapon. He examined a variety of models, visited the principal sword factories in Sheffield and Birmingham, and consulted those who could best advise him on the processes of working steel. He must have been a man who

---

[1] D. LeMarchant, *Memoirs of the late General Le Marchant* (privately printed, London, 1841), p. 44. I have found this work only in the British Museum.

could get much done in a short space of time, for by April 1797 he had had a new model sword made, and had had it approved by the Duke of York, who in that month ordered all regiments of cavalry to be re-equipped with new swords of LeMarchant's model.[1]

This exchange must have caused great expense to the nation; it was made on the terms that colonels of regiments should receive one new sword free for every old sword they could return in good condition to the Ordnance, but must pay for all new swords for which they could not give back serviceable old swords.[2] The whole business sheds a very creditable light on the keenness of both LeMarchant and the Duke. One marks the success of the Duke in dealing with two independent government departments—the Treasury and the Ordnance—and the completeness of the trust he seems to have placed in LeMarchant. The result was a great and quick improvement in the efficiency of British cavalry. No doubt the job could have been done better; 'the science of after-knowledge is so prodigious that nothing can stand against it', as one cavalryman of this period wrote in quite another context;[3] and LeMarchant is judged to have been at fault in his swordsmanship. He taught the British soldier to cut, not to thrust, and provided him with a shortish, curved cutting sword; 'after-knowledge' has come down heavily in favour of a long, thrusting sword. Very possibly LeMarchant would have been wiser to have chosen such a weapon and designed a drill for its use. The facts remain that he did bring about a great improvement, and that by trusting and using him the Duke secured as good results as he might have got from appointing a committee to consider the question and got them far quicker. Further, whatever criticisms may be made of either LeMarchant's sword or his sword drill, neither can have been very bad if Wellington considered one British squadron 'a match for two French squadrons'.

The most surprising light on the weapon training of British infantry that I have met is shed by a civilian who, as head of the field train department in the Peninsula, had the job of bringing up ammunition.

At Vittoria [he writes] each infantry soldier, on entering the field, had sixty rounds of ball cartridges...making a total of three million rounds;...from the commencement to the close of the engagement, one million, three hundred and fifty thousand rounds of ball cartridges were issued by the Field Train to the troops. Now allowing one half of these [last] to have been expended at the termination of the battle, there was still a total of three million, six hundred and seventy-five thousand rounds fired against the enemy. The French lost in killed and wounded eight thousand out of ninety thousand combatants; therefore it follows that only one musket-shot out of four hundred and fifty-nine took effect! and this calculation excludes altogether the injury inflicted on the enemy by ninety pieces of Artillery [which had fired over

---

[1] Circular to Colonels of Cavalry Regiments, 20 April 1797, WO/3/17.
[2] Ibid.
[3] T. H. McGuffie, *Peninsular Cavalry General (1811–13); the Correspondence of Robert Ballard Long* (London, 1951).

6,800 rounds between them]; at every battle in the Peninsula, except Barossa, the author remarked the same undue expenditure of ammunition in relation to the small extent of damage done.[1]

A similar, yet greater, disparity between rounds fired and casualties caused is, of course, observable in modern war, but it is more understandable today when much firing is done avowedly to keep the enemy's 'heads down' and prevent them using their own weapons. Why well-trained troops, as Wellington's certainly were, should shoot so ineffectually in the close-ordered type of battle that has been described is indeed 'a subject well worthy' of attention, as the author says.

The subject was attended to in other armies than the British when the war ended. 'A German general, of the name of von Trew, had a frame constructed, in which the musket was...so fixed as to render all motion, and consequently recoil, impossible; yet the shots...varied in their directions as well as their distances, and sometimes reached the ground within 220, and sometimes as far as 368 paces at their first fall. From this and other trials made...in Europe', it was concluded that the ammunition was faulty, the balls being ill-balanced and ill-fitting;[2] and this may explain why much fire was wasted. One may accept, too, the suggestion that the clouds of smoke created by firing made for bad shooting;[3] and poor loading, too, as has been mentioned; but, when all allowance has been made, it seems safe to declare flatly that supposed economy caused great inefficiency. British regulations permitted only thirty ball and sixty blank cartridges to be issued annually to each man for firing practice.[4] The blank rounds enabled battalions to practise various kinds of 'firings', by companies, by platoons, files, and so on;[5] only with the thirty ball cartridges could a man test his shooting against a target. I have failed to find any evidence that during the war British platoons were practised 'at extended targets, or spread sails', which was suggested after the war as a useful exercise;[6] the maxim that 'the act of aiming is the province of light troops'[7] seems to have resulted in no other troops being expected to aim. Light troops undoubtedly shot well, and much of the time spent on training them was used for 'firing ball at a mark'.[8]

The only evidence I have found of bayonet training being carried on dates from 1804. In that year a certain Captain Gordon spent from February to April 'in exercising and instructing detachments from each of the three regiments of Foot Guards and a company of the 1st battalion

---

[1] R. Henegan, *Seven Years' Campaigning in the Peninsula and the Netherlands from 1808 to 1815* (London, 1846), I, 344–6 n.
[2] Suasso, *Theory of Infantry Movements*, III, 210.
[3] *Ibid.* p. 255.
[4] Adjutant General to Lt. Col. Neville, 27 April 1805, WO/3/153.
[5] Suasso, *Theory of Infantry Movements*, III, 220.
[6] *Ibid.* p. 217.   [7] *Ibid.* p. 219 n.
[8] Circular to General Officers Commanding Districts, 25 December 1797, WO/3/31.

of the Queen's Royal Volunteers in the New System of Attack and Defence with the Bayonet'.[1] No doubt the detachments of the Guards went back to their units to act as instructors, like the cavalry detachments LeMarchant trained in swordsmanship; very possibly Gordon taught 'the New System' to detachments of the battalions, too, but evidence of his doing so seems to be wanting. Certainly hand-to-hand fighting with the bayonet was rare; small parties of men might use this weapon when mixed up in a scuffle, but, says a distinguished Peninsular surgeon, 'opposing regiments when formed in line and charging with fixed bayonets, *never* meet and struggle hand to hand and foot to foot; and this for the best possible reason, that one side turns and runs away as soon as the other comes close enough to do mischief'.[2] The writer, who knew what wounds he had had to treat, may be believed. Possibly, however, he would have seen more bayonet wounds if troops had received more training in handling this weapon, for men cannot be expected to use a weapon in which they have no confidence; confidence goes hand in hand with competence; and competence is the result of thorough training.

VII

Now to sum up. British cavalry might have been provided with a better system of drill, a better sword, and a better sword exercise than they received; light infantry companies, as distinct from the light battalions, might have been made into better skirmishers than they were; with more intelligently planned training and instruction British battalions might have made more effective use of their muskets and of their bayonets in action. When all these qualifications have been made, it still is true that in these years British infantry and cavalry became far more effective troops than they had been when war began. For this the main credit goes to the Duke of York, who created uniformity where there had previously been only disorder; this he did by steady and unremitting attention to the training of troops. David Dundas, too, was a very useful servant of his army and his country; and the Duke was either very wise or very fortunate in his choice of training officers, LeMarchant, Coote Manningham, and above all, Moore.

---

[1] Calvert to Francis Moore, 31 July 1804, WO/3/152. In addition to the units here named a number of detachments of light infantry had received bayonet instruction early in 1804 (Wynyard to Burrard, 6 March 1804, WO/3/37).

[2] G. J. Guthrie, *Commentaries on the Surgery of War* (London, 1853), pp. 15–16.

CHAPTER 6

PROMOTIONS AND APPOINTMENTS

'IN war *men* are nothing; it is *a man* who is everything.' So runs a familiar saying of Napoleon, and it is valid through every gradation of army rank. Systems of promotion are good only in so far as they succeed in securing that any body of men in need of a leader, whatever its size, shall be provided with an officer truly capable of leading it.

British regular forces in our period used different systems of promotion, with disappointingly paradoxical results. The Ordnance followed a system of blameless impartiality and unimpeachable justice, that led to results which were often deplorable; the army proper followed a system that is commonly regarded as a crying scandal but of which the results were often excellent.

The Ordnance system may be briefly dealt with. This department found officers for the artillery and engineers among the graduates of the Royal Military Academy at Woolwich, which gave an excellent military education. Its graduates were appointed to commissions as vacancies occurred, and, again as vacancies occurred, they rose step by step in rank; thus all promotion went normally by seniority. But there was no retirement age, nor any system of pensioning-off old officers. So officers clung to their commissions, and their income, literally to the death; the result was an utter stagnation of promotion. One may mark how junior was the rank of the engineers and gunners on whom Wellington relied in the Peninsula. Sir Richard Fletcher was but a major when he landed in Portugal; Jones, Burgoyne, and Alexander Dickson were only lieutenants. It is curious that such humble rank should carry such high responsibility as these young men bore; yet it was also inevitable in a branch of the service whose system of promotion virtually guaranteed that a man would be old before he became a colonel, and senile before he became a general. And though the eminent services of these men did accelerate their promotion, their rise was watched with jealousy in London, and did not carry them very high. Dickson was only a lieutenant-colonel when he commanded the artillery at Waterloo; Fletcher held no higher rank when he received his death wound in the trenches before San Sebastian. Viewed in the light of abstract justice, no system of promotion could perhaps be fairer than that followed by the Ordnance department; but judge it by results and it must be condemned as a system which cluttered the top of the service with moribund incompetence and had little reward or encouragement to offer for zeal, ability, and heroism in the lower commissioned ranks. The best that can be said for the Ordnance is that this department did begin by educating its candidates for commissions, and that a real measure of professional knowledge was to be found in every rank.

Very different were the methods of the army. In cavalry and infantry alike, there were four ways by which a man might rise in rank. The first was, of course, by purchase; an officer might buy the next step in rank above his own, and make it his property (much as till lately in Britain a doctor made a practice his property by purchase). Secondly, an officer might be promoted by brevet; thirdly, he might secure rank by recruiting; fourthly, he might be selected for promotion to succeed to a vacancy created without purchase.

I have listed these methods in the order of their normal importance, but it may be simplest to discuss them in the reverse of that order.

On promotion by selection there is least to be said. A commission was not heritable property, and so a widow could not sell one; hence when an officer was killed in action, room was made for someone to be promoted without paying any purchase price. On such an occasion a deserving sergeant might become an ensign, and an old lieutenant who had waited long might get his company. As it was exceptional for an officer to be permitted to sell a commission he had not bought, some vacancies of this kind were always likely to become available, even in peacetime.

'Recruiting for rank' also provided 'free' commissions, but it took place only in wartime when the army was being expanded. Then when whole new battalions were being raised, and old battalions augmented by new companies, many new vacancies for officers were created. Under the system of 'recruiting for rank' those vacancies were given to the men who raised the recruits to fill the ranks of the new units. This is a method both of recruitment and promotion made famous by the vivid pen of Sir John Fortescue as one of the major military abuses of the Georgian period.[1] The justice of his criticism will be examined hereafter.

Promotion by 'brevet' may be briefly explained. It was then a general and simultaneous elevation of a given number of officers from one rank to the next above it. When promotions were thus made in one mass together, it was of course impossible to find a new job at once for each man promoted, and the officers who received them had therefore to remain in the same regiments doing the same duty and drawing the same pay as they had before the brevet was made; their immediate gain was therefore slight. The advantages of a brevet were that it conveyed immediately the authority of the new rank, and that it gave its recipient a prior claim on any vacancy that might occur in that rank. Brevet was the sole method of promotion to all ranks above that of colonel, and was not used to raise officers of any lower level than captains, who might be made majors by it.

[1] *History of the British Army*, IV, 212–14.

Finally, there was the much vituperated system of purchase, but criticism of this 'traffic' in commissions is not always informed. To make a rational judgement of it, one needs to know, first, what advantages were supposed to be derived from it; secondly, how it worked; thirdly, what abuses sprang up in it; fourthly, what was done to correct those abuses, and discussion of this last point will be included in a general survey of all the Duke of York's reforms in the field of promotion.

Part of the case for permitting the sale of commissions was thus expressed by a contemporary:

In every other service in Europe it is understood that the head of the army has the power of granting pensions to officers of the army, in proportion to their rank and service; no such power exists in the head of the army in this country; therefore, when an officer is arrived at the command of a regiment, and is from long service, infirmity or wounds totally incapable of proceeding with that regiment on service, it becomes necessary to place a more effective officer in his stead. It is not possible for His Majesty to increase the establishment of the army at his pleasure by appointing two lieutenant-colonels where only one is fixed upon the establishment; nor is it consistent with justice to place an old officer upon the half-pay or deprive him altogether of his commission; there is therefore no alternative but to allow him to retire receiving a certain compensation for his former services.[1]

In other words, the sale of commissions was a convenient financial device for saving members of Parliament the unpleasantness of asking their constituents to pay taxes to provide pensions for deserving old officers; and it did this by permitting the old officer to receive on his retirement a lump sum in cash from his successor.

But this was not the only advantage. Any commission, from ensign up, could be sold, provided it had been bought; at any stage in his career, therefore, an officer could retire and be the richer for doing so. That meant that no man, who found himself ill-suited to soldiering, need stay on in the army, as do so many people today in the civil service, school teaching, and such callings, because they feel they cannot leave jobs which they dislike and do badly, when leaving the job means surrendering income and pension simultaneously. Accordingly, the system of purchase was valued as a means of keeping regiments officered by keen, young men, and there is justice in this view. There is a Shorncliffe tradition that Sir John Moore purged the 43rd and 52nd regiments of inefficient officers by making running up hill a regular and monotonous feature of his light infantry training; the fat and idle were soon glad to sell out. The last warlike expedition carried out before the end of purchase was the suppression of the Red River disturbances created in western Canada by Louis Riel in 1870; and it is striking to see what fine leaders of men the regular British officers on that expedition were—young, fit, keen, and

---

[1] *Naval and Military Magazine*, I, 2 n.

ready to give a hand on every unpleasant occasion.[1] When service was easy and soft, slack officers might well be found in regiments in the days of purchase, but they were never so readily got rid of as in those same days when purchase offered them an easy way out; and Wellington's career is an example of the system's value in bringing an able man on to high rank, while he still possessed full physical vigour.

Thirdly, the purchase of commissions was thought to be a valuable constitutional safeguard. Men had not forgotten how James II had tried to make the army an instrument of tyranny by replacing Protestant officers with Roman Catholics. But to deprive a man of a commission, which he had purchased and had not forfeited by his own disgraceful conduct, would be nothing but an act of robbery; as long as the rights of property were held sacred, it could not be done, and no sovereign could purge the army with a view to using it for a *coup d'état*. Hence, even so late as 1827, when the future Queen Victoria was already a well-grown little girl, one finds no less a man than Sir Walter Scott describing the system of the purchase of commissions as 'indispensable to the freedom of the country'.[2]

So there stands the threefold defence of purchase—a means of pensioning old officers; a means of bringing forward keen, young officers to high rank and responsibility while they were still in full vigour of life; and a safeguard of constitutional liberty. That the system was hard on poor men, who could not afford to buy, was readily acknowledged. But the general value of the system was reckoned to outweigh this evil; the poor man had in any case a chance to get promotion without paying for it as soon as his regiment went on active service (ambitious and ghoulish youngsters were sometimes heard to repine on occasions when battle produced disappointingly few casualties among the senior officers); and, finally, the system could hardly be abolished till Parliament could be persuaded to advance the large sum of money necessary to buy out all the officers who had invested their own fortunes in buying their army rank. So it lived on till that great financier and iconoclast, Gladstone, swept it away in 1870.

The way the system worked, from the very beginning of a man's army career, was as follows. He made his first application for a commission on a form issued, through the various army agents, from the Adjutant General's office. The form simply declared that the applicant fully intended to abide by the established rules and regulations of the service; the young man first had to sign it himself and submit it through the agent; and, at least after the Duke of York had become Commander-in-Chief, the applicant had also to submit a recommendation from some officer in

---

[1] G. L. Huyshe, *The Red River Expedition* (London and New York, 1871), pp. 76–80, 86–8, 112–13.
[2] *Naval and Military Magazine*, I, 2.

the service, of not less than field rank, stating that he was a suitable person to hold a commission; and next he had to deposit with the agent, through whom he secured the form, a sum of money to buy the rank of ensign. That done, he would have to wait his turn till he had the opportunity to buy an ensign's commission; when his turn came, his deposit would be handed over to the seller of the commission, and he would thereupon be gazetted as an ensign in the regiment in which he had now bought his position. His next step in rank would come in the same manner; he would again buy, and again the agent would be the medium through whom he bought. The one check on the system lay in the fact that no man could sell without permission or buy without permission; the system worked well or ill according to the discrimination with which permission was given; and that again depended on the judgement and integrity of the giver.[1]

As long as the office of Commander-in-Chief was filled, it was he who in fact gave permission to men to buy and sell, though in constitutional theory, and in form, that permission was given by the King. When there was no Commander-in-Chief, 'the patronage of the Army...[was] vested solely in the Secretary at War'.[2] And there lies the cause of most of the abuses that sprang up in the system of purchase. From the end of the American and Bourbon war in 1783 till the new war with France in 1793, there was no Commander-in-Chief, and so for a decade 'the patronage of the Army' was dispensed by a civilian minister who, for eight and a half of those years, was a peculiarly unpleasant character, namely, one Sir George Yonge, Bart. He was a wealthy west-country borough owner, whose name lives today only in a long, but uninspiring, thoroughfare in the city of Toronto and in the memory of South African scandals whose discovery happily, if belatedly, ended his governorship of the Cape, and his political career, in 1801. There can be little doubt that Yonge's conduct justified Fox's gibe at Pitt's military economies of 1792; then, when Pitt reduced the establishment of other ranks without reducing the number of officers, his great rival declared that he had adopted a method of economy which was 'the least in point of saving and the greatest in point of patronage'.[3] Indeed, it is a fact that the use of army promotion as a means of political patronage had a long and sordid eighteenth-century history. For the good of the service Pitt's own father had proposed in 1745 that officers under the rank of lieutenant-colonel should be barred

[1] Charles James, *The Regimental Companion* (London, 1803), p. 27, gives the form of recommendation for a candidate for a commission; he likewise gives the authorized prices of the various ranks.

[2] The Adjutant General to Mrs Parr, 5 November 1792, WO/3/11 in the Public Record Office.

[3] Rose cites this gibe and describes it as caustic (*William Pitt and the Great War*, London, 1911, p. 30). Perhaps it was; but after turning up the phrase in its original context in the *Parliamentary Debates*, I was left regretfully wondering whether it was indeed intended as a gibe and not as a matter-of-fact description of a natural state of affairs.

from election to the House of Commons, and Lord Chesterfield had supported the proposal, because it would prevent 'young subaltern puppys from forcing themselves by their seats in Parliament into higher posts than they are fit for';[1] but army reform did not commend itself to the Pelhams and the elder Pitt's proposal came to nothing. It was left to the Duke of Cumberland to improve matters, and his firm assertion of his right to control promotion in the army he commanded wrung a natural cry of pain from that scion of the greatest of all majority manipulators, Horace Walpole. When Cumberland was disgraced in 1757, his successor, the grand old Huguenot soldier, Sir John Ligonier, reduced the Duke of Newcastle 'to despair' by refusing to let the army's good become the plaything of political advantage.[2] So it was perhaps not accidental that the office of Commander-in-Chief was allowed to be vacant throughout the ten years' peace that followed the Treaty of Versailles in 1783. Any administration which filled this office deprived itself of a valuable means of giving 'gratifications' to 'members of parliament' (if one may adapt a phrase of Henry Fox).[3]

The recklessness with which Yonge used his opportunities for bestowing gratifications was thus described in retrospect; for promotion in his day 'no science was required, no service, no previous experience whatever: the boy let loose from school the last week might in the course of a month be a field officer, if his friends were disposed to be liberal of money and influence'. Nor indeed did the boy always require to have passed through school. 'It was no uncommon thing' for commissions to be given to babes in arms, and these babes did not even have to be male; commissions might be

obtained for a child in a cradle [continues the writer] and when he came from college the fortunate youth was at least a lieutenant of some standing by dint of fair promotion. To sum up this list of abuses, commissions were in some instances bestowed on *young ladies*, when pensions could not be had. We know ourselves one fair dame who drew the pay of captain in the ———— dragoons, and was probably not much less fit for service than some who actually did duty.[4]

These are indeed words written in 1827 of abuses that had flourished over three decades earlier; they are not on that account to be dismissed as unsound historical evidence. In part the writer speaks from his own

---

[1] Sir Lewis Namier, *Structure of Politics at the Accession of George III* (London, 1957), p. 27.

[2] *Ibid.* pp. 253-4.

[3] Basil Williams, *The Whig Supremacy* (Oxford, 1939), p. 326.

[4] 'Memoir of H.R.H. the Duke of York' by Sir Walter Scott under the pseudonym of 'the Author of Waverly' in the *Naval and Military Magazine* (1827), pp. 2 ff. Lord Londonderry (Castlereagh's younger brother) also recalled how, in the bad old days 'boys were...permitted to hold commissions, whilst they were yet acquiring the first elements of education' (*Narrative of the Peninsular War from 1808 to 1813*, 3rd ed., London, 1829, I, 4).

knowledge, and in part he is supported by contemporary evidence. A staff officer in Flanders in 1794 is found writing that 'the field officers are many of them boys and have attained their rank by means suggested by the government at home', and that 'the command of brigades devolved on young men newly come into the service, whose years and inexperience totally disqualified them for the situation. I could mention lads of one and twenty who had never been on service before.'[1] This writer again is supported by William Windham, Sir George Yonge's successor, who wrote Pitt from Flanders on 19 September 1794, 'when the line was drawn out the other day, in circumstances as critical as an army ever stood in...most of the Brigades were commanded by men too young both in age and service to be properly entrusted with the command of a company'.[2]

Such, in part, were the consequences of Sir George Yonge's administration of 'the patronage of the Army' through eight years of peace. Unfortunately the outbreak of war produced no improvement, even though it did produce a Commander-in-Chief. Lord Amherst, in his seventies, was little competent to superintend promotion or to superintend anything else. He ignored his senior staff officer, the Adjutant General, the able and enlightened Sir William Fawcett, who was reduced to writing in reply to an inquiry about promotion: 'His Lordship's arrangements for Army Promotions are generally settled between him and his secretary so that it seldom happens that I am acquainted with them till they appear in the Gazette.'[3] Unfortunately Amherst's secretary was only a civilian head clerk, not perhaps much more competent than his master. As one sample of their incompetence, it is recorded that they left 'a complete jumble' of all Sir Charles Grey's recommendations for promotion among the numerous battalions serving in the West Indies in 1794.[4]

Responsibility for the evil consequences of 'recruiting for rank' must also rest in large measure on the shoulders of Amherst; no doubt he followed suggestions made by Henry Dundas and Yonge, but as the army's chief he still had the job of making the army efficient, and he did not perform it. Though Pitt's military economies of 1792 had avowedly retained officers while discarding privates in order to preserve in peace cadres which could be expanded in war, many whole new regiments were raised as soon as war actually broke out, and staffed with green officers and filled with raw privates, they were useless beyond belief. Here is the

[1] Calvert to Dalrymple, 9 November 1794, H. Verney, *Journal and Correspondence of Sir Harry Calvert*, p. 385. On Wellington's rise from 'Ensign to Lieutenant-Colonel in less than seven years' Philip Guedalla comments, 'there was little need for a Lieutenant-Colonel to blush at twenty-four, when Kitty Packenham's brother was a Major at seventeen, and Cotton had a regiment at twenty-one and Lowry Cole at twenty-two' (*The Duke*, London, 1931, p. 40).

[2] Windham to Pitt, 19 September 1794, Rosebery, *The Windham Papers*, I, 143–6.

[3] Fawcett to Major Crawford, 5 November 1793, WO/3/11.

[4] Fawcett to Lt. Gen. Smith, 1 March 1795, WO/3/13.

Adjutant General's description of certain new battalions created in this fashion:

it will be some time before you can expect to make any use of them, as very few of the officers have served before and none of the men have ever had a Firelock on their shoulders....Four of those Irish corps you lately sent us over, viz. the 107th, 110th, 119th, and 120th, being not only almost totally unfit for any service, but not possibly to be rendered so in any tolerable time, according to General Hunter's report, are going to be reduced...the 118th [Lieutenant Colonel Talbot's] are at this moment in an open, barefaced state of mutiny and will do nothing but what they please, despising and insulting their officers in the most shameful manner.[1]

On the last sentence the only comment to be made is that soldiers who have good officers do not mutiny; and great was the bitterness good officers felt at seeing rank up to that of lieutenant-colonel given to incompetents who somehow managed to raise the required quota of men.

We want [wrote a staff officer in Flanders on 12 October 1794] a total stop put to that most pernicious mode of bestowing rank on officers without even the form of recommendation, merely for raising (by means of crimps) a certain number of men ...and relieve deserving officers from the intolerable grievance of seeing men without merit, without family or the smallest pretension to any military ability, pass over their heads and arrive at a very high, and till now very respectable, rank in the army, solely through the medium of a rascally crimp.[2]

In the light of this contemporary evidence it is hard to accuse Fortescue of exaggerating the evils of 'recruiting for rank', as it was practised when Dundas, Yonge, and Amherst ran the army. The only point in which Fortescue may be mistaken is in the amount of the blame he lays on Henry Dundas. In a letter to Lord Pelham of 30 April 1795, the Duke of York seems to lay the blame firmly on the shoulders of Amherst who allowed 'officers who have never been in the Army...to render their commissions permanent' in the rank of lieutenant-colonel if they 'would pass through the other ranks' by purchasing them.[3]

Of promotion by brevet Amherst managed to make as complete a bungle as of anything else. It was essentially a method of giving recognition to officers of long service; these were the officers who had most reason to complain of being passed over by the ignorant men who arrived at high rank by recruiting. As an act of justice to them (presumably) Amherst proposed to make a great promotion by brevet in 1794; but he dallied, and either he or his secretary did not keep his mouth shut. Rumour of the coming brevet got abroad; many officers, who did not expect to be included in it, hastened to buy rank before it in order to secure their seniority; that many of them borrowed in order to buy is likely. At last on 28 September 1794 the 'monstrous brevet' (as Fawcett

---

[1] Fawcett to Lt. Col. Hewett, April 1795, WO/3/13.

[2] Calvert to Dalrymple, 12 October 1794, Sir H. Verney, *Journals and Correspondence of Sir Harry Calvert*, p. 360.

[3] Pelham Papers, British Museum Additional MSS.

termed it) took place, but all its promotions were antedated to the first of the preceding March; so every officer who had bought rank during the summer expressly in order to get ahead of the brevet found himself robbed of the seniority which he thought he had secured and which he had spent so much to buy. By this act lasting and incurable injustice was done in many cases, and three years later the Duke of York is found deploring his inability to put the injustice right.[1] All told, there is no disputing the verdict of Henry Dundas, when he wrote to Grenville on 21 July 1798: 'Lord Amherst was a worthy and respectable old man and no one shall ever hear me say a disrespectful thing against him; but the mischief he did to the army in a few years will not be repaired but by the unremitting attention of many.'[2]

A happy thing it was for Britain that in the Duke of York she had a prince who was abundantly willing and able to give unremitting attention to the repair of Amherst's mischief, for in this field of reform one of the Duke's most valuable assets was his royal blood. In Sir Walter Scott's words, 'No rank short of that of the Duke of York—no courage and determination inferior to that of H.R.H.—could have accomplished so great a change in so important a service but which was yet so unfavourable to the wealthy and to the powerful whose children and protégés had formerly found a brief way to promotion'.[3] Scott's implication is plain enough; it required the rank of a son of George III to resist the ambitions and the political influence of 'the wealthy' and 'powerful'; in that fact, as in his age, lies such excuse as may be found for Lord Amherst's sad mismanagement. Indeed, even a royal prince, when he had been indiscreet, could not survive the resentment his reforms of promotion created among the ambitious and unscrupulous; this was the ground and this the motive of the attack that led to his fall in 1809. His attacker, Lt. Col. Gwylym Lloyd Wardle, was a former officer of a fencible regiment and in accordance with the Duke's set practice, he had been denied rank in the regular army;[4] so Wardle was a disappointed man, just as Mary Ann Clark, to whom the Duke refused to pay blackmail after she had ceased to render him the services expected of a mistress, was a disappointed woman.

The Duke's methods of repairing Amherst's mischief were necessarily threefold. He had first to make the late civilians, who had recently become proprietors of respectable army rank, comprehend, and submit to, army discipline; he had, secondly, to make them acquire a knowledge of their

[1] Duke of York to Lord Pelham, 23 March 1797, *ibid*. 33, 103.
[2] *Dropmore Papers*, IV, 264.
[3] 'Memoir of H.R.H. the Duke of York'.
[4] This regiment, the Ancient British Fencibles, raised by Sir Watkin Williams Wynn under a letter of service dated 14 March 1794, had served at Vinegar Hill in the Irish rebellion and is to be identified with that 'Welsh Regiment of Ancient Britons', which, according to Lecky, was notorious above almost all others for atrocities committed during the suppression of the rebellion (W. E. H. Lecky, *Ireland in the Eighteenth Century*, chapters IX and X).

new trade that would fit them for the rank of which he could not deprive them; how he did these things will be discussed in their proper places. His third task, which will be discussed here, was to prevent Amherst's errors from occurring again, and to that end he fenced in the whole matter of promotion with a number of very salutary rules.

He began at the beginning, with an officer's first entrance into the army. The bitterness with which that able staff officer, Sir Harry Calvert, viewed the rise of officers who entered the army in 1794 'without even the form of recommendation' has been noted. The practice (already described) of requiring all candidates for commissions to produce a recommendation from a field officer is therefore to be regarded as one of the Duke's reforms; if it did not guarantee that all candidates would be good ones, it no doubt reduced the number of applications from unsuitable people.[1] Next, by a general order issued on 12 March 1795 (before he had been six weeks in office) the Duke directed that 'all applications to him from officers on full pay for promotion, or on any other subject, shall for the future be made through the regular channel of the Colonel, or Commanding Officer of the Regiment, to which they belong, who is required to signify at the bottom of their memorials his approbation or disapprobation thereof'.[2] The purpose of this order was twofold, to secure as far as possible the promotion of good men only, and to reinforce discipline; as the Duke's private secretary explained it to Moore in 1803,

by passing under the eye of the Commanding Officer of a Regiment a great many memorials by people who are by no means deserving of consideration are...kept back, and H.R.H. is the better able to judge of those who have merit. It is also considered to have the effect of inducing young officers to look up to their Commanding Officers, who, although not able to promise them promotion, may have it essentially in their power to forward their claim to it.'[3]

So far the Duke's intentions and conduct seem perfectly sound, and yet, had he gone no farther, he would have left room for injustice. Commanding officers, like other persons in authority, run in the three standard classes of good, bad and indifferent, and have been known to hold unreasonable prejudices against individuals. The Duke was aware of this fact and therefore his general order continued:

H.R.H. does not mean by this regulation to preclude officers from addressing themselves directly to him in cases where they may deem it unavoidably necessary... but in the few instances in which this necessity may be supposed to occur, H.R.H. expects that Officers shall state very fully the particular Reasons which have induced them to deviate from this General Order.[4]

And that too seems perfectly fair.

[1] James, *Regimental Companion*, p. 27.
[2] Circular of 12 March 1795, WO/3/28.
[3] Clinton to Sir John Moore, 30 August 1803, WO/3/591.
[4] Circular of 12 March 1795, WO/3/28.

Certain other specific regulations followed. These needed careful drafting for they had to win general confidence if they were to prove satisfactory. That meant that they had to be acceptable to the custom and temper of their time; and they had also to be upheld. However, since the abuses prevailing in 1793 and 1794 were so flagrant as to make regulation conspicuously necessary, the very extent of the evil made its cure easier.

The Duke of York would have no more of the system by which 'the boy let loose from school the last week might in the course of a month be a field officer, if his friends were disposed to be liberal of money and influence'. He laid it down that no man could purchase the rank of captain till he had been a subaltern for at least two years, nor purchase the rank of major till he had served six years; and he cut out the evil of infant officers by making sixteen the minimum age at which a young gentleman could purchase an ensigncy.

The years of experience required to qualify a man for promotion to his captaincy or majority had to be served in the regular army, and no officer in the fencibles or militia was ordinarily allowed to transfer to the regulars and carry his rank with him. This rule, however, was waived on occasions when privates in the militia were permitted to volunteer into the regulars. Then a few militia officers might be allowed to accompany their men into the Army.[1]

Two other steps, also, the Duke took. He did not continue Amherst's practice of making a civilian clerk the channel for all applications for promotion, but created the new office of Military Secretary. He gave this very intimate and responsible post to able young officers with good active service records—from 1795 to 1803 to Robert Brownrigg, who was later to be Governor of Ceylon, from 1803 to 1804 to Henry Clinton who was to command British forces against Suchet on the eastern side of Spain in 1813, and from 1804 to 1809 to James Willoughby Gordon, a soldier of wide interests who was later to become a Fellow of the Royal Society and to be one of the founders of the Royal Geographical Society. The Duke also struggled hard against the corrupt practices of officers who tried to secure promotion by offering more than the regulated price to the seller of the commission they were buying or the intermediary through whom they bought. How far he succeeded here can never be known; a parliamentary commission, which studied the purchase system after the Crimean War, bluntly reported that then 'the regulation price of commissions (was) a fiction'.[2] What the Duke could do to check this practice in his day was to issue firm warnings that commissions were to be bought through no other channel than the recognized and correct one of the regular army agents;

[1] Thus in 1799 one militia captain was granted temporary rank and one ensign permanent rank in the army in cases where a militia battalion produced 80 or more volunteers for the regulars (general order of 10 October 1799).

[2] Report of Commissioners on the Sale and Purchase of Commissions in the Army, 1857, p. 23.

and, no doubt on his initiative, a clause was added to the Mutiny Act in 1807, declaring that any man who paid money to anyone acting as a go-between in arranging a sale and purchase was liable to have 'his Name laid before the King for disobedience to H.M.'s Commands'.[1] The evil of this abuse was that it gave additional advantages to the wealthy over the poor; the fact that it was legislated against proves it existed, but does not prove that in the Duke's day the regulation price of commissions was always a fiction. The 'black market' price of commissions varied, as such prices will, according to the law of supply and demand; and the supply of commissions was never larger than in wartime, when casualties created so many free vacancies.

By these means, then, the Duke of York sought to control abuses in the system of purchase and to provide some guarantee that promotion should go to those who deserved it. If he had had the power, he would probably have preferred to abolish the system. When Castlereagh consulted him about the East India Company's Army, he advised that there promotion should be by seniority up to the rank of captain, and by selection on the basis of merit to ranks above captain. This would indicate how the Duke would have liked to have managed his own army; he did in fact abolish the practice of selling the office of quarter-master in cavalry regiments; and he did not permit the system of purchase to be introduced into the Royal Staff Corps, which he created. But it is not surprising that he should fail to destroy this method of promotion which had existed almost as long as the regular army itself. That the system as he left it survived the reforming zeal of all the nineteenth-century Prime Ministers down to Gladstone indicates how hard it would have been for the Duke of York to sweep it away in his time; and he could fairly claim to have so far amended it as to ensure that it would work reasonably well in practice. His regulations that a man must serve two years before he bought a captaincy and six before he bought a majority, taken along with his reforms of discipline and training, meant that no man could buy a rank whose duties he had not learnt; and his commanding officer's certificate was some additional guarantee that he was fit for promotion in other ways too.

If, at the opening of the nineteenth century, the system of purchase was so deep rooted as to be impregnable, one might at least have expected the Duke to abolish 'recruiting for rank', of which the evils had been so glaring, and yet he did no such thing. Instead he continued the practice for reasons which he explained to William Windham in 1806 when he ineffectually tried to induce that cultivated lover of books to base recruiting policy on fact instead of theory.

In most of the Continental Powers [wrote the Duke] the Plan upon which their Armies are formed, by giving a Property to the Captains in their respective Troops

[1] General order of 20 April 1807.

or Companies and obliging them under Pecuniary risk to keep them constantly complete, makes it both an Object and Credit to them to use every exertion upon the Recruiting Service:— But in this Country...no temptation whatsoever is offered to the Officer to exert himself on the Recruiting Service [as it was normally carried on].

When, however, an officer knew that his own promotion depended on his success in persuading men to enlist, he had a strong incentive to exert himself. The result was that of 'many different Schemes...proposed and resorted to for facilitating the Recruiting of the Army...the only Plan, which has certainly to a degree succeeded, has been to permit Officers, under certain restrictions, to raise Men for Rank'.[1]

One further advantage was gained from this system of recruiting when a county magnate was permitted to raise a new battalion of which he would himself be the colonel. Then the prestige, popularity and influence of a great county family was harnessed to the recruiting service; a man of such a family 'from Local Circumstances [was] likely to procure men with much greater facility than' any obscure junior officer, with his sergeant and drummers, visiting fairs and markets in the ordinary fashion. The Duke therefore sought ways and means to use the advantages of 'recruiting for rank' and at the same time to avoid its evils.

When he first took over the command-in-chief in 1795, he indeed seems to have regarded every battalion raised in this manner as a *damnosa hereditas*. Faced with the impossibility of making serviceable battalions out of men who knew nothing and were under the nominal command of officers whose equal ignorance prevented them from teaching anything, he felt he had no resource but to break up the worst of Amherst's new levies and draft the men into good battalions that were under strength. However, he returned to the method of recruiting for rank in 1801 when 'H.M....signified His Pleasure that two Companies of one Hundred Rank and File [should] be added to the different Regiments of Regular Infantry in Great Britain', but he did so with certain provisos. He offered the chance of recruiting for rank first to those officers whose seniority entitled them to early promotion, 'the Captain Lieutenant, the two Senior Lieutenants and four Senior Ensigns'; if any of these declined to 'avail himself of the means of promotion thus offered' or failed to 'acquit himself to the utmost of his ability', the duty was to 'be assigned to some Officer of more Zeal for the Service, either to the next in Seniority from his own Regiment or to an Officer from another Corps as H.R.H. may think proper'. In no case was any 'Subaltern who has not been an Officer Two Years...eligible to obtain the Rank of Captain by these means'; and so the same standard of experience and efficiency was required for promotion by recruiting as for promotion by purchase. Finally, as an incentive to exertion on the part of the young officers involved, the levy

---

[1] Duke of York to Windham, 18 March 1806, Windsor, 12407 ff.

was to be 'completed within Three Months'; and the men must undergo the regular and strict medical inspection before they were accepted as soldiers.[1]

This experiment in 'recruiting for rank' under what the Duke called 'certain restrictions' was apparently a success for he tried it again. In 1803, when it was decided that no field officer should be a troop or company commander, a number of vacancies for captains were created, and in 41 corps of infantry and cavalry a step in rank was offered to a lieutenant on condition that he recruited thirty men, and to a cornet or ensign on condition that he recruited ten. Again, the opportunity was offered first to the senior lieutenant and cornet or ensign in the corps, and if they declined it a special report was to be made to the Duke; again there was a time limit of three months, and no officer could become a captain who had not served two years.[2]

But this attempt at recruiting did not go very far. At about the same date the Addington government launched its Army of Reserve, a conscript body chosen by lot, designed for home defence, but raised in the hope that the men, once trained, would volunteer for the regular service. Conscripts on whom the lot fell were not required to serve personally if they could bribe a substitute to serve for them, and their eager hunt for substitutes absorbed many potential recruits. Thereupon a circular letter of 13 July 1803 awarded promotion to all officers who had undertaken to recruit, whether they had got their men or not.[3]

In 1804, four eminent Irishmen were permitted to become colonels provided they raised whole new battalions on similar conditions—a time limit, and rank to go only to regular officers already qualified for it—but the colonel was free to select such officers provided they paid him no money for the rank they attained under him.

Of these, none secured its men within the time limit and all were granted considerable extensions; finally one was accepted in December 1804; two more were accepted and its officers confirmed in their new rank in February 1805;[4] and one was broken up and its men drafted to other regiments because its colonel-to-be was found to have made 'Stipulations ...with several of his officers for pecuniary consideration'.[5] After these yet another new battalion was raised in Ireland in 1805, on the same conditions, and that seems to have been the end of 'recruiting for rank'. In 1806 Windham, as Minister for War, tried to remodel the whole

---

[1] Circular to Regiments of Infantry at Home, Colonels commanding Regiments, Army Agents and the Inspector General of Recruiting, 13 February 1801 ('General Orders and Circular Letters, 1801–1806', in the War Office Library).

[2] Circular of 13 February 1801 to officers commanding infantry regiments at home to army agents and Major General Hewett; General Order of 6 June 1803, War Office Library.

[3] Circular of 13 July 1803, War Office Library.

[4] Gordon to King, 28 February 1805, HO/50/400.

[5] Same to same, 2 February 1805, *ibid.*

recruiting system, and in 1807 his whole unfortunate experiment was revised in a very practical manner by Castlereagh; thereafter, there was little occasion to resort to 'recruiting for rank'.

The Duke had been able to begin applying his new rules on promotion to the troops in Great Britain as soon as he became their commander in 1795. Ireland, however, retained its own army, under a separate Commander-in-Chief and an independent War Office, up to the union of 1801. Till then promotion in Ireland remained in the civilian hands of the Lord Lieutenant. That, to be sure, had not always been the case. Before 1767 the Commander-in-Chief in Ireland had submitted recommendations for promotion to the king and at least in form the army was under military control till then. In that year, however, Ireland received a new Lord Lieutenant who was a soldier of some distinction. This was Lord Townshend, brother to the 'Mosaic Ministry's' notorious Chancellor of the Exchequer and the man who had succeeded to the command of the British Army on the Heights of Abraham on 13 September 1759, when Wolfe was killed and Monckton wounded. Townshend had insisted that he, being a soldier, should supervise promotion in Ireland while he was Lord Lieutenant and his demand had been granted. When his stormy and unpopular Lord Lieutenancy ended in September 1772, the reason why he had controlled promotion was apparently forgotten and 'the patronage of the Army' was retained by 'Lord Harcourt who succeeded him, although not a military man'.[1] From Harcourt in turn it passed on to successive Lords Lieutenant and was used unashamedly for political ends. The result is familiar to all who know Irish history. Efficiency rotted away in regiments whose officers possessed no military qualification for the rank they held. When Sir Ralph Abercromby came to the wretched island as Commander-in-Chief, late in 1797, he found its 'army to be in a state of licentiousness which must render it formidable to everyone but the enemy', and he declared as much in a general order of 26 February 1798.[2] Holland Rose stigmatizes this order as 'incredibly foolish' and an 'outrageous insult'.[3] It may indeed have been tactless, but unfortunately it was no insult. It was on the contrary the literal truth, as Cornwallis found within a matter of months when he had to deal with the invasion, or rather raid, of the mere 1000-odd French troops who landed at Killala Bay under General Humbert in August 1798.

It was, therefore, a most fortunate thing that after 1 January 1801 George III refused to receive any recommendations for promotion in Ireland except through the Duke of York.[4] Dublin Castle, where the third Earl of Hardwicke now reigned as Lord Lieutenant, struggled hard

[1] Duke of York to Lord Hardwicke, 12 August 1801, Hardwicke Papers, B.M. Addit. MSS. 35, 349.
[2] Rose, *William Pitt and the Great War*, p. 353.
[3] *Ibid.* pp. 353–4.   [4] York to Hardwicke, *ut supra*.

to retain its patronage. On 8 August 1801 the Duke is found writing the King 'every day proves more and more the necessity of taking compleatly out of the Lord Lieutenant's hands the control of the Army...he is making every effort in his power to regain that Patronage, and states openly the importance of it as a necessary means of carrying on his Government'.[1] But Hardwicke's efforts were unavailing. The new Commander of the Forces in Ireland, General Sir William Medowes, had already received a private letter from the Duke of York ordering him, 'On all subjects relating to promotions in the Army serving in Ireland, you will direct your Military Secretary to correspond with Colonel Brownrigg to whom he will transmit Weekly the applications and memorials, with a Schedule of their contents and stating your opinion and observations on the merits of the cases referred to'. The same letter contained explicit instructions about the training, discipline and interior economy of regiments, and its date marks the beginning of the regeneration of the army in Ireland as an effective military force.[2]

All these rules on promotion by purchase and promotion by recruiting were made by the Duke out of his own sufficient authority as Commander-in-Chief, and, since he had made the rules, he was quite prepared to waive them, when good reason could be given. How freely he modified the conditions on which he permitted recruiting for rank has already been shown. More striking still is his free handling, on very rare occasions, of the rule that no young gentleman could become an officer before he had turned sixteen. The object of this rule was, of course, to end the abuse by which 'a commission (might) be obtained for a child in a cradle'. Yet that abuse had an old, lawful and not dishonourable origin. It was authorized by a regulation of Queen Anne which declared...'for the future' (a phrase indicating the practice was already old), 'no person that is not of age sufficient to serve shall be admitted into any of Her Majesty's troops, except the children of officers who have been slain or suffered extremely in the service, in which case the merits of the father may make it reasonable to show that mark of Her Majesty's royal favour to the son'.[3] The only two cases I have found of the Duke allowing youngsters to hold commissions before they were sixteen conform precisely to Queen Anne's regulation; the boys concerned were the sons of an officer killed in action under Sir Charles Grey in the West Indies. As one of them was in his turn killed in action in the Pyrenees, and the other lived to be Queen Victoria's Field Marshal Sir William Gomme, one may feel that they justified the exception which the Duke made in their favour.

Likewise the Duke had a ready sympathy for the poor but keen officers who could not afford to purchase. For their benefit he maintained a list

[1] Windsor, 10349–50.
[2] 28 May 1801. B.M. Addit. MSS. 35, 728.
[3] Cited in the Report of the Commissioners of Naval and Military Inquiry, 1840, p. xxxii.

of meritorious officers to which he referred when opportunities for free promotion by selection occurred. The confidential reports on officers, which he required, helped him to fill this list; and it was a subject on which his Military Secretary was given to making particular and confidential inquiries of first-rate officers, like Sir John Moore and Colonel Manningham of the 95th Rifles.

How well all these regulations worked in practice is a hard question to answer, and one that cannot be disentangled from the controversy over the relations of Wellington with the Duke of York, which has been raised by Mr Godfrey Davies. In that controversy there is on the one side York's criticism made to Greville, that Wellington 'was unwilling to bring forward men of talent'.[1] On the other side there are Wellington's complaints that he had not the patronage due to the commander of an army, and his assertion of March 1814 that 'the utter incapacity of some officers at the head of regiments...and the apathy and unwillingness of others' was due 'to the promotion of officers in regiments by regular rotation, thus holding forth no reward to merit or exertion'.[2]

Here, as always, one thing that helps to clarify the problem is a careful examination of chronology, and when this examination is made, Davies's accusations against the Duke lose foundation. For it is to be recalled that the Duke of York resigned the command-in-chief on Saturday, 17 March 1809 and he did not resume it till May 1811. For any frustrations Wellington suffered between these dates, not York, but his replacement, Sir David Dundas, was responsible; so for example it is Dundas who is the target of Wellington's complaint of 11 January 1811, 'I am the commander of the British army without any of the patronage or power that an officer in this situation has always had. I have remonstrated against this system in vain.'[3]

But Sir David Dundas himself got no particular pleasure out of his military patronage. One of his first and least pleasant experiences as Commander-in-Chief was to have a case of alleged over-rapid promotion made the subject of a debate and a division in the House of Commons on which the government was actually beaten in May 1809.[4] It is hardly surprising if, after that embarrassing occurrence, Sir David stuck like a limpet to the letter of the rules, and rejected all recommendations for accelerated promotion on grounds of merit. It would be equally natural if Wellington, after two years of rebuffs from Dundas, ceased to try to 'put forward men of talent'. In fact, he himself declared as much as early as 4 September 1809 when he wrote Brigadier General Alexander Campbell: 'I will give you any letter you please, but it will only subject you to the mortification of a disappointment and me to that of making

---

[1] Godfrey Davies, *Wellington and his Army*, p. 43.
[2] *Ibid.* p. 51.   [3] *Ibid.*
[4] Davies himself describes this incident (*ibid.* pp. 60–1).

another request in vain in favour of a person who deserves the King's favour'.[1]

The pity of it all is that York himself was not hostile to those recommendations on behalf of a commander's subordinates which Wellington had ceased to consider worth making. Cases of York's military secretary actually inviting such recommendations have already been noted. Godfrey Davies himself remarks that in 1808 the men whom Wellington recommended for promotion after Vimeiro got the rank he asked for them.[2] Again, after York had returned to office, he gave Wellington as strong backing as any man could ask when in July 1813 he promised him his 'cordial support in the dismissal of any officer, from the senior General to the lowest ensign'.[3] But it would seem that by this time Wellington had, as he supposed, learnt his lesson and concluded that he had no business making recommendations for promotion. The misunderstanding of the two men is perhaps best regarded as one of the unfortunate consequences of Mary Ann Clarke, who made both York and the business of promotion the subjects of a scandal at a singularly inconvenient time for Wellington.

It is, however, also to be recognized that with the best will in the world the Commander-in-Chief could not heed all the wishes of any local commander and had to be cautious in awarding promotion for merit.

Fortune has much to do with 'merit'; or, at least, distinction can only be won in battle by the man who has the luck to be in the right place at the right time. Rules applicable to a whole army cannot be too readily waived in favour of the part of it that happens to have been in action. The Duke of York's rules in particular had been designed because it was absolutely necessary to have some barrier against promotion by favouritism; and the distinction between the virtue of rewarding merit and the vice of pandering to favourites will remain a very tricky one to draw as long as merit itself remains a matter of personal judgement. Certainly the army was far better off with the Duke of York's rules, as he administered them, than it had been without them; and on that point Wellington may fairly be quoted. At the inquiry into the Duke of York's conduct over Mary Ann Clarke, Wellington was questioned and gave evidence as follows:

I know that since His Royal Highness has had the command of the army, the regulations framed by him for managing the promotion of the army have been strictly adhered to, and that the mode in which the promotion is conducted has given general satisfaction...the officers are improved in knowledge; that the staff of the army is much better than it was...that the system of subordination among the officers of the army is better than it was...and everything that relates to the military discipline of the soldiers and the military efficiency of the army has been greatly improved since His Royal Highness was appointed Commander-in-Chief.

[1] Godfrey Davies, *Wellington and his Army*, p. 54 and Gurwood, v.
[2] *Ibid.* p. 61.   [3] *Ibid.* p. 54.

Finally, in reply to another question, Wellington added: 'The improvements to which I have adverted, have been owing to the regulations of His Royal Highness and to his personal superintendence and his personal exertions over the general officers and others who were to see those regulations carried into execution.'[1]

It would be hard to pay a stronger tribute than that to the achievement of any reformer. No doubt there were still flaws that could be complained of. Unfortunately, there always will be on this side of Heaven.

[1] *Stratford's Authentic Edition of the Investigation of the Charges Brought against H.R.H. the Duke of York by Gwyllym Lloyd Wardle, Esq.* (London, n.d.), II, pp. 352–3.

CHAPTER 7

DISCIPLINE AND PUNISHMENT

I DO not altogether like this chapter heading, for it is a vulgar error to confound discipline with uniformity of conduct inspired by fear of punishment. Essentially, discipline means loyal co-operation toward a common end. It reaches its peak in the team spirit that leads a good rugby side or boat race crew to obey its coach without the suggestion of penalties ever being made; and during the Second World War a discipline of virtually this standard was reached in the British Army by those commandos which used no other sanction than that of sending an unsatisfactory man back to the unit from which he originally came. Some might indeed call a high team spirit in a military unit 'good morale', but good morale and good discipline are Siamese twins. There is no separating them. Discipline declines whenever morale deteriorates, and so does morale when discipline becomes lax, for the enthusiasm, which forms so large a part of morale, cannot co-exist with slackness that leaves unpunished the bad or lazy soldier who lets his unit down. So discipline, morale, and punishment all hang together.

What discipline is most commonly expected to produce is implicit and prompt obedience, but such obedience is by no means the whole of discipline. Intelligence is necessary too, and there are times when loyal co-operation toward a common end may require disobedience. No commander is infallible and for want of sufficiently detailed knowledge anyone may on occasion give orders which hinder, instead of forwarding, the purpose in view. Then the good subordinate will ignore his orders and act on his own initiative—as, for example, on 15 June 1815 the Duke of Saxe-Weimar ignored the instructions to move which he received and instead held the position of Quatre Bas on his own initiative; on this action the fate of the next day depended, so far as Wellington's forces were concerned; and therefore no one could call Saxe-Weimar's conduct ill-disciplined, though it was certainly not obedient.

The things that make good discipline are firmness and fairness—firmness that leaves no room for sloppy tolerance of poor conduct or half-performance; fairness that is meticulous in imposing no punishment on the man who has failed in spite of doing his best. Because an injured sense of grievance is incompatible with either good morale or good discipline, tact and understanding are as necessary as rules, regulations, and courts martial; praise for good conduct is at least as valuable as penalties for bad conduct. The qualities of 'the man at the top' are all-important; if he has moral courage, firmness, tact, and a quick appreciation of good work, he will produce well-disciplined subordinates; if he lacks those qualities, he cannot. And that is our reason for placing our chapters in the order in which they stand; as there cannot be good discipline where there are not good officers, this chapter necessarily follows the chapter on 'Appointments and Promotions'—and it must itself begin with the discipline of officers.

Previous pages have given some hint of what was wrong with the discipline of officers. All too many of them practised the shameful crime of absence without leave with no compunction and no penalties. This crime became more common as the months of war progressed through 1793 and on through 1794. Officers, who were generally men of wealthy families and sometimes Members of Parliament, were indeed not easily governed in a country which was ruled through Parliament and in which Parliament was sensitive to wealth and family connexions. No minister of cabinet rank was concerned with the army till a Secretary of State for War was appointed in 1794, nor was discipline the Secretary of State's responsibility even then; in peacetime at least administrations were often too concerned with using the army as a source of patronage to be very particular about the conduct of those they patronized; there was no Commander-in-Chief to supervise discipline till the aged Amherst was appointed in 1793, and when 'the patronage of the army' came into his hands, he showed little taste for making personal enemies or alienating people for the army's good. As for the Adjutant General, he was too subordinate an official to take a strong line with the powerful and well connected. He indeed could, and did, write letters; the records of his office contain quite sternly expressed missives bidding absent officers to return to their units. But all his industry accomplished little, as plainly appears from his own confession to a harassed major-general on 5 February 1795:

You have too much reason [he wrote] to complain of the number of officers absent on one pretence or another from their respective corps, and I have done everything I possibly can to remedy the Evil:— but unless a few severe examples are made, by either bringing some of the most culpable of the many Delinquents of this sort before a General Court Martial or by superseding them without Tryal, it will, I fear, be impracticable to put an effectual stop to this flagrant breach of all Discipline and good Order.[1]

A second offence, hardly less damaging to true discipline than this, was the reckless disloyalty with which officers felt free to criticize their superiors. It was this, in the opinion of William Windham, which destroyed the authority and usefulness of the Duke of York as commander of the army in the Netherlands in 1794. Again, it contributed much to the troubles of Moore on his retreat to Corunna, and Wellington had to win a number of victories before he won a reputation against which it was

[1] Adjutant General to Major General Small, 5 February 1795, WO/3/13.

unavailing. For this was a fault that was not easily cured. It had little opportunity to make itself felt except on active service; even then it was silenced while operations went well, but only to break out in a manner astonishing to Moore when fortune turned and orders were given that neither officers nor men were in a position to understand. It was, in short, a vice only to be corrected by much practical experience in the field.

Finally, the officers of 1793–4 were a sadly drunken lot. Fortescue writes of them in his vivid fashion:

Hard drinking...was, of course, sedulously cultivated by these aspirants to the rank of gentlemen and it was no uncommon thing for regiments to start on the march under the charge of the Adjutant and Sergeant-major only, while the officers stayed behind, to come galloping up several hours later, full of wine, careless where they rode, careless of the confusion into which they threw the columns, careless of everything but the place appointed for the end of the march, if by chance they were sober enough to have remembered it.[1]

No footnote accompanies this passage, yet there is no reason to disbelieve it. These contemptible regimental officers were no worse than some of the staff who were supposed to direct them. Stapleton Cotton, the future Lord Combermere, served in Flanders from August 1793 through 1794 and in his family was preserved the tradition that,

At this time the excesses in many regiments, and even those of the generals in command, were such as would not be credited by sober members of the profession in our own time [i.e. 1866]. In Flanders, General Erskine was never to be seen after a certain hour, however urgent the necessity for his presence; while at headquarters the officers of the staff were generally assisted to bed at night by attendants nearly as tipsy as themselves.[2]

All told, the Duke of York had plenty to do in the way of restoring discipline when he took over the command-in-chief in 1795. Most fortunately he had the personality the job required. He was a man of his word, who neither created grievances by breaking promises nor encouraged misconduct by uttering unfulfilled threats; he had an ample share of the graciousness of manner which won his elder brother the scarcely deserved title of 'the First Gentleman of Europe'; his patience was great; and his royal blood, because it made him far less vulnerable to political intrigue than any commoner could have been, was one of his greatest assets. His tools were wise regulation, reproof, the Royal Prerogative, and the full rigour of military law.

Wise regulations bearing on discipline were two—enforcing the use of the regular regimental channel of communication in applying for promotion, and the institution of confidential reports. The first has been described in our chapter on promotion, where also the statement of its

---

[1] Fortescue, *British Army*, IV, 297.
[2] Mary, Viscountess of Combermere and Captain W. W. Knollys, *Memoirs and Correspondence of F.M. Viscount Combermere* (London, 1866), pp. 30–1.

purpose was quoted, 'it is considered to have the effect of inducing young officers to look up to their Commanding Officers'; and the effect of instituting confidential reports on officers would be the same. These were probably the things which did most to bring about the great decline in drunkenness with which the Duke is credited.[1] With them may be associated another practice which says much for the Duke's patience and sense of duty. 'During the winter and spring months he held a familiar military levee every Tuesday, to which *all officers* [my italics] have access.'[2] The usual hour of attendance was 'one o'clock. It is not required that officers should be regimentally dressed on these occasions....Individuals are introduced in rotation as their names are set down, without distinction of rank.' Personal grievances, of the kind that corrode morale and injure discipline, could hardly remain unknown to so approachable a chief. That these levees must often have been tedious in extreme to the Duke can hardly be doubted, but that they were useful to the army would seem certain.

As the hardest problems for the disciplinarian occur on occasions when the wrong thing is done and bad results follow, without any clear regulation being actually broken, a couple of examples of how the Duke of York handled these situations may usefully illustrate his capacity for sound judgement and fair dealing. The first case occurred in 1795, when the newly raised, and inefficient, regiment of one Colonel Tweem was broken up (like others of the same class) so that its men could be dispersed among other and better units; but in the case of Colonel Tweem's regiment, the men mutinied before they would consent to be dispersed. The Duke, after receiving from other sources than the colonel what was evidently pretty detailed information on what actually happened, instituted no action against the men, but directed the Adjutant General to write Tweem that 'H.R.H. can only impute [the mutiny] to negligence in not having the men's accounts settled in regular and proper manner previous to their being drafted into General Fox's Regiment'; Tweem was further reprimanded for not reporting the incident and ordered to send H.R.H. an account of it.[3] Such a reprimand was about all that could be done for a colonel whose incompetence had already cost him the command of the regiment he had tried to raise, and the fault of the men was fairly regarded as too understandable to be punishable.

A less simple case arose in the summer of 1805 in the King's Regiment of Dragoon Guards. The commanding officer, a Major Balcombe, gave way to 'unsoldierlike and refractory conduct' on the part of the men,

---

[1] 'Intoxication is an odious vice; and since the Duke of York has been at the head of the army, officers have ceased to pride themselves on the insensate capability of drinking' (Sir Robert Wilson, *Enquiry into the Present State of the Military Force of Great Britain*, cited by Henry Marshall, *Military Miscellany*, London, 1846, p. 165).
[2] Charles James, *The Regimental Companion*, 7th ed. (1811), I, 2–3.
[3] Fawcett to Tweem, 24 February 1795, WO/3/13.

who also had some apparent (and this time probably imagined) grievances about their pay; and, like Colonel Tweem, Major Balcombe tried to hush the affair up without reporting it. Nevertheless, a pretty full account evidently reached the Duke, who took two steps. First, he promptly sent Balcombe's superior officer, Major General Hugonin, on 17 July, to assemble the regiment and reprove them; likewise to reprove Balcombe and the officers who had advised him; and finally to read at the head of the regiment 'H.M.'s Warrant of 1797' on the pay of Dragoons, which was also to be republished in Brigade Orders.[1] Secondly, he had Lord Chatham make a special investigation and report of all the circumstances, which the Adjutant General acknowledged in a letter of 16 September 1805; and this letter continues that H.R.H.

much laments that he is under necessity of declaring that Major Balcombe's conduct, under circumstances, which demanded his utmost Exertion and Energy, has...been marked by a want of both which totally unfits him from hereafter exercising his command in the King's Dragoon Guards with advantage to H.M.'s service. Under these circumstances, there remains no alternative to Major Balcombe, but to make his request to retire from the service; and in that case H.R.H., bearing in his recollection the length of Major Balcombe's services, and still retaining a wish to give every proof in his power of his approbation of them, will recommend to H.M. that he shall be allowed to dispose of the Commission he holds (which he did not purchase) by sale.[2]

So that incident was closed in a manner which would seem hard to criticize. No men were punished, although they had certainly deserved it. The moment for punishing passed when their commanding officer yielded, without making any arrests or laying any charges, and it would have been a breach of faith to proceed against them for offences which he had, in effect, pardoned; nothing more could be done for them than Major General Hugonin's reproof. Nor could Balcombe be punished; want of 'Exertion and Energy' is not a criminal offence. Yet the incident was not ignored, and the way it was handled would seem a model of common sense, adequate firmness, and no small degree of generosity (since Balcombe was permitted to sell an unbought commission).

A sterner penalty than Major Balcombe suffered was to deprive an officer of his commission, whether bought or unbought, without permitting him to sell it. This was indeed a very strong exercise of the Royal Prerogative, and it could not be done lightly. The celebrated case of Lord George Sackville's trial, after his misconduct at Minden, had established the precedent that a man dismissed from the service by the King could appeal to a court martial: and, therefore, though in Sackville's case the court's verdict supported the King's action, no Commander-in-Chief

[1] Calvert to Hugonin, 31 July 1805, WO/3/39.
[2] Calvert to Chatham, 16 November 1805, WO/3/39.

could recommend an officer's dismissal without being very sure of his ground.[1] Yet the Duke of York made much use of dismissal (or supersession, as it was also called), for it was by this sanction that he stamped out the far too prevalent crime of absence without leave.

The Duke was certainly, and no doubt wisely, slow to tackle this offence. His first task on receiving the command-in-chief was to get to know the army he was to rule. He undoubtedly learnt a very great deal from the Adjutant General, Sir William Fawcett, whose patience (as noted) had already been sorely tried by 'the number of officers absent on one pretext or another from their respective corps'; but he seems to have wished to acquire his own knowledge of the army for himself, and also to perfect a system of detecting the crime of absence without leave before he took action against it. Likewise any reformer does well to tackle one abuse at a time, and (as has been told) in the first summer of his command the Duke's prime task was training, to restore to the army the uniformity of manœuvre it had so long lacked. So little was done early in 1795 to compel the attendance of officers with their regiments, though during the summer some general circular letters were sent to the army agents requiring absent officers to join their corps promptly on pain of supersession without trial, if they failed to do so.[2] Meanwhile the Duke was for much of the summer touring England and inspecting troops in one military district after another; and the Adjutant General, secure now in the support of a strong chief, pressed hard to get the evidence by which the magnitude of the offence of unlawful absence could be assessed.

To obtain that evidence, it was only necessary to enforce upon commanding officers long-standing orders about sending in proper periodic returns. That these orders had in many cases been forgotten seems evident from a letter Fawcett wrote to one Lt. Col. Benson on 20 May 1795: 'concerning the Returns of the Troops', he wrote, 'it has always been the practice, in Camp as well as in Quarters, for every Regiment to send up separately to my office a Weekly State...—a Fortnight's Return of the present and absent officers—a Monthly Return on the first of every month, Forms of which I enclose herewith'.[3] The Adjutant General was thenceforth to war on all commanders who failed to be punctual with their returns;[4] and those returns were obviously not filed unread when

---

[1] It is true, of course, that a man's request for a court martial did not, and does not, necessarily have to be granted, but what the Crown has legal power to do, and what it may in fact wisely do, are often different things. The King at the beginning of the nineteenth century had still an authority in the army which required him to use his own judgement, and his position was hardly so invulnerable as that of the Prime Minister who, in 1918 with an overwhelming majority behind him, denied Sir Hubert Gough the court martial he requested.

[2] On 12 July and 24 August 1795, WO/3/13.

[3] Fawcett to Benson, 20 May 1795, WO/3/13.

[4] For example, Circular to 23rd and 88th Foot, 3rd Fencible Infantry, Royal Manx Fencibles, Loyal Tay Fencibles, 22 July 1796 (Adjutant General to 49th Regt., 5 July 1796, WO/3/15).

they reached his office; they were diligently compared with one another from week to week and fortnight to fortnight, and were sometimes sent back for correction by their authors.[1] Over and above them, in the summer of 1795 the Duke further required a special fortnightly state to be submitted from June to September which was to show the number of officers and rank and file present with each unit, the number absent or needed to complete its establishment, and the quantity and condition of the unit's clothing, weapons, and ammunition. Finally, on 5 September 1795, on his return from his tour of the Northern District, the Duke sent letters to the agents of twenty-nine specifically named regiments ordering that the colonels of those regiments be informed that any officers who were absent 'such only excepted as may be employed on the Recruiting service or be prevented by Illness duly certified by the faculty' should join 'by the 15th of this month at the latest on the failure of which they will be reported to H.M. and superseded'.

In the next spring the Duke continued this campaign against absent officers with similar letters to no fewer than forty regiments of horse and foot, including both regulars and fencibles. These letters bore results that were sometimes recorded in red ink on the file copies; as, for example, in the cases of a captain, a lieutenant, and an ensign of the 10th Regiment of Foot: '1 June, their resignations in the agent's hands'; or of two captains, one lieutenant, and five ensigns of the 12th Regiment of Foot: '28 May, Captain James recruiting, other addresses not known'. And the last entry—'address unknown'—is astonishingly frequent, but it also explains why the agent was a common channel through whom these orders were issued. It was through the agent that an officer received his pay, and therefore he might be expected to keep in touch with his agent even when his commanding officer lost track of him. However, the Duke's drive against absent officers was clearly successful; some joined, some hurried to sell their commissions before they forfeited them, others were superseded and lost the investment they had made in military rank. Years later it was stated to a parliamentary inquiry that many of the officers superseded at this time were children too young to join; and this statement is often supported by the fact that the red marginal notes on the Adjutant General's letters show that some absent officers had never joined their regiments since their appointment, and that such officers were usually ensigns, cornets, or second lieutenants.[2]

Good general rules about leave were now either revived or made. One standing regulation, which only required to be enforced, was that all leaves must end and all officers be present with their units by 10 March

---

[1] Calvert to Officer Commanding West London Regiment of Militia, 30 November 1796 and to East Norfolk Militia, 10 February 1796, WO/3/15.

[2] For example, Adjutant General to 20th and 87th Regiments, 25 May 1796; to 6th Dragoon Guards, 8 June 1796; to Royal Welsh Fuzileers, 8 June 1796, WO/3/28.

every spring,[1] but that this was often forgotten appears from a circular to General Officers Commanding Districts of 22 March 1797. These eminent officers were reminded of the regulations and ordered both to report officers who failed to obey them and to recommend successors to take their places; further, these generals were to see to it that when an officer obtained leave the name of the person granting the leave and the date on which it expired were to be clearly and accurately stated in every regimental return.[2] The Duke's firmness in this matter evidently created some dismay among indulgent senior officers who hated to refuse a man's request for leave, yet dared not break the regulations, and they endeavoured to evade responsibility for doing either by referring applications to the Commander-in-Chief. Their only reward was a blunt circular of 24 March 1798 declaring that this practice must stop, as 'it is extremely embarrassing for H.R.H. who cannot be so competent a judge of the possibility of dispensing with the attendance of officers with their regiments on urgent occasions as the General Officers in whose districts such regiments are serving'.[3] Three grounds only were allowed to justify an officer's absence from his regiment after the 10th of March—attendance in Parliament, if he were an M.P.; recruiting; and urgent private business of a nature that both required the officer's personal attention and could not be postponed.

An officer's ill health was, of course, a personal reason for which absence could not be refused, provided the ill health were genuine. That the Duke began in September 1795 by requiring illness to be 'duly certified by the faculty' has already been noted. In March 1800 he tightened this rule; thereafter officers requiring sick leave were to obtain a certificate, preferably from 'a Staff Surgeon or Physician', and 'where this, for local circumstances, is impossible, the Certificate must be signed by some surgeon of a Regiment; and when this cannot be obtained, it must be signed by some known Practitioner in Physic or Surgery', but in the last case 'the Respectability of the Signature of these Reports' was to be carefully studied by the Army Medical Board.[4] The final loophole of the pleasure-loving or work-shy officer was thus plugged.

Leave in winter time was something on which the Duke was generous; up to half the staff officers, half the captains, and one-third of the subalterns in each military district were permitted to be away at one time;[5] but spring, summer, and autumn were the months when serious training took place, and invasion would occur, if it ever came.

So far no mention has been made of courts martial. There was relatively

[1] Adjutant General to Colonel Sir J. St Clair Erskine, 2 April 1796, WO/3/15.
[2] Circular to General Officers Commanding Districts, 23 March 1797, WO/3/17.
[3] Circular to General Officers Commanding Districts, 24 March 1798, WO/3/18.
[4] Calvert to Matthew Lewis, 13 March 1800, WO/3/32.
[5] Circular to General Officers Commanding Districts, 12 October 1797, WO/3/31. Repeated on 20 November 1799, WO/3/32.

little occasion to use them to deal with officers who had a real stake in their military careers, with commissions to lose and hopes of promotion. Yet at times officers committed crimes which required a court's investigation and punishment, and courts had constantly to be used to punish the offences of other ranks; and military law must now be discussed.

That the great Sir William Blackstone did the army's discipline much harm scarcely admits of question. In his brilliantly successful 'best-seller' on the Laws of England, he writes in terms calculated to bring military law into contempt. In wartime, he says, 'more regular discipline *may* perhaps be necessary, than can be expected from a mere militia',[1] but 'particular provisions...for...the due regulation and discipline of soldiery...are to be looked upon only as temporary excrescences bred out of the distemper of the state';[2] and then he continues with the extraordinary statement: 'Martial Law [being] built upon no settled principles...is...in truth and reality no law...and therefore it ought not to be permitted in time of peace, when the King's courts are open for all persons to receive justice according to the laws of the land'.[3]

Small wonder if discipline declined in an army whose martial law was so vigorously, if absurdly, impugned by such an authority; and indeed, following Blackstone's doctrine, a sergeant, convicted in 1792 of knowingly perpetrating a fraudulent enlistment, actually appealed to the civil courts against the competence of the court martial which had sentenced him to punishment.[4] But Sergeant George Samuel Grant's plea could not be maintained, and it is indeed a pity that his case did not arise sooner than 1792. Discipline could only have benefited from an earlier judgement that the kind of martial law, to which Blackstone referred, did 'not exist in England at all', and that there was no gainsaying the authority of the Mutiny Act, against which Grant had appealed.

The facts about courts martial are, of course, that they were instituted by the Crown under the authority of the Mutiny Act; that the crimes they punished and the penalties they awarded were in most cases those expressly provided in the Mutiny Act; that, the life of the Mutiny Act being limited to twelve months only, this law was annually revised by all the collective intelligence, humanity, and legal wisdom of both houses of Parliament; and that, though the King was empowered to frame other rules and penalties than those the Act prescribed, these additions became void as soon as the Act itself ran out at its appointed time. It was then

[1] My italics; the use of the subjunctive here is an extraordinary display of Blackstone's ignorance.

[2] *Commentaries on the Law of England* (1765), I, 400.

[3] *Ibid.*

[4] A summary of the case is given by Alexander F. Tytler, *An Essay on Military Law and the Practice of Courts Martial*, 3rd ed. (1814), 23–6 n. This edition of Tytler's book, edited by Major Charles James, is made valuable by the addition of 'MS Observations...by the late Sir Charles Morgan on the first edition'; as Judge Advocate General, Morgan was the country's leading authority on military law.

well said that English military law was 'more truly and immediately formed by the people itself than any other of the existing statutes of the realm'.[1] Indeed, the Duke of Richmond (in answering criticism of his new-founded Corps of Military Artificers in 1788) declared that in his belief 'no species of trial, however popular it might be, was...more fair and candid than trials by court martial'.[2] This is a very modern-sounding statement, for those who know both civil and military law are prepared to say the same today, and there seems no reason to believe it any less true in Richmond's time than in our own. That is not to say that military law could not be severe; it could be, and was, but so far as fairness could be secured by a code, successive framers of the Mutiny Acts, through the annual deliberations of a hundred years, had done their best.

Martial law was applicable to 'every person...commissioned or in pay as an officer, or...enlisted or in pay as a non-commissioned officer or soldier'.[3] It had force over the militia during the period when those troops were assembled for training and exercise. In 1804 it was extended to apply to the volunteers when called to arms to meet an actual invasion or rebellion or insurrection within the kingdom; and officers and N.C.O.'s of the permanent training staff of these two semi-military forces were 'at all times subject to the Mutiny Act and Articles of War'.[4]

Military Courts were of three types—General, Garrison, and Regimental Courts Martial.

A Regimental Court Martial had no power to inflict the death penalty or to punish a commissioned officer. It should consist of five officers 'excepting in cases where that number cannot be conveniently assembled when *three* may be sufficient'.[5] In normal practice it consisted of a captain, as president, and four subalterns, whose sentence had to be confirmed by the regiment's colonel or commanding officer. A Garrison Court Martial only differed 'from a regimental one by being composed of officers of different regiments', and 'the governor, or other commanding officer of the garrison' approved their sentence.[6]

A General Court Martial had to consist of not less than thirteen members. It alone could punish an officer or inflict sentence of death, but the death sentence required the concurrence of at least nine of the thirteen members of the court, or of 'two thirds of the number present, where the court consists of more than thirteen'.[7] Then, as now, officers appointed to serve on courts martial swore the familiar oath not to 'disclose or discover the vote or opinion' of any fellow member of the court; then too, as now, the junior member of the court gave his opinion first.[8] Unlike the jury

---

[1] *Ibid.* p. 7.
[2] *Annual Register* (1788), p. 123.
[3] Tytler, *op. cit.* pp. 110–11.
[4] *Ibid.* pp. 114, 117–18.
[5] *Ibid.* p. 177.
[6] James, *Military Dictionary, sub* 'Courts Martial'.
[7] Tytler, *op. cit.* p. 136.
[8] *Ibid.* p. 227.

of a civil court, members of a court martial did not need to be unanimous in their verdict, and so no violence was done to the conscience of a minority. For this reason courts always consisted of an odd number of officers, so that there would not be a 'tie' in the voting. When the majority of a court, which was not unanimous in its verdict, voted guilty, only those who so voted were asked their opinion as to what the penalty should be; but the number of those who held the prisoner innocent was added to the score of those voting for the mildest of all the penalties proposed. Except in cases of urgency, courts were not permitted to sit for more than seven hours a day—from 8.00 a.m. to 3.00 p.m.; that is to say, their business was to be done by men whose minds were fresh. All evidence was taken down in writing; and either the sovereign or subordinate authority to whom the power of instituting courts was deputed had power to review the sentence. No sentence could be inflicted till the reviewing authority had confirmed it; that authority could reduce a severe sentence, but not increase a soft one; instead, it could require the court once to re-examine its own decision; but a case, after being submitted to one General Court Martial, could not be taken from it and resubmitted to another and different court for a second trial. There was, however, a right of appeal from a Regimental to a General Court Martial.

The presiding genius of a General Court Martial was a remarkable character with the still extant and paradoxical name of the Judge Advocate. His functions have altered much in a century and a half. He pronounced no judgement, though in theory he was the most ambidextrous of advocates. He was primarily a public prosecutor, bound to draft the charge and produce witnesses to prove it; but, before a court composed of officers, with no other than a military training, he stood, as he still does, as a legal expert to whom the court referred questions on points of law; and 'on every occasion when the court demands his opinion, he is bound to give it with freedom and amplitude; and even when not requested to deliver his sentiments, his duty requires that he should put the court on their guard against any deviation, either from any essential or necessary forms in their proceedings, or a violation of material justice in their final sentence and judgement'.[1] Nor was that the end of his duty to dispense legal advice. 'Another part' of his duty, 'which, though not enjoined by any particular enactment of Military Law yet has the sanction of general and established practice, is that he should assist the prisoner in the conduct of his defence.'[2] Certainly such assistance was often needed, especially by 'private soldiers, who, wanting all advantages of education, or opportunities of mental improvement, must stand greatly in need of advice in such trying circumstances';[3] yet it is extraordinary that the prosecutor should have been the man expected to help

---

[1] Tytler, *op. cit.* p. 354.   [2] *Ibid.* p. 355.
[3] *Ibid.*

the accused to baffle the prosecution. The surprise which this practice arouses is little allayed by the rider that we are not to understand that the Judge-Advocate should...consider himself as bound to do the duty of a counsel in exerting his ingenuity to defend the prisoner at all hazards against those charges which in his capacity as prosecutor, he is...bound to urge and sustain by proof.... All that is required is, that, in the same manner as in Civil courts of criminal jurisdiction, the judges are understood to be of counsel with the persons accused, [so] the Judge Advocate, in Courts Martial, shall do justice to the cause of the prisoner, by giving its full weight to every circumstance and argument in his favour.[1]

Even this seems to demand of the Judge Advocate more than can be fairly expected of any one man at one time, and that without doing as much for the accused as full fairness would require.

When the preliminaries, the swearing in of the court, the reading of the charges, had been finished, the Judge Advocate opened proceedings by stating the case and citing the witnesses for the prosecution. In a court martial, but not as a rule in the civil courts of the day, the witnesses were examined separately, and none was allowed to be in court to hear the evidence of the man summoned before him;[2] in this point certainly the practice of military was superior to that of civil courts. The evidence, when written down, was commonly checked by being read back to the witness. When the prosecution's case was concluded, the court, if requested, adjourned to give the prisoner 'as much time as may reasonably allow him to prepare himself, according to the length of the evidence and the nature of the charges'.[3] 'The statement of his defence', continues our authority, 'is generally written, and ought to be read by himself, but may be read by the Judge Advocate at the prisoner's request; and then his witnesses in support of it are examined.'[4] No counsel was allowed to speak for a prisoner nor at this date was a defending officer appointed to assist him; yet the prisoner was permitted to have counsel in court, to advise him how he should speak in his own defence; and presumably counsel might actually write out the statement he was to read in his own defence and prepare questions to be put to his witnesses. Finally, when all was finished, the entire written proceedings were read over to the court, no member of which had to keep his own notes or rely on his own memory in forming his opinion; here too courts martial seem at least as 'fair and candid' as any civil court.

All through this procedure it is hard to see what element making for fairness had been overlooked—the separate examination of witnesses, the written evidence, the adjournment to allow the prisoner to prepare his defence, permission for the prisoner to have counsel's aid in its preparation, the written statement in the prisoner's defence, which placed no

---

[1] *Ibid.* p. 356.   [2] *Ibid.* p. 248.
[3] It will be observed that in this period a court martial was not preceded by a summary of evidence.
[4] Tytler, *op. cit.* pp. xvii–xviii.

premium on skill in *extempore* speaking. All these were admirable provisions, yet it is hard to see how any of them would be very much use to
the illiterate private soldier, who could neither read the Mutiny Act,
write his defence, nor afford to hire counsel. All the wit of successive
Parliaments failed to realize that none of these elaborate provisions could
help the helpless; any assistance the prisoner might receive from his
prosecutor, the Judge Advocate, he owed to custom, not to law.

The procedure of Regimental and Garrison Courts Martial differed
from General Courts Martial in the absence of a Judge Advocate; and
they were competent to try only 'the lesser offences, or crimes which do
not infer a capital punishment'.

Minor punishments varied 'according to the degree of the crimes, and
the rank of the persons who commit them'. Officers convicted by a
General Court Martial could be cashiered, that is, deprived of their
commissions, with or without a declaration by the court of their unfitness,
'to serve his Majesty in any military capacity'; or they could be suspended,
that is, temporarily relieved of pay and duties for a period of months; and
they could be reprimanded, either publicly or privately. Other ranks could
be degraded, if they were N.C.O.'s, imprisoned, condemned to serve overseas for life or a period of years; but the commonest of punishments was
flogging. One misses from this list the common minor punishments of
the rank and file today—deprivation of pay and confinement to barracks.
The reason for their absence is simple; neither was practicable in an age
when barracks were novel and far from universal, and when the best part
of a soldier's pay was spent on buying his food.

To modern minds the most repellent thing about British discipline in
the period under discussion was the wholesale and vigorous use of flogging
as a military punishment. It does indeed seem strange that this punishment should have been used so savagely in the high summer of the
evangelical revival; that, when the active Christian conscience of the
nation laboured so earnestly to reduce, and end, the sufferings of the
black slave, the torture of the white soldier still received the annual
approval of Parliament. For floggings could, and sometimes did, end in
the death of the victim, in spite of the fact that the punishment could not
legally take place without the regimental surgeon being present to call a
halt to it; and in spite of the fact that the victim received immediate
medical care afterwards, and might take his punishment in instalments.
For punishments of 1000 lashes (and sometimes more) were not infrequently ordered, and the men who received them might have to spend
several spells in hospital between instalments before the whole punishment could be administered.

Certainly nothing is easier than to denounce so barbarous a punishment
as this, yet it baffled the wit of the authorities to devise a milder punishment that could control the appalling thugs of whom the rank and file of

the British Army was largely composed. For thugs they were: Wellington, to be sure, has received much glib abuse for describing them (in the fullest recorded version of his opinion) as 'the very scum of the earth. People talk of their enlisting from their fine military feeling', he continued,—'all stuff—no such thing. Some of our men enlist from having got bastard children—some for minor offences—many more for drink.'[1] That is certainly not a palatable statement, yet, unfortunately, it is one that the historian of recruiting must pronounce to have as much truth as can fairly be expected in any generalization. The only serious qualification to be made of it is that during the actual years of the great war with France the regular army received many men who came to it as volunteers from the militia; that the militia, because it was a conscript force, drew into its ranks a much better sample of the working class than the regular army, which was raised solely by voluntary enlistment; and that out of the militia some very good men (of whom the famous Private Wheeler was one) did pass into the army during the actual war years. But against this the point must be made that Wellington made the statement above quoted in peacetime, many years after the expiry of the last act permitting militia-men to volunteer into the regulars; and that the unpleasant types he describes were the ones whom recruiting parties most usually secured for the army. Decent working-class families abhorred the army with the deep-rooted horror that Kipling has described of a later age in his picture of the good chapel folk of Greenhow Hill.[2] But Crabbe, that most literal reporter among English poets, is our witness that rural magistrates commonly offered a young man who had got a village girl in trouble the choice between marriage and enlistment; documents on recruiting teem with records of wholesale enlistments from gaols and prison ships into the army; the criminal element was increased yet further by recruiting officers who attended quarter sessions with the power to secure a verdict of 'case dismissed' for those of the accused who would enlist and could pass a medical examination; and, finally, drunkenness and recruiting went hand in hand. If, then, the often deplored language of the Duke of Wellington was painfully forthright, it still was not inaccurate.

And the crimes of British soldiers were certainly the crimes of the scum of the earth. Their penchant for robbery and murder on active service appears with ugly frequency in Wellington's dispatches from the Peninsula. At home these crimes were rare, but desertion and drunkenness were constant. The general tone of soldier-society is thus described by a ranker of some education in a Scottish regiment:

there were few of those with whom I could associate that had an idea beyond the situation they were in; those who had were afraid to show that they possessed any

[1] Stanhope, *Conversations with Wellington*, p. 18. See also pp. 13–14.
[2] And a friend, who joined the regular army in 1913, assures me that this spirit was not dead even then.

more knowledge than their comrades for fear of being laughed at by fellows that in other circumstances they would have despised....If [a man] did not join with his neighbours in their ribald obscenity and nonsense, he was a Methodist—if he did not curse and swear, he was a Quaker—and if he did not drink the most of his pay, he was a miser, a d——d mean scrub and the generality of his comrades would join in execrating him.

In such a society it was a hard matter for a man of any superior education to keep his ground, for he had no one to converse with....Thus many men of ability and information were, I may say, forced from the intellectual height which they had attained down to the level of those with whom they had to associate; and everything conspired to sink them to that point where they became best fitted for *tractable beasts of burden*.

Blackguardism held sway, and gave tone to the whole. Even the youngest were led into scenes of drunkenness and debauchery by men advanced in years. All, therefore, with few exceptions were drawn into this overwhelming vortex of abject slavishness and dissipation.[1]

This picture of the British soldier, drawn by a ranker's pen, is not a pretty one, but it is perfectly consistent with the downright language on the same subject that has brought the Duke of Wellington so much severe criticism; and to it must be added another point—these drunken thugs were tough with a ruggedness unknown and scarcely conceivable in the decorous modern England of today. It is probably fair to regard the American soldier of the eighteenth century as not very different from the British soldier of the same period—indeed, according to Fortescue, they were often the same man, for the ranks of both sides in the American Revolution were largely filled with deserters from the other; and the private soldier's contempt for the pains of moderate corporal punishment wrung a cry of despair from no less stout-hearted a commander than George Washington. 'For the most atrocious offences, one or two instances only excepted, a man receives no more than thirty nine lashes', complained Washington to Congress; sometimes these lashes were so lightly laid on as to be 'rather a matter of sport than punishment', he continued, but even when the cat was applied with most conscientious vigour 'many hardened fellows, who have been the subjects, have declared that, for a bottle of rum, they would undergo a second operation', concluded Washington.[2] In the light of this revelation that 'many' men of two centuries ago could regard a bottle of rum as a fair equivalent for thirty-nine vigorous strokes of the cat-o'-nine-tails, it will surely be conceded that either men or rum are not today what they were in the more robust eighteenth century; and the problem of the disciplinarian appears in a new perspective. In spite, then, of what seems the desperate severity of courts martial which awarded hundreds of lashes as a single penalty for convicted soldiers, the punishment of flogging lived on because responsible

[1] Donaldson, *Recollections of an Eventful Life*, pp. 84–6.
[2] Jared Sparks, *The Writings of Washington* (New York, 1847–52), IV, 118.

British legislators dared not limit the use of what was regarded as the surest means of controlling an army so largely drawn from the criminal class.

For flogging was effective. There is no point in objecting to this statement that the French Army managed to do without it, or that, in spite of it, the discipline of the British Army broke down deplorably on occasions when, as in 1809 and 1812, it had to retreat. The French Army, being a conscript force that received a fair cross-section of the nation, was composed of a much better class of men than the British, and yet it dispensed with flogging only at the cost of making much more lavish use of the death penalty.[1] That, by and large, flogging was effective in maintaining an adequate degree of subordination, even in an army where many soldiers were criminals, is evident from Wellington's repeated observation that, while atrocious crimes were all too frequently committed by soldiers in isolated detachments, his men were usually well behaved while serving with their own units. When separated from their units, the men had too sporting a chance to 'get away with' robbery or murder; under the eye of their own officers and N.C.O.'s detection was too certain and punishment too severe for the same temptation to exist.

And there lay the prime stumbling block of flogging's opponents. For they existed, and they were eloquent, long before the punishment of the cat was abolished; they were easily able to show that it was cruel, beastly, degrading, and liable to abuse; they were not able to show that it did not do its job of maintaining subordination or point out any other punishment that could be relied on to do the job equally well. And (more curious still to the modern mind) the punishment was not really resented by those who were liable to it.

I have never found any evidence [writes David Hannay of the navy before 1815] that flogging as a punishment given for proven offences against discipline or good order in the ship was looked upon as a grievance. On the contrary, when inflicted by a captain, who, however severe he might be, was just, it was considered by the best elements in the crews as their protection against unruly spirits swept into the fleet by the press or the criminals imported from the gaols.[2]

So was it in the army. The terms in which rankers are found to support the severity of the army's discipline are striking. The first witness may be John Stevenson, described as 'Forty Years a Wesleyan Class Leader, twenty-one Years in the British Foot Guards, Sixteen a Non-Commissioned Officer'.[3] 'They talk of the lash,' wrote Stevenson, 'I was never any more afraid of the lash than I was of the gibbet, no man ever comes to that but through his own conduct, just the same as thousands come to the jail and

---

[1] Stanhope, *Conversations with Wellington*, p. 18.
[2] David Hannay, *Naval Courts Martial* (Cambridge, 1914), p. 67.
[3] John Stevenson, *A Soldier in Time of War* (London, 1841), title-page.

177

penal settlements';[1] and if there were plenty of men who came to the lash in the army, it was because

> of those who voluntarily enlist, some few are driven by poverty...[but] some have disgraced themselves in their situation or employment, many have committed misdemeanours which expose them to the penalties of the law of the land, and most are confirmed drunkards—in fact, generally speaking such as have been the pests of their neighborhoods, the annoyance of all respectable persons, the plague of the magistracy, and the trouble of the parish officers.[2]

Next, one may cite James Anton, who rose from the ranks to become Quarter-Master-Sergeant of the 42nd Highlanders.

> Philanthropists, who decry the lash [says Anton] ought to consider in what manner the good men—the deserving, exemplary soldiers—are to be protected; if no coercive measures are to be resorted to in purpose to prevent ruthless ruffians from insulting with impunity the temperate, the well-inclined, and the orderly-disposed, the good must be left to the mercy of the worthless....In civil society, the mechanic, the labourer, yea even the pauper, can remove from his dwelling or place of abode if he finds himself annoyed by a troublesome neighbour; but the good soldier cannot remove without this despicable demon of discord accompanying him, and yet we are told that the lash is not to be used. The good soldier thanks you not for such philanthropy; the incorrigible laughs at your humanity, despises your clemency, and meditates only how he may gratify his naturally vicious propensities.[3]

And, finally, there is Private Wheeler's defence, written in 1816, of Wellington's alleged severities: 'the army...could not be kept in the order so essential to its well-being if some examples had not been made...such punishments were necessary to deter others.'[4] At the other end of the scale corporal punishment was upheld in Parliament by men of the stamp of Palmerston, 'genuinely sympathetic with human suffering and intolerant of brutality' as he was;[5] and also of Wilberforce who, in 1812, replied to the proposal to abolish flogging by saying that 'when he considered what a huge and multifarious body an army was, he should be afraid of adopting suddenly so material a change in what was deemed to be so essential to its discipline, on which depended entirely the management and government of it'.[6] It would then seem wise for the modern commentator to be more thankful that he lives in an age which can dispense with flogging than ready to criticize the ages that used it; but if one hesitates to criticize, one need not assert that the power to employ the lash was never abused,[7] nor need one give credit for any very lively sense of proportion

---

[1] Stevenson, *op. cit.* p. 140.　　　　　　　　　　[2] *Ibid.* p. 153.

[3] James Anton, *Retrospect of a Military Life during the most eventful Periods of the last War* (Edinburgh, 1841), p. 11.

[4] Captain B. H. Liddell Hart (ed.), *The Letters of Private Wheeler, 1809–1828* (London, 1951), p. 196.

[5] H. F. C. Bell, *Lord Palmerston* (London, 1936), I, 39.

[6] *Parl. Deb.* xxi (1812), 1287.

[7] It was stated in Parliament in 1842 that no fewer than four full colonels in the British Army at that date carried the scars of floggings received before they rose from the ranks. *Parl. Deb.* lxii (1842), 531.

to the members of a court which could order a man the penalty of 1900 lashes for a single offence.[1]

Yet reform was on the way, and it began, not in Parliament, but in the army itself. The cowardly and indecent custom (introduced from Prussia to France as a 'reform' in the reign of Louis XVI), which permitted an officer to strike soldiers at random with his cane, died out in England under the Duke of York's rule, so that in his day the British Army became one in which no officer dared strike a soldier, and no blow could be given without due legal sentence; and that was something. It was a good deal, too, that the old barbarities of 'riding the wooden horse', picketing, and running the gauntlet were obsolete by the end of the eighteenth century.

Royalty's influence was firm but cautious on the side of humanity. In 1807 it fell to George III to review the case of a private in the 54th Regiment whom a General Court Martial had sentenced to 1500 lashes for mutinous conduct; and the King minuted the papers. 'It appearing to His Majesty that a punishment to the extent of 1000 lashes is a sufficient example for any breach of military discipline, short of capital offence; and as even that number cannot be safely inflicted at any one period, His Majesty has been graciously pleased to express his opinion, that no sentence for corporal punishment should exceed 1000 lashes.'[2] As relations between father and son were close, it is hard not to believe this minute reflects the Duke of York's, as well as the King's, opinion; and at an early date after his reappointment to the Horse Guards the Duke returned to this subject in a confidential circular to commanding officers. This letter stated:

There is no point on which H.R.H. is more decided in his opinion than that, when officers are earnest and zealous in the discharge of their duty, and competent to their respective situations, a frequent recurrence to punishment will not be necessary... but H.R.H. has reason to apprehend that in many cases sufficient attention has not been paid to the *prevention of crime*. The timely interference of the officer, his personal intercourse and acquaintance with his men (which are sure to be repaid by the soldier's confidence and attachment) and, above all, his personal example, are the only efficacious means of preventing military offences; and the Commander-in-Chief has no hesitation in declaring that the maintenance of strict discipline, without severity of punishment, and the support and encouragement of an ardent military spirit in a corps without licentiousness, are the criterions by which H.R.H. will be very much guided in forming his opinions of the talents, abilities, and merit of the officers to whom the command of the different regiments and corps of the army are confided; [and further, since the function of a regimental court martial was] enquiring into...*small offences*...it is H.R.H.'s positive command that on no pretence whatever shall the award of a regimental court martial hereafter exceed 300 lashes.[3]

---

[1] In India in 1825. This seems to be the 'record'; but the local Commander-in-Chief reduced the sentence to a mere 1200 lashes (Marshall, *Military Miscellany*), p. 194.

[2] *Ibid.* p. 191.

[3] Cited by Marshall, *op. cit.* pp. 184–5.

'Modest and late' will no doubt be the cynic's comment on the royal efforts of both King and Duke to mitigate the brutality of military punishment. The King's 'opinion, that no sentence for corporal punishment should exceed 1000 lashes' was not a positive order, and later cases did occur of General Courts Martial exceeding that number; and the Duke's circular letter, dealing as it did with regimental courts only, imposed no limit at all upon General Courts Martial. That criticism is true, but it takes no account of the difficulty of the situation the royal pair had to handle. The army contained many officers grown old in the service who were inured to flogging as the natural means of maintaining discipline; and it was fairly said that too prompt and vigorous interference with the old custom of the army would have caused 'Commanding Officers, who had been checked in their practice by such a regulation', to attribute 'every irregularity in the regiment to the Duke's orders'.[1] The Duke's letter, on the other hand, left them free to punish very adequately, but made it pretty plainly in their interest to do so as little as possible. At about this time too the Duke began to require semi-annual returns from all regiments of punishments inflicted.

Commanding officers themselves could take a much bolder line than royalty, as the scope of their responsibility was narrower; and many among them made as little use as they dared of corporal punishment. Indeed Wellington was long after to state to a parliamentary committee: 'From the time I entered the army it was the desire of every commanding officer I have ever seen, and who knew his duty, to diminish corporal punishment as much as possible.'[2] In that statement he is supported by the ranker, John Stevenson, who has already been quoted as saying that he 'was never any more afraid of the lash than...of the gibbet'. Officers were indeed accused of sadistic callousness, but, retorts Stevenson, 'there is a class of writers who provided they can so pander to a vitiated taste as to obtain a dishonourable profit, are reckless of principle, honesty and truth...these veracious and trustworthy gentlemen have...been endeavouring to mislead the public...[about] the character of the officers of the army and navy, [representing] soldiers and seamen...as exposed to tyranny compared to which the horrors of West Indian slavery are mild'.[3] No doubt, continued the writer, among the many officers of the British Army, there were some brutes who abused the authority entrusted to them, but in twenty-one years' service Stevenson had apparently not met one.

Many experiments were made by the decent class of officers who attempted to maintain discipline without the lash. Sir Charles Napier describes the alternative tried by a commanding officer in Guernsey when he decided never again to flog a drunkard.

---

[1] Marshall, *op. cit.* p. 186.
[2] Cited in the debate on the Mutiny Act, 1842 (*Parl. Deb.* LXII (1842), 536).
[3] Stevenson, *op. cit.* p. 149.

The Colonel, accompanied by the Surgeon, went to the guardhouse and felt the drunkard's pulse; he was declared to be in a fever. Nothing could be more true. He was therefore put in a blanket, and four soldiers bore him through the barracks, his comrades all laughing at the care taken of him; on reaching the hospital the patient was put to bed and *blistered* between the shoulders, fed on bread and water for a week, and then discharged cured. He was then brought on parade, when the Commanding Officer congratulated him on his recovery from the fever, and sent him to join his company, where he was laughed at and jeered by his comrades for the space of a week. Many others underwent the same treatment; but the joke, though very amusing to sober soldiers, soon began to be none to the drunkards. There was considerable pain and uneasiness—some bread, plenty of water; but no pitying comrades—no commiseration—no mercy. The experiment was completely success- ful. Not a man of that regiment was flogged in Guernsey from the time the men were treated with blisters; and after a fortnight there was no such thing as a man drunk for guard or parade.[1]

This was an experiment of a kind which some individualists can try successfully, but which depends too much on personality to be fit for general application; and the punishment was still corporal, for the opera- tion of blistering was far from painless. A more valuable, because more generally applicable, step was taken by the Grenadier Guards when serving in Sicily in 1807. They tried 'a close kind of military confinement, when the soldier was off duty...combined with punishment drill'. Their Regimental Courts Martial used 'solitary confinement' as a 'common sentence...in Cadiz in 1811 and 1812', and brought the practice home with them to Knightsbridge barracks in 1814.[2] This punishment was nicknamed 'billing up'; Wellington held that it was useful as long as the power to flog remained in reserve; but '"who would", he said, "bear to be billed up but for fear of a stronger punishment? He would knock down the sentry and walk out!"'[3]

In these ways, then, with royal interference and experiments by humane commanding officers, the movement toward the obsolescence of flogging began in our period; and all but obsolete it became long before Parliament abolished it (or so one would gather from the experience of Lord Roberts; Parliament did not abolish flogging till 1881, and the grand total of floggings which Roberts had to witness in a military career that began in 1852 was, precisely, one).

Meanwhile, in the period when flogging was actively in use, there were two ways in which a soldier sentenced to this punishment could try to evade it.

The first, open only to men sentenced by Regimental or Garrison Courts Martial, was to appeal to a General Court Martial. It was not necessarily a wise thing to do. The General Court Martial might not only confirm the sentence of the regimental court, but increase it, if the appeal

<hr />

[1] Marshall, *op. cit.* pp. 159–60. [2] *Ibid.*
[3] Stanhope, *Conversations with Wellington*, p. 18.

seemed to have been made without due reason. Yet such appeals were embarrassingly popular; if they did not always, or even often, enable a man to escape the consequences of regimental conviction, they certainly postponed the infliction of the sentence. Even that was boon sufficient to make appeals a regular nuisance: 'I cannot help taking this opportunity of suggesting to you the Expediency of discouraging Soldiers from appealing from a Regimental to a General Court Martial', wrote Fawcett to one Lt. Gen. Rooke on 9 August 1798; 'this is usually done solely with a view to procrastination, and except in very particular instances cannot be necessary for the Investigation of Crimes and irregularities, on which Regimental Courts Martial are competent to form a judgement.'[1] Finally, this right of appeal was all but closed by a decision of the Judge Advocate General that it existed only in cases where the soldier's pay was concerned. Precisely what that decision means is not very clear; that it was unfortunate in that it virtually deprived the victim of injustice at the hands of a Regimental Court Martial from having his case reviewed by a higher authority seems likely; that it was necessary, to enable officers to attend to their regular duty, instead of being constantly summoned to sit, thirteen at a time, on General Courts Martial, which were needless more often than not, seems likelier still.

When this attempt to evade the lash failed, there was still one opening left. The man sentenced could appeal to the Commander-in-Chief to have his sentence commuted to one of service for life in some garrison overseas. Though the Duke of York objected to courts martial using transportation itself as a punishment, he rarely seems to have turned down a soldier's own petition to serve overseas in lieu of receiving a flogging in England, at any rate at first. He demanded certain safeguards. At that time, when tropical hygiene was so little understood, expectation of life in many colonies was short indeed, and the Duke permitted no sentence to be commuted to transportation without a written 'Paper containing the Soldier's request to serve on a Foreign Station';[2] and if the man had originally enlisted under some limitation of time or place, he must volunteer for 'General Service'. Subject to the Commander-in-Chief's approval, he could then be dispatched to the recruiting depot, where his passage was in due course provided.

Thus a regiment serving at home got rid of an unwanted scoundrel, and a short-handed regiment serving abroad, in circumstances that made recruiting a perennial difficulty, received a trained soldier. So far the commutation of sentence would seem ideal for both, but in fact this was not a happy way of providing for the defence of the overseas empire. The criminal element became more than ever top-heavy in foreign garrisons, and (thanks no doubt to its habitual intemperance) frequently lacked the

[1] WO/3/18.
[2] Wynyard to Whitelocke, 7 December 1801, WO/3/34.

physical fitness required by climates that were hard on the healthiest of men. Too often it was found that these men 'on their arrival at the place of their destination...become the Inhabitants of the General Hospital, and their bodily Infirmities do not allow the effect of strict discipline to be resorted to for the Amendment of their Morals', wrote the Adjutant General to the War Office on 21 December 1801.

In short [he continued] after a very serious Expence being incurred in their Transportation they are more calculated to spread contagion in more ways than one in any Corps they may join than to add to its effective strength. H.R.H. [the Duke of York] is equally aware of the bad consequences of setting these men at liberty and is therefore desirous that the Secretary of War would be so good as to take an opportunity of submitting the Circumstances above stated to the consideration of H.M.'s Ministers in order that they may decide on the most eligible mode of disposing of persons of the above description.[1]

The results of the cabinet's deliberations appear to have been that men volunteering to serve overseas in order to escape punishment were permitted to do so only if a medical inspection pronounced them fit to serve 'on any foreign station';[2] and that men whose fitness to serve in the tropics was doubtful, might be judged 'proper Subjects to be sent to any Corps stationed in the back Settlements of Canada'.[3] Men who were fit for neither might apparently 'meet the punishment due to their Crimes', and continue to serve at home or be discharged.[4]

These decisions seem well judged for the purpose of preventing foreign garrisons from being loaded down any further with useless criminals, but still did nothing to solve the problem created by the numbers of unfit men who had already commuted sentences of flogging for life service overseas. How acute that problem had become appears from a letter written in October 1802 by the governor of the Leeward and Windward Islands, Lt. Gen. Grinfield, in the following terms:

I must beg to call your attention to a set of men sent here as Soldiers and denominated Culprits, who are proscribed from returning to England, and many of them are unfit for and useless as Soldiers; the turning them adrift without provision or subsistence, besides the apparent Cruelty, is a measure I cannot take upon my self to authorize, and yet these men are, as by the Return herewith sent, increasing very much upon the remaining Regiments....I should humbly hope H.R.H. will take this matter into his consideration, and give directions with respect to those who are incapable of Service, as their remaining here is a great expence to Government and Burthen on the Regiments to which they belong, and a great inconvenience in point of accommodation, as they must be provided with room in Barracks when tolerably well, and in Hospitals when sick.

[1] Calvert to Matthew Lewis, 21 December 1801, *ibid.*
[2] Wynyard to Hewett, 5 February 1802, *ibid.*
[3] Adjutant General to Hewett, 22 January 1802, *ibid.*
[4] Wynyard to Hewett, 5 July 1802, *ibid.* Let it be noted that I have deduced the cabinet's decision from these two cited cases, which follow shortly after the Duke's appeal for a decision; I have not found that decision explicitly stated in any document.

The return Grinfield enclosed is dated 14 October 1802 and shows that since the beginning of 1799 the eleven regiments serving in the Leeward and Windward Islands had received no fewer than 1207 culprits; of these about thirty (the number is not exactly given) had been made N.C.O.'s 'from good behaviour'; in addition to the culprits there were between three and four hundred deserters who had 'been sent from the different depots in England as bad Characters, but concerning whom' Grinfield had 'no specific instructions', and of these '33...were brought before a Medical Board at Barbadoes on the 18th September, 1802, and were considered by the Board totally unfit for any Service'.[1]

On receiving Grinfield's letter the Duke of York promptly gave permission on his own authority for all culprits whose good conduct had won them promotion 'to return to their respective Regiments in England',[2] but he felt unable to give any directions about the others till he had consulted the ministers, and out of his consultations there came certain new rules. These were, first, that any man, who had petitioned to serve overseas for life in order to avoid corporal punishment and who, after seven years' service there, could produce a certificate of good conduct from his commanding officer, would be considered to have expiated his former offences; thereafter, he would be as free to return home as any other soldier in the regiment in which he was serving. Further, any culprit who was serving overseas as a result, not of his own choice, but of a definite sentence to transportation awarded by court martial, might be released from his sentence by royal permission; and to obtain that he must submit a humble petition to the King.[3]

It is clear from these regulations that the Addington cabinet again failed to grasp the problem which the Duke and Grinfield had successively brought before them; they did nothing more 'with respect to those who are incapable of Service' than permit such invalid culprits as had earned certificates of good conduct to return (a strong temptation here to colonial governors to place a very loose interpretation on 'good conduct'); and one fears that even the men who earned the permission were rarely grateful for it. Long acquaintance with a sunny climate often makes Englishmen flinch from the rigours of their native land; that rum was cheap and plentiful in the West Indies is certain; that mulatto women became a tie which bound many soldiers to the islands of their exile is likely; and men who had once served in the West Indies generally did not wish to come home. At any rate, when the 45th Regiment and a detachment of the 70th Regiment were called home in 1801, the Duke of York, in reporting their arrival to his father, commented: 'Both Corps are perfect skeletons, having as usual allowed such men as chose to turn out

---

[1] Brownrigg to Sullivan, with enclosures, 3 December 1802, WO/1/624.
[2] *Ibid.*
[3] Adjutant General to General Grinfield, 18 April 1803, WO/3/36.

Volunteers to enlist into Regiments remaining in the West Indies.'[1] However, these ineffectual regulations seem to have been the best that were forthcoming; as such, they provide another reason for thankfulness that the navy of Napoleon was never equal to the navy of Louis XVI, or some valuable colonies might have changed hands pretty cheaply.

In the letter books of the Commander-in-Chief one occasionally finds reference to misdemeanours that hardly admitted of punishment, such as malingering, and cases where men deliberately mutilated themselves in order to be discharged as unfit. Nothing could be done with the latter, except to dismiss them with ignomy. With malingerers the Duke could deal very summarily and not unshrewdly, as in the case of a man claiming some undiagnosable trouble in the knee, on which a puzzled general consulted the Horse Guards and received the terse reply: 'H.R.H.....is pleased to direct that you cause Thomas Raven to be blistered for the supposed disease in his knee. This treatment, if the man is really disordered, may contribute to his cure, and if he is an Imposter, will most probably deter him from repeating the Imposition.'[2]

This chapter has so far dealt with the infantry and cavalry who formed the army proper, to the exclusion of the various Ordnance Corps, for three reasons: first, it was in the army that reform was most conspicuously called for; secondly, in the Ordnance archives preserved in the Public Record Office there is little material comparable to the letter books of the Commander-in-Chief, which shed so much light on the affairs of the Army; thirdly, the Ordnance and army both were ruled by the same Mutiny Act, so what has been said of the one under this head applies as well to the other.

In general, it may be said of the older Ordnance troops that their officers were far less liable than those of the army to be guilty of the abuses which the Duke of York had to clean up. Unlike the army, they never lacked a Commander-in-Chief to keep an eye on slackness or misconduct, for there was always a Master General of the Ordnance; and for the ten years preceding the war, when a headless army was drifting into such abject condition, the Ordnance was ruled by the keenest and most wide-awake of all Masters General, the Duke of Richmond. Further, every officer in the artillery and engineers began his military career by being schooled to discipline in the Royal Military Academy at Woolwich, to which the army had no counterpart (till the Royal Military College was founded in 1801); thus the young army ensign had nowhere to receive any military training save the regiment he joined, and prior to the Duke of York's reforms, the schooling he received there was quite as likely to teach him military vices as military virtues. As the Engineers had no other ranks, they had naturally no problem with deserters, or thieving or

---

[1] Duke of York to George III, 4 July 1801, Windsor, 10277.
[2] Calvert to Este, 31 August 1804, WO/3/37.

drunken privates. Discipline of other ranks in the Royal Artillery regiments seems to have been good; that it became very bad in the Royal Artillery drivers during the long, lax reign of Chatham has been noted, and a reform of the drivers, intended by Lord Moira, was scotched by Chatham's return on the fall of the Ministry of all the Talents. As for the Corps of Royal Military Artificers, they were anything but models of good discipline. They became, says an authority who had seen much of them,

permanently fixed at their respective stations, both at home and abroad; where they remained for life, in. . .a state of vegetation; so that there were [by 1811] a vast number of men who had actually grown grey in the Corps. . . .Everywhere they intermixed with civilians; they married in a proportion unknown in any other corps. . .the superior pay, too, of the Royal Military Artificers, which in a well regulated corps, such as His Majesty's Life Guards, etc., invariably adds to the respectability of a soldier had of course the directly contrary effect in a neglected one. And. . .to all these evils, which in process of time would have broken the military spirit and ruined the character of the best troops that ever existed, was added a most ill-judged system of [recruiting by] receiving volunteers from regiments of the line. . . a system by which commanding officers of these regiments got rid of their worst men.[1]

But nobody cared, very much, about the Royal Military Artificers, till Wellington's costly lack of skilled specialists in field engineering for his sieges caused this very unmilitary body to be metamorphosed into the Royal Corps of Sappers and Miners and turned over for effective training to the author of the above description, Major C. W. Pasley.

[1] C. W. Pasley, *Course of Military Instruction* (London, 1817), ii, iv. It should be noted that this writer limits the evils of recruiting volunteers from the line to those companies only of the artificers which were stationed in the West Indies and Gibraltar. I have omitted that limitation because I find the artificers were recruited in this way at home as well as abroad.

CHAPTER 8

MILITARY EDUCATION

THE real history of formal education for war in England begins only in 1741, when a warrant of King George II founded the Royal Military Academy at Woolwich. Even then the purpose of the foundation was to provide officers for the artillery and engineers alone. The academy thus founded may be likened to a small public school where 48 or (after 1782) 60 youths, dressed in a military uniform, ignored most public school subjects, and studied intensely subjects which the public schools ignored. Greek had no place at Woolwich; a very modest amount of Latin was demanded as a gentlemanly entrance requirement only; but French and drawing were important and mathematics overwhelming. So far, indeed, the contrast between Woolwich and the eighteenth- and nineteenth-century public school is strong. In other ways Woolwich was ahead of the public school of the day. Before the public schools had learnt the value of organized athletics, fencing was a regular exercise required of all at Woolwich. Discipline in its two parts, both commanding and obeying, was taught by a sort of 'prefect system' under which 'corporals' and 'heads of rooms' were entrusted with authority over their fellows, and Dr Arnold himself could not have improved on the language in which corporals were solemnly bidden to be an example to those under them.[1] Religion was treated as a matter of great importance, at least in so far as attendance at Sunday church parades was compulsory; and here again the academy recalls the Victorian, and the modern, public school.

When it first opened, Woolwich taught a very practical outdoor syllabus, in addition to academic studies. The date of its foundation, 1741, will be remembered as the year in which Brigadier Thomas Wentworth's siege of Cartagena in the West Indies failed so signally. Much blame for the failure has been placed on Wentworth's own caution, nor is it all undeserved. But Sir John Fortescue points out that 'there was but one engineer in (Wentworth's) whole army who was in the least competent to carry on a siege, and there seems to have been considerable difficulty, first in getting him to the scene of action at all and secondly in getting him to work when he reached it'.[2] And Sir John might have added that, within two weeks of the opening of the attack on Fort Boca Chica, this solitary engineer passed beyond all danger of work in this present world when

[1] W. D. Jones, *Records of the Royal Military Academy* (Woolwich, 1851), p. 59. I regret that I find that in working with this book on two different occasions, I took my references in different ways—first, by page numbers, second, by dates. The chronological arrangement of the book, however, makes either reference equally easy to find.
[2] *History of the British Army*, II, 65.

yellow fever consigned him to the next.[1] An army so destitute of expert leadership could hardly be expected to succeed.

The foundation of the Royal Military Academy seems to have been a prompt reaction to Wentworth's experience and the weaknesses which it revealed—or so its prescribed course of training would suggest. A dummy fortress was to be erected 'near the Warren at Woolwich...made of earth and turfed' and consisting of 'two Demi-Bastions, Two Flanks and a Curtain between them, with a Ditch, Ravelin, Covertway, Place of Arms and a Glacis'. Every other summer this imposing dummy was to be attacked by the students, 'under the direction of the Engineers belonging to the Ordnance'. The instructions continued with precision: 'Parallels shall be drawn and Trenches opened....Batteries shall be raised by the Besiegers, at proper distances and in proper places....Mines shall be made by the Besieged to blow up the Batteries, and the Besiegers shall also carry on Mines to make breach.' Meanwhile the mock siege was to be frequently interrupted by 'the Chief Master (who) shall...give lectures and instructions on the reason for the several operations therein performed'. Finally, once every year there was to be 'a General Examination ...before the Master General or, in his absence, the Lieutenant-General and principal officers of the Ordnance', and 'an exact account' was to be 'kept of every one's proficiency'.[2]

It would be very hard to improve on these exceedingly practical instructions for training engineers in their duties. In the process of time the biennial attack on the mock fortress seems to have been dropped. In 1792, however, the cadet at Woolwich still had to master a very exacting theoretical syllabus before he could be 'reported fit for a public examination for a commission in the Royal Corps of Artillery and Engineers'.[3] The length and nature of this syllabus defy full quotation and it is therefore consigned to an end-note at the close of this chapter. Here it is only necessary to remark that the very full requirements of the mathematical course included a great deal that would now be called Physics; that lectures were given in Chemistry too; that a very exacting course in Drawing was required; and that the French course would probably be regarded as severe indeed by a modern schoolboy, for in addition to an abundance of the grammar and exercises expected in the study of any language, the cadets also had to learn that neglected orphan of modern examinations, 'Pronounciation' (sic).

The Chemistry was a new addition to the syllabus. In 1788 Dr Allen Crawford first was hired to give chemical lectures at the academy which could be attended by any Ordnance officers who applied for leave for the

---

[1] So I am informed by my friend, John Ogelsby, whose doctoral thesis for the University of Washington dealt with the British West Indies in this period.

[2] Jones, *Records of R.M.A.* pp. 3–4.

[3] *Ibid.* p. 45.

purpose. He was heard with great attention by the cadets, who took good notes in notebooks which they handed in to the doctor for marking and correction.[1] From that time forward chemistry continued to be taught, and in 1798 an advanced course in physics (or, at any rate, 'natural philosophy') was added.[2]

If one may take it at its face value, this Woolwich syllabus probably provided the most thorough, all-round scientific education to be had in England, if not in Britain, at the time. Certainly the academy's teaching staff was distinguished. The 'Mr Sandby' who taught drawing was none other than that most attractive minor master of water-colour, Paul Sandby.[3] The Professor of Mathematics, and author of some of the textbooks used, was the same Charles Hutton who was a Fellow of the Royal Society and whose computation of the density of the earth won the praise of Laplace.[4] The Professor of Chemistry, Dr Crawford, was likewise outstanding among scientists of his day.[5] It should not therefore be surprising that when the British government later wanted someone to make scientific observations at places as far apart as St Helena in the Atlantic Ocean, at Toronto in Canada West, and at Fort Chipewyan, in the remote north of what were then called the Hudson's Bay Territories, the choice fell on an engineer officer, the future Sir John Henry Lefroy. Likewise, by teaching at Woolwich, Sandby made his influence felt far beyond Great Britain, for, writes a curator of the Royal Ontario Museum, 'most of the artists working in Canada in the early period were army officers, many of whom had received their training at the Royal military Academy...under Paul Sandby'.[6] What is here said of art in Canada is likely to be true of many another place where British garrisons were stationed, from the West Indies to the Cape, to India and on to the penal colonies in Australia; and Sandby's 'influence is usually strongly felt among his pupils'.[7]

The education given to the cadets was the same for all. No distinction was made at the academy between those who were to be gunners and those who were to be engineers; every cadet was to be equally trained for both; and that was sane because the biggest job for either gunner or engineer— the conduct of a siege—required the close co-operation of them both. (It later became a wartime practice, however, for engineer candidates to spend an extra six months at the academy.)[8]

Though the excellence of this syllabus is, on paper, conspicuous, the really important question was (as it always is), what real standards of proficiency were actually reached by the young gentlemen who studied it?

---

[1] *Ibid.* pp. 41–2.
[2] *Ibid.* p. 69.
[3] *Dictionary of National Biography.*
[4] *Ibid.*
[5] *Ibid.* where his Christian name is given as 'Adair', though Jones, *Records of R.M.A.*, calls him Allen Crawford.
[6] F. St G. Spendlove, *The Face of Early Canada* (Toronto, 1958), p. 26.
[7] *Ibid.* p. 46.
[8] Jones, *Records of R.M.A.* p. 75.

Here Woolwich was subject to an ebb and flow of standards unknown to ordinary schools. It was founded to fill vacancies in the armed forces; in peacetime those vacancies were few and training was then exceedingly thorough; in wartime vacancies were many, the need for officers was pressing, and then standards declined. Standards were probably never higher than during the peacetime administration of the Duke of Richmond. The vacancies that then occurred were filled by the duly prescribed competitive public examination. The future seniority of the candidates in the corps was regulated by their standing relative to one another in the examinations. An added nervous hazard for the candidates was provided by the presence of the Master General of Ordnance himself, for with characteristic thoroughness in dealing with all Ordnance matters, the Duke of Richmond obeyed George II's old instructions and attended examinations whenever he could. But the following summary of thirty years' teaching history at the academy, written by its Lieutenant Governor in 1814, shows how intimately the achievement of high standards was related to the number of vacancies in the Ordnance Corps:

At the termination of the American War in 1783 [he wrote] there were 241 Officers in the Artillery, of which 17 were supernumerary Lieutenants; the Officers of the Engineers were 68 in all. The first public examination of cadets at the Royal Military Academy, after the above period, was held in 1786; at that time the 17 supernumerary Lieutenants had been taken into the Regiment (of Artillery) and three vacancies had occurred, two of which were filled up by cadets, the other being given to an Officer of the line, who had acted as Assistant Engineer during the war. The next public examination was held in 1787 for 5 Commissions, there being a similar number of vacancies. In the year 1788, there were 11 vacancies and 11 Commissions were given away on an examination. In 1789 there were 6 vacancies which were all filled up by examination from the Academy. In 1790, owing to arrangements on an appearance of war, the vacancies became more numerous, but of the 23 which were then subsisting, 8 only were filled up, no more Cadets being deemed qualified at that time; for the same reason but 5 cadets were promoted in 1791, when the vacancies had increased to 35 on account of an augmentation of two companies of Artillery for India, and in 1792, the last year of the peace, only 6 cadets were considered eligible for promotion, although the vacancies then amounted to 38. This circumstance, together with the augmentations, which took place on the breaking out of war, rendered it necessary to diminish the required extent of qualification, and by degrees reduced it very low, which caused the examinations to be discontinued.[1]

No other guarantee of the accuracy of the figures here stated is needed than the fact that the Lieutenant Governor, who wrote this letter, was the same fanatically exact William Mudge who had made his name by his work on the Ordnance Survey. But for the same reason one may hesitate a little before accepting too tragically the statement that the standard of qualification became 'very low'. Mudge's own standards were very severe; and his successor was to lower the entrance qualification to the

---

[1] Jones, *op. cit. sub* 31 May 1814.

academy which he had established, on the ground that he demanded more algebra of fourteen-year-old boys than they had a chance to learn 'in the provincial schools of this country'.[1]

When the demands of war made it evident that either the artillery must go short of officers or the academy must lower its examination standards, Richmond took two steps. In 1793 he enlarged the academy with 30 additional cadets (making a total of 90),[2] and in August 1794 he lowered the qualification for a commission. He then stated that he did

not mean to recommend any Gentleman Cadet for promotion who has not been examined and found qualified in the following branches of study, viz:— Arithmetic and Logarithms; Algebra, as far as Quadratic Equations; the first four books of Euclid; Mensuration, including Trigonometry and Heights and Distances; Practical Geometry; the general systems of Vauban; the definition and explanations of Artillery in general, and the construction of a piece of Ordnance, illustrated by 24 Drawings; they must also be able to read and translate French.

Whenever the Master-General receives a satisfactory report that any Gentleman Cadet is perfectly qualified in all these branches [continued Richmond] he will be ready to recommend him to His Majesty for promotion. [Professors and masters were urged to do their best, but the warning was added] Cadets...must be sensible that without their own exertions nothing can avail, and they will do well to consider what they may lose by neglecting the present opportunity, for as several Gentlemen are studying for Commissions out of the Academy, and others are daily presenting themselves, the vacancies in the Regiment will probably be soon filled up, after which the qualifications expected from a Cadet to entitle him to a Commission will be very different.[3]

Cornwallis's appointment as Master General caused a wavering in policy. First, he ordered an immediate promotion of cadets to vacancies in the artillery and engineers without any apparent regard for their academic qualifications;[4] second, as if disturbed by the consequences of that act, he reaffirmed the qualifications laid down by Richmond in August 1794 as a minimum for a commission.[5] At this time, too, a form letter was adopted to warn the families of unsatisfactory cadets that their boys were being inattentive or idle.[6] The pressure put on the cadets to work seems to have been effective—at any rate, the numbers of them who sought private tuition in the evenings from the academy's instructors were so large, that special rules governing private instruction had to be drafted.[7] In 1797, Cornwallis felt able to restore academic requirements for a commission which had been waived in 1793.[8] In 1798 the number of cadets was again increased; 100 were to receive free instruction at the academy (60 for the King's, and 40 for the East India Company's forces), and a number of additional cadets were allowed to come to Woolwich, to

[1] Col. W. H. Ford to Lord Fitzroy Somerset, 30 September 1800, *ibid.* p. 114.
[2] *Ibid.* p. 51. [3] *Ibid.* p. 53.
[4] *Ibid.* pp. 54–5. [5] *Ibid.* p. 55.
[6] *Ibid.* p. 57. [7] *Ibid.* pp. 58–9.
[8] *Ibid.* p. 63.

take instruction from two local private schools under the inspection of the academy's officers. During Cornwallis's absence in Ireland the reports on cadets (which were regularly sent to the Master General) went to the Lieutenant General of the Ordnance, Sir William Howe, and he continued to watch standards jealously.

But then Pitt fell, Addington came in, and, with Chatham as Master General, the Irish Ordnance was incorporated with the British as a result of the Union of 1801. A result of the amalgamation of the Irish and British artillery was an admitted decline in standards; and when Chatham suggested that promotion from the academy to the forces might again be made on the results of a competitive public examination, attended by the Master General, he was discouraged.

It is only step by step [wrote the inspector of studies at the academy] that we can approach the extent of qualifications which the cadets attained in the last peace, or make it creditable to produce them at a Public Examination, and in the meantime [continued the writer] it seems highly expedient at least to prevent the increase of vacancies; both these objects may be kept in view by promoting periodically for some time to come a few of the best qualified cadets without Public Examination, [and] lessening the number of promotions according to circumstances[;] by these means vacancies may be kept within bounds while the cadets, by remaining longer and longer at the academy, will by degrees become older and better informed previous to getting their Commissions. Some improvement will be constantly going on, but the academy has been so excessively drained of late, that it must require a little time to recover the disadvantages thereby occasioned.[1]

The 'little time' that was wanted, however, was not granted. This report was written on 2 June 1802. Barely a year later Britain was again at war, and gravely short of engineer officers to plan and construct defences. The crisis could only be met by expansion in which co-operation with the army helped to save Woolwich from being 'excessively drained'. Extra cadets from Woolwich were sent to the junior branch of the Duke of York's new Royal Military College at Great Marlow (which will be described below) and successfully prepared for Ordnance requirements. The draft of this plan, approved by Chatham in March 1803, is summarized as follows:

the Muster Roll of the Cadet Company to contain 153 names, but recommended to be increased to and kept at 180 or very near it, so as to have 40 Gentlemen ready for promotion every year after the present one. Further, that when the Establishment is complete, viz: 100 Cadets at Woolwich, 60 Ordnance Cadets at the College (i.e. Great Marlow), 15 or 20 India Cadets at [the] College, there should be, over and above, from 5 to 10 Extra Cadets admitted and studying at such private schools, as their friends may prefer, ready to replace immediately at the College any that may be drawn from thence to Woolwich.[2]

In actual performance this programme was surpassed. In July 1806 the establishment of the Royal Military Academy was increased to 200 cadets

[1] Jones, op. cit. p. 74.   [2] Ibid. p. 75.

for the King's service, and 46 for the East India Company.[1] That autumn 188 were in residence at Woolwich, with 60 more at the junior branch of the Royal Military College at Great Marlow, making a total of 248;[2] in March 1807, the total at both places was 246, and thirteen extra cadets were studying 'with their friends' to qualify themselves for places at the Academy as soon as promotions should create vacancies.[3]

One may fairly suppose that these increases in numbers did much to save the academy from being excessively drained, and therefore did enable cadets to 'become older and better informed previous to getting their Commissions'. One may mark too that in April 1793, when the first demands of war fell upon an Academy which was still at its peacetime strength of only 60, the Duke of Richmond, in giving commissions to 14 cadets, had made their future promotion conditional upon their continuing their studies successfully.[4] Unless this precedent was later rejected (a point on which evidence is lacking) the qualifications of artillery and engineer officers should not have suffered too badly. Certainly it is a fact that some of the service's best officers graduated in what would seem some of the leaner years for educational standards. Thus Alexander Dickson received his commission in 1794; John Fox Burgoyne in 1798; and John Thomas Jones in 1798; therefore the conclusion that, through all the ups and downs of war, the academy did on the whole provide the essential services for which it was founded would seem a fair one. It may still, however, be worth noting how much the efficiency of the academy was due to a generous absence of any interdepartmental jealousy on the part of the Duke of York. The Royal Military College was his foundation and pet hobby. He permitted it to be used for the convenience of the Ordnance Department from 1803 till after his fall from office in 1809. In 1810 a new arrangement for training gunners and engineers for the East India Company's service made it possible for the Royal Military Academy at Woolwich to take and teach all its own cadets under its own roof.[5] Only then did the Royal Military College become a purely army institution.

The army proper was far less fortunate than the Ordnance Corps. When the great war with France began it had no military academy to form young officers. Then all young officers normally came to their regiments with no previous instruction and they learnt nothing but what the regiment taught. They were supposed to read the regiment's standing orders; to be drilled on squads in squads by the adjutant, and to read the manual.[6] But, says a satirist of the 1780's, under the guise of advising younger officers: 'On coming into the regiment, perhaps the major or adjutant will advise you to learn the manual, the salute, or other parts of

[1] *Ibid.* 1 July 1806.   [2] *Ibid.* 27 October 1806.
[3] *Ibid.* 26 March 1807.   [4] *Ibid.* p. 50.
[5] *Ibid.* p. 90.
[6] Charles James, *Regimental Companion* (London, 1813), 1, 84.

the exercise; to which you may answer that you do not want to be a Drill-sergeant or corporal—or that you purchased your commission and did not come into the army to be made a machine of.' (And if it is the satirist's function to exaggerate, it is still none of his business to invent.)[1] Many regiments, too, had little competence to teach in the 1780's.

But this casual system ceased when the Duke of York took over the army. Under him it was affirmed that 'Commanding officers of regiments are equally responsible for the instruction and improvement of the officers under their command as they are for the drill of the men'. Every officer was expected within two years of his joining the army to be 'capable of commanding and exercising a troop or company in every situation...[to] be perfectly acquainted with its interior management, economy and discipline; and...[to render] himself competent in every respect to the duties of a field officer'. It was likewise 'indispensably necessary that every officer should be instructed in each individual circumstance required of a recruit or soldier...[and] accustom himself to give his words of command, not only with energy and precision, but with that confident manly voice, which at once discloses that he is perfectly master of the subject'. Inspecting Generals were directed 'to make the most strict enquiries and observations on' the qualifications of a regiment's officers. If they found any 'who either from incapacity or inattention [were] deficient in any part of their duty', they were required to report them to the Commander-in-Chief, 'in order, in the first instance that they [might] on no account rise to a higher rank till they [had] proved themselves equal to...the duties attached thereto, and, in the event of continued negligence or incapacity, that they [might] be removed from the service'.[2] These measures, coupled with the firm enforcement of Dundas's drill and the suppression of absence without leave, put an end to the ignorance of British officers which Jomini had marked as one of the great weaknesses of the service. As noted elsewhere, Jomini points to the year 1800 as the date by which this reform of the army was fully accomplished.[3]

Even, however, when this simple, practical programme was in fact carried out, it still taught the young officer nothing but regimental routine and the manoeuvres of a battalion, and England was almost destitute of means to teach him more. Our very language possessed pitifully few books on the military art. Richard Kane's *Campaigns of King William and the Duke of Marlborough together with a system of Discipline for a Battalion of Foot* was excellent as far as it went, but it had not been reprinted since 1747 and it did not contain very much. Humphrey Bland's manual, though it won the praise of James Wolfe, was still more antiquated.[4] Sir William Fawcett had done a national service by translating

---

[1] *Advice to Officers of the British Army*, pp. 59–60.
[2] James, *Regimental Companion* (London, 1813), I, 88–9. [3] *Supra*, p. 3.
[4] Humphrey Bland, *A Treatise of Military Discipline* (London, 1727).

Marshal Saxe's *Reveries* in 1757 and the King of Prussia's regulations for cavalry in 1757 and for infantry in 1759; but they too must have become pretty scarce by the 1790's; Henry Lloyd's *History of the late War in Germany* was (and is) excellent, but bulky and expensive; Thomas Simes may perhaps be called a military writer of some importance, but he was certainly not brilliant. His works are spotty, ill-arranged, too often encumbered with trivial detail, and, to say the best, rather dull.[1] These, with David Dundas, about exhaust the list of English military writers available on the eve of the French Revolution. The important continental writings of du Bourcet and von Saldern were left untranslated in their original languages; and it is doubtful how far a translation of Guibert, made at some date prior to 1786, would still have been readily available in the 1790's.

It is then understandable that some parents who desired a successful military career for their sons tried to get them instructed on the continent. George III had sent Frederick, Duke of York, to Germany, where he obviously learnt a very great deal. So too, on a humbler scale, Dr Moore took his son, the future Sir John, to Germany, and at Brunswick hired a sergeant to give him daily tuition in the Prussian exercise. The parents of the future Duke of Wellington, preferring France, sent their boy to the Military Academy at Angers, but their choice was unique and the Duke could not remember any other British officer who was instructed there.

Practice in the higher branches of the military art was even harder to come by than books on its theory. In wartime, indeed, considerable bodies of troops were sometimes assembled in training camps; on these occasions battalion officers were given valuable experience in handling their own men and some practice in co-operating with each other. But these camps were static; the cherished legal rights of private property hemmed in the training areas; the only private owner of land who could be expected to devote his property to the purpose of training troops was the King. As the Duke of York wrote in 1800, 'Windsor Forest is the only ground in the South of England at your Majesty's disposal capable of containing, and furnishing space for exercising a Large Body of Troops'.[2] So in the most favourable circumstances a war of manœuvre could never be practised, except in the face of a real enemy, and war itself was virtually the only school for war in which the British officer of the eighteenth century could make a practical study of the higher branches of his trade. The best that can be said for this system (if it may be so called) is that few things are more instructive than first-hand observation of the blunders of the uninstructed; and in British campaigns of the eighteenth century there is no

---

[1] Thomas Simes, *A Military Course for the Government of a Battalion* (London, 1777); *A Treatise of Military Science which Comprehends the Grand Operations of War* (London, 1780); *The Military Guide for Young Officers*, 3rd ed. (London, 1781).
[2] Duke of York to George III, 24 April 1800, Windsor, 9548-9.

want of object lessons of this kind. Yet it was a costly and haphazard way to educate commanders. Meanwhile, Prussia every year concentrated great masses of troops for her annual manœuvres and maintained an *Ecole militaire* at Berlin. France too assembled training camps in time of peace, and had her military colleges at Brienne and Angers. In Austria likewise neither the practice nor the theory of war was neglected in time of peace.

Thinking British soldiers were not blind to the difficulties they faced in preparing themselves for their own calling. David Dundas in 1788 stressed the need of practical manœuvres in the field when he grieved that 'we had not the same opportunities of assembly that all well disciplined armies annually have'.[1] At about the same date the Duke of Richmond was concerned for the theoretical side of an officer's training and pressed upon Pitt a plan for founding a national military college. In the cabinet Richmond's colleagues had approved his scheme, but only to drop it later as a political hot potato in the face of the anti-military prejudices of the British Parliament and people. The large-scale manœuvres, which Dundas so rightly regarded as indispensable to efficiency and sound training, were even less possible. They could not be attempted without the concentration of troops. To that, magistrates all over England would object, because it would withdraw from their districts the dispersed and petty detachments of troops on which they relied to uphold law and public order. It would likewise almost certainly involve expenditure which it would be unpleasant to defend in Parliament, and, were it done in spite of these obstacles, the lack of sufficiently spacious training areas was calculated to defeat its purpose. So, the exercising of the Guards in the oft-fought 'Battle of Hyde Park', and modest field days by the Dublin garrison in Phoenix Park, remained Britain's best, and wretched, substitute for serious manœuvres.[2] The due price of her parsimony and prejudice was paid when war caught her with senior officers who, having rarely manœuvred as much as one battalion at one time, knew not how to handle brigades and divisions.[3] Competent staff officers were almost as rare as experienced generals.

The weakness of an army incapable of training officers for any higher duty than the management of a battalion should in any case have been obvious to the Duke of York, who had attended the training camps, as well as the courts, of Vienna and Berlin; but his experience in the field in 1793–4 was of a nature to impress Britain's need of a trained staff on any-one's mind. As Adjutant General he then had under him successively Sir James Murray (who changed his surname to Pulteney in 1794) and General James Craig. Each was a capable officer, but it would not appear

---

[1] *Principles of Military Movements*, appendix, p. 87.
[2] *Ibid.* appendix, pp. 87–8.
[3] Stanhope, *Conversations with Wellington*, p. 271.

that either had the assistance he required to deal adequately with the faults in discipline and training from which the British Army was found to suffer.

The Quarter Master's branch was still more sadly weak. The position of Quarter Master General was filled, first, by an engineer, Colonel Moncrieff, until he was killed at Dunkirk, and then by Lt. Gen. Henry Fox. How far Fox ever performed the real duties of his position is doubtful. In a recent and valuable book Mr S. G. P. Ward writes that Fox was constantly commanding 'detachments on enterprises quite unconnected with his staff appointment', and suggests that he lacked military science.[1] But Fox did not leave his staff duties without cause. As Sir Harry Calvert wrote in November 1794, 'The want of general officers to command brigades has... been an evil of the most serious nature, and has been attended by the very worst consequences... General Fox is too much occupied with his staff appointment to be reckoned as a major general, though his zeal induces him to come forward as such whenever he can'; and since Calvert goes on to say that the command of brigades had 'devolved on young men newly come into the service, whose years and inexperience totally disqualified them for the situation,'[2] Fox is hardly to be blamed if, in his zeal to court the din of arms, he was more frequently under fire than at his desk. The army in which he served so variously was confronted with such a grim choice of difficulties that his staff duties may well have been less important than the sundry 'enterprises quite unconnected with his appointment' on which he is found engaged.

A fact less conspicuous, yet hardly less serious, than the shortage of general officers is the absence of a single English officer of any consequence among the staff serving under Fox in the Quarter Master General's department. His assistants there were two Hanoverians, Major Sontag and Captain Offeney, one Austrian, Major Lindenthal, and a Lt. van Zulikom. One is tempted to guess that the last two were serving primarily as liaison officers from Britain's allies, Austria and Holland, and that the main burden of the work was borne by the two Hanoverians. The Hanoverian Army could provide no more, for it was itself hardly any better off. The great Scharnhorst (who served through these campaigns as a gunner officer in the Electoral forces) wrote later, 'Posterity will hardly believe that we campaigned in the neighbourhood of Mouscron, Menin, Werwicq and Courtrai without possessing a plan of the country, and that we fought over it without making any reconnaissance, although a couple of engineers could have made a sketch of it in five or six days.... We can almost say that the Duke of York and General Walmoden possessed no general staff.'[3]

[1] S. G. P. Ward, *Wellington's Headquarters* (Oxford, 1957), p. 20.
[2] H. Verney, *Journals and Correspondence of Sir Harry Calvert*, pp. 384–5.
[3] Cited by Ward, *op. cit.* p. 21.

After attempting to command troops in the field under these conditions the Duke of York cannot have been under any illusions as to how much his country had suffered from the failure of Richmond's scheme for creating a staff college. It became his object to found such an institution himself if he could somehow overcome the prejudices which had ruined Richmond's plans; and in 1798 he saw his chance.

In that year there came to Britain a distinguished foreigner named Francis Jarry. This man was a French professional soldier, who, with the curious disregard for the place of his birth which was almost as characteristic of eighteenth-century warriors as of modern professional athletes, had joined the Prussian Army. He had served through the whole of the Seven Years War on the personal staff of Frederick the Great, and was one of twelve men whom the King personally instructed in the duties of the Quarter Master General's department. He was the head of the *Ecole Militaire* at Berlin from the end of the Seven Years War till the death of Frederick the Great; and it is most probable that the Duke had met him there during his years in Germany. When the French revolutionary war broke out, Dumouriez persuaded Jarry to return to France and he held a high command in the army that won Jemappes. Later he left France as an émigré, and in 1798 he is described as offering to run a military school in England. No living British general in 1798 had qualifications approaching his, and the Duke of York received his offer gladly.

This offer was the seed from which both the Royal Military College at Sandhurst and the Staff College at Camberley were to grow, but the plan proposed was modest indeed when compared to those two imposing establishments. The facts about its opening seem to be exceedingly simple. Jarry was in a commonplace, yet tragic, position. Like many exiled French aristocrats, he was out of a job in a foreign country. Some in that position, like Chateaubriand, tried to earn their daily bread by teaching. General Jarry wished to do the same, but where Chateaubriand toiled over irregular French verbs and corrected sentences as a tutor in a private family, Jarry apparently took his own house in High Wycombe and then invited the Commander-in-Chief to fill it with pupils whom he would instruct in the higher branches of the art of war. Such, at any rate, is what seems implied by a circular letter of the Adjutant General of 12 December 1798. The first paragraph of this letter informed commanding officers of the school's purpose, and requested them to nominate officers to attend it. The second paragraph continues:

General Jarry will on the 10th of March be established at High Wycombe in the county of Buckingham and be ready to receive such pupils as have obtained H.R.H.'s approbation and Leave of Absence from their Regiments for that purpose. The number will be limited to thirty, each of whom on his Admission must pay into the hands of Messrs. Cox and Greenwood, Treasurers of the Establishment, the sum of Twenty Pounds, independent of which he must be prepared to provide himself with such books and instruments as General Jarry may think necessary; and as much of the instruction will be given actually in the Field, it is very desirable that each officer should be provided with a horse, for which forage will be allowed.[1]

In this scheme there was much admirable ingeniousness. Though nothing is said of domestic details, the officers would presumably pay as usual for their own messing, and bring their own batmen with them, in which case housekeeping and service would be amply provided. Jarry's salary was to be £500 and the students' tuition fees would cover this sum, and leave £100 over for extras; and so, by these apparently quite private arrangements, Britain was to be provided with a small staff college run by the most eminent instructor in Europe. Except for the forage of a few horses, which could hardly be noticed in the annual army estimates, not a penny of expense was asked of the nation.

But the plan broke down in spite of the pains taken to ensure that only officers capable of benefiting from the instruction given should be admitted to the college. 'General Jarry', continues the circular letter, 'speaks very little English, therefore his lectures will be given in the French language'. When the school finally opened on 4 May 1799, after some delay owing to Jarry being ill, his 'lectures...were greatly admired ...by all who could understand them—but being confined to the higher branches of the military art, and delivered in a foreign language, they were quite lost on the generality of officers'.[2] It was also unfortunate that, to youthful British eyes, General Jarry's foreign ways appeared eccentric, and there was some very improper ragging. So almost at once a superintendent had to be appointed to assist Jarry; also an adjutant, a draughtsman to teach drawing, a professor of French and a professor of Mathematics. The net result was that, instead of paying for itself, the college had to be assisted in the very first year of its existence with the sum of £1003. 11s. 7d. out of the 'Army Extraordinaries' account.

Luckily, however, the Duke of York had a second string to his bow. This was the same Major (now Lt. Col.) John Gaspard LeMarchant who had just designed a new sword for the British cavalry and taught them how to use it.

LeMarchant had long been revolving various schemes of military education in his mind, and the Adjutant General's circular letter of 12 December 1798 apparently stimulated him to approach the Duke on the subject. At any rate, in January 1799 he laid before York a rather grandiose plan for an army college. The Duke, after reading it carefully and sympathetically, advised LeMarchant that it was impractical. It demanded a great outlay of public money; it could not succeed until people's prejudices, which had wrecked Richmond's scheme, were removed; and prejudices could only be removed by proving them ground-

---

[1] Adjutant General's Circular of 12 December 1798, WO/3/19.
[2] D. LeMarchant, *Memoir of Major General LeMarchant*, chapter vi.

less, a task which would require stronger arguments than any in Le-Marchant's draft. However, the Duke concluded to LeMarchant, 'If you will revise your plan, and accompany it with all the details necessary for satisfying the public, it shall have my warm support'.[1] As an earnest of that support the Duke appointed LeMarchant to serve at High Wycombe as Jarry's assistant.

The events that followed this interview present a curious picture in the story told by LeMarchant's son. The younger LeMarchant may well have been hazy on dates and details (for example, he supposes that Jarry only came into the scheme *after* his father had first approached the Duke, though a comparison of his own dates with the Adjutant General's correspondence proves this to be mistaken), yet the general outline of his story need not on that account be wrong. Those general outlines show the Duke as betraying no outward interest in founding a national military college. Instead the relatively obscure Lt. Col. LeMarchant is busily employed on what would now be called a publicity campaign. For this he had certain strong advantages—a good appearance, an attractive manner and a wide acquaintance. In the months when he was teaching the sword exercise, he had come into contact with colonels of yeomanry regiments all over the country. The yeomanry were fashionable and well-to-do, their colonels were commonly persons of influence, sometimes members of Parliament, and even owners of rotten boroughs. Many colonels, taken by LeMarchant's enthusiasm and impressed by the prospectus which he circularized to them, declared their readiness to support his scheme. Finally, the Duke turned LeMarchant loose upon the cabinet itself, in whose hands a draft of the college prospectus had long lain unconsidered; and, with the particular help of Huskisson, Le-Marchant was at last successful in winning Pitt's consent to have his scheme formally examined and reported on by a committee of generals.

So far the success seems all LeMarchant's, but in the background the Duke had been far from idle. He had given liberally of his time to LeMarchant, working and reworking over the scheme, pointing out objections and preparing answers to them. He had had his staff—his private secretary, and the Adjutant and Quarter Master Generals—work on it too. He had particularly demanded that great desideratum of politicians, a statement of the proposed expense, before he approved the plan. He had then forwarded the plan to the ministers, and, at least so far as the written record goes, had never complained of their neglect of it, till months later he placed them in the embarrassing position of being confronted with its slighted author, LeMarchant. By that date too he was able to point to the actual existence of an infant college, to the fact that it was under a most distinguished instructor, and yet was in danger of foundering because officers were too ill-prepared to digest his instruction. The argument was

[1] LeMarchant, *loc. cit.*

therefore available that either the existing college must be expanded with more preparatory instruction and instructors, or a promising start must be thrown away. Finally, one can only suppose it normal that the Duke would be asked to suggest names for the committee of generals who were to pronounce judgement on LeMarchant's scheme,[1] and a heavily weighted committee it was. The Duke himself presided; it included both the past and present Adjutant Generals, Sir William Fawcett and Harry Calvert, and the Quarter Master General, David Dundas—all men who had nursed the scheme from infancy; also Lt. Gen. Harcourt, who evidently favoured the scheme, because he consented to be the college's first governor. Somehow LeMarchant himself was added to this distinguished collection of high-ranking officers, and if the other four generals and noblemen on the committee had been united in opposition (a point on which there is no record), they would have been comfortably outvoted.

Yet LeMarchant's scheme did not come through the committee's hands unscathed. Of three points he had proposed, only two were accepted—a junior college for training future officers, and a staff college for teaching the higher branches of the art of war. The third, the creation of a 'Legion', or department for giving free education to the sons of N.C.O.'s and serving soldiers, was dropped. It is described as being dropped at the instance of David Dundas, who urged that it would lead to too much promotion from the ranks; and this, according to Dundas, was something which in France had led to much desertion because men disliked taking orders from their former equals. It seems odd that this objection to part of LeMarchant's scheme should be raised at this stage by, of all people, Dundas, who had had a considerable hand in shaping the scheme as it came before the committee. One is tempted to suspect the Horse Guards staff of permitting this proposal to stand in the scheme only in order that it might be dropped at the last, as a sop to the politicians' desire for economy. Anyway they now pruned it out, and on returning the matter to the ministers they succeeded in winning a qualified approval for the plan they had thus cheapened. It took time, of course, to win even that. The wheels of cabinet government did not turn fast, but Jarry's existing private school for staff officers was at last adopted as a national institution and formally named the Royal Military College by a warrant of 24 June 1801. Eleven days later, the Duke of York wrote his father to confirm arrangements that had evidently been informally made already—the appointment of LeMarchant as Lieutenant Governor, of Greenwood as treasurer, and some arrangements, not easily understood now, about transferring professors of various subjects to High Wycombe.[2] These last, of whom there were four, were men who deserve some sympathy; they had been needed, LeMarchant had selected them some time earlier, but

---

[1] *Ibid.*
[2] Duke of York to George III, 1 July 1801, Windsor, 10275–6.

their positions remained obviously insecure, and their salaries almost certainly unpaid, till such time as the slow procedures of government at last produced the Royal Warrant; and the younger LeMarchant describes the delays in the latter as being so provoking as to drive his father almost to the point of resignation.[1]

At last, then, the plan seemed safely launched, yet LeMarchant was still not satisfied. The warrant of 24 June 1801 was a very bald document. It gave the new staff officers' training school the name of 'The Royal Military College' and it created a board of governors. But it laid down no rules for the conduct of the teaching, or standards of admission; and it said nothing about the creation of a junior branch.

Each omission was a disappointment to LeMarchant, the first no less than the second. A year before the warrant of 24 June 1801 was issued, he had written Harry Calvert a forceful letter in which he said:

If the Appointments to Offices, the Public Examinations conducted (*sic*) together with the Application of the Charities (i.e. the free education in the junior department) are left to every succeeding governor to regulate according to his own views, the Charity will be perverted, the Appointments made a source of patronage and the Public Examinations will be conducted by favor, to the Disgrace of the Establishment.

If the power to abuse rests with those in authority, *with time* that abuse of power is certain to happen; therefore a Charter, in which these and every Regulation is specified, will place the laws of the college under the immediate protection of the Crown. Whatever alterations times and circumstances may render necessary, it will be in His Majesty's power to make, but these alterations will be the effect of Deliberation and not inconsiderably done. Under such high authority there is no danger that whatever changes may be made will be directed to venal purposes.[2]

To the modern eye LeMarchant's conviction that George III was a sufficient guarantor of honesty may seem stranger than his certainty that want of regulation would make abuses sure. Yet each conviction was justified by experience. LeMarchant, and all his generation, had seen the army corrupted by politics before 1795 and restored by Royal authority thereafter. And, in due course, the college's governing board did produce the regulations, which were established by a Royal Warrant dated 9 December 1801.

In part these regulations deal with normal, and dull, matters of routine. What the warrant has to say about educational standards is revealing and important.

To be admitted to the college an officer had to be at least nineteen years old, with at least two years of regimental service behind him, and he must be 'well grounded in a Knowledge of Discipline and the interior care of a troop or a company'. Academically, he had only to know the first four rules of arithmetic and enough French to begin the first French course the college provided. And the point most likely to strike the modern

---

[1] D. LeMarchant, *loc. cit.*
[2] LeMarchant to Calvert, 17 June 1800, WO/1/620.

reader is the extremely elementary nature of the instruction given in the first division of each course at the college. Yet it is to be remembered that boys could enter the army at no greater age than sixteen; also that before reaching the college they had all had at least two years in which to forget their schooling. It was, then, only realistic for the first classes to be elementary, as the early difficulties of General Jarry had shown.

So in the first division of French the officer-student merely learnt irregular verbs and did simple exercises. In the second division he studied syntax, did more exercises and had to 'read and construe the Lectures of the Department on Military Surveys'. That done, he passed into the third division, where he continued doing exercises, did some more syntax, and construed 'the Lectures of the Department on Fortification'. From this he proceeded in the fourth division to read 'a work entitled "The Hussar", "The Instructions of the King of Prussia to his Officers"', and the lectures on Castrametation, Grand Guards and Reconnaissance. In the fifth division he had to read and construe 'The Instructions of the King of Prussia to his General Officers', and the lectures of the Department on the March and Movements of Armies. Here it is interesting to see how, when Napoleon was already master of France, and a good deal more than France, it was still Frederick the Great who was regarded as the ideal example and teacher of the art of war. The French authors now thought important, Guibert, Bourcet and du Teil, had no place in the curriculum.

In mathematics, the student officer began with nothing more advanced than fractions and decimals; and from these he proceeded into the second division to study the rules of proportion, square and cube roots, and the use of logarithms; then he advanced to geometry. In the fourth division he took up trigonometry and its use in the field for measuring heights and distances; lastly he had to be taught the use of the theodolite in surveying.

As surveying was the end to which all his instruction in mathematics led, it is not surprising that drawing is the next subject on the list; and it was no more intended to make the student an artist than was the French course intended to make him appreciate Voltaire and Rousseau. The end to which the drawing course led up was the sketching of ground. It began with an explanation of the nature of plans and the properties and uses of mathematical drawing instruments. In the first division there was also a little of 'delineation of Figures by the Eye, from Examples and Models', but this was for the very practical purpose of learning 'to judge accurately of Shapes and Proportions and of acquiring Command of Hand'. There followed practice in shading and the application of colour, and 'observing Ground in comparison with a Plan, for the purpose of acquiring distinct and complete ideas of the nature and value of the representation which Plans of the Ground convey'. The third division of drawing took the student out of doors and taught him to draw and shade hills with a brush and pen, after examples in adjacent country (and there are plenty of hills in the High Wycombe end of Buckinghamshire). He was also coached in 'forming an eye to Distances and Angles on Horseback', and sketching ground under the instruction of a master. Finally, in the fourth division, he had to sketch ground without a master, and to go out with a group of fellow pupils to make sketches of ground which, when finished, could be joined together so as to make one general plan of the country.

After drawing, the next two subjects listed are field fortification and a study of the German language.

Field fortification began theoretically with instruction about the terms employed, the materials to be used and tracing on paper the works described in the lectures; finally the student had to trace camps on the ground and to apply 'the Principles of Attack and Defence with reference to local features of the Country and Lectures that have been given'. German begins with the rudiments of grammar and ends with reading 'The King of Prussia's Instructions to his General Officers'.

Then, on the top of all that has thus far been learnt, come two courses which involve the practical application of the knowledge gained. The first deals with reconnaissance; the reconnaissance of ground for a given number of columns in route of march; reconnoitring the route of a column advancing; estimating the labours of opening the several communications, the number of artificers required and the time required to clear the route of march of a column; and detailing the same on a plan. The student then had to reconnoitre ground for a given number of troops to take up a defensive position and to plan a chain of posts and batteries to cover it. Finally, he had to reconnoitre ground suitable to encamp a number of troops preparatory to an offensive, 'having particular Attention in taking up the Ground, to the Movements of the Army, by providing the readiest Means of Directing its Operations'.

This course is thus mainly a training in the movement of a single column. The final course deals with the co-ordination of the movements of several columns. The student had first to calculate the time of a column's march under various circumstances, and the times of several columns relative to one another. Then he had to reconnoitre routes for these several columns to advance, and to form them on the march in conformity to the field of battle they were to occupy. He must further regulate their 'March and Arrival on the Field...relatively to the manner of deploying; whether with a view to encamp or to form an order of battle'. Having practised all these calculations according to the requirements of the offensive, the student had next to prepare them for the retreat and defensive. And his last exercises consisted of learning 'to estimate the Resources of a Country in green and dry Forage; in Cattle and Grain; Horses and Carriages; together with Population'; and 'to draw out Plans of Resources, Plans of Operations, of Position and of Cantonments'. When he had learnt all these things, and had proven his knowledge in an oral examination, he passed out of the college, qualified as a staff officer; and his name was registered at the college for the Commander-in-Chief's information.

But not only were the subjects of study prescribed; the rate of progress was also regulated. The subjects were themselves closely interrelated, and no man was to progress in one field beyond the point which his knowledge of another field permitted. The student was not to begin to learn German till he was in the fifth division of French; nor was he to begin the study of fortification till he had reached the third division of mathematics, which dealt with geometry. He was not to begin sketching ground from nature till he had trained his eye to judge distances and had gone through practical geometry. Thus at no point was he allowed to start on the more advanced subjects till he was enabled, by his thorough knowledge of the simpler, to understand what he was about.

But enough of the senior department of the Royal Military College. It will be remembered that a junior branch had also been proposed; to this we must now turn. It was founded, also by Royal Warrant, in the spring of 1802. That warrant prescribed a twofold purpose; to educate some (but by no means all) of those who from early life were intended for the military profession; and, secondly, 'to afford a Provision for the Orphan Sons of those meritorious Officers who have fallen or been disabled in the Service of their Country as well as for the Sons of those Officers in our Military Service who, from pecuniary difficulties, might not otherwise be able to give them an adequate Education'. The school was to contain 100 cadets, who were to enter upon three different establishments. First, there were to be 30 sons of officers who had either died or been maimed on active service; these 30 were to receive their education, board and clothing free of all expense. Next were to be 20 sons of officers actually in the service; these were to pay £40 per annum in return for which they were to receive education, board and clothing. The last category was to contain 30 sons of noblemen and gentlemen and 20 cadets of the East India Company's service; these were to pay £90 a year for their education, board and clothing. The cadets were thus drawn from very varied sources, some from almost pauper homes, and some from the wealthiest homes in the land; and so it may perhaps be appropriate to mention here one provision that was eminently wise in view of these differences of circumstance; namely, that no cadet was on any account to be allowed by his parents or friends to come up to the college with a greater sum of money in his possession than one guinea. Nor, though a boy's people might allow him pocket money, was he ever to receive more than 2s. 6d. a week. Without some such rule it would have been difficult for cadets to live on an equality at the college. In a similar fashion some English public schools still attempt to regulate the amount of pocket money that boys are allowed by their parents.

Next we come to the entrance qualifications. No cadet could be admitted to the college who was not over thirteen and under fifteen; and to prove his age he must produce a 'sufficient Certificate of the time of his Birth'; and he must be mentally and physically fit. He must also pass certain educational tests before he could enter the college; he had to be able to write a good hand and to be well grounded in grammar and arithmetic.

The subjects in which they were to be instructed were, according to the warrant, 'Mathematics, Fortification, and general Principles of Gunnery and Artillery Service'. They shall also be taught drawing of plans, military movements and perspective; likewise the knowledge of tactics, military geography and history; together with the German and French languages. (The twenty cadets of the East India Company were excused learning German on the ground that it could be of no use to them; however, as provision was to be made for their instruction in oriental languages, they escaped nothing but, rather, were worse off.) 'Frequent lectures shall be given on Natural and Moral Philosophy.' Athletics were there too. Riding and fencing, the use of the sabre and swimming are also to be included among their acquirements; but one is glad to notice that dancing, which was originally proposed, was after all omitted. Public examinations were to be held from time to time and no cadet could be recommended from the college for a commission in the army until he had passed a leaving examination and had 'obtained a Certificate thereof, signed by such Commissioners as shall be present at the Examination'. Any cadet who after four years at the college failed to pass the leaving examination would have to quit the college, unless he could show that his failure was due to continued ill health or some other unavoidable interruption of his studies.

So much for the theoretical side of a cadet's education at the college. For learning the practical part of their profession, they were formed into a company. Four would act as commissioned officers, one being a captain lieutenant, two lieutenants and one an ensign; there were to be five sergeants, ten squads of nine each and one supernumerary. Thus they would learn their drill and manœuvres actually on the parade ground and would begin at the beginning of it, in the position of private soldiers. For this purpose they were to have two military instructors; one inspector of a company who must hold the rank of a subaltern in the army; and one company sergeant major who must have served in a regiment of the line.

To supervise the whole of their education, on both the practical and the theoretical side, there was to be a superintendent. The man who filled this post must not be under the rank of captain in the army. He was to receive orders from, and make reports to, the Governor or Lieutenant Governor of the college; and he was diligently to superintend the studies of the pupils and to be responsible for the discipline and interior regulation of the department.

The junior department of the Royal Military College was not situated at High Wycombe, but at Great Marlow. As, however, Great Marlow and High Wycombe are but four miles apart it was possible for the two departments to be under one and the same governing authority; and the last section of this warrant of March 1802 deals with that authority. A collegiate board was to govern the internal officers of both departments; it was to consist of the Governor, the Lieutenant Governor, and the commandant of each department; to form a quorum, at least three of these four must be present, and either the Governor or Lieutenant Governor had always to preside. When all four attended, and their opinions on any matter were equally divided, the president, that is, the Governor, was to have a casting vote. They were to assemble for the dispatch of business at least once a month. Before them were to be held the public examinations of both departments of the college, which were apparently oral; but when they met for the purpose of conducting examinations, one or more members of the Supreme Board were to attend and take their seats at the Collegiate Board; and no final passing-out examination could be held without a member of the Supreme Board being present. The President of the Supreme Board was to select the member or members of this board who were to attend the examination. This rule was presumably a safeguard against the examinations being conducted by favour, one of the abuses which LeMarchant had been so sure would creep in unless specially guarded against. This seems the more likely because the Collegiate Board had to examine, not only the cadets, but also prospective teachers, when a situation at the college fell vacant; and on these occasions it was not necessary for any of the Supreme Board to be present. The Collegiate Board was in addition responsible for the financial business of the college; they had to call for tenders for furnishing the supplies needed by the college and to make contracts for them; but no contract was to be entered into for a longer period than one year. They were to examine all accounts, and at the expiration of every quarter to send a statement of them to the treasurer of the Supreme Board.

That is the story of the foundation of the Royal Military College and of its constitution. The new institution did not get off to a very good start. The assembling of young officers together for the purposes of study was something so new in the army that the first batch of the young men did not realize its importance; and it was difficult to get them to work as hard as they should. In December 1802 we find the Adjutant General writing to General Harcourt, the Governor, that the Commander-in-Chief was disappointed with the reports of the progress made by the pupils. Their backwardness had been attributed to their inexperience and youth; but, the Duke of York pointed out, the Collegiate Board should inquire more strictly and fully into the qualifications of candidates before they were admitted, and if this were properly done there need be no more waste of instruction upon idle officers.[1] In the following April we find that His Royal Highness was still disappointed with the reports from the senior department; some officers were absent without leave; and some had secured leave for reasons which the Duke thought quite inadequate. Even when leave was granted on Sundays, he disapproved of it; and he gave orders that one captain who was absent without leave was to be 'no longer considered as belonging to the college', and a lieutenant who had overstayed leave was to be warned.[2] And these admonitions of the Duke, coupled, as the second was, with a severe example, seem to have had their effect for they did not need to be again repeated.

This much we learn from the Commander-in-Chief's official correspondence. From other sources too we find that discipline at the college was not at first all that it should have been. General Jarry, who was old, eccentric and a foreigner, was mocked by some of the young officers, a number of whom greatly insulted him by smashing up a number of models of field fortifications he had taken the trouble to make. The young men responsible for this stupid performance were sent back to their regiments; but General Jarry never repaired the models. Again, one day two officers were out walking by the river, and saw an old farmer fishing from a boat. They hailed him, and demanded that he should row them up the river. Very obligingly he did so; but before he had gone far, they leapt upon him, tipped him overboard, and rowed away themselves in his boat. The farmer had, fortunately, fallen into a shallow stretch of water and was able to struggle ashore. He then went and informed LeMarchant, who was furious when he heard, and promised to punish the officers most severely; but against this the farmer protested; he was a Quaker, he said, and he desired nothing less than to get his fellow human beings into any sort of trouble. Then why, asked LeMarchant, had he reported the officers if he did not wish them punished? In order, he replied, that LeMarchant might tell them not to do it again. And so these officers were let off; but not all those who misbehaved themselves had Quakers to intercede for them, and LeMarchant, who was not a man to suffer fools gladly, managed with time to improve the discipline of the senior branch.[3]

The boys in the junior department at Great Marlow also gave trouble at the start, and trouble, at that, of a serious nature. On 19 August 1804 General Harcourt had to report that nine cadets had entered into what was described as 'a mutinous conspiracy'. Precisely what this consisted of we are not told; but the Duke of York certainly took it most seriously,

---

[1] Adjutant General to Harcourt, 11 December 1802, WO/3/35.
[2] Same to same, 6 April 1803, WO/3/35.
[3] The incidents in this paragraph are drawn from Denis LeMarchant's memoir of his father, chapter VI.

for he reported it to the King, and ordered all the culprits to be solemnly expelled. For this ceremony all the cadets of the junior department were to assemble under arms, and every officer and student of each department was to attend. It was then publicly to be pointed out to the culprits that by civil law the offence they had attempted would have subjected them to transportation as felons, and if submitted to a military tribunal 'would subject them to a most ignominious death' (so their offence, whatever it was, certainly seems serious). They were then to be informed that the King had ordered them to be expelled with every mark of infamy and that they were thereafter to be held unworthy of the honour of serving His Majesty in any military capacity. And when this announcement had been made in the 'manner...best calculated to impress the minds of the other cadets with a just sense of the enormity of the offender's guilt', every vestige of the dress and uniform of the college was to be stripped off them by a drummer, their swords and arms were to be broken, and they were to be solemnly dismissed from the college. 'Measures', the instructions continue, 'must be taken for their immediate removal from the college'; but let us hope time was allowed them in which to replace the 'dress and uniform of the college' with civilian garments with which the cadet had to supply himself. When this extraordinary performance had been concluded the commandant was to report it to the Adjutant General for the Commander-in-Chief's information, stating to what class the culprits belonged and whether any of them held commissions; for if they had commissions, they were to be deprived of them.[1]

It is clear then that those in authority over the Royal Military College had a number of difficulties to overcome before the institution was all that could be desired. But that the college was of great value to the service there can be no doubt. As will be gathered from what we have said above the duties of a staff officer were not light, and at the senior branch those duties were thoroughly taught. Jobs were soon found for them. In the winter of 1802 a number of them were employed to make a survey on the coast[2] (and here it may be remembered that a failure to make a survey of their border was one of the principal errors for which the Duke of York had blamed the Dutch in 1794). When the invasion scare of 1805 was at its height and it was necessary to improvise brigade staffs for the volunteer units, pupils still actually at the college were detailed in the event of invasion to repair hurriedly to places of assembly to serve with the generals who were to command volunteer brigades. One crusty lieutenant general, who had been told that in the event of the enemy landing, he would be joined by a couple of officers from Wycombe, replied that he supposed the young gentlemen would inform him what use he was to make of them on their arrival at Kettering; and to him the Adjutant

---

[1] Wynyard to Harcourt, 23 August 1804, WO/3/37.
[2] Calvert to Harcourt, 1 January 1803, WO/3/35.

General answered that the officers had been selected by the Commander-in-Chief from among the students of the senior branch of the Royal Military College 'for the purpose of ensuring you the immediate aid of intelligent officers'.[1] Besides creating a supply of officers competent for staff work, the college must have done good by diffusing through the army men who understood surveying and field fortification.

And if there still be doubts as to the value and success of the Royal Military College they may be laid to rest by a comparison between the first warrants that founded it and the warrant of 1808 that altered and reconstituted it. The differences between them are mainly slight and trivial. The required age and terms of service of candidates for the senior department are increased. The instructions about the conduct of studies are briefer and less detailed. The instructions about the management of its financial concerns are far more detailed. But the chief and greatest alteration deals with the junior department, which was quadrupled. In the place of one company of cadets there were to be four. They were moreover to receive the pay of 2s. 6d. a day. This should be sufficient evidence of the value of the college in the opinion both of the government and the parents of prospective officers.

The credit for the founding of the institution is, obviously, divided. It was LeMarchant who carefully elaborated and thoroughly worked out a plan of what was needed and thereby produced an ideal which could be aimed at if not achieved in every detail; it was LeMarchant again who, as Lieutenant Governor, was able, under Harcourt, to guide the infant institution along the path he would have it take. It was the Duke of York who, foreseeing that the introduction of a full-fledged college was not immediately practicable, secured the achievement of the modest beginning from which it was possible within three years to develop most of what LeMarchant had envisaged; how much else besides he contributed by means of advice and warning to LeMarchant we cannot assess, though LeMarchant's son acknowledges a debt. These two are chiefly responsible. There were others who bore a lesser but valuable part. Huskisson was certainly one of these, and Sir Harry Calvert another; while it would seem the Duke's successive private secretaries, Brownrigg and Clinton, contributed much. But, unable as we are to say how much or how little each contributed, the sum of their effort was beyond doubt an asset to the army and so to the nation.

[1] Calvert to Harcourt, 21 August, and to Manners, 5 September 1805, WO/3/39.

APPENDIX TO CHAPTER 8

The following is the syllabus of the Royal Military Academy in the early 1790's, extracted from W. D. Jones's *Records of the Royal Military Academy* (Woolwich, 1851), pp. 45 *seq.*

FORTIFICATION

(1) The definitions and explanations of the works of both Regular and Irregular Fortification, correctly wrote and understood.

(2) The construction of the 1st, 2nd and 3rd Systems of M. DeVauban, described on paper.

(3) The same of M. Coehorn's System.

(4) The same of M. de Cormontaingne's System.

(5) Irregular Fortification described on paper.

(6) The Attack and Defence of Fortified Places.

(7) The Art of Mining.

(8) The Elements of Field Fortification.

(9) How to trace on the Ground; Permanent and Field Fortification, with and without Mathematical Instruments.

(10) To take Plans with and without Instruments.

(11) Theory and Practice of Levelling.

(12) How to estimate the works of a Fortification, viz. Revetments, Ramparts, Ditches, Batardeaux, Powder Magazines, turned and joined Arches.

(13) To produce a fair copy of the book containing Calculations, Plans and Sections relative to the Estimates.

(14) To produce the complete course of the above neatly drawn, containing the Plans, Sections and Geometrical elevations, composed of 68 Plates.

(15) To produce the Field Book containing the practice on the ground, the tracing, and works of Permanent Fortification, Surveying and Levelling.

Printed and Manuscript Books made use of in the above Course

The Course of Fortification from M. Landmann, Comprised in 68 Plates.

The Estimates from M. Landmann's Manuscripts.

Surveying and Tracing outworks on the ground, from M. Landmann's Manuscripts.

The Attack and Defence of Fortified Places, by Mr Muller.

Playdell's Field Fortification.

ARTILLERY

(1) The definitions and explanations of the several parts of Artillery; also, tables containing the general dimensions and construction of Guns and Mortars, correctly wrote and understood.

(2) The general construction of Brass and Iron Guns, Sea and Land Mortars and Howitzers, described on paper.

(3) The general construction of Ship and Garrison Carriages, Travelling Carriages, Land and Sea Mortar Beds, described as above.

(4) The same of the Iron Work for Ship, Garrison and Travelling Carriages.

(5) The different kinds of wood made use of for the several sorts of Gun Carriages and Mortar Beds.

(6) How to find the weight of Guns, Mortars and Howitzers.

(7) To find the quantity of Powder which a Chamber contains.

(8) To find the diameter of Shot and bores of Guns.

(9) To find the weight of Shot and Shells.

(10) To find the number of Shot and Shells contained in a Pile.

(11) To ascertain the number of horses necessary to draw the different natures of Ordnance.

(12) The number of men required to construct a Battery in one night.

(13) To produce a complete course of the above neatly drawn, containing the Plans, Sections and Geometrical elevations, composed of 57 Plates.

Printed and Manuscript Books made use of in the above Course

The Course of Artillery from M. Landmann, in 57 Plates.

The construction of Artillery from Major Bloomfield, Inspector, of the Royal Artillery.

Muller's Artillery.

MATHEMATICS

(1) *Arithmetic*, in all its parts.

(2) *Logarithms*, their nature, use and construction.

(3) *Geometry*, the theory from Euclid's Elements 4 first Books.

(4) *Algebra*, from the first Elements, to the Solution of Cubic and higher Equations.

(5) *Trigonometry*, with Heights and Distances.

(6) *Mensuration*, in Superfices and Solids, in Theory and Practice, with Surveying and Measuring of Artificer's Works, Buildings, Timber, etc.

(7) *Conic Sections.*

(8) *Mechanics*, including motions equable and variable, Forces, constant, variable and percussive, Gravity, Sound and Distances, Inclined Planes, Projectiles, Practical Gunnery, Pendulums, Centres of Gravity, Percussion, Oscillations and Gyration, Ballistic Pendulum, etc.

(9) *Fluxions.*

(10) *Hydrostatics and Hydraulics*, including the pressure, motion and issuing of Fluids, the filling and exhausting of Vessels, etc., Specific Gravities of Bodies, Syphons, Pumps, Diving Bells, etc.

(11) *Pneumatics*, including the nature, properties and effects of the Air and the Atmosphere, with the Air Pumps, Syringes, Condensing Engine, Thermometer, Barometer, with the method of measuring altitudes by the Barometer and Thermometer.

(12) *Practical Exercises*, concerning these and various other branches, as the weight and dimensions, and piling, of Shot and Shells, bulk or capacities of various vessels or figures to contain certain weights of powder, distances by the motion of sound, concerning the effects of variable and constant forces, etc.

(13) *Resistance of Fluids*, as water, air, etc., with their action or bodies in motion, etc.

(14) *Gunnery*, Robin's new principles of Gunnery, Experiments, particularly with the Ballistic Pendulum.

Printed and Manuscript Books made use of in the above Course

Books. Dr Hutton's Arithmetic, Logarithms, Mensuration, Conic Sections and Select Exercises; Tracts; Mr Robin's Gunnery, the 1st vol. of his Works; Professor Simpson's (of Glasgow) Elements of Algebra; Rossignal's Geometry; Bonnycastle's Algebra; Simpson's Algebra for application to Geometry.

Manuscripts. Dr Hutton's Fluxion's, Mechanics, Hydrostatics, Pneumatics.

The above Course of Mathematics is correctly wrote down by the Gentlemen Cadets in their books, with Drawings applicable to the several parts of it.

DRAWING

With the 2nd Drawing Master

Figure Drawing, the several parts of the human figure, from Drawings by the Master.

Perspective, in Theory and Practice; 1st Theory of Perspective; 2nd Putting Planes in Perspective; 3rd Elevations; 4th Measures and proportions of Figures at different distances; 5th Lights and Shadows; thus far with the Jesuit's Perspective.

With the 1st Drawing Master

With Mr P. Sandby, putting Perspective in practice by copying from Drawings, which qualifies them for Drawing from nature, teaches them the effect of Light and Shade, and makes them acquainted also with Aerial Perspective; then to proceed to take views about Woolwich and other places, which teaches them at the same time to break ground, and forms the eye to the knowledge of it.

THE FRENCH LANGUAGE

Grammar and Pronounciation thoroughly learned and the practical application of it.

Translation, from English into French, and from French into English, the translation wrote down and made correct.

Exercises, particular exercises to be given them to perform in the Language, chiefly on subjects that have a military tendency.

CHEMISTRY

The Gentlemen Cadets generally attend two, and often, three, courses of Lectures in Chemistry, the theory and practice of it; they make notes during the Lectures, which are thirty-two in number, these they enter into fair books, which are given them for that purpose, and which are most copious on the heads relative to Artillery, as gun powder, the materials that compose it, metals, etc.

The Gentlemen Cadets are also taught Fencing and Dancing, the Exercises of Small Arms, and Light Field Pieces.

CHAPTER 9[1]

MANPOWER

RECRUITING in Britain in the period 1793–1815 is a subject large enough for a whole book. Indeed Fortescue has written a whole book on manpower in the period after the Treaty of Amiens alone.[2] Elsewhere, too, he has stated that 'in the years 1802 and 1803 there were passed no fewer than twenty-one Acts of Parliament and at least two principal codes of regulations, all designed to raise men for the defence of the realm, voluntarily or by compulsion. Many of these Acts were mutually contradictory or mutually destructive, though not drawn with any such intent; and frequently they conflicted with the two codes of regulations which themselves could not be harmoniously worked together.'[3] The subject of manpower is therefore not merely so large but also so complex that in a work of this nature only a sketch of it is possible.

That sketch must start in the days preceding France's declaration of war in February 1793, for the very first effect of war was to expose what the peacetime miserliness of Parliament had done to recruiting. From 1660 to 1792 the government had kept the soldier's daily wage down to 6d. a day, and out of it had expected him to buy all his food, and to replace any article of equipment or clothing that was worn out, stolen, or lost before it was officially due to be replaced. But the cost of living was rising against the soldier through all these long years in which his rate of pay remained unaltered. The result in 1790 was that from sheer poverty the wretched private was 'unable to satisfy the common calls of hunger, and being without any hope of relief he naturally deserted in despair'.[4] Such was the state of the army when Pitt desired to fling it into action against the veterans of Suvorov in an attempt—happily frustrated—to wrest the Black Sea port of Oczakov from Catherine II. This war scare, however, had probably one fortunate result. It lent force to the arguments of Sir

---

[1] As it has been suggested that this chapter is misplaced and should come earlier in the book I had better explain my reasons for leaving it to come nearly at the end.

There were, in effect, not one, but two British armies in the period covered, namely, the Ordnance troops under the Master General, and the cavalry and infantry under the Commander-in-Chief. Since the manpower problem affected both, this chapter needs to come where it can apply to both, i.e. either first or last. Objections to putting it first are (a) that, as men are useless till you have some competent organization to make use of them, the chapters on training, discipline and education seemed to have a fair priority; and (b) there is the chronological point that, as the manpower problem was the last one to which an effective solution was found, the last place in the book is the most reasonable one for it to occupy.

[2] *County Lieutenancies and the Army* (London, 1909).
[3] *Historical and Military Essays* (London, 1928), p. 211.
[4] Fortescue, *British Army*, III, 520.

William Fawcett, the Adjutant General, when he urged that the lot of the private soldier must be improved. So in the next year, 1792, the amount of stoppages that could be legally made from the soldier's pay was limited and a ration of bread was actually issued to him free, at a cost to the nation of no less than 10½d. per man per week. 'The general result of these reforms', writes Fortescue, 'was that the soldier not only received enough food to keep him alive, but the magnificent sum of 18s. 0½d. a year—over and above all deductions for food and clothing.'[1]

But not even so bright a prize as 18s. a year was temptation enough to make the British working man eager to sign away his whole life and freedom, and, though recruiting improved, the army's ranks were still wasted and thin when it was suddenly called into action against France.

It is, of course, usual for a power to begin recruiting vigorously at the outbreak of war in order to increase its peacetime strength. But Britain's task was to recruit in order to bring her army up to its nominal peacetime strength. The results were immediately seen in Flanders. The second British brigade sent there, as early as April 1793, was such a raw rabble of new-raised men as to be 'totally unfit for service'.[2] Such was the handicap with which the army began 'the great war with France'.

The next startling point, which the researcher encounters, is the fact that this greatest war which Britain had yet faced was the first in which her statesmen lacked the moral courage to take the men they needed for victory by direct conscription for offensive service. Previous British governments, from the days of William III even to those of Lord North, had not flinched from impressing at least the workless for active service.[3] Only one such attempt was made by Pitt's government and its successors, and that attempt was only made in 1796, when the chance of swift victory had been let slip. It consisted of two acts of Parliament; one applied to England,[4] the other to Scotland;[5] they were referred to as the 'Quota Acts', because each aimed to raise a given number of men, called a 'quota', from every parish; each was so ill-drawn as to require the passage of another act 'to explain and amend' it in a matter of weeks; each was full of loopholes; neither made any serious attempt to secure that the army received men fit for service, or even that it received men at all. Thus any parish which preferred not to meet its quota by compelling men to serve was permitted to buy its way out of its responsibilities by paying a fine; and no statement of physical standards of any kind prescribed what sort

---

[1] *Ibid.* p. 521.

[2] Calvert to John Calvert, 26 April 1893, in Harry Verney, *Journals and Correspondence of Sir Harry Calvert* (London, 1853), p. 67.

[3] Lord North's act is 18 Geo. III, cap. 53; it rather closely follows 30 Geo. II, cap. 8.

[4] 37 Geo. III, cap. 4, passed on 11 November 1796 and amended by 37 Geo. III, cap. 24, passed 30 December 1796.

[5] 37 Geo. III, cap. 4, passed on 11 November 1796 and amended by 37 Geo. III, cap. 39, passed on 27 March 1797.

of men were required. Military men were left hoping that in these matters 'H.M.'s printed Regulations and Instructions, bearing the date of 20 September last, for carrying on the recruiting service' would be accepted as defining what constituted a satisfactory recruit.[1] Accordingly, some receiving officers were provided with army surgeons to inspect the fitness of the men; others were instructed to employ for the purpose 'some Surgeon of Reputation in the Place, the expence of which will be defrayed by the War Office'.[2] But these precautions might as well have been left untaken. Regulations printed for the direction of military men had not the force of law for civilians; and the civil magistrates charged with executing the acts were given power to compel the receiving officers to take whatever men they chose to provide. This power was abused sufficiently freely to compel some reference to physical standards in the amending acts;[3] but even so those measures did no more than authorize the rejection of children under eighteen who had not yet grown to be 5 feet 3 inches tall and of older men under 5 feet 4 inches. Finally, the acts laid down no procedure for dealing with recruits who seized the first opportunity of deserting. These were evidently numerous; and all that the receiving officers could do was to keep in their 'Possession the Certificates of such recruits as have deserted' till the amending and explaining acts were passed[4] (but where would the deserters be then? And how were they to be recognized and apprehended?).

Such was the first and last attempt to provide Britain with an offensive force by compulsion during the great war with France. That acts as imperfect as these were never renewed is less wonderful than the fact that any government could think them worth the time Parliament wasted in passing them in the first place. Yet their failure need not perhaps be unduly regretted. There is nothing very admirable about a system of compulsion which applies only to those who are both workless and voteless—a defect which these acts shared with their more efficient predecessors.

The next fact the student encounters is that while so little was done to build up an offensive force to win victory abroad, a whole series of auxiliary forces were raised for no more decisive purpose than fighting defensive battles on British soil. Such battles could, of course, have been at least as successfully fought by a properly recruited body of regulars; and, except in Ireland, the navy was in fact to prevent them from being fought at all. Yet these defensive forces were not only raised, but raised in

---

[1] Adjutant General to Lt. Col. Enys, 10 December 1796, WO/3/30.

[2] Adjutant General's Circular, 1 December 1796, *ibid*.

[3] For example, the receiving officer at Kingston on Thames is found asking the Adjutant General's support for rejecting a man made unfit for service by venereal disease (Adjutant General to Major Armstrong, 17 December 1796, *ibid*.).

[4] Adjutant General to Major Armstrong, 17 December 1796, and to Major Bygrave, 23 December 1796, *ibid*.

a manner injurious to the regular army, the one force available for the offensive action which can alone bring victory.

The first of these auxiliary forces was, of course, the militia, raised under the authority of the Home Office. Their regiments were filled with temporary soldiers raised by conscription for home defence in wartime only. The men were selected by ballot, but were not required to serve personally provided they could find a substitute.[1] Few wished to serve personally, and for a man who did not 'it was a matter of urgency to find someone at once' to take his place. But the substitute expected to be well paid, so the 'club' method of insurance was common, and, with a limited field of prospective 'substitutes', the market rose. In 1803 Sergeant Butler received 'no less than £20 for entering the Militia as a substitute for a Mr. G'.[2] Here the militia came into immediate and direct competition with the regular army. The substitutes were naturally men ready by choice to enter the life of a soldier for a price; as such they were precisely the men whom the army might otherwise have gained as recruits.

The second auxiliary force was the volunteers, also raised by the Home Secretary. Service with them had an irresistible appeal for the self-seeking and the thrifty, because any man who enrolled in them and achieved a very modest standard of training was secure from being balloted into the militia. He was thus safe in person and safe in pocket, free even from the need of paying insurance premiums; he had as well the added privileges of being excused from paying the annual tax on his hair powder, and on his horse also, if he belonged to a mounted (or yeomanry) unit; and prior to 1803 he was generally permitted to be quite useless to his country, too.

Even after 1803 the volunteer remained only a part-time soldier, available for home defence alone; his discipline continued to be milder than that of either militiaman or regular; his freedom from the ballot remained one cause that made the militia hard to fill; the difficulty of filling the militia continued to keep the price of substitutes high; the high price of substitutes continued to make it hard for the regulars to find recruits. However, the volunteers, and still more the militia, did have this value; in proportion as they added to the security of the country against invasion, they released regulars for service overseas. The great plans for a British counter-attack in northern Europe, which were made in 1805 only to be frustrated by the disaster of Ulm, would probably have been impossible had there been no volunteers.

The last, and possibly the most useless, auxiliary force was provided by the fencible regiments. These were units of horse and foot raised by

---

[1] On the subject of ballots and substitutes, see Fortescue, *County Lieutenancies*, pp. 15–17.

[2] T. H. McGuffie, 'Bounty Payments in the Napoleonic Period', *Army Quarterly* (1946), p. 276.

voluntary enlistment for home defence only for the duration of the war. They also weakened the regulars by taking men who might otherwise have joined the army proper and strengthened the nation's potential striking force for foreign service. Their quality is perhaps sufficiently indicated by the discovery in 1799–1800 that some fencible cavalry were mounted on horses discarded by the regular cavalry. The Duke of York had no use for any of them; and in 1799–1800 he had most of them broken up and disbanded. In general it may be said of fencible regiments, as it was said of Charles I, that nothing in all their lives became them like their dissolution; then many of their men volunteered for really useful service in the regulars. Barring a few colonial units, none was employed after 1801.

So much for the army's competitors; now for the organization of the recruiting service.

In the American and Bourbon War of 1775–83 an Inspector General of Recruiting had been wisely appointed to supervise the business of raising men. His headquarters were located at Chatham, a spot so conveniently close to the capital and suitable for embarking troops to proceed overseas that it is at first surprising to discover that the recruiting depot was moved to the Isle of Wight in 1803. There is a sufficiently likely explanation of the move, however; namely, that Chatham was in fact far too handy to London. From Chatham the newly enlisted man could all too speedily take himself off and be lost as a deserter among the teeming masses of an ill-policed great city. The Isle of Wight, girdled by a pretty formidable moat, was a much safer place for assembling numbers of men who were tempted to enlist for a handsome 'bounty', were commonly made drunk in the process, and were liable to lose interest in soldiering as soon as the bounty was spent (and the bounties rarely outlasted the hangover).

This office of Inspector General of Recruiting seems to have survived the American War at least till 1789, when William Fawcett, the Adjutant General, wished General Henry Fox (the famous politician's very capable and decent brother) to be appointed to it. But, to Cornwallis's regret, the Secretary-at-War, Sir George Yonge, overruled Fawcett and gave the job to John Graves Simcoe who, though 'a very good and respectable man', was not Fox's equal for doing business.[1] Simcoe, however, had the merit of being a candidate for the Cornish borough of St Mawes, which duly sent him to Parliament in 1790, and there he presumably voted to the full satisfaction of his political superiors, for in the very next year he moved on to better and higher things as the governor of Upper Canada. If the inspectorate of recruiting was filled at all after 1791, its occupant was an incompetent nonentity and the quality of the men who were approved and accepted for service in Flanders in 1793–4 was shocking. As early as April 1793, when the war was barely two months old, Harry Calvert was describing the new men sent out from England as 'worse than any I ever

[1] Ross, *Cornwallis Correspondence*, i, 448.

saw, even at the close of the American War'.[1] A year later another consignment of recruits, who fell under Calvert's eye, 'much resembled Falstaff's men and were as lightly clad as any Carmagnole battalion'.[2] Such were the consequences of want of inspection coupled with a reckless use of the system of 'recruiting for rank' (which has been described in the chapter on promotion).

Clearly then the recruiting department was much in need of reform when the Duke of York became Commander-in-Chief, and reforms were made. Now General Henry Fox, who had served with distinction in Flanders, did become Inspector General of Recruiting.[3] In 1798 he was succeeded by General Hewett,[4] who was in turn succeeded by General Whitelocke in November 1804.[5] In 1806 the appointment was abolished. The work attached to it was not neglected but added to the duties of the Adjutant General, and the unfortunate Whitelocke, who was perhaps best fitted for an office job, went off to lose any reputation he possessed on the deplorable Buenos Aires expedition.

Apparently in 1795, too, fifteen recruiting districts were organized in England, four in Scotland, and five in Ireland. Over each was placed an Inspecting Field Officer, with a staff of 'an adjutant, a sergeant major and requisite number of depot sergeants'.[6] In 1796 'a hospital mate' was added to the staff to examine the recruits physically;[7] and in 1802 the hospital mates were replaced by better qualified District Surgeons.[8]

That was the framework of the recruiting organization. The actual gathering of the recruits from 'civvy street' was done by parties sent out for the purpose by individual regiments and working under the general supervision of the Inspecting Field Officers. A normal recruiting party consisted of a subaltern or captain, a sergeant, a few trusty men, and sometimes a drummer. The work fell mainly on the sergeant. His job was not an easy one, and the following description of it, though written a score of years after Waterloo, is a fair enough picture of his problems.

Recruiting [says the author] is a trade which like all others requires experience, and many an unfortunate serjeant has been the victim of incautious zeal in his first essay. There are in every town a considerable number of young men who have previously

---

[1] Verney, *Diaries of Sir Harry Calvert*, pp. 67–8. [2] *Ibid.* p. 187.

[3] I have not found the date of Fox's appointment. On 15 March 1797, however, the Adjutant General wrote him, to define a disputed point about his authority over recruiting detachments left at home by regiments on foreign service (WO/3/31).

[4] The first reference to Hewett as Inspector General which I have found is in a letter of 14 November 1798 from the Adjutant General to Simcoe (WO/3/32).

[5] Hewett's last letter in the Home Office papers is dated 20 November 1804; Whitelocke's first is dated 22 November 1804 (HO/50/399).

[6] This was done 'at an early period of the war', says Henry Marshall, *Military Miscellany* (London, 1846), p. 72. I presume the date to have been 1795. Certainly Calvert's description of the recruits arriving in Flanders in 1794 implies there was no proper inspection in that year; equally the Inspecting Field Officers must have existed by 1796 or they could not have had hospital mates 'added' to their staffs in that year.

[7] Marshall, *Military Miscellany*, p. 61. [8] *Ibid.* p. 63.

been rejected as unfit to serve.... These men gladly avail themselves of the serjeant's anxiety to procure recruits, take his enlistment money, and put him to the expence of supporting them till brought up for medical inspection, when of course they are discharged. As this loss must be borne by the serjeant himself a few such mistakes teach him to be cautious, and he then finds candidates for enlistment become comparatively scarce, though, perhaps, other parties, longer in town can procure them for their corps without any difficulty.[1]

He soon finds that all the martial strains of the 'spirit-stirring drum and ear-piercing fife...' are of little avail and that he might bawl himself hoarse in proclaiming the merits of his corps without adding a single recruit to its ranks; he therefore changes his mode of attack and wisely determines to follow the example of those who have had longer experience in the service. Finding nothing is to be done without an extensive acquaintance in the town, he visits the public houses and places of amusement frequented by tradesmen during their idle hours, where he generally spends his evenings and furnishes many a tale of campaigns he never served, and foreign adventures he has never witnessed, to his gaping auditors....[2]

Once established in the public houses, and in favour with the publicans, the sergeant was on the road toward overcoming his difficulties. But those difficulties were still great.

The first, which existed only in wartime, was of course the ease with which those who wanted it could obtain what was called 'the careless freedom of military life'[3] with no obligation to incur the dangers of foreign service, by simply offering themselves as militia substitutes. The second was the heart-felt objection of decent working-class families to seeing their sons become soldiers, and one meets this time and again in the memoirs of rankers who served in the Peninsular War. A third was soon to be provided in men's lively fear of service in the yellow-fever-ridden West Indies, where the four years 1793–6 cost the British Army not less than 80,000 men lost to the service, including 40,000 actually dead; and the latter figure exceeded 'the total losses of Wellington's from death, discharges, desertion, and all causes from the beginning to the end of the Peninsular War'.[4] The fourth was the wretched poverty that went hand in hand with the supposedly 'careless freedom' of a soldier's life. The low pay of the soldier has already been described. Here it is only necessary to add that, after the introduction of a free bread issue in 1792, nothing more was done to make the serviceman's life attractive till 1797. Then the panic created by the naval mutinies suddenly scared Parliament into belated and modest generosity; the soldier and sailor both were awarded the new wage of 1 whole shilling a day. But even that did not mean very much. Prices were rising, too, and sharply; wages in civil life followed prices, albeit slowly and inadequately. In 1800, so Marshall calculates,

---

[1] This sentence is misleading unless one remembers it was written in peacetime. It gives a very false idea of the difficulty of making good wartime losses and achieving wartime increases.

[2] From 'On Recruiting the Army', by 'a Practical Recruiter', in the *United Service Journal*, vol. III for 1837, pp. 436 ff.

[3] *Ibid.* p. 437.   [4] Fortescue, *British Army*, IV, 496.

the wage of a soldier was 7*s*. 7*d*. a week, while an 'artisan's' was 18*s*.; in 1806 the weekly wage of a soldier with less than seven years' service was still 7*s*. 7*d*.; the artisan's had risen to 28*s*.[1] So the soldier's lot remained from three to four times as wretched as that of the civilian lower classes.

. Even more miserable than the army's men were its women. A marriage allowance was paid to the militiaman's wife, but none to the soldier's. Married quarters in barracks were primitive to the point of indecency. Soldiers' wives were expected to make themselves useful by doing laundry and other chores till the regiment went on active service; then they were required to put up with indefinite, and perhaps final, separation without any means of support, for soldiers' wives were permitted to follow their husbands on active service only in the proportion of sixty women to every thousand men.[2] The wretchedness of those women who had the misfortune to love and marry soldiers was by no means overlooked in high places; it was in fact well known, but the only reform to which the imagination of officialdom could rise was an attempt to suppress matrimony itself. 'Marriage', so the regulations ran, 'is to be discouraged as much as possible. Officers must explain to the men the many miseries that women are exposed to, and by every sort of persuasion they must prevent their marrying if possible.'[3] These words might not have been out of place in the mouth of the Grand Master of some medieval crusading order urging a young knight to live up to his vows of chastity; but they were printed in 1795.

Grimly out of date as this directive may sound, the course it inculcated was still the best that a good conscientious regimental officer could do for one of his own men. He could not provide a marriage allowance or decent quarters; only Parliament and the taxpayer could provide these things, and they did not care. Indeed, as one studies the treatment of the soldier in this period it is hard to remember that England in the eighteenth century had experienced a great religious revival; that Wesley had preached, and Watts written hymns in that age; that in the very years of the war the evangelical movement was at its height and the slave trade to meet its end. The wave of pious indignation that delivered the black underdog from his oppression cared nothing about hard bargains driven with white underdogs. So far as this age went, the poet was wrong who wrote

> Our God and soldier we adore
> When at the brink of peril, not before.
> The danger past, they're both alike requited,
> Our God forgotten and our soldier slighted.

[1] Marshall, *Military Miscellany*, p. 68.
[2] For example, 'Women only in the proportion of Six to every Hundred Men will be permitted to embark. They should be carefully selected, as being of good Character and having the inclination and ability to render themselves useful; it is very desirable that those who have children should be left at home' (General Order for Troops destined for Continental Service, 15 April 1807, War Office Library).
[3] *Rules and Regulations for Cavalry* (1795 ed.), p. 74, in the War Office Library.

Even at the brink of peril the one thought that the British public and Parliament gave to their soldier at the dawn of the nineteenth century was how to get him as cheaply as possible.

It is, therefore, not surprising that recruiting was a difficult business. That is why, as late as 1806, the Duke of York still had a good word to say for the system of recruiting for rank. It gave officers a very strong personal interest in enlisting men; but, as noted elsewhere, very strict conditions had by then been prescribed to prevent abuses.

The prime incentive for getting men of course lay in the bounty. This was a sum of money provided partly to pay for clothing and equipping the recruit, and partly to induce him to volunteer by giving him a handsome bonus out of the residue. Indeed, the bounty worked two ways as an incentive. The hope of receiving it induced the recruit to enlist; determination to secure the best part of it made the recruiting sergeants very industrious in getting their men. And the sergeants must be conceded to have been very successful in this last part of their activities.

I had my bounty paid with strict exactitude [writes one man who enlisted in London and was then marched to Maidstone]. Unfortunately for me [he continues] the party into which I was thrown bore no resemblance at all to a well regulated regiment. The barracks were filled with small detachments from a countless variety of corps [as might be expected in any recruiting depot] and the sergeants and corporals...seem to me at this distance of time to have been selected from the very scum of the earth. Like a band of harpies they pounced upon us recruits and never let us loose from their talons till they had thoroughly pigeoned us. We were invited to their rooms of an evening—introduced to their wives who made much of us— praised, favoured, screened and cajoled, till our funds began to run out; and then [when the recruits could no longer stand the drinks], the sergeants would have nothing more to say to us.[1]

James Donaldson, who enlisted in Glasgow, received 'about 4 guineas' from his bounty when his necessaries were paid for. With the exception of a few shillings it was all sponged out of him at the depot. This time the sponging included putting on a dinner for the sergeant who conducted him and his fellow recruits from Glasgow to Dunbar. The sergeant also let it be known that it was proper for the conducting N.C.O. to receive 'a present' from recruits 'when they receive their bounty.... "What is the usual sum?" said one. After some hesitation the sergeant replied "Five shillings each"—and proceeded to accept it.'[2]

Not all recruits, however, were as simple as these boys from Glasgow. Instead some made a profession of collecting bounties. Rifleman Harris tells of the execution of 'a private from the 70th Regiment [who] had deserted from that corps, and afterwards enlisted into several other

[1] From 'Reminiscences of a Light Dragoon', *United Service Journal*, vol. II for 1840, p. 456.
[2] *Recollections of an Eventful Life, passed chiefly in the Army*, by a Soldier (Glasgow, 1825), pp. 77–8.

regiments; indeed I was told...that sixteen different times he had received the bounty and then stolen off'.[1]

Such a man was obviously a losing prospect for the recruiting sergeant, yet those of them who added experience to a good knowledge of men still did pretty well. The methods used by one of the more successful may be worth quoting.

There was no wonder, [at his success, he said modestly] no wonder at all. I knew Glasgow well...knew the minds of the young fellows better than they did themselves —for I had been a weaver myself and a lazy one too....The truth is, you could scarcely catch a weaver contented. They are always complaining. Therefore you would never have much trouble enticing them to enlist...the best way was to make up to the individual you had in your eye, and, after bidding him the time of day, ask him what sort of a web he had in. You might be sure it was a bad one, for when a weaver turns lazy, his web is always bad; ask him how a clever handsome-looking fellow like him could waste his time hanging see-saw between heaven and hell, in a damp unwholesome shop, no better than one of the dripping vaults of St Mungo's church, when he could breathe the pure air of heaven, and have little or nothing to do, if he enlisted for a soldier; that weaving was going to ruin, and he had better get into some berth, or he might soon be starved.[2]

Ploughboys, the sergeant went on, had to be hooked another way. They were to be gulled with fine stories of their chances of becoming sergeants, or even more.

If you saw an officer pass while you were speaking, no matter whether you knew him or not, tell [the yokel] that he was only a recruit a year ago; but now he's so proud he won't speak to you; but you hope he [i.e. the yokel] won't be so when he gets his commission.

If that line failed, the sergeant played on the ploughboy's stomach with wonderful stories of cheap and abundant provisions 'in the place where your *gallant honourable* regiment is lying'. That rarely failed to make an impression, but it was then necessary to get 'quickly to work before his high notions' evaporated. 'You must keep him drinking— don't let him go to the door without one of your men with him, until he is passed the doctor and attested.'[3]

'Heroics', talk about 'glory, honour, laurels, drums, trumpets, applauding world, deathless fame, immortality and all that' quickly bowled over 'sentimental chaps'. They were 'the easiest caught of all'.[4]

When a man had good 'sales resistance', the 'last resource was to get him drunk, and then slip a shilling into his pocket, get him home to your billet, swear he enlisted, bring all your party to prove it, get him persuaded to pass the doctor as it will save the *smart* should he be rejected. If he

---

[1] *Recollections of Rifleman Harris*, ed. Henry Curling, with an introduction by Sir John Fortescue (London, 1928), p. 3.
[2] *Recollections of an Eventful Life*, pp. 167 seq.
[3] *Ibid.*   [4] *Ibid.*

passes you must try every means in your power to get him to drink, blow him up with a fine story, get him inveigled to the magistrate in some shape or other, and get him attested; but by no means let him out of your hands.'[1]

This is a pretty sad tale of trickery almost all through, but there seems little reason to doubt it. The sergeant's story is perfectly consistent with the observation of our earlier witness who stigmatized recruiting N.C.O.'s as 'the very scum of the earth'. The recruit was not the only person who might be tricked, either. There was the Inspecting Surgeon who might find some physical defect, particularly in the matter of height. When that was doubtful it was 'a common plan...to keep the recruit in bed up to the hour when he is brought to the subdivision officer to be measured; for strange as it may appear to those who are not versed in such matters, most men are taller by at least a quarter of an inch when newly risen than after walking about for a few hours'.[2]

Finally, there was the magistrate before whom the recruit had to swear the oath that actually made him a soldier and laid him open to the penalties of desertion if he absconded. The magistrate was supposed to satisfy himself that the recruit was a genuine volunteer, that he was sober, and knew what he was doing. But, said the Glasgow sergeant, 'as for the magistrates, we knew whom to go to on these occasions. You know it was all for the good of the service.'[3] And that last point was hard to set aside. The crisis of a great war does much for elasticity of conscience.

Yet not all recruits who joined the army were tricked into it. Many volunteered only too eagerly, and, because these men raised special problems of discipline, they have been discussed elsewhere. Here it need only be repeated that many convicts gained release from gaol by volunteering for the army; many still unconvicted criminals were happy to get the charges laid against them dropped by enlisting; other genuine volunteers were 'the sturdiest of our yeomen, who, having increased the population of their parish without permission of the clergy, are glad to escape the consequences by sheltering under the license of the camp'. These, continues the writer retrospectively, 'once constituted the great mass of recruits from country districts, where military ardour seems by no means so readily excited as among the crowded population of towns'.[4]

There was yet another class of volunteer, at once pathetic and unreliable. It has been shown that English wages for the lowest labourers in civil life were such as should prevent any sensible man from enlisting, but

---

[1] *Recollections of an Eventful Life*, pp. 171–2.
[2] 'On Recruiting for the Army' by 'A Practical Recruiter', *United Service Magazine*, vol. III for 1837, p. 438.
[3] *Recollections of an Eventful Life*, pp. 171–2.
[4] 'On Recruiting the Army', *United Service Journal*, vol. III for 1837, p. 438. But, adds the writer, the new provision for bastards under the Poor Law of 1834 largely cut off this supply of men.

English poverty was a mild thing when compared with the destitution of the poor across St George's Channel. The result was that very many Irishmen enlisted in English regiments even before the Union; and when Ireland was torn by rebellion and invasion in 1797–8, English regular battalions were so full of Irish that the government dared not use them in the crisis.[1] That is why the voluntary services of battalions of militia and fencibles were accepted for the suppression of the rebellion, in spite of the storm of criticism the measure aroused in the House of Commons; and the government's best excuse, that the militia were the 'troops which could at this moment most conveniently be spared' was both far from convincing and at the same time the nearest approach to the truth that they dared tell.[2]

These were the methods of, and the sort of men secured by, what may be called normal recruiting. They were rarely sufficient for the needs of a nation at war. Therefore other methods had to be sought.

In 1790 a Highland captain called Macdonald, hurrying to join his regiment at Newcastle during the Nootka Sound crisis, pondered 'many plans for raising men expeditiously'. It occurred to him 'that if a bounty was offered to *volunteers* from the *regiments of militia*, a body of men fit for active and immediate service might be formed'; and he ventured to suggest his idea in writing to the War Office.[3] There it received every attention that could be expected for any good idea submitted to a government department presided over by Sir George Yonge; namely, it made no discoverable impression whatever. But five years passed, Sir George Yonge was dispensed with, and the same idea was somehow proposed to Lord Spencer, First Lord of the Admiralty and to Cornwallis, Master General of the Ordnance. This time the result was an Act of Parliament 'for augmenting the Royal Regiment of Artillery and providing Seafaring Men for the Service of the Navy, out of the Private Men now serving in the Militia'.[4] 'The usual Allowance of Bounty' was offered as an encouragement to 'the Private Men' to come forward, but unfortunately nothing was done about encouraging the militia colonels. Their pride was wounded at being regarded 'merely as recruiting officers for the Artillery';[5] a protest against the 'extraordinary and unprecedented' measure was solemnly recorded in the journals of Parliament; and all Cornwallis got was a reinforcement of 'four hundred very bad recruits',[6]—the men, presumably, whose departure was regarded as a gain, not a loss, by the

---

[1] 'As almost the whole of the Recruits for the Infantry of the line are Irish, it would be by no Means a politic measure to send any of the regular Battalions to Ireland' (Duke of York to George III, 22 April 1797, Windsor, 8409).

[2] Henry Dundas on 19 June 1798, in *Parl. Deb.* 1st series, XXXIII, 1505.

[3] The letter is printed in James, *Regimental Companion* (London, 1812), I, 503–4.

[4] 35 Geo. III, cap. 83.

[5] Ross, *Cornwallis Correspondence*, II, 290.

[6] Cornwallis to the Duke of York, 25 September 1796, Chatham Papers, PRO/30/8/241 *seq.*

militia colonels. After this beginning no one would expect volunteering from the militia to prove a valuable way of augmenting the regulars; yet in fullness of time it was to prove the best device of all.

It may seem odd that the army was excluded from this act for recruiting the Royal Artillery and the navy. But the army was not overlooked. The Duke of York was simultaneously arranging to get men from the fencible regiments to volunteer on similar terms to serve in the regulars. This could be, and was, done on the authority of the Commander-in-Chief without an Act of Parliament. Each fencible man volunteering received a bounty of 5 guineas; and colonels of fencible regiments were permitted to give a bounty of 10 guineas to recruits coming forward to replace the volunteers. The volunteering began on the authority of a circular letter on 17 August 1795,[1] but it seems that protests soon began to flow in from fencible commanding officers who were pained at seeing their regiments depleted, and a second circular of 9 September 1795 acknowledged the right of a fencible colonel to veto a volunteer's transfer. One may fairly guess that that was enough to ensure that the only volunteers the army got were men of whom fencible colonels were glad to be rid; and what looks very like confirmation of that guess is found in another letter from the Adjutant General, written on 28 October 1795, and ordering 'all the Regiments of Fencible Cavalry in Great Britain...to put an immediate stop to the further Raising of Recruits and to the purchase of Horses for their respective Corps'.[2] If the fencibles could neither meet the enemy on his own soil nor produce men who would do so, there was little point in permitting them to compete with the army for recruits for those duties of home defence which the militia existed to perform.

An old and wise American proverb warns against the folly of 'sending a boy on a man's job', but a job may still have to be attempted even when no men are forthcoming, and so in 1797 the army turned to recruiting boys. 'Healthy lads under 16 years of Age who are likely to grow may be taken as low as Five Feet One Inch', ran the Horse Guards directive. Six regiments of foot were detailed to receive them 'in Consideration of the difficulty of obtaining Recruits of a proper description'. The Duke of York added a number of very particular cautions for the management of boys. 'It will be needless to suggest to you', the Adjutant General wrote at his behest, 'the necessity of more than ordinary regularity in the Articles of Messing, Cleanliness and Conduct in Quarters, which can only be enforced...by the unremitting care of the Officers and N.C.O.'s of the Regiment.' The boys were to begin their training by drilling without arms; then they were to be issued with 'Fuzees'—lighter weapons than the regulation musket.

[1] Adjutant General's Circular, 28 October 1795, WO/3/28.
[2] Adjutant General to Officers commanding the 9th, 16th, 22nd, 34th and 56th Foot 2 December 1797, WO/3/31.

H.R.H. [the writer continued] recommends in general terms the utmost Mildness and Lenity as the best modes of establishing Discipline and attaching the Lads to H.M.'s service and commands me to suggest for your consideration the expediency of establishing a Regimental School for the instruction of such of them as discover Abilities in the necessary Qualifications of reading and writing, with a view of their becoming hereafter useful and valuable N.C.O.'s.[1]

Boys had the merit of being cheap. Their bounties amounted to no more than 5 guineas a head (although it was wartime) with an additional £2. 5s. 0d. allowed to the officer commanding the recruiting party which enlisted them. £1 of this sum was to be paid to the party at the boy recruit's final approval; and 'in case the Recruit is brought by any person not Military, the officer is permitted to reward the Bringer with 10s.', which was 'to be deducted from the £1 allotted for the party [sic]'.[2] One fears this repellent sort of recruiting would involve more kinds of party than one; in fact, the whole thing smells of an unpleasant and bibulous trade in children;[3] and quite certainly it meant that for several years six regiments of foot would be unfit for service. Unfortunately the scheme also seems to have been a success—enough of one, at any rate, for another regiment to be put on 'the Boy Establishment' early in 1800; and still more boys were recruited in 1805.

The need to provide what Captain Macdonald had called 'men fit for active and immediate service' remained. The attempt to get volunteers from the militia was therefore tried again in 1798, without encouraging results; but then in 1799 yet another act permitting militiamen to volunteer into the regulars was passed, and proved, up to a point, an overwhelming success. The militia colonels offered no hindrance; the militiamen were equally astonished and delighted with their bounties; enthusiasm was vast and drunkenness glorious. A rendezvous for the new volunteers was appointed at Barham Downs in Kent; thither the militiamen

came tumbling down...in every possible conveyance—post coaches, post chaises with six horses, caravans, tilt-carts, flying waggons &c. &c., leaving the officer to plod his way on foot, with two or three who had either spent or lost their money before starting. They talk...of the folly of sailors in spending their money—soldiers can be equally fools on similar terms. Several, when they could no longer get rid of their money by the suddenness of embarkation, very quietly put the one and two pound notes between slices of bread-and-butter and ate them like sandwiches.[4]

But the better part managed to drink, instead of eat, their money. The bonanza of the publicans of Canterbury was interrupted only by the news

---

[1] *Ibid.*   [2] *Ibid.*

[3] But one marks that this recruiting of boys antedates even the first Factory Act by twelve years. One's indignation should therefore perhaps be moderated. These children taken into military life need not necessarily have been worse off than those employed in civil life. Much would depend on the quality of their officers; and drilling in the open air was certainly a healthier occupation than toiling in factories, or sweating underground in mines for an unprescribed number of hours.

[4] 'Recollections of the British Army', *United Service Magazine*, vol. IV for 1836, 184.

that Mr Pitt and Mr Dundas were coming for a *feu de joie* to be fired in honour of Sir Ralph Abercromby's successful landing in Holland. Then

a general sweeping was made...of Canterbury and all the adjacent villages; and by three o'clock in the day every man able to stand or walk was brought into camp. We were drawn out in single line extending from near the race course to the Half-Way House; and in due time the Premier and Mr Dundas appeared in front, and seemed much pleased to see so strong a muster. The ceremony of priming and loading was gone through very decently, and the *feu de joie* commenced; it might better have been called a *feu d'ivresse*, for there were certainly not five hundred men quite sober. It was not thought prudent to attempt a march past.[1]

Evidently a very good time was had by all, except perhaps those sober, civilian inhabitants of Kent who were not gainfully employed in the liquor trade. But one or two pernickety points rather spoil the general impression left by this lively picture of a jolly recruiting picnic. On earlier occasions when militia volunteering was attempted, it had proved unsuccessful; militia colonels had been offended at being treated as recruiting officers, as Cornwallis found. 'Depend upon it [this kind of recruiting] will disgust your most respectable Militia officers, and many of them will leave it', Henry Dundas warned Castlereagh in 1807.[2] But in 1799 the militia officers were not disgusted and their men were not hindered from coming forward; and the reason for the scheme's success, as Dundas further explained to Castlereagh, was that 'the prospect of an aid to a revolution on Holland was then in the view of every person, and the draft from the Militia for such an object was universally popular'.[3] In other words, the men were only gained by making the purpose for which they were wanted such widely public knowledge that any alert enemy could not fail to become as well aware of it as the militia colonels. No wonder, then, that so many of these gay volunteers on Barham Downs were to die to so little purpose among the sandhills of Alkmaar or that General Brune and the defenders of Holland were found so well prepared to thwart the object for which the men were drafted. Indeed Parliament itself, with a generosity unusual among belligerent powers, gave the enemy a broad hint of what the men were wanted for by enacting that the militia volunteers were not for service anywhere in Britain's far-flung empire, but in Europe only, for the duration of the war and for six months after, or for five years, whichever might be the shorter.

Again the invasion of Holland for which these men were wanted had already begun when the drafts assembled on Barham Downs with a view to speedy embarkation; the success of Abercromby's skilful and fortunate opposed landing was announced while they were there; the men's drinking of their bounty was actually interrupted by orders for embarkation. (Likewise, among Wellington's difficulties on the Talavera in 1809 Napier

---

[1] 'Recollections of the British Army.'
[2] Londonderry, *Castlereagh's Correspondence*, VIII, 78.
[3] *Ibid.* p. 79.

remarked that many of his men were militia volunteers, and they had so recently joined the regulars that they were still wearing the insignia of their militia units which the regimental tailors had not had time to alter.[1] Here Oman, scenting the misunderstanding of a man who had merely served in the Peninsular War, hastened with academic omniscience to correct the false impression the soldier gave; the militiamen, said Oman, were fully trained soldiers before ever they joined the regulars.[2] Oman's fact is correct; the militiamen could indeed perform all the movements of the manual exercise with mechanical perfection and were admirably instructed in Dundas's manœuvres. The soldier's point still stands, however, in spite of academic correction. The strength of a unit in action should be the strength of a team, in which the men know each other, their N.C.O.'s and their officers, and the N.C.O.'s and officers know their men. This last-minute reinforcement of the army with militia volunteers in 1799 and on other occasions could not possibly create a team; it could only throw together a scratch side.) Nevertheless the system did produce excellent recruits. Pitt turned to it again in 1805 in an attempt to secure 17,000 men; Windham used it to provide 4000 men from Ireland in 1806;[3] as will be shown, Castlereagh later made it a permanent system for filling the regulars; and scenes of mass drunkenness, like the one recorded on Barham Downs, remained an ugly and invariable part of the process, to the legitimate grief of militia officers.[4]

The new war which followed the Treaty of Amiens found Henry Addington still in office, and the sober common sense which appears in his other measures also marks his rearmament of Britain. This time the increase of the forces was made hard by the very preparedness with which Addington entered the war. There was the less slack for the nation to take up, because so much of her manpower was already in the services. Even in 1802 Addington had looked ahead and revised the Militia Acts, empowering the government to call out a force of 50,000 balloted men for home defence as the 'Old' Militia, and half that number more as the Supplementary Militia. The Old Militia were embodied in March 1803, before the final rupture of relations, and the Supplementary Militia as soon as war was declared. So by 1 July 1803 'there were already 70,000 men in the militia'[5]; and most of them must have been already in a fairly advanced state of training. This was a very solid contribution to the security of the country. The total of militia and regulars in Britain,

[1] *Peninsular War*, book VIII, chapter 2, 'Observations'.
[2] *Wellington's Army* (London, 1913), p. 210.
[3] Fortescue, *County Lieutenancies*, pp. 145, 165–6.
[4] 'What has most revolted the feelings of Militia officers to this species of measure has been the scene of disorder and indiscipline which has been introduced into their respective regiments during the...volunteering', wrote Castlereagh in 1807 (*Correspondence*, VIII, 56).
[5] George Pellew, *Life and Correspondence of the Rt. Hon. Henry Addington, first Viscount Sidmouth* (London, 1847), II, 203.

amounting together to over 130,000 men, provided a much stronger force than there was any likelihood of Bonaparte acquiring the means to ferry across the Channel at this time.

It was, of course, certain that Bonaparte would use all his energy to increase his shipping, and therefore it was necessary for Britain to expand her forces to meet the increased number of troops which her enemy would become able to land. Addington proceeded to do so, with a measure intended to supplement ordinary recruiting and firm-based on the army's experience of receiving volunteers into the line from the militia. That experience, as noted above, had shown that once the men who had entered the militia had become used to a soldier's life, they were very ready to volunteer into the regular army. The commanding officers of militia regiments, on the other hand, strongly objected to spoiling their battalions by losing good men, and felt injured at being regarded 'merely as recruiting officers'. Therefore Addington now brought forward a plan for raising an 'Army of Reserve' modelled on the militia but designed from the first to provide volunteers for the line.

The men, like militiamen, were to be conscripted by ballot; they might either serve as principals or pay a substitute to take their place. They were not, of course, compelled to serve outside the United Kingdom, but they might at any time volunteer for general service. Three acts on these lines were intended to produce a total of 50,000 men, 34,000 from England, 6000 from Scotland, and 10,000 from Ireland. Though officially entitled 'Additional Force Acts', they are better known as the Army of Reserve Acts.

Fortescue expressed his opinion of these measures with his usual vigour in a curt entry in his table of contents, which runs 'Utter Failure of the Army of Reserve'. He supported that opinion with figures, of which the following are a fair sample.

By the 1st of May, 1804 [he writes] when the Act was acknowledged to be dead, the Army of Reserve had produced a nominal total of 45,492 men, of whom 2,116 had been discharged as unfit or for other causes, 589 had died, and 5,561, nearly one ninth, had deserted or been claimed as deserters by other corps, leaving 37,136 as nominally effective. Of these, however, 7,000 were young and undersized and had to be drafted into garrison battalions until they could grow up. Thus while paying for 45,000 men the country gained the immediate services of little more than 30,000.[1]

But here Fortescue's own figures make it impossible to agree with his savage verdict on Addington's act. As no government can prevent the occurrence of death, it is not fair to blame Addington for the loss of the 589 reservists who had died. The one-ninth recorded as lost by desertion is certainly a large proportion, but fair criticism would require Fortescue to show whether it was exceptional in an army in which desertion was an

[1] *County Lieutenancies*, p. 73.

all too commonly committed and an all too rarely detected crime; unfortunately there is evidence that it was by no means exceptional.[1] The enlistment of boys, who had to be put in garrison battalions till they grew up, or of weaklings who had to be discharged, was unfortunate; but it points to failure in the act's execution by local authorities rather than to defects in its drafting. Nor, in the long run, were the growing boys to be regarded as a dead loss; and even garrison battalions had a place, albeit a minor one, in the business of national defence. On the other hand, the 30,000 effective men, whom the act did produce, were a greater force than that which Napoleon had conquered at Marengo. Further, though Fortescue does not mention the fact, before too long 19,553 of those men had already volunteered for general service. Many of Addington's contemporaries therefore thought the Army of Reserve Acts a very great success. In fact, Castlereagh, whom Fortescue himself called 'the ablest Minister who has ever presided at the War Office',[2] seriously considered reviving them in 1807;[3] and Henry Dundas, who had at least an abundance of experience, urged him to do so.[4]

Let it then be granted that the Army of Reserve Acts were an incomplete success; it is still beyond dispute that they made a very notable increase to the strength of the country. The solid value of these acts remains after one has taken into account errors in their drafting, the difficulties of carrying them into effect, and even the burden which they threw upon the Lords Lieutenant of the counties, who had to execute them (a class from which Fortescue was descended and for which he had a most lively sympathy).[5] It is true indeed that the cost of substitutes was raised uncommonly high by the balloting for the Army of Reserve so soon after the completion of both the Old and the Supplementary Militia; it is true, too, that the competition of the Army of Reserve caused the Duke of York to drop a scheme for having certain officers earn a step in rank by recruiting a given number of men, as has been told elsewhere. But in 1807 Addington's brother could claim in debate that during the operation of the Army of Reserve 'the regular recruiting had not diminished [by] more than one fourteenth, as was demonstrated by documents laid on the table' of the House of Commons;[6] and his statement went uncontradicted. It was, unfortunately, to be rather a long time before any government hit on a more successful scheme for strengthening the country than Addington's much abused, but eminently valuable, Army of Reserve.

---

[1] For example, on the very next page Fortescue records that of 3481 recruits raised by 360 ordinary recruiting parties in the last six months of 1803 '291 deserted'—not a very much lower proportion; and these recruits were volunteers, not conscripts.

[2] *County Lieutenancies*, p. 177; also, p. 234.

[3] Londonderry, *Castlereagh's Correspondence*, VIII, 80.

[4] *Ibid.* p. 55.

[5] *County Lieutenancies*, p. 77 n. 1.

[6] *Parliamentary Debates*, 27 July 1807, p. 952.

The very raising of the Army of Reserve made possible the development of another reform. When he received the men, the Duke of York did not form them into new regiments. Instead, he used them to provide more second battalions for existing regiments. A prime purpose of these second battalions was to gather and train recruits and to furnish drafts to keep their first battalions constantly up to strength. This system proved its value in the Peninsular War, but after Waterloo it was abandoned in the name of economy, and for long was forgotten. After many years, however, it was adopted in a not very dissimilar form by a certain Edward Cardwell who held office under the great Mr Gladstone, and then, of course, with the name of 'the Cardwell System' it was promptly hailed as a notable sign of that progress which so conspicuously marked Victoria's reign. Relatively few remember that Cardwell was only reviving York's system of seventy years before.

Another military institution which was revived in Victoria's reign, and for which Addington and York did much, was that of the Volunteers. Volunteer units for home defence had, of course, been raised before, in the American and Bourbon War of 1775–83 and between 1793 and 1801 in the war with the French Republic. Though they had never been troops of any very distinguished reputation, it was natural that they should be revived when a new war threatened, and out of them the Duke of York and Mr Charles Yorke (successively Secretary-at-War and Home Secretary) with Addington's backing made a very large and by no means contemptible army.

No pretence can be made that the civilian authorities began by realizing all that needed to be done for the volunteers or by foreseeing how valuable a force they could become. That the civilians began by feeling an evident jealousy over any apparent interference by the Commander-in-Chief must be conceded; that they continued to suspect him of seeking to extend his own patronage through the force is true. Yet they submitted to many of his demands and showed a very creditable spirit of co-operation. The story can only be summarized here. Those who want detail, especially on the civilian side, may find it in Fortescue's *County Lieutenancies and the Army*.

Here it will be enough to say that in 1802 Addington took steps to preserve the volunteer system that had grown up during the late war. In June 1803 he extended it with a code of regulations, defining services and pay, which was known as the 'June Allowances'. In July he encouraged volunteering with a Levy en Masse Act empowering the government 'to drill every able-bodied man whether he liked it or not'.[1] In August he issued a second code of volunteer regulations known as the 'August Allowances'. The 'June Allowances... offered pay to the men for eighty-five days exercise in the year and required of them an agreement to serve

[1] Fortescue, *County Lieutenancies*, p. 66.

232

within their Military District'.[1] The August Allowances, granted to the late volunteers who came forward under the threat of the Levy en Masse Act, provided them with pay for only twenty days' exercise and required them to serve anywhere in the kingdom. More confusion was created first by a ruling of 18 August 1803, that the number of volunteers was in no county to exceed six times the Old Militia; and by another ruling of 31 August that 'all' offers to serve as volunteers were to be accepted, but those exceeding the quota laid down on the 18th were to be carried as supernumeraries 'without any allowance for pay, arms or clothing and without claim to exemption from any ballot'.[2]

Out of these confusions there certainly came much trouble and correspondence for the Lords Lieutenant. Fortescue has by no means overlooked them. The raising of all these men, to a total of 380,000 in Great Britain and 70,000 in Ireland, created a demand for arms which, as told elsewhere, the Ordnance had no means to supply. On this ground too there accumulated grievances which Fortescue has faithfully and extensively reported. Finally, the volunteers were not subject to military law except when called out on permanent duty; hence some units were distinguished for an extraordinary want of discipline, as is again described in the lively pages of Fortescue.

The facts Fortescue states are beyond dispute, yet it is hard to accept his very unfavourable verdict on Addington's management of the volunteers. The raising and arming of 450,000 men is never a small job. To do it efficiently requires great experience and great mastery of detail. Addington's cabinet were not experienced men, naturally, for the country had never attempted so vast a task before; and the burden of the detail fell very heavily upon their own shoulders, for the civil service of their day was but a pigmy compared with the staff that assists a modern minister. They had little chance to correct their own mistakes, for they were in office for less than a year after the war broke out. Yet they did raise a part-time force of 450,000 men and in due course that force was armed.

The efficiency of the volunteers depended, of course, on the quality of their training, and that equally naturally depended on their discipline. Though Fortescue has collected numerous and (as he puts it) some 'extremely interesting' examples of ill-disciplined volunteers,[3] Addington and his colleagues had not failed to provide a pretty threatening sanction to control them. Freedom from being balloted for the militia or the Army of Reserve was a prime attraction that made volunteer service popular; therefore, when volunteers were disorderly or incompetent, the obvious step was to disband them and promptly ballot them for compulsory service. Unfortunately some Lords Lieutenant of counties were too weak to take this vigorous step. Men whose moral strength was like

---

[1] *Ibid.* p. 75.   [2] *Ibid.* p. 78.
[3] *Ibid.* p. 107.

that of water, forever dribbling downhill, found it easier simply to report cases of indiscipline to the Home Secretary and thus deposit their problems in the lap of a man who had none of the local knowledge necessary for solving them. But by the better men the strong step of disbanding bad volunteers was uncompromisingly taken, with excellent results. It is hardly a coincidence that Devon, where in July 1803 the Lord Lieutenant had disbanded a whole battalion of volunteers 'and swept every man of them into the ballot for the Army of Reserve',[1] was also the county where General Simcoe was soon able to report that 'he had over 2,000 Volunteers fit for immediate service'.[2] Again it is hardly a coincidence that in Scotland, where the ballot was especially unpopular, Lord Moira, the local commander and an excellent officer, declared himself ready to meet any enemy in the field with volunteers alone, unsupported by any regulars.[3]

Of the training of the volunteers Fortescue writes: 'Being left to themselves, these amateur soldiers, of course, aped their professional brethren; the hours [of training] were zealously devoted to the classical eighteen manœuvres of David Dundas.... All this was utterly useless.'[4] Instead Fortescue thought that the volunteers should have been trained as a species of irregular light infantry. For this view he could claim support from the parliamentary speeches of Robert Craufurd, later the bold and able, yet erratic and unwise, leader of the Light Division in the Peninsula;[5] he could also quote the statement of General John Money, 'You cannot make men equal to regular troops in twenty-four days' drill, but you can make them good sharp-shooters in ten days; whereas long tedious drills weary the peasantry'.[6]

Fortescue is a formidable authority; in Money and Craufurd he has formidable supporters too. Yet the present writer finds himself in disagreement with almost every point of Fortescue's opinions on the training of the volunteers.

In the chapter on training I have endeavoured to describe what was required of light troops. Here I may repeat David Dundas's statement that though their skirmishers were 'loose, detached, and numerous', such troops always needed 'a firm reserve...to rally upon',[7]—the necessity lying in the fact that the skirmishers' greatest danger was in being caught in dispersed order by cavalry, whom only troops in close order could repel. Dundas's other statement that the attacks of light infantry should be co-ordinated—or, as he put it, 'connected'—also bears repetition.[8] I may further repeat that no less an authority than John Moore heartily approved of de Rottenburg's manual for light infantry training; also John Macdonald's description of the French light infantry as a 'waspish soldiery',

[1] Fortescue, *County Lieutenancies*, p. 99.   [2] *Ibid.* p. 118.
[3] *Parliamentary Debates*, 11 July 1806, p. 1087.
[4] Fortescue, *County Lieutenancies*, p. 117.
[5] *Ibid.*   [6] *Ibid.* p. 117.
[7] Dundas, *Military Science*, pp. 13–14.   [8] *Ibid.*

experts in the art of using cover and marksmen who shot 'with unerring certainty'.[1] Then, when these things have been repeated, one may fairly ask how light troops were to retain 'a firm reserve...to rally upon' if none of them had ever learnt the drill which was required of firm, substantial bodies of infantry of the line and which Dundas provided? Or how they were to be expected to co-ordinate their movements in extended order if they knew not even the much simpler business of making co-ordinated movements in close order? To these questions there is no very obvious answer. Therefore de Rottenburg was surely right when he insisted on the opening page of his light infantry manual that troops should never begin their light training till they had perfectly mastered their close-order drill. One may also remark that even to recognize each of the fifty-odd separate bugle calls used to convey orders to light infantry called for more training in what might now be called 'musical appreciation' than quite a few tone-deaf men can receive.

Then there are those arts of using cover and of marksmanship which were among the essential skills of the light infantryman. No one who has tried to teach fieldcraft is likely to agree that newly raised troops can quickly learn the art of using cover, especially if they are townees. (The mere business of crawling can be found strangely exhausting. Some men persist in the notion that if their heads are down their backsides must necessarily be down too, often as this proves a patent *non sequitur*. Others again are slow to grasp the value of shadow.) As for marksmanship, one can agree that a man with a naturally steady hand and good eye may soon learn to shoot well in good conditions at a clear target at a known range; but, till he gains experience, the same man commonly shoots very erratically indeed in the field where he has to guess his own ranges and judge how to aim off for wind. That is true even with the small, conical bullet, the high-powered propellant, and the flat trajectory of modern weapons; it was so much the harder to shoot well with the fixed backsight, the bulky spherical ball, the weak powder, and consequently high trajectory of the usually unrifled weapons of 1800. All round, then, one may concur in the view that it would have been desirable to turn the volunteers into sufficiently skilled light infantry, but one cannot believe it practical. For them Dundas's manœuvres provided the best training just because it was the simplest.

Fortescue is also mistaken when he describes the volunteers as 'left to themselves' in the matter of training. The Duke of York saw to it that they were not. It would take too long to trace here all his negotiations on this subject with the Home Secretary, Charles Yorke. Briefly, however, he secured the appointment in every district of Inspecting Field Officers whose job was to inspect the volunteers once a month, to report their

[1] John Macdonald, *Instructions for the Conduct of Infantry on Actual Service*, translated from the French, etc., II, xxxix–xl.

effective numbers, the state of their equipment, and the quality of their training. Thanks to these reports the Duke knew which volunteers he might trust in the face of an enemy, and which were best left for the police duties called 'Internal Defence'; he was also able to have some disbanded. From this system, too, the volunteers in turn gained the advantage of professional oversight and advice. Further, the Duke so organized his Inspecting Field Officers as to be able to form them conveniently into brigade staffs, ready to handle the larger formations into which the volunteers would have to be assembled if ever they were called out to serve against an invader. In fact the neatness and practicality of all the Duke's arrangements for making the most of the services of these amateur soldiers seem wholly admirable. These arrangements ran to the provision of transport for regimental equipment and 'horse buses', as it were, to hasten the march of inland units toward an invaded maritime county.

Thus guided (not controlled) by the Commander-in-Chief's department, many of the volunteers made rapid progress. Though Fortescue's opinion of them was low, he did not fail to cite, with characteristic honesty, evidence that ran against his own verdict. Thus he quotes the confidence (described above) of Simcoe and Moira in the Devon and Scottish volunteers respectively.[1] He notes what one might expect, namely, that the volunteers generally improved rapidly in 1804. He finds the behaviour of the volunteers of Derbyshire and West Yorkshire on the occasion of a false alarm in 1805 most praiseworthy.

To these frank admissions by Fortescue, other evidence may be added. David Dundas himself was soon reporting Pitt's 3000 Cinque Ports Volunteers as fit to act with the regulars. As early as February 1804, an Inspecting Field Officer in Lancashire described the 1st Manchester and Salford Regiment of Volunteers as 'highly disciplined and in every other respect fit for immediate service'. Of the 2nd Manchester and Salford Regiment he added: 'I cannot do other than Report this Regiment as equally fit for immediate Service'; and he said the same of the Oldham Volunteers and the Ashton-under-Lyme Volunteers.[2] Here one may remark that Fortescue concedes that wealthy country gentlemen could sometimes make good units out of volunteer recruits from their own docile tenantry; but this report describes a whole group of excellent regiments made out of townees from urban areas, and that in little more than six months. Just one month later Lt. Gen. Fox is found writing an almost equally strong report on the volunteers of the Home District, which covered the counties of Middlesex, Hertford, and Berkshire.

Having seen a considerable proportion of these Corps myself in each County of the District [he stated] I have the satisfaction of observing that there appears without exception a general zeal and ardor for the Public Service although from a variety of

[1] *County Lieutenancies*, p. 139.
[2] Lt. Col. Maxwell to Prince Frederick William, 26 February 1804, HO/50/396.

circumstances some are infinitely more forward than others; but the majority of them (both Cavalry and Infantry) are in my opinion fit to be joined to Regular Troops; indeed much more so than many new raised Corps and Bodies of Recruits I have frequently seen join an Army on Service and who have upon joining almost immediately been opposed to the Enemy and have behaved well.[1]

And Fox spoke with the authority both of an ex-Inspector General of Recruiting, who knew the business of turning raw civilians into respectable soldiers, and of an active officer who had distinguished himself in the face of the enemy.

To sum up, probably the fairest judgement on this great force of amateur soldiers which Addington raised was that of Cornwallis, than whom no living Englishman had more often or more successfully led troops into battle. 'Government have acted properly', he wrote in December 1803, 'in endeavouring only to make [the volunteers] as much soldiers as it was possible to render a force so composed, and no man, whether civil or military, will persuade me that 300,000 men, trained as the volunteers at present are, do not add very materially to the confidence and to the actual security of this country.'[2] So when all reasonable objections have been made, it would still seem that in their management of the volunteers Addington and Yorke showed a thoroughly sound understanding alike of what the country needed for its defence, and of what it was practical to do. One cannot but feel that Fortescue gave too much heed to the oratory of their parliamentary critics, forgot as he read of things which went wrong how often things which go right remain unreported, and made too little allowance for the real difficulties of any government in the opening months of a great war.

On 9 May 1804 Addington resigned. Through the opening months of the year Pitt and Grenville had gradually drawn toward Fox in what struck Cornwallis as a 'coalition...full as profligate as that of Fox and Lord North'.[3] But in fact the coalition was never consummated. Addington, a convinced supporter of the royal prerogative, carefully timed his resignation when Pitt was 'not now pledged to any man' in order to prevent the King's 'closet being forced' by a union of Pitt and the hated Fox.[4] The rest of the story is familiar. George III refused to accept Fox, Grenville refused to serve without him, and Pitt was left to form a cabinet in which Lord Melville, whose reputation was so soon to be tarnished, was almost his only colleague of first rank.

Pitt faced other difficulties too, and these may fairly be described as of his own making. He had rashly attacked Addington's government with the charge: 'No one measure for public defence can they truly be said to have originated, whereas several they have enfeebled and retarded.'[5] But

---

[1] Fox to Calvert, 14 March 1804, *ibid.*
[2] Ross, *Cornwallis Correspondence*, III, 509.   [3] *Ibid.* pp. 510–11.
[4] Abbot's diary for 29 and 30 April 1804, cited by Pellew, *Life of Addington*, II, 280–1.
[5] On 23 April 1804, cited by Fortescue, *County Lieutenancies*, p. 127.

Hiley Addington, Henry's brother, vigorously insisted that 'we had at present, after a war of ten months, a greater regular army than we had at the end of the last war which had lasted ten years';[1] and if Hiley's description of the length of the war with the French republic smacks more of rhetorical licence than of sober arithmetic, his main point was still unanswerably true. Pitt's criticism thus committed him to surpassing a man who had conspicuously surpassed himself. Therein he undertook more than he could perform.

That Pitt's Volunteer Consolidation Act did indeed make some improvements in the great amateur army, which Addington had raised, may fairly be conceded. But the real need was to increase the regulars. In his attempt to meet this need Pitt introduced a hybrid scheme, bred out of the wretched Quota Act of 1796 by Addington's Army of Reserve Act of 1803. The Quota Act was the dominant parent of this mule, which in too many places proved as sterile as mules are usually found to be.

Pitt's aim was to get away from the ballot which, by encouraging a trade in substitutes, led (in the modern economist's phrase) to 'spiralling' bounties. Accordingly, he required each county to raise a given quota of men from its various parishes. The parish officers were somehow to produce the men, on pain of a £20 fine for each man deficient; and they were forbidden to accept men from places more than twenty miles away in the same county or ten miles away in a neighbouring county. The fines paid went to the general recruiting fund. As in Addington's act, the men were to be enlisted for home service only, for five years or till six months after the end of the war. When raised, the men, like Addington's, were to be used to build up the second battalions of the Duke of York's Cardwell-type system, and it was hoped they would volunteer for general service. Parish officers were encouraged to do their duty by a reward of one guinea for each man they raised. Simultaneously the men of the Supplementary Militia were to be fused with those raised by the Army of Reserve, and the Army of Reserve Act was repealed.

Pitt hopefully christened his misbegotten measure the Permanent Additional Force Act; but its permanence endured only from 25 June 1804, when it was passed, till 23 May 1806, when it was repealed. In those twenty-three months it produced only 13,000 recruits (less than half the effective total Addington's Army of Reserve Act had produced in six months), though the number Pitt had expected and required in under two months, namely, by 1 August 1804, was no less than 20,000. Of the 13,000 actually achieved in two years, 2800, over one-fifth, deserted,[2] and how many of the rest really met the required standards of fitness for service is a question never likely to be answered.

The cause of the act's failure was that a majority of the parish officers

---

[1] *Parliamentary Debates*, 10 April 1804, p. 135.
[2] Fortescue, *County Lieutenancies*, p. 160.

simply would not try to enforce it or attempt to understand it. As one Mr Lee, member for Waterford County, stated, on the authority of figures submitted to the House of Commons, 'In England there were no less than 14 counties, in which not a man had been raised by the parish officers; and in the large county of York, which ought to have produced 5,674, no more than 407 had been raised altogether in the last 18 months. He thought it a great objection to the bill that, in the course of 18 months, it could not be understood by those whose duty it was to execute it.' His own Irish county was indeed credited with raising over a hundred men, but 'he could say, from his own certain knowledge that...the number was entirely made up of men under the size of 5 feet 4 inches, who had been handed over to the parish officers by the serjeants who had been recruiting other descriptions of service'.[1] Likewise the Leicestershire parish officers were credited with raising 200 men; but again a member who knew the county, one Mr Babington, stated that they too were undersized men, raised by recruiting sergeants and handed over to the parish officers (presumably after failing to pass their regular medical examination).[2] In short, parish officers seem in general either to have glumly calculated the cost of the deficiency fines and prepared to pay them; or to have tried to evade them by buying the recruiting sergeants' rejected men and passing them off as their own parish levies.

Yet the Permanent Additional Force Act still had its friends. The Duke of York reported it useful for connecting regiments with counties and providing men for second battalions,[3] and after Pitt's death his colleagues fought hard for it in the House of Commons. The ostensible reasons for their struggle were, first, that if only the parish officers could be made to do their work properly, many petty villages, too small individually to be worth the attention of recruiting parties, could collectively produce a valuable number of men; and, second, that in the last months of its life the act really had begun to function. In part this was due to the fact that the authorities winked at infringements of the twenty-mile clause; in part it was due to nascent co-operation between the parishes and the Inspecting Field Officers of the recruiting service. The results were described in the following not very luminous statement by Spencer Perceval which will be quoted *verbatim* in order to give every reader a chance to understand the act's effects as best he may:

In the 50 weeks ending the 14th of last March [i.e. 1806] it produced above 9000 men. In the last 15 weeks it had produced an average of 258 per week, which would give 13,200 in the year; in the last 10 weeks an average of 277, or 14,600 in the year; and in the last five weeks, an average of 356 per week, being at the rate of above 18,000 in the year.[4]

[1] *Parliamentary Debates*, 6 May 1806, p. 17.
[2] *Ibid.* p. 16.
[3] Duke of York to Windham, 18 March 1806, Windsor, 12407–18.
[4] *Parliamentary Debates*, 17 April 1806, p. 792.

Perceval's apparent point was that the authorities charged with executing the act had achieved a recent spurt which they might conceivably maintain.

But one doubts whether these were the real motives for the final vigorous defence of this bad act. It may well be that its defenders clung to it simply as a lesser evil than the approaching alternative. For Pitt's death on 23 January 1806 had unleashed delirium at the war ministry. His cabinet colleagues had been unable to carry on without him; Fox and Grenville had taken office with Windham as Secretary of State for War and Colonies; and Windham had come to power intent upon root-and-branch changes in the army which Fortescue, with apparent but unaccountable sincerity, denominated 'reforms', even though he acknowledged their failure.

For the past three years Windham had been the critic of successive recruiting measures proposed by other war governments. It might, then, be imagined that he would bring to office some concrete, practical, and fully thought-out plan for improvement. Yet his own mind seems often to have been far from clear as to how he would transmute into fact the theories on which he dilated with graceful periods, alliterative phrases, and classical quotations.

Certain things indeed were more than clear in Windham's programme. With an unpardonable phrase, which Spencer Perceval did not let him forget, Windham had mocked the volunteers as 'painted cherries which none but simple birds would take for real fruit',[1] and that force could expect little sympathy from the new minister. Windham also cited the results of Marengo and Austerlitz as evidence that the only force which counted was a regular army; and he had vigorously denounced the bounty and the ballot.

So the strengthening of the regulars without ballot and with minimum bounties was his business. To achieve it, he proposed three things— better pay, pensions, and short service—and over the Duke of York's reasoned protest he swept away the Additional Force Act.

By improved pay, Windham averred, 'a better description of men will be induced to enter the army',[2] yet he saw dangers ahead if the pay became really good. 'If you could raise the pay to 5s. a day, you would never want soldiers', he told Parliament, 'but, besides the objection of expence, ...you cannot increase the pay to such an extent, without rendering the army licentious.'[3] So there is one plain self-contradiction by a muddled mind. Windham simultaneously wanted to raise the pay to get better men, and feared to raise it lest he corrupt these paragons of his own recruiting. The course he chose to steer between this Scylla and Charybdis was to leave the private's pay at 1s. a day for his first seven years' service, to raise it to 1s. 6d. for the next seven years, and to 2s. for a further and

---

[1] *Parliamentary Debates*, 21 May 1806, p. 319.
[2] *Ibid.* 3 April 1806, p. 666. [3] *Ibid.* pp. 663–4.

final period of seven years. In other words, his method of inducing 'a better description of men...to enter the army' was to invite them to wait seven years for 6d., and this in a country where, as has been seen, some of the poorer classes had so little idea of what to do with a pound note as to be capable of putting it between slices of bread and butter and eating it. Rarely can even Windham have sounded less convincing than when he tried to pretend that he had found in this enticement a real means to lure men into the army. His promise of pensions to retired soldiers was a yet more distant carrot to lead men into their country's service, but it imposed an immediate and a severe burden on a war-strained Treasury. (It is still, however, something for which Windham's humanity deserves much credit, whether it served an immediate practical purpose or not.)[1]

Windham's only other idea on how to make the army popular was to offer an easy escape from it with short enlistments. Normally men enlisted for life, but short enlistments for three years' service had been tried in the American and Bourbon War. When accompanied by high wartime bounties these short enlistments had produced plenty of recruits, but when the war ended their effect on the army was disastrous; masses of time-expired men left the ranks in a very short period, creating gaps it was found impossible to fill. After that unfortunate experience short enlistments rather naturally received no very serious consideration for the next twenty years. Then in 1804 the Duke of York asked a number of very experienced officers for their opinion of short enlistment as a means of filling the army. Six men—Generals Fox, Lord Harrington, Whitelocke, Pulteney, Lord Mulgrave, and Lord Moira—thought well of it; two more —Dundas and Cornwallis—also favoured it, provided no discharges were granted in wartime; one—Craig—was not hostile, but did not believe it would fill the ranks in wartime; four were uncompromisingly hostile, and of these four two spoke with special authority, namely, Hewett who had now some six years' experience as the Inspector General of Recruiting, and Moore who incisively replied: 'If limited service and enormous bounties could tempt men to enlist, would the Army of Reserve and Permanent Additional Force be incomplete now?'[2]

The generals, therefore, could not as a whole be called enthusiastic for short enlistment. Windham, however, seems in any case to have set little stock on the advice of mere generals. He preferred that of an ex-sergeant turned journalist, the redoubtable William Cobbett, with whom he had hatched some obscure plan for limited enlistments. So he now introduced a scheme whereby every man would be automatically discharged after he had served seven years, regardless of whether the country was at war or

[1] Yet it is symptomatic of the deep contradictions in Windham's character that he could uphold so sadistic an amusement as bull-baiting, which he actually defended in Parliament on 2 April 1800 as 'a long used and manly exercise'! And on 2 April 1802 he described another attempt to legislate against it as 'a combined effort of methodism and jacobinism'.
[2] Cited by Fortescue, *County Lieutenancies*, p. 162.

at peace, unless he preferred to re-enlist for the extra 6*d.*; he would again be automatically discharged after fourteen years of service unless, for another 6*d.*, he preferred to re-join for a third term of seven years. In favour of this scheme, Windham quoted the opinions of the generals, whose answers he interpreted as being seven in favour of the change, six against, and one doubtful; but, alleging them to be confidential, he coyly declined to print those opinions for the inspection of his critics.[1]

His scheme had only to be explained for a storm to burst. Cobbett was soon writing to upbraid him for mangling their original plan, as he had understood it;[2] and in the House of Commons one of those very generals who were supposed to have written opinions favourable to limited enlistment immediately rose to voice his outspoken dissent from Windham's scheme. This was James Pulteney, who declared the facts about the Duke of York's inquiry of 1804 to have been that the question on which the generals had been divided was the 'principle of enlisting men for limited instead of perpetual service; but on the subject of dismissing the soldier in the midst of a war, at the end of 7 years, 11 out of 13 were decidedly against it; and 2 others, who declared no opinion, might fairly be supposed to be against the principle also'.[3]

So the slim majority of generals, which Windham claimed for his scheme, was changed into a solid phalanx of hostility at the same time that he forfeited the support of his only sergeant. The broad opinion of the plan held by informed, practical men in the House of Commons was probably sufficiently summarized in a single sentence by the member who declared his detestation 'of every limb of the Minerva which had lately sprung from the rt. hon. secretary's brain'.[4]

Nevertheless, Fox and Grenville commanded a majority; Windham had the stubbornness of a doctrinaire too lost in the fog of his own phrases to see the sense of other men's objections; and his act went through. Perhaps the most repellent part of it was the provision that unpaid fines due under Pitt's Additional Force Act from parishes which had not raised their quota of men should all be remitted. It may be true, as Fortescue felt, that it would have been hard to collect them, for they amounted to a total of £1,800,000;[5] but Windham's action in effect rewarded those who broke the law of the land and penalized those parish officers who had conscientiously made some attempt to obey it. And that is surely the negation of good government.

Windham also virtually destroyed the great army of volunteers, which Addington had created, Pitt had improved, and the Duke of York had done so much to make useful. Windham's objection to the volunteers

---

[1] *Parliamentary Debates*, 17 April 1806, p. 781.
[2] Rosebery, *Windham Papers*, II, 295.
[3] *Parliamentary Debates*, 30 April 1806, p. 963.
[4] Mr Bastard, *ibid.* p. 1014.
[5] *County Lieutenancies*, p. 164.

was due, partly to the notion that they were excessively expensive in themselves; partly to the familiar fact that their exemption from balloted service sent up the price of militia substitutes, and the price of bounties for regular recruits spiralled as a result; and partly to the belief that they were useless as troops. Spencer Perceval suggested that he had the best of personal reasons for the last view. He declared himself afraid...

that the rt. hon. gent. had taken all his ideas of the volunteers from the corps which he himself commanded, the Felbrig volunteers...that corps in itself united everything which the rt. hon. gent. had been so accustomed to condemn...in the first place, of all the corps which subsisted in the county of Norfolk, this was the only one in which the commander had taken the title of colonel, all the rest of the volunteer commanders in the county were content with being merely captains. The composition of this corps was also somewhat singular. There were 73 privates, but no staff, no field officer, no captain, no subalterns, and only two sergeants which was of course too little to instruct the men in all they ought to do. The rt. hon. gent. seemed to wish to exemplify in his own corps all the imperfections which he complained of in the volunteer system. If at any time he saw in Hyde Park, or anywhere else, such an appearance of discipline as staggered his opinion, he immediately comforted himself with the recollection of his own corps in the country, and of their indiscipline and want of subordination.

But, said Perceval, so far as the volunteers in general went, 'the reports of the inspecting officers were...quite in opposition to this opinion';[1] and another member of Parliament, Sir Henry Mildmay, stated that 'by summer of 1806 most of [the volunteers] had been reported fit to act with troops of the line'.[2] Apparently, then, the strength which the volunteers gave the country, and which Cornwallis had valued even three years earlier, had now grown very respectable.

Yet Windham's attack went on, in defiance alike of irony and of solid argument. He suspended the ballot for the militia, in the hope that a limited bounty would keep it filled by voluntary recruiting; and by that stroke he removed the sanction—fear of the ballot—which had been valuable in keeping the volunteers efficient. He swept away their Inspecting Field Officers, without whose services their training could not be supervised nor the value of individual units made known to the Commander-in-Chief. Likewise, he docked the volunteers' training allowances, reduced the number of days they were required to drill, and refused to give any guarantee that they would receive any future clothing allowances. So he left them, having in the name of economy destroyed everything that made them efficient, but without by any means abolishing their whole expense to the nation.

Even Windham could see that the crippling of this force weakened the country and that some substitute must be provided, so he had also committed himself to a sort of rehash of Addington's Levy en Masse Act.

[1] *Parliamentary Debates*, 6 June 1806, p. 21.   [2] *Ibid.* 3 July 1806, p. 905.

He could not, of course, use that act, for the pledge had been given that it would not be enforced if enough volunteers came forward; and more than enough volunteers had offered their services. Therefore Windham repealed the Levy en Masse Act, and substituted a Training Act, which was intended to compel the population to undergo training in batches of 200,000 men per year chosen by ballot from the militia lists in every county. They were to be paid one shilling for each of their twenty-four days' training, but could be excused altogether for the price of a £5 fine.

The debate on this act displayed Windham's incompetence in an almost pitiable light. He could give the House no clear answer as to whether volunteers would or would not be balloted. He had limited his bill to England only, and could give no satisfying reason for excusing the Scots from service. But he hinted it might be applied to Scotland in 'two or three years',[1] and thereby provoked Castlereagh to suggest that 'if he wished to make an experiment merely...[he might]...try it on a much narrower scale and...confine, for the present, this boon of his to the county of Norfolk' alone.[2] He had just crippled the volunteers on the plea of economy; but his new compulsory training scheme would cost £240,000 per annum in wages to the trainees alone, without counting the pay of their instructors and without the smallest visible prospect of efficiency. For he provided no officers for this mass of men, or military law to control them. He simply intended that a sergeant should give the men military instruction, while the village constable stood by to furnish disciplinary assistance somehow. But how? On this question, the report of the debate runs:

Mr Spencer Stanhope wished to ask whether the men, when at drill, were to be under the command of the sergeant or of the constable who was to stand over them? He was anxious to know what the rt. hon. gent. meant on this head as, being a deputy lieutenant, enquiries might be directed to him on this head.

Mr Windham replied that the sergeant would instruct them and the constable would stand by.[3]

This fatuous evasion produced 'a loud laugh from the opposition'. But neither question nor laughter could get a straight answer from Windham; and Spencer Perceval rose to divert the House with a picture of the constable solemnly taking 'the man to prison, if he did not turn out his toes properly or obey the signals of "eyes right" or "eyes left" with sufficient promptitude'.[4] Canning followed by challenging the Lord Advocate of Scotland to take all the time he pleased to frame, if he could, a bill for his own neglected country that would 'devise...a description of force...less efficient...than the 200,000 men who were to be drawn out in splendid array under a few constables and drill sergeants'.[5]

[1] *Parliamentary Debates*, 26 June 1806, pp. 847.
[2] *Ibid.* 25 June 1806, p. 847.   [3] *Ibid.* 27 June 1806, pp. 863–4.
[4] *Ibid.* p. 864.   [5] *Ibid.* 5 July 1806, p. 914.

When General Sir James Pulteney wanted the number of training days doubled for the sake of increased efficiency, Windham answered: 'It was true that under the bill of 1803 [the Levy en Masse Act] the men were to be trained 40 days, but then 20 of these days were Sundays, and these were here given up.... He himself earnestly wished to preserve the reverence for the Sabbath. He had shewn it when he wished to suppress the growing evil of Sunday Newspapers.'[1] And the mind is left wondering how this man, who apparently felt more concern over the evil of not observing Sunday than over the danger of invasion, had ever seemed to anyone a fit person for a Ministry of Defence. Windham displayed his lack of any sense of reality again in his ideas that his trainees should have no uniforms; that they should be given a sort of training 'which it will be very easy for them to acquire'; that this training would enable them either to act as 'an armed peasantry, or to recruit immediately whatever losses the regular army might receive' from an enemy. Then, claimed Windham, the regular army, if beaten, 'could immediately repair the disaster and would rise like Antaeus, when flung to the earth, with redoubled vigour'.[2] The facts, of course, were that if any men of an armed peasantry without uniforms were captured when harassing an invader, the laws of war permitted them to be shot without mercy as *francs-tireurs* instead of being treated as prisoners; and that twenty-four days' training, especially of such irregular training, was too little by half to make them fit reinforcements for the line. Nevertheless, the Training Act passed the House of Commons on 6 July 1806.

In March 1807 the Ministry of All the Talents fell, after passing one great measure, the abolition of the slave trade. It is deservedly remembered for that act of idealism and courage—idealism on behalf of the underdog and courage to defy the powerful West India lobby, the great vested interests of Liverpool and Bristol and all the gloomy forebodings of the many amateur economists who believed that abolition meant commercial ruin. It seems but fair to recall here the great humanitarian achievement of this ministry as a balance to the summary, which must now be given, of its unrelieved military failure.

When Pitt died and his government fell, the country had been made strong by over 300,000 volunteers, of whom by 1806 most had been reported fit to act with the line. Hence the government had felt able to plan an invasion of North Germany and that invasion was to be massive. The nation was so strong that the government could aim to throw ashore against the left flank of the French a force intended to amount to not less than 60,000 men.[3] Though the scheme failed, for reasons in part beyond

[1] *Ibid.* 27 June 1806, p. 863.　　　　　[2] *Ibid.* 3 April 1806, p. 681.
[3] 'Memorandum relative to the Projected Expedition, for the Consideration of the Cabinet. Downing St., October 21, 1805', Londonderry, *Castlereagh's Correspondence*, II, 25–9; including the Hanoverians of the King's German Legion, 'the army for offensive operations' was expected to 'exceed 70,000 rank and file'. On 3 November Castlereagh

the government's control,[1] a Britain which could even plan such a stroke was in terms of real force a greater world power than she had been since the days of Marlborough.

Such was the condition in which Castlereagh had left his country when he resigned from the War Ministry in February 1806. On his return to office fifteen months later he found its strength wasted and gone. The volunteers were no longer the valuable defensive force which they had been when he left office. Discouraged as they were and stripped of the Inspecting Field Officers who provided them with supervision and a staff, their efficiency was so withered that Castlereagh could describe them as a mere 'fleeting and inapplicable mass'. Not a day's training had been done under Windham's precious National Training Act. The regular army which in 1805 had had an expeditionary force and shipping ready to deliver at any moment an unforeseeable blow at any part of the enemy's extended coastline, was now unequal even to home defence, so that maritime counties were garrisoned largely by the militia.[2] Abroad, Britain's allies, Russia and Prussia, who had checked Napoleon sharply at Eylau and remained still undefeated, were clamantly demanding British aid, especially in cavalry. But, thanks to Windham's notions of economy, the means to send that aid were no longer to hand. The Whigs had given up the fleet of military transports which Castlereagh had kept in pay so as to be ready at any time to strike the enemy without warning. They had retained only enough ships to keep up necessary communications with the Channel Isles and Ireland; of these few, only one was a horse transport.[3] In short, the country which fifteen months earlier had been strong at home and formidable abroad was now weak at home and impotent abroad.

Such were the military consequences of the Ministry of All the Talents. They left their successors helpless to intervene while Britain's great enemy instructed the Duke of York to form 'the present disposable force into one connected army for active service' (*ibid.* p. 36).

[1] This plan was, of course, drafted before the government had heard of the Austrian disaster at Ulm on 20 October 1805, and nearly six weeks before Napoleon's decisive victory at Austerlitz over the allies in whose aid the invasion was planned. The Duke of York, on hearing of it, sent Pitt a vigorous clear-headed memorandum, showing that an attack on Holland, the intended target, could not succeed without the benevolent neutrality of Prussia and could not be launched in winter. (Windsor.) As late as 5 December the friendship of Prussia was relied upon (*Castlereagh Correspondence*, II, 72); on 23 December operations against 'the French army in force to the southward' were substituted for the reconquest of Holland. But on 29 December Castlereagh's 'suspense relative to affairs on the continent' was 'very painfully relieved by the confirmation of the disaster to our allies' at Austerlitz (*ibid.* pp. 95–6). On 5 January 1806 Castlereagh wrote Pitt 'if we can bring away 10,000 (recruits from Hanover), we shall have made a good campaign of it' (*ibid.* p. 105). On 4 February the order to re-embark the troops already on the continent was dispatched (*ibid.* p. 127). The number re-embarked was 'over twenty-six thousand strong, for the King's German Legion had increased by one-third during its stay in Germany' (Fortescue, *British Army*, v, 296).

[2] Fortescue, *County Lieutenancies*, p. 175. This situation was caused in part by the need for more garrisons overseas, and was not wholly due to Windham's blunders.

[3] Londonderry, *Castlereagh Correspondence*, VIII, 47–8.

won new triumphs, first at Danzig, then at Friedland. As a sequel to the last came Tilsit, and Russia was transformed from a friend into an enemy. This was a disaster which dwarfed all the petty, but still humiliating, failures of All-the-Talents' strategy in the Dardanelles, Egypt and Buenos Aires. Castlereagh's one compensation for the desperate but fruitless efforts he made to support his allies lay in the fact that the troops and the shipping, which he could not assemble in time to act before Friedland, were available to neutralize part at least of the results of Tilsit by mastering the Danes and securing their fleet in August 1807.

Apart from this stroke at Copenhagen there was nothing that Castlereagh could do for the moment but rearm his country. It would be an error to accuse him of coming to office with any detailed and thought-out scheme for this. Indeed when the Duke of York and Sir Harry Calvert successively brought forward well-conceived and logical long-range schemes of military reorganization he rejected them.[1] Possibly he was right to do so—not because the soldiers did not know what would be militarily good for the country, but because Castlereagh, as a House of Commons man, was better placed to judge how much good to the country Parliament would permit him to do.

So Castlereagh tackled the job of rearmament in his own way, a way that reveals three facets of his greatness—a tireless readiness to work, a clear sense of perspective, and openness of mind. His readiness to work enabled him to master a mass of detail; his sense of perspective saved him from ever getting lost in it; his openness of mind led him to consider any suggestion, whatever its source, without prejudice. Out of varied expedients he built a system which proved equal to meeting Britain's needs for the rest of the war.

His two big jobs were to make his country secure at home and formidable abroad once more.

To the first, security at home, Windham's Training Act contributed nothing, for its own author had found himself unequal to any attempt at enforcing it in the nine months that separated its passage into law and his own fall.

The only resource was, therefore, to revive the volunteers. In a closely considered memorandum Castlereagh declared that they could all be left with the twenty-four days' pay for training which Windham had conceded, but they must have a clothing allowance. They must also have their Inspecting Field Officers without 'whose superintendence Government could have no security for the faithful application of the allowances granted...[or knowledge] of the state of their discipline and numbers'. These were the first essentials 'toward enabling His Majesty to employ his Regular forces...with effect against the enemy'.[2] They were duly done;

---

[1] These schemes are described by Fortescue, *County Lieutenancies*, pp. 176, 224–5.

[2] Londonderry, *Castlereagh Correspondence*, VIII, 51–2.

and some of the dismal reports, which soon came in from the revived Inspecting Field Officers, may have influenced Castlereagh's later policy toward the volunteers.

Next Castlereagh examined the state of the regulars. As had been forecast, the short service scheme had failed wretchedly. It is indeed true, as Fortescue records, that the number of men raised by voluntary recruiting in 1806 and 1807 was much larger absolutely than in previous years, but it was also true that the men were raised at much greater cost and that even so they were insufficient. In 1805–6, as Castlereagh put it, 'the recruiting parties did not exceed in number 405' but in 1806–7 'they had been increased to 1113 exclusive of above 400 extra recruiting officers,.... this extraordinary increase in the number of recruiting parties' was not only 'highly prejudicial to the discipline and efficiency of the army, but... so much extra expense incurred for the levy of men'.[1]

Windham had endeavoured to spur recruiting yet further by threatening to disband 54 second battalions and place their officers on half-pay if they did not raise 400 men each in six months. In spite of these strong measures, however, Castlereagh found that 'upon a comparison of the effectives of the Army with the establishment as voted by Parliament', there was still 'a deficiency of about 35,000 men'.[2] And this deficiency existed in spite of something unpleasantly like a breach of promise on Windham's part. For, according to Castlereagh, Windham 'had certainly held out an expectation to all those men who had served 21 years in the army that they would be immediately discharged; but prudence would not allow him to venture on this step and in the face of his own principles he abstained from discharging these men, who were very numerous and who were still in the service'.[3] Castlereagh also noted that of the 35,000 men deficient 23,000 were required to complete '54 battalions now at home... to an average strength of about 700 a battalion'.[4]

There was a twofold problem here; first the general raising of men, and, secondly, strengthening a large number of very weak battalions. These were second battalions of the Duke of York's Cardwell-type system, formed out of the Army of Reserve and repeatedly drained to maintain their first battalions. Of them Castlereagh wrote 'Nothing can appear more perfect than the system of second battalions if they can have the double quality of being reasonably efficient in themselves for the purposes of home defence, while they, at the same time, feed their first battalions on foreign service'. But when Castlereagh wrote these lines the system was keeping '16,000 men [enlisted] for general service dispersed over 56 battalions, each too weak for use'.[5]

[1] *Parliamentary Debates*, 13 August 1807, p. 122.
[2] Londonderry, *Castlereagh Correspondence*, VIII, 55.
[3] *Parliamentary Debates*, 22 July 1807, p. 868.
[4] *Castlereagh Correspondence*, VIII, 55.
[5] *Ibid.* p. 65.

It was impossible, continued Castlereagh, to raise the needed total of 35,000 men without exciting 'the opposition of some considerable class of interests, both in and out of Parliament'. But he did not flinch from that and considered two methods—'the one is a draft from the Militia leaving that defensive force gradually to repair its numbers; the other is some very active local assessment, to be enforced by a fine, etc., which, like the Army of Reserve Act, shall be competent to extort a large number of men from the parishes in a short space of time'.[1]

Of these two, the Army of Reserve had a number of friends. Among them was old Henry Dundas, now Lord Melville, who wrote Castlereagh, 'I never could figure a reason the Army of Reserve was laid aside, unless because it was necessary to run down the administration which introduced it'[2]—a curious admission from a member of the cabinet which had done the laying aside! But Castlereagh had grave doubts of another Army of Reserve. The effectiveness of that measure had depended on the £20 fine imposed on balloted men who refused to serve. But now, after Windham, fines had fallen into contempt 'from their enforcement being always neglected, and latterly wholly abandoned by an express enactment'.[3]

Accordingly, there was nothing for it but a new demand upon the militia, for which, indeed, the time was unusually appropriate. In 1807 the men who had entered the militia in March 1803 had only a few months to wait for their discharge after completing their five years of service; they would all have to be replaced in any case; all were fully trained; and, in the matter of bounty, it would be at least as cheap to get the men to volunteer from the militia as to try to recruit them from civil life after their discharge. So Castlereagh demanded a total of 28,000 men from the militia—21,000 from Britain and 7000 from Ireland. The men came forward very well, and a total of 27,505 were secured.[4]

A loss of so many was, of course, all but crippling to the militia for, thanks to the disuse of the ballot and reliance on voluntary enlistment, it too was under strength. On 1 July 1807 it had only 77,790 effectives against an establishment of 95,823.[5] The damage to the militia was, of course, foreseen, and a cure was found in the revival of the ballot. This produced the expected protest from Windham, the usual scramble for substitutes and the inevitable crop of insurance societies. But the first-line strength of the country—the regular army—was made good. In due time the militia did 'gradually repair its numbers'. By March 1808 the militia of Great Britain and Ireland were reported only 8110 short of their requirements.[6]

There was less complaining, too, among militia officers than had been expected. But, in truth, militia officers must have been coming to regard

---

[1] *Ibid.* p. 55.
[2] *Ibid.* p. 80.
[3] *Ibid.* p. 55.
[4] Fortescue, *County Lieutenancies*, p. 186.
[5] *Ibid.* p. 202.
[6] *Ibid.* p. 196.

these drafts on their regiments as an inevitable evil. Since Cornwallis first offended the militia colonels by treating them as 'recruiting officers to the Artillery' in 1796, and since the gay volunteering of the fellows who gathered on Barham Downs in 1799, Pitt had taken his 9000 militiamen for the army in 1805[1] and Windham had taken 4000 from the Irish Militia in 1806.[2] Castlereagh's draft in 1807 was not the last either. He was to take another 28,492 in 1809,[3] Palmerston still another 11,453 in 1811.[4]

Though ordinary recruiting alone could not keep the army full it did provide a valuable 12,000 men in addition to the militia volunteers. Castlereagh did not abolish Windham's scheme of limited enlistment. He revived enlistments for life, however, and let the recruit choose on which of the two alternatives he would serve.

With the regulars reasonably well brought up to strength and the militia repaired, Castlereagh's job was still unfinished. He relied heavily on the volunteers for home defence, but their strength had greatly declined, from a total of 330,116 in 1805 to 294,148 on paper in 1807, and of the latter figure only '240,000 were under arms at the last inspections' of the year.[5] A number of disturbing reports also indicated that their discipline had fallen sadly since the days when most of them were judged fit to act with the line.[6] It therefore seemed desirable to disband bad units, though this could only make the force numerically weaker still. Again Castlereagh was thoroughly impressed with the basic good sense of Windham's opinion that the whole manhood of the nation should be trained to arms, although as a practical man he never doubted that Windham's scheme could not work. Likewise he had not forgotten Addington's useful act creating a Supplementary Militia by the compulsion of the ballot. Finally, one valuable thing at least had come out of Windham's training scheme—new lists of men of military age had been made out. From all these materials Castlereagh concocted a new force, tentatively called the Sedentary Militia but later named the Local Militia.

This force, as finally created, did not conform to Castlereagh's first wishes. He would have liked to disband all but 100,000 volunteers of the best sort in the large towns of Great Britain, to train all able-bodied men between 18 and 30 in the use of firearms and then to form by an annual ballot a Sedentary Militia of 200,000 to be trained in drill for twenty-eight days a year. Men of this Sedentary Militia were to be free to enter the army, navy, marines or regular militia and to be replaced by ballot.[7]

---

[1] *County Lieutenancies*, p. 145. 17,000 was the number for which Pitt hoped and 9000-odd was the number he got.

[2] *Ibid.* p. 166.   [3] *Ibid.* p. 223.

[4] *Ibid.* p. 257.   [5] *Ibid.* pp. 198, 209.

[6] *Ibid.* pp. 198–200.

[7] This project is contained in an undated 'Memorandum on a System of Defence' printed on pp. 113–24 of *Castlereagh's Correspondence*, VIII, where it almost immediately follows a letter to Lord Chatham dated '31 December 1807'.

But this scheme, which would have made Britain into a very powerful state indeed, was apparently judged unpractical. Instead, Castlereagh merely created a Local Militia designed to make good the deficiencies of the volunteers and in any case not to exceed the number of 308,934 men. The immediate need in 1808 stood at 60,000 men. These were to be raised by voluntary enlistment, or when that failed, by ballot with no substitutes accepted. Service under the ballot was compelled by heavy fines or imprisonment. Volunteer infantry corps were invited to transfer themselves bodily into the Local Militia, in return for a bounty of 2 guineas a man. The new force was to be formed into battalions with a proper compliment of officers, and with a regimental staff which was to be on permanent pay. Local Militiamen were to serve for four years, during which, and for two years afterward, they were to be exempt from the ballot for the regular militia. They were required to undergo twenty-eight days' training a year, either in their own or a neighbouring county, but no farther afield. They could be called out to suppress riots, but not for more than fourteen days in a year, and those days were to count as part of their training. Finally, the Local Militiaman remained free to enlist in the regular army at any time.[1]

The advantages of this scheme were that it empowered the government to train initially a greater number of men than Windham himself had envisaged, but it also possessed the machinery for discipline, as Windham's scheme had not. The invitation to the volunteers to transfer to the Local Militia likewise provided a means of bringing the men of that force under the regular discipline that some volunteer units needed badly. Similarly the transfer of the volunteers, wherever it happened, would give to the Local Militia the officers whom it might otherwise have been very hard to find in sufficient numbers.

As soon as the acts were passed, pressure began to be brought to bear on the volunteers. Returns were called for and inefficient units were disbanded and swept into the ballot.

A year's experience brought to light certain flaws in the Local Militia and on 27 March 1809 Castlereagh introduced a new bill to amend the original act. The amending bill permitted the filling of the Local Militia by voluntary enlistment or by ballot at any time without orders from headquarters. It also permitted Local Militiamen to enlist as volunteers in the regular militia as well as in the army, but forbade them to join either during the annual period of training. The cost of the force was reduced by repealing a section of the previous act which stipulated that a bounty of 2 guineas must be given to recruits who voluntarily enlisted. Instead local authorities were permitted to give a bounty not exceeding 2 guineas, and the bounty originally offered to volunteers who chose to transfer was abolished.[2]

[1] Fortescue, *County Lieutenancies*, pp. 210–14.   [2] *Ibid.* pp. 228–9.

When he introduced the amending act, Castlereagh was already able to claim considerable success for his original scheme. After one year's life the Local Militia already numbered 250 regiments, with an average strength of nearly 800 men each, and a grand total of 195,161 men. Of these some 125,000 had transferred into the Local Militia from the volunteers. More such transfers were encouraged in June 1809, by the warning that volunteer infantry units could expect no further grants for clothing. From that date forward the volunteer infantry steadily dwindled till they were dissolved in March 1813 in order that their weapons might be sent to help arm the Prussians for the War of Liberation.[1] The volunteer cavalry, called yeomanry, survived the war and is familiar to students of the unhappy years that followed 1815 as a sort of auxiliary police force.

Various criticisms, not overlooked by Fortescue, may be made of Castlereagh's work. There was friction between the two different militias.[2] There were difficulties with discipline in some Local Militia units.[3] Castlereagh also perhaps allowed his Local Militia to grow too big too fast, so that too many men became eligible for discharge at the same time.[4] But, by compelling the volunteers to be efficient and by creating the Local Militia he did give Britain a stronger, better disciplined force for home defence than she had ever had. With the defence of the homeland thus secured it was again possible to use the regular army for offensive operations; and, thanks once more to Castlereagh, the regular army was never stronger than when the Spanish revolt broke out in 1808. By normal recruiting added to his draft of 27,500 militiamen the army received an increase of 40,000 men in a single year. The system Castlereagh created proved sufficient to meet the country's actual needs for the remainder of the war.

As one reviews the story of Britain's manpower problem, when she faced revolutionary and Napoleonic France, one cannot help being struck first by the surprising failure of Pitt in this, and in other fields, as a war leader and inevitably one asks why a man of such great gifts failed so consistently. It is true that he became Premier with none of his father's military training, experience or interests. His early mistakes of 1793-4 may perhaps be fairly condoned as those of a novice. But by 1804-6 the bitter lessons of defeat should surely have taught an able man something at least of the art of making war. For war is very largely a matter of managing detail right, and Pitt was a master of detail; he had proved that abundantly before 1793. Yet his errors in 1804-5 were curiously similar to those he committed in 1793-9. In both periods he failed to grasp the essentials of the recruiting problem. The main feature of his Permanent Additional Force Act—the use of local civilian officials to recruit soldiers

---

[1] *County Lieutenancies*, pp. 260-70.   [2] *Ibid.* p. 272.
[3] *Ibid.* pp. 231, 243-9.
[4] *Ibid.* p. 265.

—came straight from the miserable Quota Act of 1796. Here his recipe for success was to rely on instruments already proved incompetent.

A case might perhaps be made for arguing that there was real growth in Pitt's strategical thinking. The diversion of Major General Sir James Craig and 6000 men to the Mediterranean in 1805 was forced upon him, partly by the Russians, partly by the importance of making Sicily secure. Aside from this, British strategy in 1805 was free from that mania for dispersing too few troops on too many jobs, which had contributed so much to France's survival in 1793–4. The plan of 1805 for throwing a single expeditionary force, over 60,000 strong, against the French left flank in Germany at least showed a sound understanding of the principle of 'concentration'. But no one can certainly claim this scheme as Pitt's. It matured only after Castlereagh had been War Minister for some months, and then—like the Alkmaar scheme of 1799—it was vitiated by unconsidered matters of detail. As the Duke of York pointed out, the first condition of its success was Prussia's sympathy, which alone could make it possible to secure transport. But that country's sympathy was hardly to be bought for less than the cession of Hanover, which Pitt was not prepared to offer. No battering train to master fortified places was available; yet Pitt's original hope was to invade eastern Holland, which was girdled with fortified cities. Finally—perhaps the most crippling weakness of all—the government that launched this plan was devoid of any sense of the supreme importance of timing. Pitt's first exchanges with Russia were made before Christmas 1804.[1] The major objects of the coalition were defined in January 1805.[2] Thereafter negotiations were stalled by Russia's demand that Britain surrender Malta; that, however, was not a sufficient cause for abandoning hope; and hope itself was cause enough to warrant the preparations necessary for playing an effective part in the expected contest. Yet no preparations appear to have been undertaken at all till after Castlereagh became War Minister in July. As has been seen, Castlereagh lost little time in getting to work on his job;[3] but he was not ready to lay any detailed plan for continental operations before the cabinet till 21 October.[4] Meanwhile Mack and all his Austrians had laid down their arms at Ulm on the day before. Here Pitt and Camden both stand convicted of want of realistic foresight.

And yet again one asks, why should a man with Pitt's breadth and capacity of mind fail so signally? The truest answer is probably to be found not in any defect of mind but in his weaknesses of personality—in his shyness and his aloofness. He dominated men so much more easily than he confided in them. A tremendous worker himself, he had little knack of getting others to work for him. Instead, he far too often pre-

---

[1] Rose, *Pitt and the Great War*, p. 516.
[2] *Ibid.* p. 522.
[3] For example, in his creation of the disposable force described on pp. 32–33 above.
[4] Londonderry, *Castlereagh Correspondence*, II, 25.

ferred attempting things himself to letting competent and responsible persons do them for him, and he took more upon his own shoulders than all his abilities could have performed, even if he had known what was required for the performance.[1]

The second point which emerges from this study is, surely, that Addington has been much underrated. Far from being a feeble blunderer, he was an unflashy man of very sane common sense. He kept Britain strong in peace. He was much more practical than Pitt in devising measures to make her still stronger in war. When the time came to strike, he was found ready to strike—witness the swift recapture of French West Indian colonies so lately restored by the Treaty of Amiens. His finance was sound, and he was in no hurry to squander British money on bribing other powers to try to pull his chestnuts out of the fire.

Finally, as one studies the detail of military administration, one cannot but feel an ever-growing admiration for that ogre of the Whigs whose manner of death was to win him the unkind title of 'Carotyd-artery-cutting Castlereagh'. In capacity for hard work, in grasp of reality (both as to needs and to difficulties), in indifference to uninformed or otherwise foolish criticism, in the *tact des choses possibles*—in all these things Castlereagh was first rate. One may grant that only a Wellington could have won the victories which brought England glory and safety out of the Peninsula. The fact remains that Castlereagh's work provided the troops with whom Wellington fought, just as the Duke of York's reforms made them fit to fight with.

---

[1] Perhaps I have expressed this too mildly, and would better have described Pitt as an incurable meddler in other people's business. Witness Rose's statement on pp. 530–1 of his *William Pitt and the Great War*; 'apart from the defence of a weak government against a strong Opposition, Pitt transacted very much of the business of the War Office and Foreign Office, besides assisting the Admiralty and the Commander-in-Chief'. Let it be granted that any Premier must be very closely interested in foreign policy, but in Castlereagh Pitt had a man better able to do the work of the War Department than any other man—Haldane doubtfully excepted—who has held that office; and the very idea of a layman like Pitt offering assistance to such experienced and technically proficient administrators as Barham and York smacks of impertinence.

COMMISSARIAT DUTIES

IT has been suggested that the appendix on the commissariat here presented might well be omitted from this study of how the British Army was prepared for effective service in the field. Nowadays such a suggestion is no doubt comprehensible. In our modern age of luxury the scholar has come to take his three square meals a day almost as much for granted as the air he breathes. It is easy to forget that actual famine, which last occurred in France as recently as 1855, was only banished from western Europe by the spread of railways and the opening up of virgin wheatlands in the New World. Even in the Second World War, troops encountered little or none of such hardship as was suffered in Paris during the siege of 1870-1 when rats were sold for food at 50 centimes each, and all the varied livestock of the zoo in the Jardin des Plantes went by way of the slaughterhouse to the tables of such Parisians as were lucky enough to receive a share. Hence many who served in the forces came, like civilians, to take their rations as a matter of course, forgetting both the elaborate supply organizations which delivered those rations and the varied modern inventions which made delivery possible. The historian, however, should remember that the method of preserving foods by boiling them in sealed tins was not discovered till 1809, nor used in war till the Royal Navy first received canned meats in 1813; that railways made little contribution to war till the second half of the nineteenth century; and that the motor lorry and the air drop are twentieth-century innovations.

Moreover, even today, with all our modern aids, the supply of food to his troops is still one of the first problems a general has to solve in any operation he undertakes. So in 1939 General Sir Archibald Wavell (as he then was) praised to a Cambridge audience Socrates' description of the good commander, beginning 'the general must know how to get his men their rations', on the ground that this description puts first 'administration, which is the real crux of generalship';[1] and he declared it unfortunate that 'in most military books strategy and tactics are emphasized at the expense of the administrative factors'.[2] From this last sentence one may perhaps conclude that most military books available in the 1930's were less realistic than at least some of their predecessors two centuries or so earlier. Certainly Thomas Simes, writing in 1780, had no doubts on the matter. 'Famine', he roundly declared, 'makes greater havoc of an army

---

[1] On p. 14 of his first Cambridge lecture on 'Generals and Generalship', reprinted in his posthumous *Soldiers and Soldiering* (London, 1953).

[2] *Ibid.* p. 22.

than the enemy and is more terrible than the bayonet. Time and opportunity may repair other misfortunes, but where forage and provisions have not been carefully provided, the evil is without remedy. The main and principal point in war is to procure plenty of provisions, and destroy the enemy by famine.'[1] In 1800 Napoleon stressed the same point when he wrote Berthier (who was then busily preparing for the crossing of the Alps which led to Marengo) 'votre plus grand travail dans tout ceci sera d'assurer vos subsistances'.[2]

In the face of the witness of such varied military authorities as these (for Socrates, like the others, had been on active service) it would hardly be pardonable to leave this study of the British Army devoid of any description of how the basic duty of feeding horse and man in the field was carried out. Therefore we print here a short manuscript on the duties of commissariat, which was written in 1796 by the experienced British commissary, Havilland LeMesurier, and is preserved in the Chatham papers in the Public Record Office. The *Dictionary of National Biography* credits LeMesurier with writing two manuals on the supply of armies, *Commissariat Duties in the Field*, published in 1796, and *The British Commissary*, published in 1798. Both are exceedingly rare now, so the printing of this manuscript, which appears to be the first draft of his earlier work, should be useful to serious students of war.

Points likely to surprise the modern reader of LeMesurier's work are, first, the fact that the Commissary was not a soldier, but a member of 'the Civil Administration of an Army'. He was not a very kindly regarded civilian either; indeed, 'the prejudices of society against a Commissary almost prevent him from receiving the common respect due to the character of a gentleman', as Wellington put it.[3] Secondly, the Army's 'Civil Administration' was appointed by and responsible to the Lords of the Treasury, not to the Commander-in-Chief who had nevertheless to give it orders. Thirdly, after all Britain's wars of the eighteenth century, Commissaries were still 'only employed in time of War and sought for at the moment of active operations'. The Treasury, in short, chose to regard all the varied duties of supplying troops engaged in active operations as simple enough to be performed by wholly inexperienced and untrained men—a conveniently economical theory in peacetime, which regularly proved a most costly delusion in war. Fourthly, though no army could operate effectively without moving, and no movement was possible without ample commissariat transport, the Treasury set its face against maintaining a permanent British waggon train.

On the last point, LeMesurier's own experience led him to believe the Treasury's policy was right. In Belgium, Holland and Germany he had

---

[1] Thomas Simes, *Treatise of Military Science* (London, 1780), p. 6.
[2] *Correspondance de Napoléon I*, VI, no. 4279.
[3] To Colonel Gordon, 19 December 1810, Gurwood, vol. VII.

found he could manage very well with 'waggons of the country' hired on sufficiently precise contracts. His support of this theory, one can only suppose, must have contributed to its survival; and, most unhappily, it did survive until 1854 when the British Army found itself required to campaign in a land which possessed neither contractors to provide the 'waggons of the country', nor any very noticeable supply of the waggons themselves. Then the nation learnt, most expensively, that even to maintain the siege of Sebastopol, it needed the Royal Waggon Train which, founded in 1855, became the ancestor of the Royal Army Service Corps.

A perhaps disappointing feature of LeMesurier's manual is the fact that, while he has much to teach on methods of accounting, he has relatively little to tell of the actual collection and distribution of the army's provisions. Yet that in itself was the natural result of a system under which the commissary was so much more directly responsible to a Treasury which insisted on accurate accounting than to a Commander-in-Chief who merely wanted his men and horses to be properly fed. Further, what LeMesurier does have to tell about the actual supply problem is enlightening.

In particular, he most strikingly reveals the traffic problems of an eighteenth-century army with the number of 9600 waggons found necessary to move forage alone for British and allied troops in the German campaign of 1760. One has only to think of the probable condition of an eighteenth-century road over which a mere one thousand waggons had passed in wet weather to realize why war was so largely an affair of summer campaigns.

Then, all unnoticed by LeMesurier, there was the nightmarish problem of defending a convoy of waggons. And here Carlyle invites quotation. In describing Frederick II's convoy bringing from Troppau supplies needed to maintain the siege of Olmutz in June 1758, he writes:

The driving of 3,000 four-horse wagons, under escort, ninety miles of road, is such an enterprise as cannot readily be conceived by sedentary pacific readers;—much more the attack of such! Military science, constraining chaos into the cosmic state, has nowhere such a problem. There are twelve thousand horses, for one thing, to be shod, geared, kept roadworthy and regular; say six thousand country wagoners, thick-soled peasants; then hanging to the skirts of these, in miscellaneous crazy vehicles and weak teams, equine and asinine, are one or two thousand sutler people, male and female, not of select quality, though on them, too, we keep a sharp eye. The series covers many miles, as many as twenty English miles (says Tempelhof), unless in favorable points you compress them into five, going four wagons abreast for defence's sake. Defence, or escort, goes in three bulks or brigades: vanguard, middle, rear-guard, with spare pickets intervening;—wider than five miles, you cannot get the parts to support one another. An enemy breaking in upon you, at some difficult point of road, woody hollow or the like, and opening cannon, musketry and hussar exercise on such an object, must make a confused transaction of it.[1] [And Loudon, the most alert of Austrians, made such 'a confused transaction' of this particular convoy that Frederick had to raise his siege and withdraw in failure.]

It is again of interest that LeMesurier should detail three methods of supplying troops—by magazines, by contractors and by direct requisition. The interest of this point lies in the fact that it contradicts a commonly accepted supposition that French armies of the Revolution discovered a new system of subsistence, this supposed novelty consisting of simply 'living off the land' by requisitions, or by plain, crude plundering. It is further supposed that this system gave French armies a new mobility, by freeing them from dependence on magazines, from the drag weight of a slow-moving waggon train and from anxiety over their lines of communication.[2]

This assumption, if not wholly in error, is at least at fault in its emphasis. In general all armies had to live on the produce of the land where they were campaigning in the days before railways or modern methods of food preservation enabled them to live on supplies from afar. To this, as to all generalizations, exceptions may indeed be noted. The Elbe might enable a Prussian Army campaigning in Saxony to live in part off a magazine in Magdeburg; or the barges on the Oder might supply an army campaigning in Silesia from magazines in Breslau. But the distances involved in these cases were not very great. Wellington's reliance on the sea to bring in supplies successively at different Peninsular ports in 1813 offers another striking exception, but one possible only for the army of a nation which had command of the sea. So, since the bringing of supplies from a great distance was normally impracticable, the armies of every nation had necessarily to live upon the land where they campaigned.

The methods used were common to all armies. The French of the Revolution did in fact use magazines. Napoleon himself relied on them—not very satisfactorily—when he began his Italian campaign in the spring of 1796;[3] amassed them again on a vast scale to support his new invasion

---

[1] Thomas Carlyle, *History of Frederick II of Prussia*, book XVIII, chap. XII.

[2] This idea is expressed as neatly as may be by three recent and able authors who write of French revolutionary armies 'Since they lived on the country, they carried less baggage. They thus freed themselves from the restricting magazines which had held eighteenth-century war in a straightjacket' (R. A. Preston, S. F. Wise and H. O. Werner, *Men in Arms*, New York, 1956, p. 181). But was eighteenth-century war always held in a 'straightjacket'? The phrase may fairly apply to the operations of Marshal Saxe, manœuvring carefully among the Barrier fortresses of Belgium; or to the unhappy flounderings of commanders of the calibre of Soubise and Contades. But is it an apt description of Marlborough's conduct in the Blenheim campaign? Or of his swift exploitation of victory after Ramillies? Or of Charles XII's lunge across the Ukraine? Or of Frederick's activity in the Seven Years War? Or even of Cornwallis's marches in the Carolinas? Or of the campaigns of Suvorov? Surely the rational answer to these questions is 'No'.

[3] Holland Rose, *Life of Napoleon I*, I, 86.

of Italy in the spring of 1800;[1] and recommended their use to Massena in the spring of 1811.[2] In the little-studied Italian campaign of 1799 the Austrians and Russians captured very considerable French magazines as they advanced victoriously westward.[3] Wellington's dispatches record the repeated formation of large French magazines in Spain.[4] An essential corollary to a system of magazines was a waggon train to shuttle between the magazines containing supplies and the troops who needed them. And one of the advantages which Napoleon is reported as claiming in 1805 from his fruitless threat to England was the fact that it enabled him to keep up the complete waggon trains which would be most useful and ready for a war with Austria.[5] After the revolution, too, as well as in the days of Louis XV, French commanders often relied on contractors to keep their armies supplied, in very much the manner described by LeMesurier. So one of the unpleasant surprises Russia held in store for Napoleon was the discovery that he could not 'here, as in other campaigns, . . . meet with concerns which for gold, or preferably paper, would deliver what was required; but that where there was no proper administration, there could be no contractors'.[6]

So far the French methods after the Revolution were the normal ones of the eighteenth century. The reverse is true, too. Like the leaders of revolutionary French armies, commanders of the eighteenth century had made their troops live on the produce of the countryside in which they were campaigning. The taking of requisitions from either friendly or hostile peasants, as described by LeMesurier, was no novelty lately learned from the enemy. Thomas Simes, the military writer already quoted, had published in 1780 two very detailed and practical drills, one for securing 'green forage' from the fields in which it grew,[7] the other for collecting 'dry forage' from the barns in which it had been stored.[8] One task in the

---

[1] Napoleon's supply arrangements in 1800 are summarized in my article 'War and Civilian Historians' in the *Journal of the History of Ideas* (January 1957), p. 91, but see, in particular, *Correspondance de Napoléon I*, VI, 4626. On his supply arrangements in 1805, see p. 263 n. 3, below.

[2] Berthier to Massena, 29 March 1811. Printed by J. T. Jones, *Journal of Sieges in Spain*, 3rd edition, III, 207.

[3] For example, at Pizzighettone a magazine sufficient to maintain 30,000 men for two months (Jomini, *Histoire critique et militaire des Guerres de la Revolution*, livre XIV, chap. LXXXVI). When Mantua fell, after a long investment, it was found to contain rations for another six months, a provision greatly exceeding the ordinary needs of a garrison (*ibid.* livre XV, chap. LXXXIX).

[4] For example, Wellington to Beresford, 10 June 1811, in Gurwood, vol. VII; to Lord Liverpool, 8 August 1811, to Henry Wellesley, 29 August 1811, to Lord Liverpool, 9 January 1812, in Gurwood, vol. VIII.

[5] A. Fournier, *Napoleon I; A Biography*, translated by A. E. Adams (London, 1911), p. 354.

[6] Jean Hanoteau (editor), *With Napoleon in Russia; the Memoirs of General de Caulaincourt, Duke of Vicenza*, English translation (New York, 1935), p. 141.

[7] Simes, *op. cit.* pp. 196–204.

[8] *Ibid.* pp. 205–11. Dry forage, explains Simes, means 'oats, barley, hay, chopped straw &c.' (*ibid.* p. 13).

latter operation was to estimate how many sheaves a given village could produce; and here Simes quotes with approval a method detailed by so early a writer as Puysegur.[1] He quotes with similar approval the maxim 'To distress the enemy more by famine than the sword is a mark of consummate skill'.[2] And that was the purpose of the great Frederick's invasion of Bohemia in September 1745 after Hohenfriedberg—to eat up the country by living off the land, and then to withdraw, leaving behind him fields and barns too stripped of forage and provisions to enable his enemy to pursue him back into Silesia.[3]

The great rule in this game was always to forage toward your enemy, and to be the first 'to get possession of the forage between the two armies...beginning with the fields at the greatest distance, and reserving the nearest to last'.[4] The enemy naturally could not be expected to remain a passive spectator of this stripping of the countryside on which he too wished to live. That is why such well-elaborated drills as Simes describes had been worked out for foragers before the 1780's; for the first part of those drills consisted of establishing 'the chain' of troops whose job was to protect the foragers as they mowed the fields or emptied the barns of the area allotted to them.

Like French revolutionary troops after them, the Prussian soldiers of Frederick the Great had handmills for grinding their own grain in the field. Right useful they were too; by their means, runs our author, 'you will not only spare your magazines, but will...frequently be enabled to continue in a camp, which otherwise you would have been obliged to quit; besides, fewer convoys will be required'.[5]

All told, then, French revolutionary armies had little to add to the art of living off the land in war. It was well understood and widely practised before them. It was, in fact, inescapable that similar conditions should impose the same general line of conduct on all armies. So in harvest time, and for a bit later, you could forage and support your troops on what you found in the countryside. In the autumn, too, you must lay in magazines, before frost and mud hampered you, if you wished to make a spring campaign. If food supplies for your men ran short, you could expect sickness and desertion; and if spring caught you without ample hay in store, or without transport to carry it, you could make no great manœuvres till the new growth of summer provided green forage enough to support your horses.[6]

These things being so, one may well ask what there was that was novel in the supply of French armies. For there is indeed some truth in the

---

[1] Simes, *op. cit.* p. 207. [2] *Ibid.* p. 205.
[3] Thomas Carlyle, *History of Frederick II of Prussia*, book xv, chap. xii.
[4] Simes, *op. cit.* p. 14. [5] *Ibid.* p. 9.
[6] For this reason the start of Wellington's advance from Portugal in 1813, which led him by way of Vittoria to the French frontier and beyond, was delayed till May. The result of his delay was a race against time, involving a good deal of anxiety before Vittoria was won.

opinion that there was a revolutionary change between normal eighteenth-century warfare and that of the nineteenth. The question of what caused the change is still more easily asked than answered. Three things may be suggested—good luck, new roads and a new standard of ruthlessness.

Luck, manifested in the weakness and division of their opponents, early enabled the French to carry the war on to enemy soil, and to live there by requisitions, instead of distressing their own people. This was great luck indeed, to which perhaps the survival of the revolution is due. A government like the Directory was unpopular enough even when the main burden of supporting its armies was borne by foreigners.

Turning to roads, one may repeat that the last third of the eighteenth century was the age of enlightened despotism, and that road building was one of the commonest expressions of despotic enlightenment. The great trunk roads which Arthur Young admired in France had been made in Spain by Charles III, and Frederick the Great, Maria Theresa and Joseph II had not been unprogressive in Germany either. But, in Wellington's phrase, every new trunk road helped to destroy 'the cheap defence of nations, an unimproved frontier'. Where the way was made easier for the waggons of commerce, and the stage coaches of civilian traffic, it was also made easier for armies; and as one observes the novel range and swiftness of manœuvre practised by French revolutionary armies, one must recall the work of Macadam's continental counterparts. So the 'grand chemin de Durlach à Stuttgart', on whose right Lannes and on whose left Ney were directed to forage in September 1805, obviously helped to hasten Napoleon's swift advance to Ulm; and the historian of war cannot afford to neglect the history of highways. They revolutionized strategic manœuvre by making great movements of troops easier than they had ever been before, since the decay of that network of military highways by which the Romans had bound their empire together.

The new standard of ruthlessness had very wide effects. It began at the top. Humane men of the eighteenth century had supposed Voltaire to be joking when he quipped that the English shot unsuccessful admirals *pour encourager les autres*. But it was the function of the French Revolution to take the *philosophes* seriously, and for a while this fatal form of encouragement became almost one of its established techniques. So when Lafayette and Dumouriez were successively beaten in 1792 and 1793 they both found it healthiest to seek sanctuary in their enemies' camp—a thing without precedent in eighteenth-century war. The execution of Houchard in 1793 warned French generals that they did not have to fail, but only to score insufficient success, in order to lose their heads as well as their commands. Custine's death reinforced the lesson. Inevitably, this new practice brought a new type of man to high command, a type of man much more ready to gamble than the Dauns, Broglies or Saxe-Cobourg-Saalfelds who had served the Old Regime. The revolutionary government did not fail to give these new commanders the means with which to gamble. The system of conscription, begun in 1793, provided them with lives to squander.

Thus supplied, French generals could afford to run risks from which commanders of laboriously enlisted, long service, professional troops of the Old Regime had fair reason to flinch. Their new attitude was expressed most brutally by their emperor when he declared that he had an income of 200,000 young men a year; or, in his famous interview with Metternich at the Marcolini Palace in Dresden, that he did 'not take much heed of the lives of a million men'. This attitude in turn engendered a new doctrine of battle as the means of gaining swift decision—the doctrine later made classic by Clausewitz when he wrote the words, 'Only great and general battles can produce great results'; or again, 'Let us not hear of generals who conquer without bloodshed'.[1] In the face of this new doctrine the old maxim—'to distress an enemy more by famine than the sword, is a mark of consummate skill'—was cast aside. Napoleon himself rejected it even when it would most have aided him.[2]

Quick decision, won by battle, either put a sudden end to the war or started an advance into new, and as yet unforaged, territory. Either way the commander could ignore the prudential advice of Simes, who had warned that in foraging 'the General should take care to leave sufficient grain, not only to enable the husbandman to live, but also to sow his ground; particularly if he foresees a probability of the next campaign being carried on in the same country'.[3] Still less did the French heed LeMesurier's maxims, given below, that, in foraging by requisition, it was 'even, if possible, more urgent that the Peasant should be paid regularly than the Contractor'; or that requisitions formally made in the enemy's country entitled 'every Individual in the latter to the protection of his private property'. Instead, French commanders foraged with unprecedented callousness and rapacity; 'they take everything and leave the unfortunate inhabitants to starve', as Wellington said of Massena's troops in 1810.[4]

In due season, this vigorous foraging did set French generals free from embarrassing lines of communication, and the need to defend them. So

---

[1] Cited by B. H. Liddell Hart, *The Ghost of Napoleon* (London, 1933), p. 126.

[2] Namely, in the Waterloo campaign. On this occasion, said Wellington on 18 May 1834, 'Napoleon...was certainly wrong in attacking at all. There were four armies going to enter France—before the harvest—and in a country much exhausted by the last campaign. We should have been reduced to many straits for subsistence—in fact, I don't hesitate to say the Prussians were already in great difficulties...Napoleon might, after providing for the other frontiers, have stationed himself on the Meuse with nearly 300,000 men. He might have played again the same game which he played so admirably the year before...[when he] manœuvred from one invading army to another and attacked them separately....[He] might have given us great trouble, and had many chances in his favour. Instead of this, by Waterloo he put an end to the war at once. But the fact is, he never in his life had patience for a defensive war' (Stanhope, *Conversations with Wellington*, pp. 59–60).

[3] Simes, *Treatise of Military Science*, p. 206.

[4] Wellington to Lord Liverpool, 21 December 1910, Gurwood, vol. VII.

in 1810 Wellington found it 'astonishing' that Massena could remain before the lines of Torres Vedras so long. 'It happened unfortunately', he wrote, 'that the Indian corn harvest...was on the ground at the moment of the enemy's invasion';[1] with that for a start, and later with 'meat only and such vegetables as they could pick up' the French somehow managed to maintain their ground before Wellington's lines for a full month. They were so 'indifferent about their flanks or rear or communications', that no manœuvre against their flank was worth attempting as a means of levering them out of their position.[2] Likewise in the summer of 1812 Marmont was enabled to ignore his communications by feeding his army on ripening grain mown in the fields where it grew; and, till he blundered at Salamanca, he gained thereby a great advantage over Wellington, who, refusing to live by pillaging his allies, could not neglect his communications. So too Napoleon in 1805, advancing against Austria through a well-tilled countryside at a date when the unthreshed harvest must still have been stacked in the fields, could live easily upon the land.[3]

Thus far French commanders of the revolution did indeed gain real advantages by cutting loose from magazines and transport columns. But in doing so they took risks impossible for any commander who had a wise regard for his army's welfare. At other seasons than during or after harvest, or when operations went awry, the results of their far too casual reliance on the countryside were often disastrous. For this reason Napoleon's troops suffered greatly in the Polish winter of 1806–7, when even the emperor's own pet pig, reserved for a Christmas banquet, disappeared mysteriously from its sty (and the Emperor's guardsman, the future Captain Coignet, who could easily have told his master where it went, had the best of reasons for not doing so). In the 1812 campaign recklessly casual supply arrangements did much more than the Russian winter to destroy the French Army. Thirteen years earlier these Russian sufferings of Napoleon's men had been foreshadowed in miniature in even so sunny a land as Italy in the autumn of 1799. Then, writes Jomini, 'les routes étaient couvertes de soldats expirant de froid et de faim.... Tant de

---

[1] Third letter of Wellington to Lord Liverpool, written on 27 October 1810, Gurwood, vol. VI.

[2] Wellington to Lord Liverpool, 3 November 1810, Gurwood, vol. VI.

[3] See his instruction to Murat of 21 September 1805, 'Le général Lannes vivra des réquisitions qu'il fera sur la droite du grand chemin de Durlach à Stuttgart; les pays de la gauche nourriront le maréchal Ney sur la route jusqu'où passe le maréchal Soult; Soult, les pays situés sur la gauche de sa route jusqu'à la route de Davout; et Davout, les pays qui sont sur sa gauche' (*Correspondance de Napoléon I*, no. 9249). Yet even on this campaign Napoleon formed considerable magazines—namely, one of 100,000 rations of biscuit at Goettingen (*ibid.* 9119); two more of 300,000 and 600,000 rations of biscuit respectively at Wurzburg and Strassburg (*ibid.* 9218); and one at Augsburg of 1,000,000 rations of biscuit, flour sufficient for another 2,000,000 rations of biscuit, 300,000 bales of hay and 100,000 pints of eau-de-vie (*ibid.* 9425). This last letter also refers to 'les moyens de transport de la compagnie Breidt', which I have not identified but would seem to be the name of a firm of German contractors.

souffrances relachèrent les liens de la discipline. Les soldats, voyant qu'on abusait de leur patience, abandonnèrent en foule les drapeaux pour rentrer dans l'intérieur.'[1] Hunger, leading to sickness, straggling and the cutting off of stragglers so reduced Massena's army before Torres Vedras that on 27 October 1810 Wellington reported to Liverpool 'I calculate that a reinforcement of 15,000 men would not give him so good an army as he had at Busaco'.[2] To those who complained of the cost of supporting a British Army, with all the expense of magazines and transport, Wellington retorted that if the British were to 'go on as French troops do, without pay, provisions, magazines or anything...we must form such a Government as exists in France, which can with impunity lose one half of the troops employed in the field every year, only by the privations and hardships imposed on them';[3] and years later he remarked to Lord Stanhope 'the French armies were made to take their chance and live as they could, and their loss of men was immense. It is very singular that in relating Napoleon's campaigns this has never been clearly shown in anything like its full extent.'[4] Even an income of 200,000 young men every year could not indefinitely meet the cost of campaigns conducted in this fashion.

An army could be almost as much crippled by the loss of horses as by the loss of men, and the French managed their horses very badly too. Caulaincourt records the loss of as many as 10,000 horses in the first week of the advance into Russia—with the inevitable result that waggons with essential supplies had to be left behind or troopers march on foot.[5] Still more disastrous losses were caused on the retreat by the neglect of so simple a precaution as rough-shoeing horses to enable them to stand up on icy roads.[6]

In the long run, then, the casual French system of living by requisition or pillage, and their indifference to precautions which conservative soldiers were wise enough to take, brought more disadvantages than advantages. For a striking example here one may point to the British invasion of south-west France in 1813–14. Wellington stuck by LeMesurier's precept that it was even more important to pay peasants punctually than contractors. He was at pains to pay them in their own money, calling on experienced counterfeiters in the British Army to come forward and turn good English guineas into gold Napoleons—in an army so largely recruited from the criminal class as the British he had no trouble finding all the skilled forgers of false coin he could use. The magic of gold, promptly paid, gave Wellington a more regular supply in France itself than Soult could wring out of his fellow countrymen for the support of their own

---

[1] Jomini, *op. cit.* livre xv, chap. xcvi.
[2] Gurwood, vol. vii.
[3] To Lord Wellesley, 26 January 1811, Gurwood, vol. viii.
[4] Stanhope, *Conversations with Wellington*, p. 86.
[5] Caulaincourt, *op. cit.* p. 49.
[6] *Ibid.* pp. 161–2.

army.[1] The goodwill bought by prompt payment was as important as the regularity of supply. Everywhere the burden of French requisitions notoriously did much to take the gilt off liberty, equality and fraternity, to turn the Frenchman from a deliverer into a hated foreigner and at last to rouse the storm of *Befreiungskrieg*.

So much for the excellence of LeMesurier's advice on prompt payment. It brought a regular supply of forage for horses and flour for men. Regular rations were in turn essential to good health, good discipline and full battalions. But there is one matter which LeMesurier does not even mention—the supply of meat. As indicated by Massena's experience before Torres Vedras meat was easier to provide than bread. The troops' meat could march on its own hoofs till it was wanted and the rear of an advancing army presented an almost 'wild west' appearance in the great, but ever diminishing, droves of cattle which followed the marching men. The job of acting as 'cattle guards' was one that required 'at times the strongest and most active men in the regiments. These men are frequently out at night and their marches are always more fatiguing than those of the other soldiers.'[2] Thanks to the presence of these herds of cattle, some old-fashioned eighteenth-century soldiers held that 'All carriages belonging to any army ought to be drawn by oxen...[then] such as get maimed, must be killed and eaten, to be replaced by others out of the magazines'.[3]

Both French and British regulations required that all slaughtering and butchering of cattle should be done at night and that no meat should be issued to the troops till the following morning. For the ration was weighed out to the men, and if it were issued before it had had time to lose weight by cooling and evaporation, the soldier would be robbed of his due. Yet no gourmet will regard the twelve hours or so which passed between the slaughter of the commissariat bullocks and the ration issue as a sufficient time for the meat to become properly 'hung', and the luckless soldiers' almost unvarying diet must have been *bœuf à la rigor mortis*. For this reason, as well as for its simplicity, the preferred method of cooking was boiling. Even so life on the staff of a commander like Wellington, who insisted on eating the same rations as his men, was thought hard, especially if he also insisted on rising and marching at dawn; ('*J'en ai pris en horreur les deux mots*, daylight *et* cold beef', recalled Wellington's Spanish liaison officer, Alava, years after the Peninsular War was over).[4]

Two points more about these droves of cattle before we leave them and let the reader turn to LeMesurier. How were they fed? For fed they must have been if they were to have any meat on their bones to feed the soldier after they were slaughtered. Obviously the simplest way of feeding them

---

[1] Napier, *Peninsular War*, book XXIV, chap. 3.
[2] Wellington to Colonel Torrens, 15 April 1812, Gurwood, vol. IX.
[3] Simes, *op. cit.* p. 104.
[4] Stanhope, *Conversations with Wellington*, p. 29.

was to let them do their own grazing. But this takes time; and when his grazing is done, the ox must also chew the cud, which wastes more time because he will not do it on the move; nor, under the best conditions, does he move fast. Some twelve miles a day, or at most fifteen, would be all that an army's beef cattle could be expected to march, and any troops who did more would, in effect, be running away from their own rations—never a popular military manœuvre. Therefore, one suspects, the beef supply very possibly did more to limit the mobility of armies than even the much abused waggon trains and magazines.

The second question is—where were the army's cattle fed? When an army was stationary, they could no doubt be pastured in convenient meadows (like the herd of one thousand head of bullocks which Napoleon collected at Bourg on the eve of crossing the Alps in 1800); and if proper rent was paid, no injury would be done to the local farmer. But one cannot believe that fodder was hauled for cattle in mobile operations. It was hard enough to carry a proportion of fodder for the cavalry and artillery horses. One can only suppose that an advancing army's droves of beef cattle very commonly fanned out and grazed as they travelled—to the utter ruin of all crops along the line of march. This certainly was the normal way of feeding the innumerable mules of the Spanish muleteers who formed Wellington's baggage train;[1] and there, it may be presumed, is one reason why the marches of the 'cattle guards' would be 'always more fatiguing than those of the other soldiers', as they tramped hither and yon over the fields behind their charges. It was also a reason why, as Wellington put it, 'War is a terrible evil, particularly to those who reside in those parts of the country which are the seat of the operations of the hostile armies'.[2]

[1] Compare Major General Long's observation that these animals were 'fed chiefly in the fields'. McGuffie, *Peninsular Cavalry General*, p. 100.
[2] To Brig. Gen. Cox, 14 May 1810, in Gurwood, vol. VI.

A SYSTEM FOR THE BRITISH
COMMISSARIAT

By HAVILLAND LeMESURIER, Esq.,

*late Deputy Commissary General to the Army serving
on the Continent of Europe*

1796

To their Excellencies General Count Wallmoden, Commander of the Combined Army and Lt. Gen. David Dundas, Commanding the British Troops, late on the Continent of Europe, this System simplified under their Command and written at their desire is with every sentiment of gratitude and respect inscribed.

I. INTRODUCTION

THERE is not an article of expense in the Contingencies of an Army but must in some measure depend on the abilities and integrity of its Commissaries. The Commander in Chief, occupied with the great movements and general plans, cannot stoop to the inspection of articles of running expense, neither can the Military Departments be taken off from the detail of their duty to examine and control them. In fact, the Civil Administration of an Army is an object of such magnitude as to demand the whole attention of the persons entrusted with it; who, although necessarily under the orders of the Commander in Chief, do nevertheless receive instructions from and report to the Lords of the Treasury, as being alone accountable to Parliament for the expenditure of all grants. Experience shows, that notwithstanding Commissariat Expenses have been commented upon in and out of Parliament from the Duke of Marlborough's time to this day, no one has attempted to bring a System forward which may obviate the inconvenience of sending Men abroad to exercise functions which are perfectly new to them. The truth is, Commissaries are only employed in time of War, and sought for at the moment of active operations; it should however be remembered that the importance of their office is not to be estimated by the length of their services but by the weight of its responsibility. For instance the Assistant Commissaries, sent out to the Continent during the late Campaigns, received no other information from the Treasury than notice of their appointment and verbal orders to join at Head Quarters. Had the nature of the Service been previously known to those Gentlemen, or at least had General Instructions been delivered them on their arrival, their minds would have been relieved of much anxiety, and their Accounts would from the beginning have regularly been brought forward; now as the saving to the Country must ever be proportionate to the punctuality of its Agents, it may be fair to ask, how many millions would have been saved in the seven years war, the late American war, and the present numerous Commissariat Establishments had a uniform system been adopted and followed?

With a view to remedy these inconveniences, and to call the attention of able men to the consideration of some plan which may procure to the Armies a more regular supply when on service, and to the country a greater security for the due expenditure of its treasure, it may be a most profitable study to consider the duties of the different Civil Officers as founded in theory and practice, from the Commissary General downwards, and by examining the system hitherto adopted on the Continent, obtain such fixed principles as shall be applicable to providing the smallest Corps, as well as the greatest Armies.

II. OF A COMMISSARY GENERAL

This is the only Civil Officer of the Army (the Commissary of Accounts excepted) who receives his Instructions direct from the Treasury. In the seven years war he was called Intendant General and the office was filled successively by Mr. Orby Hunter, General Pierson and Sir George Howard, each of whom granted Warrants for payment of supplies, and the Commander in Chief did then as now give his Warrants for the contingencies. In the Austrian and Prussian services he generally is the oldest Lieutenant General in the Army. In the present war the Commissary General has been decorated with no military rank, but his Commissions and his Instructions show the great power a Commissary General is invested with.[1] He is ordered as Superintendent and Director of Forage, Provisions, Necessaries and Extraordinaries to consult the Commander in Chief as to the places where Magazines are to be laid up, the quantities to be provided, and the removal and delivery thereof; and under such directions it is his duty to provide those Magazines and every other Extraordinary the Army may stand in need of. By his Instructions he is to draw and negotiate all Bills on the Treasury, and even those drawn on the Pay Master

---

[1] See copies in Appendix A, nos. 1, 2, 3.

General are to be negotiated by him; in short, whether this Officer be called Intendant or Commissary General, he is responsible for the providing of the Army in every situation, and with him rest the direction and control of every article of expense.

Invested with such extensive powers, his situation is the more arduous as much is to be done by him on the spur of the moment. The fullest confidence must be placed in him by the Commander in Chief, else the latter would be cramped in his operations, whilst the other could not exercise that discretion he ought ever to keep in mind, of incurring just so much and no more expense than is required for the due performance of every service. A frequent and daily intercourse will in consequence be kept up between them; hence it follows that however inconvenient the Military Departments may think it to crowd their Quarters, the Commissary General should always be fixed as near the Commander in Chief as possible; for his presence must on reflection be found as necessary to the due regulation of a march as that of the Quarter Master General or any other Officer in the Army.

As the Commissary attends the Commander in Chief daily for orders and to make his reports, so should he at certain hours render himself accessible to persons of every description. It is a most essential part of his duty to obtain information of every kind: the Civil Polity, the interior resources, the roads, rivers or canals of a country are objects which obviously he must acquire a knowledge of, but which he will be deceived in unless he can have information from various sources and compare and digest the opinions and views of different people; for interest rules mankind, and no one comes near an Army without an interested motive. By thus opening the sluices of information he will not only obtain useful knowledge as to the country, but will be furnished with the only means in his power of checking abuses in every Department: for no Contractor will seek to corrupt subordinate Officers while he finds himself admitted to the presence of the Chief, and abuses will be attempted with extreme caution when so watchful an eye is known to pervade every part of the Administration. But while oral communication is insisted on as necessary to draw forth resources and check abuses, it is as indispensably required that all money transactions should be committed to writing. Every Tender should be written and signed; the supply of an Army must not depend on the caprice of any man, and it is well known that persons in general are much more tenacious of their bond than of their word; but above all it is incumbent on the Commissary General to prove that he has at all times used diligence to procure Tenders and that he has accepted the best. The unaccepted Tenders are the fair and proper Certificates of prices to be produced by him, and they come within the meaning of the 5th articles of his Treasury[1] Instructions; for the Certificate of two respectable merchants

---

[1] See Appendix A, no. 3.

abroad may at any time be obtained with a little management when a mere cover is intended, while a discreet Commissary General will be cautious of disclosing his transactions to the merchants of the Country he is in, which he must do if he requires bona fide Certificates of them; and as to the Certificates of Magistrates it is well known that they are little to be depended upon.

In truth the money transactions are the most burthensome part of a Commissary General's duty. They are the more discouraging as with every anxiety and regularity on his part, it is not possible to shut every avenue to suspicion, neither will the World scarcely ever be brought to do justice to his integrity. There is however a mode of relieving his mind from part of the burden and of satisfying the rational and thinking part of mankind. The 5th article of his Instructions point to this.[1] He is there ordered 'to submit his Vouchers *on the spot* to the inspection and examination of persons appointed for that purpose'. If he is determined to be punctual, he will never fail so to do at the end of every month; he will also insist on his examinations taking place while the memory is fresh, the difficulties of the service apparent, and the Commander in Chief at hand to do justice to his exertions. In all matters of Contracts in particular, it is of the utmost importance to him that copies he makes shall accompany his Monthly Accounts; as by that open line of conduct he challenges enquiry while in his power to profit from the animadversions of others. Thus while millions pass through his hands he may never have accounts outstanding for more than one month's expenditure, and if he pursues that line toward others which he himself follows, every expense will be liquidated as soon as incurred, and by his punctuality he will draw to himself every nerve and every purse upon a scale of economy proportionate to the competition.

III. OF DEPUTIES COMMISSARY GENERAL

Such being the complicated duties of the Intendant or Commissary General, Government gives him Deputies, which were called in the seven years war Commissaries General of supply and now Deputies Commissary General.[2] These officers are on every occasion the representatives of the Commissary General and in his absence must perform his functions. They generally are two in number, and it is necessary they should be more than one if the Army be at all considerable or the service active, for since the Head must be relieved from the labour of detail, it will be found greatly to facilitate the operations if the Department of one of the Deputies be specially directed by him to attend to the mode of supplying the Army and watching it in all its parts, while the whole attention of the other is taken up in superintending the Accounts and bringing them regularly forward. Unquestionably the duties of these officers should be kept distinct from

---

[1] See Appendix A, no. 3. [2] See copy of their Commission in Appendix B, no. 1.

those of the Issuing Commissaries, and whatever may be the pressure of the moment, it is more advisable for them to appoint a person who is not a Commissioned Officer to make the Issues and do the duties of an Assistant Commissary, than to undertake that laborious detail and make themselves accountable for it in the first instance; whereby they would be taken off from that watchfulness over the whole which alone can spy defects, and would be deprived of leisure to apply a remedy. Their communication with the Commissary General must be direct and their reports incessant.[1] They are like hands to the head. They are not only to arrange and witness his transactions but may even be empowered to draw on the Paymaster for the contingencies of the Department, and if their Accounts are made up the 15th and last day of every month (a rule which experience has shown to be productive of the happiest effects) no time will be afforded for errors to multiply and the Commissary General will be perfectly safe in delegating that trust.

IV. OF ASSISTANT COMMISSARIES

The late Commissary General on the Continent having from motives which do him honour, obtained for these officers War Office Commissions which entitle them to half pay, they now have two Commissions, the additional one being for 5/- a day paid at the Treasury. On them rests the execution of the Commissariat Duties. They have to distribute the Bread, Forage, Straw, Fuel and Candle to the Troops, and every other Extraordinary the Service may require. It is their duty to see the Troops provided comfortably to General Orders, and that every article be good in kind and the quantity full in tale and weight. If they form Magazines, it therefore is incumbent on them to keep a very watchful eye over Contractors and their own Magazine-keepers; the first will do all in their power to defraud, and will turn the carelessness or corruption of the meanest labourer to profit, by passing off inferior qualities or lighter weights than their Contracts specify. Besides personal inspection and those local arrangements which will suggest themselves to the intelligent mind, the Commissary will find it necessary to give a separate responsibility to every Magazine-keeper, and to keep an account open with every store under his charge, for since he may as he sees occasion empty one store before another, he can by this precaution ascertain the fidelity of the people under him without waiting for the final delivery of his Magazine.

When the Assistant Commissary forages the Army in the field, he must in like manner charge himself with every article received, whether procured from an established Magazine, from a Contractor, or by Requisitions in the Country, for which he will be discharged by his Issues to the Troops.

---

[1] See in the Appendix B, no. 2, form of a weekly General Return of the Magazines of the Army.

In short, there is not an article of Entry or Issue but must be exactly and immediately accounted for.

In the Appendix will be found the formula of Returns of Magazines, Accounts of Entries and Issues, Abstract of Disbursement and Account Current, being those which latterly were printed for the use of Assistant and Acting Assistant Commissaries on the Continent. In the Appendix will also be found General Instructions to Assistant Commissaries. They were drawn up by the late Commissary General in 1794, and delivered to all Assistant Commissaries who joined the Army from that period: some alterations will be found suggested, and a part of them was temporary, but the foundation is correct, and unless such are drawn up and delivered to every Commissariat Officer *before* he enters upon Service, it is impossible that the duties of the Department can be uniformly carried on.

With these General Instructions every Assistant Commissary must therefore comply, and according to them will he be made responsible. Above all he must keep his accounts so closely made up as to transmit them with the Vouchers on the 15th and last day of every month. It is well known and has been felt that there are situations where the Issuing Commissary is so uncomfortably situated that he has not even the conveniences of an Office to open his papers in, and it is acknowledged that where many bundles of Papers are to be sorted and taken account of, such a situation would be a fair plea for delay. But it is positively insisted upon that no Commissary ought ever to stand in that predicament. He ought never to have more than fifteen days' accounts and Vouchers to carry with him. He requires no superfluous papers. Pen and Ink he must have to make his Issues, every necessary Clerk (and men who can read, write and understand the first rule of arithmetick are everywhere to be found) must be allowed him, and instead of finding it a hardship to make up his Accounts twice in the month, he will be happy when the day arrives to get rid of his Vouchers. The mode of making them up by Abstract prevents the necessity of carrying Books of Account, and printed forms will enable the most ordinary Clerk to set his Vouchers in order. If example were necessary to enforce so plain a precept, so indispensable an injunction, it could be alledged that the Commissaries with the left wing of the Army at and after the retreat from Holland in January, February and March, 1795, had every possible difficulty to encounter, being harrassed by the enemy on the outposts and by Austrians and Prussians in their quarters, yet they never failed producing their Accounts on the appointed days; after that period, that is from the 1st of May, 1795, to the breaking up of the Commissariat in March, 1796, the Officer in charge of the Department received the Accounts of *every Accountant* under his orders twice in the Month, and transmitted them monthly with his own to the Office of Accounts. In fact, no other mode can be satisfactory, for since the Commissary General takes Credit for all he pays to the inferior Accountants, the

Accounts of the Department are not completely delivered in unless their Vouchers accompany his own.

The instructions given the Assistant Commissaries comprehend the duties of the Acting Assistant Commissaries. These are either the most intelligent of the Commissariat Clerks, or other persons, who when Assistant Commissaries are not in sufficient numbers are appointed to act in their stead. It would be extremely improvident were Government to send out as many Assistant Commissaries as are adequate to provide for the Army in every situation, and it would be unwise to shut the door of promotion against the Commissariat Clerks and others who show capacity and zeal. As to these, their numbers must wholly depend on the nature of the service and grow out of the occasion.

For the greatest part of the time the Continental Army was assembled, the Field Bakery was under the direction of an Assistant Commissary; this is mentioned merely to introduce the observation, that forming part of the Commissariat, and the Bakery Accounts running necessarily into minutiae, everything suggested to urge punctuality and deprecate procrastination will apply with additional force to this branch of the service. The detail of the duties of the Director of the Bakery are, however, too complicated, and in many respects too mechanical, to find a place here.

V. OF THE WAGGON TRAIN

The great engine in the hands of the Commissariat, on which the movements of an Army depend, is a proper establishment of Waggons. In all Wars where a British army has taken the field great abuses have unfortunately prevailed in this Department, and it even now remains a question whether Government ought to purchase Waggons and Horses and form temporary establishments, or whether the Army should be provided with a Train by Contractors.

In the seven years war there was a General Contractor for the Waggon Train, and his Contract was kept up until the very year before the peace, when Government bought the Train from him. In the American War, Waggons were considered almost as a privilege by the Departments to which they were attached, until the arrival of the Gentleman last sent there as Commissary General who found it necessary to make great reforms in that branch of service. The same Gentleman, when he went out to the Continent with the late Army, made use of the Waggons of different Contractors, but in the beginning of 1794 an experiment was made by raising a Corps called the Corps of Royal Waggoners and purchasing Waggons and Horses. Of this Corps little need be said, as its miserable state became proverbial in the Army; it failed completely in every part, and the only trace remaining of it is a heavy charge on the half-pay list for the reduced Officers.

The idea of this Corps was probably taken from the fine well-regulated establishment of Austrian Waggons. This is a standing establishment, kept up in peace and war, having Officers and Men trained to the Service, and a system improved and perfected through a succession of years. Unquestionably a great Military Power like Austria, to which a Waggon Train is necessary in Peace as well as War, acts wisely in point of resource and economically in point of expense, to make and keep up an establishment of its own Waggons, in preference to throwing them into the hands of Contractors; but it is obvious that the excellence of the Austrian system consists in the discipline of the Individuals who compose it, all of them being made acquainted with their duty from their youth; such a set of men (to say nothing of the difficulty of purchasing and organising hundreds or thousands of Waggons when other Services press) it is utterly impossible for Britain to procure upon the spur of the moment.

Bad, therefore, as were the Contract Waggons in the campaign of 1794, they certainly did far better Service than the Royal Corps of Waggoners. The Contractors did not pay their Waggoners regularly and probably committed depredations in drawing Forage for more horses than were effective; many were the complaints against them and various their excuses; both were in some respects reasonable, and both led to the consideration of a better system as soon as opportunity was afforded to put it to the proof.

Accordingly the Royal Train was sold, and every purchaser of not less than fifty Waggons was admitted to the advantages of a Contract for all the Waggons he purchased; he was ensured the duration of his Contract for three months, and was only to deposit one-third of the cost, allowing the remainder to be paid out of his earnings. The form of Contract and the pay of the Waggon were previously fixed, and by this mode a most advantageous Sale was procured, while a new set of Contractors were introduced, with the additional advantage of obliging the old Contractors to reduce their prices and to come under the same terms.

In the Appendix will be found a translation of one of the original Contracts. The discipline of the Service was maintained by obliging every Contractor to obey the orders of the Officers appointed to command the Train, and rendering him responsible for the conduct of every individual employed under his Contract; every pretext for not paying his Waggoners their subsistence was prevented by settling his accounts twice every month; the Waggoners were afforded protection by having an immediate appeal to the Officers of the Commissariat, who were totally independent of the Contractors, and set over them to order and inspect their proceedings; abuses in drawing Forage were checked, by obliging every Contractor to render an account of the whole number of Rations drawn by his men and horses every month; and lastly an Assistant Commissary was appointed over the whole as Inspector of the Train, and to report weekly to the Commissary General on its effective strength and actual employment.

Doubtless many a more ingenious system may be devised, but none has hitherto been put into practice by a British Commissariat so successfully as the present; for every Regiment of British Cavalry late on the Continent may be appealed, to say, whether any complaint of irregularity or insufficiency was ever preferred after they were provided with Waggons under the new Contracts; whether the complaints that had subsisted against that branch of the Service was not then done away; and whether the Horses and Waggons were not always kept in condition for service. It is therefore unquestionably in the interest of Great Britain that every Commissary should provide the Army with Waggons of the Country on Contract, (binding the Contractors in such a way that their Waggons may be as much under Military Orders as if they belonged to the Crown) for in that case the expense is certain and the Waggons kept in pay no longer than they absolutely serve; and it must equally be the wish of the Army to be attended with such Waggons and Horses, because they are conducted by men whose interest it is to keep them up in the best possible condition and consequently which are to be depended upon in time of difficulty and extraordinary movements.

As for the number of Waggons a Train should consist of, that can be ascertained by no rule. The resources of the Country and the nature of the operations must direct the judgement. An advancing Army requires a large and effective Train, else the General cannot be sure of his operations: a retreating Army needs but a small one because it falls back upon resources and will most effectually distress the enemy by sweeping the Waggons as it moves. In both cases the richness or poverty of the Country will make a wide difference. With the Army on the Continent it was understood a number of Waggons sufficient to carry two days Forage and three days Bread was always to remain with the Regiments, besides those attached to the Departments; these it must be remembered are exclusive of Hospital and Bakery Waggons and the various necessary Transports.

VI. OF REGIMENTAL RECEIPTS

It being contrary to a Commissary's duty to issue any article under his charge without being furnished with a regular receipt, it follows that the form of that receipt should be perfectly known and invariably used. This can only be enforced by General Orders, and assuredly it is one of the first that ought to be given out. In the British Service these Receipts are called Requisitions or Returns. Both appellations prevail and both without impropriety; for one Corps will draw up the Receipt in the form of a Requisition, another in the shape of a Return, whereby neither are in strictness a complete voucher until the person who brings it to the Commissary witnesses the Issue, although in point of fact the additional signature can seldom be obtained when the Army forages in the field.

The informality of these Receipts on the part of British Troops on the Continent led to serious evils. It engendered an Office which became respectable by the talents of the Gentleman who filled it, but which in itself was never defined as to its relative situation with the commissariat, or at best was an Assistant to the Adjutant General under another name. This officer had been appointed under the name of Inspecting Commissary for the ostensible purpose of inspecting the quality and weight of the forage, but he moreover did receive wherever he happened to be (for the Office was dispensed with elsewhere) all Requisitions for Forage and Bread; against them he gave his cheque or *Bon*, as it was called, with which the Forage was obtained for the Commissary. As, however, the Inspecting Commissary had certainly no right by virtue of his Office to order any Issue, he afterwards used to present a Return of all he had given orders for (except the broken periods issued between one Foraging day and the other) to the Adjutant General, who signed it as a matter of course, and that Return became the Commissary's voucher. Thus were there three Vouchers for one Issue: the Original Requisition, the Inspecting Commissary's *Bon*, and the Adjutant General's sweeping return: but the last neither comprehended the broken periods, nor what was drawn by Detachments of the same Regiments at a distance. The evil was at last felt, and before the British Cavalry left the Continent the Regimental Receipts were brought direct to the Assistant Commissary.

It may be asked, how the Commissary could issue upon the Inspecting Commissary's *Bon*, when his orders are to take only Regimental Receipts? —The answer is that no Commissary durst refuse doing what General Orders point out. The Regiments were ordered to carry their Returns to the Inspecting Commissary and not to him; therefore he had no alternative but to accept the Bon, or make the Issues without a voucher.

There however were *Bons* of another description. These were the Commissary's own cheques, which were sometimes given to Regiments to account for deficiencies when he could give part but not the whole of the Requisitions, and at other times when he was obliged to give orders for the Forage to Contractors or Magistrates. It is greatly to the honour of the Commissariat that only one man, and he a foreigner, was found to take advantage of this multiplication of Vouchers. The integrity of the Commissaries was so little exposed to suspicion, that it scarcely was perceived the Commissary could take credit for the whole of the Regimental Requisition, while the holder of the Bon for the deficiency of the Issue could sell or obtain Forage for it elsewhere. It was not till after the system now submitted was enforced, that the practicability of the fraud came to light. One Commissary finding himself obliged to send the Returns of his Magazines and the Vouchers on the 15th and last day of every month, could no longer avoid showing the regular Entries and Issues of his Magazine; alarmed at the deficiencies which appeared in his Forage

Accounts, he accused his Clerk of issuing his Bons a second time, instead of destroying them as soon as complied with, and brought him to a Court Martial; when it appeared that both were leagued with Contractors, and such matter of crimination came out against himself, that in his turn he was tried, convicted and cashiered with infamy.[1]

The results of these observations will be that in every case there should if possible be only one Voucher for one Issue. The mode of accomplishing this must be simple, and it is adopted by those who certainly have most experience: for every German Corps or German Officer who draws Forage, or any other article from the Commissariat, sends a mere receipt.[2] This prevents further writing or trouble, because the Receipt may be presented in the open field and is itself a complete Voucher: all that is required is for the Regiment to order its Forage Party to bring back the Receipt if the quantity be not obtained, and the Quarter Master or Foraging Sergeant to give a Receipt for what they get if only a part can be had.

VII. OF FORAGING AN ARMY BY MAGAZINES

Before an Army takes the field the means of supply must unquestionably be ascertained. To answer this Magazines are formed and placed in situations to assist the General's plans. They remove all apprehension of want and give confidence to an Army.

Without entering into discussion whether too great a stress be not in general laid on the necessity of having *large* Magazines, it is necessary to remark that this is by far the most expensive mode of Foraging an Army. The expense of a Magazine Establishment is great and the waste considerable. Whenever purchases are made in a country, prices will advance in proportion to the size of the Magazine. It will also be remembered that when an Army moves from its Magazines, the cost and waste of removing them will often amount to infinitely more than the original price; that the removal is often impracticable, and that every Waggon employed on that service is an addition to the expense and takes off from the resources necessary for the General Operations. It was calculated in the seven years war that 9600 Waggons were required to transport the mere Forage for 30,000 Horses from the nearest Magazine in Cassell to the seat of operations at Giessen.[3] However, if active operations are intended, the expense must be submitted to and in proportion to the resources of the Country will the contents of the Depot be increased or diminished.

The material point to be considered is the conveniency of Land and Water carriage, because the price of articles, and the assistance to the Army, will be found proportionate to the expense and facility of the

[1] See the Charges and Sentence in Appendix E, no. 1.
[2] E, no. 2. Translation of a German Forage Receipt.
[3] See in Appendix F Extract of a letter from H.S.H. the Duke Ferdinand of Brunswick to the Marquis of Granby, dated Paderborn, 24th April 1760.

transport. Should small Depots of nine to thirty days provision be established, they will be found to possess great advantages over extensive Magazines; abuses are immediately seen because the quantities are small; they occasion no great advance in price; they are easily transported, or if they fall into an enemy's hands the mischief is of little importance.

VIII. OF FORAGING BY CONTRACTORS

But the great advantage of small Depots consists in the art of placing them as a reserve to give confidence to the troops, and to counteract the failures or be combined with the exertions of Contractors. These are a set of men without whom an Army cannot subsist. They may be classed under two descriptions. One, the great Contractors who deliver specifick quantities into Magazines under the care of an Assistant Commissary within a given time; the other, those Contractors who engage to furnish indefinite quantities to certain Corps during a March on the outposts, or in Camp or Quarters at a distance from the main body. Contracts of the latter description should be made subject to be revoked by either party on giving warning,[1] for the Commissary General must reserve to himself the power of reducing prices as he becomes better acquainted with the resources of a Country, else he may fear to make engagements on the spur of the moment when the nature of the service may require it, and he will deprive himself of the advantages of competition by tying up his own hands. The chief point to be gained is, to persuade every Contractor that if he individually should keep back, others will be found to come forward. Competition must therefore be established, and it can only be procured by the most scrupulous punctuality in settling and paying Accounts. If a British Commissary General once establishes his character, by never putting off a payment, by paying all the engagements he has made with the same punctuality a private merchant holds himself bound to do, he will find a throng press upon him for the preference of his commands; but if Contractors are put off after having made their deliveries, and do not touch that payment they had calculated upon to face their private engagements, each will fall off from the Army, and none will be left but some man of great capital who can afford to run the chance of delay, and build his calculations upon a monopoly of the Contracts.

It is clear that the independence of the Commissariat can never subsist while the Army is in the hands of one great Contractor.[2] He cannot act by himself but has of course a number of Sub-Contractors. They all, from the chief downwards, have no spur to their exertions but the plus and minus of

---

[1] A reduction in price from month to month took place on the Continent during nearly the whole of the year 1795, making a total saving which it does not belong to the Writer to calculate.

[2] See in Appendix G Extract of a letter from H.S.H. Duke Ferdinand of Brunswick to the Marquis of Granby, dated Wavern, 25 May 1760.

gain; they cannot upon extraordinary occasions make a sacrifice of property to the success of military operations; even if they fail in their Contracts, they generally will find plausible reasons for their failure, since they must of necessity be protected from loss by the enemy or military events, and they know the Commissariat cannot do without them; but what is more, a Commissary General by thus setting a bar between him and the Sub-Contractors, who after all are the efficient men, deprives himself of the proper sources of information, and in the moment of difficulty may expose the Army to sudden want.

Unquestionably a great task is imposed on the Commissary General by obliging him to make a number of Contracts where only one would discharge his responsibility, but if he establishes competition he will never be at a loss for tenders; and if he has Depots in reserve so disposed as to afford assistance to different points of the Army whenever any Contractor fails, he will force the Contractors to make their engagements good, and keep the troops secure of their supplies independently of them all.

IX. OF FORAGING BY REQUISITION

The first care of a Commissary General when an Army comes into a friendly Country must be to fix a rate with the Government for every article of provisions. If the Army comes for its protection, the terms ought to be moderate, but at all events they should be known. Differences with the peasants will thereby be avoided, and the Army will draw forth all their resources with good will instead of forcing part from them with the point of the bayonet. It is even, if possible, more urgent that the peasant should be paid regularly than the Contractor, and whenever he applies direct to Head Quarters it will be good policy never to put him off, were it only with a view that he may have sufficient confidence to retain his Waggons and Horses, instead of sending them away from the Army; for if that resource be properly secured an immense retrenchment may be made in the Waggon Train, and supplies will be transported with astonishing expedition in every case of emergency.

In an enemy's Country the Requisitions are of a different nature. Doubtless the British nation wars not with the poor cottager, and every relief will be afforded him that humanity can dictate and sound policy does not condemn. But there no formality will be required except the order of the Commanding Officer; nevertheless it must never be forgotten that where Requisitions are made, or are levied, a compact arises between the Army and the Country which entitled every individual in the latter to the protection of his private property.

The last kind of Requisition is that made with the sword even in a friend's Country. No set of men will tamely starve whilst provisions are within their reach, and if fair means will not procure them recourse must be had to violence. In such case it is the bounden duty of the Commissariat to make the necessity apparent, to methodise the measures and to procure fair compensation.

X. OF PROVIDING MONEY FOR AN ARMY

The acknowledged credit of Great Britain in every part of the World gives a British Commissary General every facility which the Country he is in can possibly afford. He possesses an unlimited credit on the Treasury of Great Britain, and (provided the Lords Commissioners will on their part order his bills to be accepted with the punctuality expected from men of business) can never want money as long as Trading Towns are within his reach. As however the resources of a Country may sometimes be limited and it may from thence follow that circuitous modes must be found, in which case a concurrence of drawers would counteract each others means, the negotiating of all Bills, not only for the Commissariat Expenses and the subsistence of the troops but also for every other service that may arise, ought of necessity to be placed in the hands of one man; and accordingly the late Commissary General on the Continent was invested with the sole power of negotiating them.

It is stated in the 3rd article of the Treasury Instructions[1] that the produce of these Bills should be deposited in the hands of the Deputy Pay Master General, who pays only on the Commissary General's Warrant. This certainly is the regular mode, and is to be followed as closely as possible, but when an Army is in motion, and perhaps in an Enemy's Country, it is extremely desirable for the Commissary General to have other Depots of cash besides the Military Chest, and it will save great expense and risk whenever he can make it convenient to pay by Drafts on the bankers and merchants who negotiate the Bills at a distance. These bankers and merchants will of course be made to subject themselves to produce the required Certificates of rates of Exchange and value of money, and to transmit their Accounts and Vouchers at the same time and with the same regularity as the Accountants under the Commissary General's orders; so that they will be equally checked and controlled by the Commissary of Accounts, and the public purse be as fully guarded by this mode as it possibly can be by the other.

In this branch of the Commissary General's duty, constant foresight is required: the sinews of War is Money, and without it the parts of an Army cannot hold together.

XI. OF A COMMISSARY OF ACCOUNTS

This Officer (as has already been observed) receives his Instructions direct from the Treasury, and although by his Commissions he is put under the orders of the Commander in Chief, he is directed to follow only such

[1] See Appendix A, no. 3.

Instructions as he may from time to time receive from the Lords of the Treasury.[1] His duties are strongly marked. They consist in detecting frauds; in examining and auditing Accounts; in making enquiries into every article of expenditure so as to be enabled to check the Commissary General's Contracts, and every other disbursement made for the Army; and especially in entering all Accounts in his Books, so as to control the several Accountants, to keep every branch of the service distinct and to bring the whole expense of the Army under one view.

His powers are of the negative kind. The Commissary General is ordered by his Instructions to submit all his Vouchers to his examination, and of course he has a right to demand every explanation that can lead to the forming of a perfect judgement of the money transactions of the Army; neither will he certify any Account until he is fully persuaded of the correctness of the costings, of the fairness of the purchases or payments, and of the regularity of the Vouchers. Should he have doubts it is his duty to state them to the Commissary General in the first instance, or if the case requires it to the Commander in Chief, and lastly to the Lords of the Treasury. He is sent to the Army for the purpose of watching the public purse, to give the alarm if it is opened improperly, and since his sanction must be obtained before the Army Accounts can be passed, he himself is responsible in the second instance if mal-practices should be detected.

Such are the advantages derived to the Country from having a branch of the Office of Comptrollers of Army Accounts attached to an Army. It is only 'on the spot' that a right judgement can be formed of the difficulties of the service or a just estimate made of its expense. Prices vary from local situation and arbitrary laws: in Germany especially, when the Government changes at every step, no general rule can be adopted, and it would be as unwise to fix a rate of prices by General Orders for all Germany, as for Government at home to fix a rule for the Armies in every quarter of the globe. Nothing can therefore be more wise, or more comfortable to the feelings of a great Accountant, than the appointment of an office that shall regularly discharge him from the weight of his papers, whose duty it will be to provoke his justification on every doubtful point while the transaction is recent and open to explanation, and whose neglect to do it at the time will be his best excuse, should he be taxed with want of regularity afterwards. The Country has in fact no substantial control over a Commissary General but through this Office. It is stated by the Commissioners for examining of the Public Accounts in their seventh Report, presented to the House of Commons on the 18th of June, 1782, that 'a Voucher for a payment for the extraordinary Service abroad is and of necessity must be allowed on the Office of Auditors of the Imprest, if it contains a certain number received, the signature of the person receiving,

[1] See Appendix H, nos. 1, 2, 3 with the Note added.

and a just computation, and agrees with the Abstract, it being then deemed and admitted as a fair Voucher'. Any man conversant in business will feel that such Vouchers are not difficult to be produced at a distance of time and place, although no man will dare submit a false Voucher of such a description to a Public Office *on the spot* within fifteen days of the time of payment.

Calculated as was this Office to ease the Accountant and guard the money of the Public, experience has shown that it can bring distress on an Army and increase the burden of its expense. In the seven years war a Commission of Accounts was sent out without whose Certificate no account was paid. In the present war, it was a standing order of the Commissariat on the Continent, until the beginning of the year 1795, that 'before payments were made, the Account on which they were made must be certified by the Commissary of Accounts'.

At first view it may be said, the Commissary General makes the Contracts, but as he cannot pay them until certified by the Commissary of Accounts, they are a check on each other. This argument is specious, but fallacious. In the first place the Contractors know only the Commissary General, and if after having fulfilled their Contracts, they must be sent away to dance attendance on another Office, they have a right to complain of deception, and most assuredly they will quit the Army as they did in both the Wars alluded to.[1] In the next place every man of business knows that prompt payment is the life of business. The Contractor will feel by far more anxiety to obtain his money for the past than to enter into any new Contract and supposing a case to arise where pressed by his engagements he cannot get his Accounts passed at the Office of Accounts, may he not attempt corruption to gain his Certificates? A similar attempt may certainly be made at the Commissary General's Office, but at least the Contract, the payment and the Voucher must undergo a revision; whereas lastly the reference *before* payment destroys control. The Certificate of the Officer of Accounts is final. There is no check on him, no revision of his sentence; if he is satisfied no man can complain; in his own Office are the Vouchers, and the grounds of his decisions remain in his own breast. Surely it never was the intention of Government that any payment should be made without being checked, and the obvious meaning of the Instructions to the Commissary of Accounts goes to his examining everything that is *done*, but in no event to take away the responsibility with which another Officer is invested.

Undoubtedly the mode of referring accounts before payment relieves a Commissary General from a disagreeable part of his responsibility, but if

---

[1] Those who know the Writer will believe he is the last man to detract from the merits of the Contracter General who attended the late Army on the Continent whose exertions were often astonishing and always liberal; his extensive means enabled him to wait for his payments, but every other Contractor left the Army in the Spring of 1794, and he thereby became its Sole Contracter.

in doing so he casts off the responsibility which Government laid on him in the first instance, for the purpose of obtaining the examination and control of another Office in the second instance, he runs counter to his Instructions, and leaves his Contractors at the mercy of an Officer over whom there is no check.

Another great evil arising from the reference before payment will be its interference with the examination and control of the Accounts of the different Accountants. It was given as a reason by the Commissary of Accounts on the Continent for not passing the Accounts of the Commissariat more readily that it was out of his power to give sufficient attention to them while ordered to march with the Army. The bustle of moving his papers so often and the clamours of the people demanding money by whom he was beset, occupied (he said) his whole time. Whereas the necessity for that Officer's paying attention to the sorting and methodizing papers in his Office requires his being at a distance from the general operations for no one will deny that it is in his power if kept free from interruption to examine and arrange Accounts however voluminous, especially when transmitted every month; in this consists the chief use of his Office, and it is only by beginning well that so desireable a Service can be carried through. It is therefore much to be lamented that the Commissions of this Office were dated in March, 1793: They should be coaeval, else confusion will ensue, and if once confusion arises from delay, the activity of military operations will preclude the possibility of establishing order. The Forage Accounts of an Army are those in particular which are generally overlooked, yet that will be found the most vulnerable part of the Commissariat System. In the charges against the Assistant Commissary already mentioned, it will be seen that he was connected with Contractors in a way that could only be detected by examining his Forage Accounts. It is also evident that no check lies upon his Regiments or Departments in drawing of Forage, unless regular Accounts are kept of all they draw. How desirable therefore it is, how indispensable a duty it becomes, for the Commissary of Accounts to keep an Account open with every Regiment, so as to enable him to report from time to time to the Commander in Chief and to apprise the Commissary General, what are the quantities of Forage and Commissariat allowances drawn by each Department and Corps.

Let it not be said this is impossible. If the Commissary of Accounts is suffered to remain free from interruption, if the Commissary General transmits to him regularly every month all the Accounts of the Accountants of the Army, what can possibly prevent his reducing them to order? A Forage Abstract may serve as his model how to keep his Forage Accounts open. There he will find the name of the Regiment or Department and the quantity drawn for. Let him have all the Abstracts copied in a kind of Journal and from thence posted under different kinds of Account.

As for any mischief that may arise from disclosing the strength of the Army, none can. It is but too true that in a British Army the effective combatants bear but a small proportion to the numbers fed. In July 1795 it was found that the Commissariat provided for 45,000 persons, while the effective strength scarcely exceeded 20,000 men. The returns of the effective men rest with the Adjutant General, and they only are necessary in a military point of view; but an enemy would be grossly deceived who should calculate the strength of our Armies by the number of Rations issued, and these are all which the Commissariat need be informed of.

XII. CONCLUSION

The avowed design of this Essay being to establish a practical system for the British Commissariat, care has been taken to confine these observations to what is strictly Commissariat. What is said of providing Bread and Forage in Germany may, it is believed, apply to every other Necessary for an Army in all parts of the World, and the mode of accounting for Entries and Issues will also serve for every general article of supply. Much stress has been laid on the necessity of keeping the Office of Accounts aloof from the contamination of Army followers, and making it an Office of control over the Accountants but in no instance (for cases of extraordinary exception belong to no rule) allowing it to interfere with payments to Contractors. It has been proved by experience that no competition can be maintained unless the Commissary General fulfils his own bargains. It is insisted upon that the Commissary of Accounts can keep a clear and distinct Account of all the money transactions of an Army provided they are regularly laid before him, but that he cannot be answerable for their examination at the time and on the spot, if he is obliged to follow the Army, and is subject to be interrupted by the settlement of Accounts with persons demanding payment. It is shown that this is the only system which affords security to the Public, because the operations of the Commissary General are thereby controlled by the Office of Accounts, while no Control lies over the latter; and if the Copies of all Contracts are transmitted and the Accounts and Vouchers submitted within the month, not only the Commissary of Accounts, but the Deputies Commissary General, and every person, whether in or out of the Department, can form an opinion of prices, and of the fairness of the transactions.

If the line here laid down is followed, and the responsibility of the Department subdivides among its members, each will bear his proper proportion and the weight which may be supposed to bear on the Commissary General for the settlement of his Accounts, will be relieved or taken off by one of his Deputies. There need only further be declared, that all what is now recommended (save a part of what is laid down on the duty of the Commissary of Accounts) has been put in practice on the Continent from the month of January, 1795 to the month of March, 1796.

In the early part of that period every difficulty was combined that could justify delay in the production of Accounts, afterwards the Army had no interruption from the enemy, but it was kept moving from one Cantonment to another, divided into several Camps, put again into Cantonments, and lastly marched home, so as to have passed over in a North, East and West direction all the part of Germany contained between the Ems and the Elbe as far as Frankfurt to the South. By following the system here laid down, no Corps, however distant or however small, suffered want; and by submitting the Copy of every Contract, with his own and the Vouchers of every Accountant under him, at the beginning of every month to the Commissary of Accounts (which Vouchers have all been by him fully examined and allowed) but making it his rule to settle and pay for all his engagements in the first instance, the Officer in charge of the Commissariat had the satisfaction to quit the Country within a month after the troops had reached the place of their discharge, without having any demand on his Administration unpaid. Everything wound itself up. No claim has since been preferred, and if any should ever arise hereafter, the punctuality established in the Department would of itself be fair evidence that the claim itself must be unfounded.

APPENDICES

A1

COMMISSARY GENERAL'S COMMISSION BROOK WATSON ESQR, COMMISSARY GENERAL OF STORES, PROVISIONS, AND FORAGE

(Sgd)
George Rex

(L.S.) George the Third by the Grace of God, King of Great Britain, France and Ireland, Defender of the Faith, etc To Our Trusty and Well-beloved Brook Watson, Esqr Greeting; We do by these presents constitute and appoint you to be Commissary General of Stores, Provisions, and Forage to our Forces serving on the Continent now under the Command of our most dearly beloved Son, His Royal Highness Lieutenant General the Duke of York; You are therefore carefully and diligently to discharge the Duty of Commissary General for Stores, Provisions, and Forage, by doing and performing all manner of things thereunto belonging as well as by inspecting the Rates and Goodness of the Stores, Provisions, and Forage of *Entered* Our said Forces as by viewing and taking an Account of all the Remains *with the* of Stores, Provisions, and Forage bought for the Use of Our said Forces *Secretary* upon Removal of Camp and Quarters; and We do hereby authorize *at War.* You to inspect the buying and delivering of Stores, Provisions, and *(Sgd)* Forage for the use of Our said Forces, whether the same be done by *Mr Lewis* Contractors or others, as likewise to settle and adjust all Accounts relating thereunto; And you are to observe and follow such Orders and Directions from time to time as you shall receive from Us, our said most dearly beloved Son, or other your superior Officer, according to the Rules and Discipline of War, in pursuance of the Trust we hereby repose in you. Given at our Court of

St James, the Twenty Seventh Day of February 1793 in the Thirty Third of Our Reign.

By His Majesty's Command,

(sgd) Henry Dundas.

A2
COMMISSARY GENERAL'S WARRANT

Brook Watson, Esqr to be Superintendant and Director of Forage Provisions, etc to the Army under the Command of the Duke of York.

(sgd) George Rex

George the Third by the Grace of God, King of Great Britain France and Ireland, Defender of the Faith, and so forth, To all whom these presents shall come Greeting. Know ye that We reposing special Trust and Confidence in the Prudence, Skill and Integrity of our trusty and well beloved Brook Watson, Esquire, to be Superintendant and Director of Forage Provisions, Necessaries and Extraordinaries of Our Army now serving on the Continent of Europe under the Command of Our Dearly Beloved Son Frederick Duke of York and Albany have nominated and Do by these presents nominate and appoint the said Brook Watson to be Superintendant and Director of Forage, Provisions, Necessaries and Extraordinaries of Our said Army; hereby giving the said Brook Watson the full power and Authorities hereinafter mentioned but subject nevertheless to the Control of Us and our High Treasurer or Commissioners of Our Treasury for the time being, strictly commanding the said Brook Watson to follow such Instructions and Directions touching the execution of his Office, as he shall receive from Us, or from Our High Treasurer or Commissioners of Our Treasury for the time being. And we hereby authorize and impower the said Brook Watson to procure and provide Waggons, Horses, Wood, Straw and all other Necessaries and Conveniences commonly called Contingencies for the Use of Our said Army, as to the Places where Magazines of Forage should be laid up and the Quantities to be provided at each place, and as to the Removal and Delivery thereof to such places as the Necessity of the service may require; and for the purposes aforesaid Brook Watson is, with the Consent and Direction of the Commander in Chief of Our said Army for the time being to make such Contracts and Agreements, as shall be necessary, and take Care that the same be faithfully performed and that the Supplies provided be duly distributed to the Army. For the due execution whereof all Commissaries Officers, Agents, Ministers and Contractors employed or to be employed in any of the affairs aforesaid, are to pay Obedience to the Directions of the said Brook Watson. And for the greater Encouragement of the said Brook Watson well, duly and diligently to discharge the duties hereby required of him, We are graciously pleased to allow the said Brook Watson the sum of Four Pounds by the Day, the same to commence from the date hereof and to be payable for and during his Continuance in the due Execution of the said Office or until Directions to the Contrary shall be given by Us or by Our High Treasurer or Commissioners of Our Treasury for the Time being. Given at our Court at Saint James this first day of March, 1793, in the Thirty Third Year of Our Reign.

By His Majesty's Command

signed W. Pitt
signed Mornington
signed Rd Hopkins

A3

COMMISSARY GENERAL'S INSTRUCTIONS

Instructions to Brook Watson, Esqr Superintendant and Director of Forage, Provisions, Necessaries and Extraordinaries of the Army now serving or to serve on the Continent of Europe.

Whereas His Majesty has been pleased by Warrant under His Royal Sign Manual, bearing date the first day of March 1793, to appoint you to be Superintendant and Director of Forage, Provisions, Necessaries and Extraordinaries of the Army now serving or to serve on the Continent of Europe under the Command of His Royal Highness Frederick, Duke of York and Albany with Directions to follow such Instructions and Orders touching the Execution of your said Office as you shall receive from His Majesty or His High Treasurer or the Commissioners of the Treasury for the time being.

FIRST. You are forthwith to repair to the Army on the Continent of Europe to take upon yourself the superintendance over the several Departments and to be considered responsible for the Expenditure of all Money, Provisions, and Stores.

SECOND. You are to draw all Bills for the Extraordinary Service of the Army and also to negotiate all such Bills, as shall be drawn by the Deputy Paymaster of the Force to your Office for the pay and Subsistence of the Troops taking Care that the same are negotiated at the most favourable rate of exchange that can be obtained and at the least possible Commission.

THIRD. You are to deposit in the hands of the Deputy Paymaster General all the money you shall procure for Bills negotiated by you as aforesaid, and to issue your orders on the Deputy Paymaster General for such payments as you shall find necessary.

FOURTH. You are to obtain the authority or approbation of the Commander in Chief for all expenses incurred by you.

FIFTH. You are to take a written Voucher for the due payment of all Articles purchased by you, with a certificate of two reputable Merchants annexed thereto that the same were bought at the Market-price of the time, and on payment thereof the Receipt of the party is to be attested by at least one Witness. You are to submit the said Vouchers to the Inspection and Examination upon the spot of such Person or Persons as may hereafter be appointed for that purpose, who are to certify that the same are regular, correct and complete, which Certificate is to be laid before the Commander in Chief for his Approbation and Signature.

SIXTH. You are to make up your Cash Account once in every two months and to transmit a copy thereof with One set of Vouchers to us, or to the Lords Commissioners of the Treasury for the time being.

SEVENTH. You are to keep a like Account of the Receipt and Issue of all Provisions and Stores which shall have been purchased by you or that may come into your hands, which Account with proper Vouchers for all your Issues is to be laid before the Person or Persons to be appointed, as aforesaid, to be examined by him or them and afterwards submitted to the Commander in Chief for his Approbation and Signature and transmitted to Us or the Lords Commissioners of the Treasury for the time being.

EIGHTH. When any Provisions or Stores are damaged, lost, destroyed or plundered you are to obtain special Certificates thereof for your Indemnification without which you will not be allowed Credit for the same. You are to be particularly attentive to the preservation of all Stores and Provisions committed to your Charge and to give positive orders to your Deputies and Assisstants for that purpose, as you will be responsible for the whole.

NINTH. You are to obey all such further Orders and Instructions as you may from time to time receive from Us or from the Lords Commissioners of the Treasury for the time being or from the Commander in Chief now or for the time being. Given under our Hands at the Treasury Chambers, Whitehall this ninth Day of March One Thousand Seven hundred and Ninety three.

signed Wm Pitt
signed Mornington
signed Bayham

B I

DEPUTY COMMISSARY GENERAL'S COMMISSION

Havilland Le Mesurier Esqr. Deputy Commissary General of Stores, Provisions & Forage
   George R

(LS) George the Third by the Grace of God King of Great Britain, France and Ireland, Defender of the Faith etc. To Our Trusty and Well beloved Havilland Le Mesurier Esqr Greeting. We do by these presents constitute and appoint you to be Deputy Commissary General of Stores, Provisions and Forage to Our Forces serving on the Continent under the Command of Our most dearly beloved Son, His Royal Highness General Frederick, Duke of York. You are therefore carefully *Entered* and diligently to discharge the Duty of Deputy Commissary General *with the* of Stores, Provisions and Forage by doing and performing all and *Secretary* all manner of things thereunto belonging as well as by inspecting the *at War* Rates and Goodness of all Stores, Provisions and Forage of Our said *sgd* Forces as by viewing and taking an Account of all the Remains of Stores, *Mr Lewis* Provisions and Forage upon Removal of Camp and Quarters and we do hereby authorize you to inspect the buying and delivering of Stores, Provisions and Forage for the Use of Our said Forces, whether the same be done by Contractors or others as likewise to settle and adjust all Accounts relating thereunto, and you are to observe and follow such orders and directions *Entered* from time to time as you shall receive from Us, Our said dearly be- *with the* loved Son or other Your superior Officer, according to the Rules and *Commissary* Discipline of War, in pursuance of the Trust We hereby repose in you. *General of* Given at Our Court at St James the Seventeenth Day of June 1794, *Muster* the Thirty fourth Year of Our Reign *sgd Wm* *Woodman*

By His Majesty's Command
sgd Portland

APPENDIX B

B2

GENERAL RETURN OF MAGAZINES

General Remain of the King's Magazines on the....of........179.... at night

Date	Name of Magazine	Pounds			Pounds		
		Biscuit	Wholemeal	Rye Meal	Oats	Hay	Straw
	Bremen	500,000		1,000,000	1,000,000	400,000	
	Quackenbruch	—	1,000,000		2,000,000	1,500,000	
	Hoya				1,000,000	2,000,000	
	Hammeln		2,000,000	2,500,000			600,000
		500,000	3,000,000	3,500,000	4,000,000	3,900,000	600,000

C1

WEEKLY MAGAZINE RETURN

Return of the State of the King's Magazines
at on....the....of...., 179.., at Night

	Pounds					
	Biscuit	Wheat Meal	Rye Meal	Oats	Hay	Straw
Remained in the Magazines on —— of —— 179— at Night, as per last Return						
Received into the Magazines since that period; Together						
Issued out of the Magazines since that period						
Remains in the Magazines this —— of —— 179—						

(signed) N. N.
Assist. Commissary

C2

ACCOUNT OF ENTRIES & ISSUES

Account of Entries into the King's Magazine at N.

Date	From whom received	Pounds			Wheat Meal		Rye Meal		Empty Sacks	Loaved Bread		Pounds Biscuit	Pieces Turff	Pounds Candles
		Oats	Hay	Straw	Sacks	Pounds	Sacks	Pounds		Wheat	Rye			
1795 May 2	Contractor N.N. by Billander J. Meyer	500,000	—	—	—	—	—	—	800	—	—	—	—	—
16	Contractor N.N. from 16th to 31st	500,000	200,000	40,000	—	—	—	—	800	—	—	—	—	—
20	By 50 Contract Wag-gons of Joseph Schipfer from Mr. Asst. Commissary N.N.	—	—	—	—	150,000			600					
		1,000,000	200,000	40,000	—	150,000	—	—	2,200	—	—	—	—	—
	Remained by last Return	50,000	80,000	—	50	—	340	70,000	3,000	—	—	4,000	—	—
	Issued up	1,050,000	280,000	40,000	50	150,000	340	70,000	5,200	—	—	4,000	—	—
		500,000	248,000	36,000	—	—	340	24,000	4,000	—	—	—	—	—
	Remains	550,000	32,000	4,000	50	150,000	—	46,000	1,200	—	—	4,000	—	—

Account of Issues out of the King's Magazine at N.

Date	To whom issued	Pounds			Wheat Meal		Rye Meal		Empty Sacks	Loaved Bread		Pounds Biscuit	Pieces Turff	Pounds Candles
		Oats	Hay	Straw	Sacks	Pounds	Sacks	Pounds		Wheat	Rye			
1795 May 2	To Mr. Assistant Commissary N.N. for the King's Bakery, Per Abstract of Stores	— 500,000	— 248,000	— 36,000	—	—	340 —	24,000 —	— 4,000	—	—	—	—	—
		500,000	248,000	36,000	—	—	340	24,000	4,000	—	—	—	—	—

N.. the —— of —— 1795
(signed) N.N.
Asst. Commissary.

19-2

C 3

Abstract of Issues out of the King's Magazine at N from .... to ...., 1795

Number of Voucher	Date	Name & Rank of Officers signing	From what Regiment, Detachment or Corps	For how many Days	Pounds			Wheat Meal		Rye Meal		Empty Sacks	Loaved Bread		Pounds Biscuit	Pieces Turff	Pounds Candles
					Oats	Hay	Straw	Sacks	Pounds	Sacks	Pounds		Wheat	Rye			
	1795		Hessian Life														
84	May 1	Captain A....	Dragoons...	1–4	4,000	6,000	1,600	—	—	—	—	—	—	200	—	1,500	24
85	,, 3	Major B....	Salm Hussars.	3–6	6,000	9,000	2,400	—	—	—	—	—	—	300	—	2,300	32
86	,, 8	Captain C....	Hannover	8–11	6,000	9,000	3,000	—	—	—	—	—	—	500	—	3,000	30
87		— —	Artillery...														
88		— —	— —														
					16,000	24,000	7,000	—	—	—	—	—	—	1,000	—	6,800	86

APPENDIX B

C4

ABSTRACT OF DISBURSEMENTS

Month of

. . . .

Abstract of Disbursements made for the Public Service by —— from the 1st of ——
to the —— of ——, 179—, inclusive.

Date	Number of Voucher	To whom paid	For what Service	Westphal: Currency		
				Rdrs.	JW	d

C5

ACCOUNT CURRENT

Dr. Brook Watson, Esqr., Commissary General, in Current Account with

Date		Westphal: Currency			Date		Westphal: Currency		
		Rdrs.	JW	d			Rdrs.	JW	d

C6

GENERAL INSTRUCTIONS TO ASSISSTANT COMMISSARIES

Instructions to NN A: Assisstant Commissary to the Army in the Service of Great Britain commanded by His Royal Highness the Duke of York and Albany etc etc.

1. You are strictly to obey all such orders as you may from time to time receive from the Right Honorable the Lords Commissioners of His Majesty's Treasury, His Royal Highness the Commander in Chief for the time being, the Commissary General for the time being or any your Superior Officer according to the Rules and Discipline of War, taking care whenever the nature of the service will permit to have such orders in writing.

2. You are to take Care that proper Storehouses or places of Deposit be provided for all His Majesty's Stores, Provisions and Forage committed to your Charge, and you are to keep clear, concise and exact Accounts of all the said Articles, showing your Receipts, Issues, Condemnation Losses, and Remains* *which Accounts you are to make up weekly, if the nature of the service will admit, but at least at the end of every month and transmit to me or the Commissary General for the time being.*

3. Whenever any Stores, Provision and Forage are to be received into His Majesty's Magazines under your Charge you will demand from the Masters or Conductors of the different Vessels or Waggons employed in carrying them, their several Bills of lading or Way Bills, marking the Quantity they have in Charge of every Article for the Commissariat, and receive the different Articles accordingly, granting discharges or receipts for whatever may be delivered to you.

4. You will have the Quality of the Articles inspected by proper and discret [*sic*] persons and if any thereof be found insufficient or short in Weight or Tale, specify the same in your Receipts.†

5. You will also mark the days of arrival and discharge of any Vessels or Carriages from which you receive Stores, Provisions or Forage and if you detain them beyond a reasonable time for their delivery, minute your reasons for such detention.

6. Whenever any Stores, Provisions or Forage are to be forwarded from any of the Magazines under your Charge to some other destination, you will furnish the Masters or Conductors of the Vessels or Carriages you may employ with proper Bills of lading or Way Bills specifying the Quantities of the different Articles in their Charge, taking double Receipts for the same, one to be sent to the Officer of the Commissariat, or other person to whom the Articles are consigned.

7. If the Exigency of the Service should at any time require you to purchase Stores, Provisions or Forage, you are, besides the proper Voucher for the payment of the purchase money, to annex to every such Account a Certificate of two respectable Merchants or Magistrates of the place that the said Articles were bought at the fair market price of the time.

8. When any Stores, Provisions or Forage are damaged, lost, destroyed or plundered, you are to obtain special certificate thereof from the Officer Commanding for your Indemnification without which you will not be allowed Credit for the same, and you are to be particularly attentive to the Preservation of all Stores, Provisions and Forage Committed to your Charge and to give positive orders to

* 'which Accounts you are to make up on the 15th and last day of every month and transmit the same with the Vouchers to me or to the Commissary General for the time being'.

† 'and make an immediate report thereof'.

this effect to all persons employed under you as you will be responsible for the whole.

9. For the purpose of obtaining the proper Voucher required for your Indemnification, in the Case of any Stores, Provisions or Forage being found unfit for service, you will apply by letter to your Commanding Officer, requesting him to order a Survey to be held thereon and to grant you a certificate specifying the several Quantities, which shall be condemned as unfit for service. Before any Survey shall be requested you will apply to the Commissary General if within your reach.

10. You are not to lend exchange or sell any of the Stores, Provisions or Forage committed to your Charge on any Account whatever.

11.* *Your authority for issuing Stores, Provisions and Forage will be the Returns of the effective Men and Horses of the different Corps signed by such Officer as may be appointed for such service by the Commander in Chief or the Officer commanding the particular Corps or Detachment and you are to take receipts for the Quantities you issue corresponding with the said Returns.*

12. [Omitted, but with footnote saying 'This relates to the Allowances in Flanders and varied during the Campaigns'.]

13. You are not to issue back Rations or Portions to any Person.

14.† You are to provide the means of Transport by Land and Water in the following Cases:

(*a*) For the Transport of sick and wounded to the Hospital.

(*b*) For the Transport of Cloathing, Necessaries and Camp Equipage from Regimental Store Houses or Depots to the Regiments, but not after these articles are distributed to the men, there being a sufficient number of Bat Horses for Carrying them on a March.

* Art 11. This Article could not apply to German Troops, who never send Returns to the Commissary, as is set forth more at length under the head of 'Regimental Receipts'. The whole of this Article might be comprised in the following words 'Your authority for issuing Stores, Provisions and Forage will be a Regimental Receipt according to the form in General Orders'.

The different Allowances for Bread, Forage, Camp Straw and fuel are the following: viz.

Bread	*To the British: One Pound and a half of Wheat Bread per day to each Man, and six Women per Company, if effective, to be allowed the same.* *To the Foreign Troops. Two Pounds of Bread baked of 2/3 Rye and 1/3 Wheat to each Man per day.*
Forage	*To the British. Heavy Cavalry and all Draft Horses attached to the British Corps Thirteen Pounds of Oats and nine Pounds of Hay each Horse per day.* *To the British. Light Cavalry and all other British saddle Horses Eleven Pounds of Oats and nine Pounds of Hay.* *To the Foreign. Cavalry and Infantry Horses Ten Pounds of Oats and Ten Pounds of Hay each Horse per day.* *To the Contract Waggons of J. Dubois, G. Petethan and G. Devaux Ten Pounds of Oats and Ten Pounds of Hay each Horse per Day.*
Camp Straw	*To every six Men. Thirty six Pounds in forming the Camp and Twelve Pounds every Week after during its Continuation.*
Wood in Camp	*To every hundred and fifty Men, half a Cord per day including all Regimental Officers.* *A Lieutenant General may draw one sixth and a Major General one tenth of a Cord of Wood per day if necessary.*

† This article is subject to variation.

(c) For the Transport of Bread and Forage as well as Camp Straw and Wood whenever the Waggons attached to the different Regiments for these services shall be found insufficient; on this head you are to take note of the following regulations:

The Army throughout is provided with a sufficient number of Waggons attached to the Corps for transporting their Bread from the Magazine to Camp.

On Marches the Troops are to carry three days Bread themselves and if Bread for a greater number of days is issued to them, it must be carried in the Waggons just mentioned.

The British Troops are also provided with a sufficient number of Waggons for transporting Forage, Straw and Wood from the Magazines to the Camp and on Marches the Regimental Horses are to carry their Forage for three days, Cavalry as well as Infantry, and if a greater number of Days is issued to them, it must be carried on these Waggons.

The foreign corps are not provided with Waggons for transporting Forage, Straw and Wood from the Magazines to the Camp and therefore must be supplied with what is necessary for these services, when occasion requires. The Bread Waggons however attached to the Troops of Hesse Cassel are so constructed as to be capable of aiding in the Transport of Forage, Straw and Wood; it is therefore only necessary to furnish them occasionally with what may be deficient.

The Regulation of the men carrying three days Bread and the Horses three days Forage on a march obtains in the foreign Troops as well as the British.

The number of Waggons which may become necessary for the Services stated in this Article cannot be exactly limited; it must be according to Circumstances; But it will be your duty to be particularly careful to keep these demands within reasonable bounds, and not to grant Waggons on every slight application. When Head Quarters are at hand you will do right not to give any without a requisition from the Quarter Master General, or an Officer in his Department authorized for the purpose.

When no Waggons or boats belonging to the Commissariat are at your Disposal or when they are insufficient you must provide what is necessary by Requisition to the Imperial Civil Commissary, or, if none is at hand, to the Magistrates whose duty it is to command them from the Inhabitants of the Country. Waggons and boats so provided are to be paid by the Commissary General at certain established rates; you have therefore nothing to do with the payment of them, but are only to grant Certificates of the services rendered by them specifying their numbers and the time during which they were employed.

15.* Fuel and Straw for Encampments you are also to obtain by Requisition to the Imperial Civil Commissary, or the Magistrates, whenever the King's Magazines under your charge do not contain a sufficient Quantity of these Articles. You will give receipts to the Imperial Civil Commissary or to the Magistrates for what they furnish and keep the Regimental Voucher for the delivery in your own possession.

16. You are to keep separate Cash Accounts to be made up and transmitted to me† as those mentioned in the 2nd Article of these Instructions and you are to take duplicate receipts to serve as one in my name for all Cash Disbursements, which must be witnessed by at least one known respectable person.

17. You are to make frequent reports to me on the different heads of business under your Charge and state all Cases of doubt or difficulty, that you may receive further Instructions thereon; if any unforeseen Circumstances should arise not

---

* This Article is of too local a kind to make a General Rule.
† Art 16 'with the Vouchers'.

provided for by your Instructions, and the nature of which will not admit of the delay necessary to receive my orders thereon, you are to state the same with your opinion of the proper course to be taken to the Officer Commanding in your District, and, that done, act according to his Directions, giving him such Communication of your Instructions as the case may require.

18.* The Allowance of Fuel and Candles to Troops in Garrison are as follows:

Each room to be allowed	$\frac{1}{8}$ of a Cord of Wood per Week from			6 July	to 26 Oct
	$\frac{1}{4}$,,	,,	,,	26 Oct	,, 30 Nov
	$\frac{1}{2}$,,	,,	,,	1 Dec	,, 31 May
	$\frac{1}{4}$,,	,,	,,	1 June	,, 5 July

One Chaldron of Coals (36 Bushels) equal to 3 Cords of Wood
A Lieutenant General to receive for 5 Rooms

A Major General	,,	,,	,, 4	,,
Brigadier General Colonel	,,	,,	,, 3	,,
Field Officers	,,	,,	,, 2	,,
Captains	,,	,,	,, 1	,,
Two Subalterns	,,	,,	,, 1	,,
Twelve Serjeants, Corporals, Drummers and Rank and File	,,	,, 1	,,

Each Room One Pound of Candles per Week from 1st November to 1st May
Guard Rooms 3 Candles of Ten to the Pound from ditto to ditto

A Cord of Wood is a pile 4 feet wide
8 ,, long
4 ,, high

A Chaldron of Coals: 36 Bushels each weighing 75 Pounds.
Given at Tournay, this 28th day of May 1794.

(signed) Brook Watson Comm^y General

D 1
TRANSLATION: WAGGON CONTRACT

The undersigned engages to furnish for the service of His Britannick Majesty One hundred good Waggons with one Driver and four good horses to each, able to draw on unpaved roads 1500 lbs and on paved roads 3000 lbs Weight under the following Conditions, Viz:

FIRST. He will be paid for each Waggon the sum of four Dutch florins per day, and the payment will be made every fortnight on producing Returns of the Waggons and effective Horses, which have done duty, Certified by the Commanding Officer of the Train.

Each Draught Horse will receive a Ration of Forage of 10 lbs of Oats and 15 lbs of Hay, and each Waggoner one portion of Bread per day.

SECOND. The undersigned makes himself responsible as well toward the Commissary General, as toward the Commanding Officer of the Train, for the good

* Art 18 This Article is subject to variation.

conduct of every Individual employed under the present Contract and accountable for whatever may be done contrary to the service; he binds himself to make good every deficiency that may arise from Theft or Negligence in the Transport of Stores upon his Waggons, unless the same can be proved to have been taken by superior force, it being left with him in such case to stop the amount from the pay of such Brigadiers and Waggoners as participated in the fraud.

THIRD. The Brigades will be under the Command of Officers of the Corps of Royal Waggoners, or such other officers as may be appointed for the purpose, to whom the undersigned will make his report every day, according to the annexed formulary.

FOURTH. To every Ten Waggons there will be a Brigadier at two florins per day and to every hundred Waggons two Chief Brigadiers at three florins, an Inspector at four and a fourier likewise at four florins per day, who will all be under the immediate orders of the Commanding Officer, although paid by the undersigned Contractor, who is to make the same payment monthly in the prescence of an Officer of the Crown.

FIFTH. Each of these Individuals shall be mounted at the Contractor's Expence and none will receive a Ration of Forage unless the Commanding Officer of the Waggon Corps certifies that he is duly mounted and able to execute the service. Each of them will receive One Portion of Bread per day, the same as the Waggoners.

SIXTH. The undersigned will propose to the Commanding Officer of the Train the Individuals that he is desirous of placing in the Contract, and the latter will have the right to reject or to accept them, if he sees cause, on the Condition nevertheless that he gives his reasons in writing to the Commissary General if the Case requires it.

SEVENTH. The Waggon Park shall always be general, with the Distinction however of the several Contractors' Waggons which are to be numbered and to bear the name and number of the Contract in Red Characters, to which Article the undersigned will conform.

EIGHTH. There will be provided at his Expence two or three large Tents in the Park attached to his Contract to lodge the Brigadiers and Individuals who may be there on duty.

NINTH. He shall not have the power of making any Deduction from the Pay of his Waggoners or other Individuals, except in the Case set forth in Article 2 when the same must be done in the presence of One of His Majesty's Officers; neither can he under any pretext put off their payments; but in case the said Contractor should have money or effects entrusted to him by these Individuals he will cause an account thereof to be drawn up and transmit a Copy to the Commanding Officer of the Train.

TENTH. The Undersigned will transmit every month a summary Return (according to the annexed formulary) of the Bread and Forage received from the different Magazines for the Men and Horses of his Contract to the Commanding Officer of the Train to whom he shall always apply to examine and certify his Forage Reports.

ELEVENTH. To each Convoy there will be One or more Chief Brigadiers, according to the Exigency of the case, who will have a General Forage Bill (according to the annexed formulary) which is to be produced at the different Stations to the Commissaries, who issue the Forage, for their signatures and brought back to the Commanding Officer of the Train.

TWELFTH. At every foraging, when at the Park, each Brigadier will make his separate Receipt and the Fourier of the Contract will make the General Receipt signed by himself and the Contractor and examined by the Commander of the Park, who shall fix foraging days to avoid confusion.

THIRTEENTH. In case a Waggon should be taken by the Enemy, he will be paid six Louis D'or for a Waggon and Eight Louis D'ors for a Horse, provided it is proved that the Loss was not occasioned by the fault of the Contractor or his Agents, and that the Waggon and Horses were effective.

FOURTEENTH. In case of accident amongst the Horses the undersigned will be allowed to do the service of One Waggon with three Horses only, provided it is for no longer space than Eight Days, after which term the four Horses must be complete, or the Waggon will not be paid for.

FIFTEENTH. The Contractor shall not under pretext of Sickness amongst his Waggoners excuse himself from service as he must take care always to have a sufficient number of Waggoners and Horses in reserve, as well as a certain Quantity of Harness of every kind. The number of Horses in reserve will be fixed at Thirty to every hundred Waggons and the number of supernumerary Waggoners to Ten; these will receive One Portion of Bread for each man and One Ration of Forage for each Horse.

Done and passed in Duplicate at Delmenhorst,

11 May 1795
(signed) Petithan
(L.S.) Accepted.

(signed) Havd Le Mesurier
Dy Comm^y Genl.

(signed) J. N. Daiwaille.
qua teste

D2

DAILY REPORT OF A WAGGON CONTRACTOR

Report of the Stations and Condition of N.N's Contract Waggons in His Britannick Majesty's Service the —— of ——, 179—, at Night

Department, Regiment or Corps to which the Waggons are attached	In which Camp or Place	Inspectors	Fourriers	Chief Brigadiers	Brigadiers	Drivers	Waggons	Carts	Horses
To the Hessian Regiment Prince Frederick	Neunhaus	—	—	—	—	6	4	2	22
To the 8th Regt. of British Light Dragoons	Brinkum	—	—	—	—	6	6	—	24
To the Hannoverian Life Guards	Wildeshawen	—	—	—	—	8	5	3	29
To the Brigade of Hesse Darmstadt	Gehrde	—	—	—	1	11	10	—	42
To Mr. Asst. Commissary Longden	Cloppenburg	—	—	1	3	40	36	—	150
To Mr. Asst. Commissary Greet	Quackenbrück	—	—	—	2	17	15	—	63
Remains in Park in good Condition & fit for Service	Nienburg	1	1	1	6	25	20	5	119
Unfit for Service at Present	do.	—	—	—	—	7	4	—	11
	TOTAL	1	1	2	12	120	100	10	460

Nienburg, the 3rd of August, 1795
(signed) N. N.
Contractor.

E 1

CHARGES AND SENTENCE OF THE COURT MARTIAL ON I.B.

At a General Court Martial held by order of L. General Dundas at Brinkum the 14th September, 1795, of Major General Dundas was president I. B. Esqr, Assisstant Commissary of Stores and Provisions, was charged by Havilland Le Mesurier, Esqr, Deputy Commissary General with the following Crimes, vizt

FIRST CHARGE. With having defrauded Government of the sum of two thousand seven hundred Guilders Brabant Currency upon a forged Receipt, dated Thourout, 12 March 1794, knowing it to be a Forgery.

SECOND CHARGE. With having fraudently given the Contractors H & E & Co a Certificate of Deliveries into the King's Magazine at Quackenbrügge, as received from the 8th to the 23rd April, 1795, for Two hundred and seventy seven thousand, Eight hundred and fifty Pounds of Oats, and Ninety two Thousand, seven hundred and Twenty eight pounds of Hay, which quantities never were delivered into the Magazine, whereby the Crown was defrauded to the Amount of Thirty thousand six hundred and Eleven Guilders, Dutch Currency.

THIRD CHARGE. With having been in Partnership with Contractors and others in deliveries made into the King's Magazines under his Charge, by which means the Crown was defrauded of various sums.

FOURTH CHARGE. For combining with his clerks and Magazine keepers to defraud the Crown and allowing them a share in the illegal Profits made by the Purchase and Sale of the King's Forage and Stores.

OPINION OF THE COURT

The Court having maturely considered the Evidence brought against the Prisoner in support of the four Charges of which he stands accused, together with his defence and the Evidence he has produced to substantiate his Defence, is of Opinion

UPON THE FIRST CHARGE

That the Evidence is not adequate to a Conviction and the Court does therefore acquit the said I. B. of the first Charge

(signed) R. Dundas, Maj. Gl.
President

UPON THE SECOND CHARGE

The Court finds the Prisoner I. B. guilty in Breach of the first Article of the 15th Section of the Articles of War; it does therefore sentence him to pay into the hands of Brook Watson, Esqr. Commissary General, or his order for the use of the Crown, the sum of Thirty thousand six hundred and Eleven Guilders Dutch Currency, being a sum which he partook of and which Government has been defrauded of, with his Knowledge and by his Assisstance and culpable Conduct, and also to forfeit the sum of One hundred Pounds sterling, to be applied and disposed of as His Majesty shall direct and appoint, and also to remain in Prison until such time as the said Thirty thousand six hundred and Eleven Guilders, Dutch Money, and the said One hundred Pounds Sterling are so paid accordingly

(signed) R. Dundas, Maj. Gl.
President

UPON THE THIRD CHARGE

The Court finds the Prisoner I. B. guilty of Breach of the 1st Article of the 13th Section of the Articles of War, it does therefore sentence him to pay into the hands of Brook Watson Esqr, Commissary General or his order for the use of the Crown the sum of Two thousand and fifty Guilders, Dutch Money, being a sum which he has partook of and which Government has been defrauded [of] with his Knowledge and by his Assistance and culpable Conduct, and also to forfeit the sum of One hundred Pounds Sterling to be applied and disposed of as His Majesty shall direct and appoint: and to remain in Prison until such time as the said Two thousand and Fifty Guilders Dutch Money and the said One hundred Pounds Sterling are so paid accordingly.

(signed) R. Dundas, Maj: Gl:
President

The Court does likewise sentence him to pay into the hands of Brook Watson, Esqr, Commissary General, or his order for the use of the Crown, the sum of Two thousand, One hundred and sixty florins, Dutch Money, being a sum which he has partook of and which Government has been defrauded of with his Knowledge and by his assistance and culpable Conduct; and also to forfeit the sum of One hundred Pounds Sterling, to be applied and disposed of as His Majesty shall direct and appoint;— and to remain in Prison until such time as the said Two thousand one hundred and sixty florins Dutch Money, and the said One hundred Pounds Sterling are so paid accordingly.

(signed) R. Dundas, Maj. Gl.
President

UPON THE FOURTH CHARGE

The Court find the Prisoner I. B. guilty in Breach of the 22nd Article of the 16th Section of the Articles of War. and it does sentence him from his scandalous and infamous Conduct as unworthy to remain in His Majesty's service to be cashiered with every mark of Infamy and disgrace.

And the Court further adjudges that the Prisoner I. B. shall stand amenable and remain liable for all such other sums in which he has been a party concerned to defraud Government during the period of his being Assisstant Commissary as may hereafter be proved against him in a Court of Civil Judication

(signed) R. Dundas, Maj: Gl:
President

E2

TRANSLATION OF A GERMAN RECEIPT FOR FORAGE

The undersigned acknowledges by this present that the 14th Hanoverian Regiment of Light Infantry received for the 1st, 2nd, 3rd, & 4th, of June for 4 days:—*Four hundred and sixty seven Rations of Oats at 10 lbs. Four hundred and sixty seven Rations of Hay at 10 lbs. Two thousand, four hundred and Eighty Port* of Bread at 2 lbs.* from the Magazines of His Britannick Majesty at Cloppenburg.

Cloppenburg the 1st of June 1795
(signed) v, L. Col

4,670 lbs of Oats
4,670 „ „ Hay
4,960 „ „ Bread

F

Extract of a Letter from H.S.H. Duke Ferdinand of Brunswick, dated Paderborn 24 April 1760, to L. General the Marquis of Granby.

Posons par Exemple que l'Armée qui agira en Hesse fut de Nouveau aux Enverons de Giessen, cette Armée exigera au dela de trente mille Rations par jour et comme nous n'avons encore en Hesse que le Magazin de Cassel, il faudrait non seulement en faire sortir chaque jour 600 Voitures; mais aussi les fair relever à Frizlar, à Ziegenhayn, & à Marpurg, de façon que pour fournir à l'armée le fourage complet d'un seul jour aux environs de Giessen, il faudrait avoir en Chemin 2400 Voitures. Ces mêmes Voitures en retournant à leur Station ne pourront charger de nouveau, que le troisième, cinquième et septième jour, apres quoi il faut leur accorder quelques jours de repos, tant pour faire respirer les Chevaux, que pour permettre au paysan de vacquer à ses affaires, mais pour remplir le vuide entre ces jours, que je viens de nommer, il faut encore 2400 Voitures pour le seconde, quatrième et sixième et huitième jour, de manière que dans la premiere huitane, il faudrait avoir journellement 4,800 Chariots, en accordant à ces Voitures huit jour de repos, il faudrait encore 4,800 Voitures pour relever les premiers, de façon que l'Armee exige pour le seul article de fourage 9600 Voitures, il s'en faut beaucoup qu'on doive compter d'en trouver pour cette Besogne la quatrieme partie en Hesse.

Les Provinces voisines y Concoureront, mais elles ne pourront jamais fournir le nombre de Voitures demandées en meme temps pour d'autres besoins.

Il est donc impossible de pourvoir l'armée de fourage par des Transports tirés des Magazins, soit de celui de Cassel, soit d'autres Magazins.

G

Extract of a Letter from H.S.H. Duke Ferdinand of Brunswick to the Marquis of Granby, dated Wavern, 25 May, 1760

Quant à l'offre du Major*** je Vous dirai que je ne suis point du sentiment qu'un Entrepreneur général, du fourage nous convienne. Voicy mes Raisons:

1º. Il est vrai qu'il serait fort Commode pour le Commissariat d'avoir un Entrepreneur general, mais l'Armee en souffrirait et on aurait tort de se fier a ses promesses qu'il ne pourrait réaliser, si je même lui supposais la meilleure volonté du monde et le moins d'Envie que possible, *qualités qu'on ne vante cependant pas beaucoup au sujet du Major****.

2º. Si le Commissariat fait son devoir comme j'ai lieu de l'esperer des arrangements pris à present, je pense qu'il vaut mieux de mettre au profit de la Couronne ce gain souvent immense, qu'on est obligé d'accorder aux Entrepreneurs generaux.

3º. La moindre difficulté est de faire ses achapts. Le seul point difficile est de trouver des voitures pour les Transports, tant pour former les Magazins que pour en transporter le necessaire à l'Armée. Si vous voulez vous donner la peine de Vous informer sur les détails de cette Branche du Service aupres du Commissariat, vous trouverez qu'ils sont immenses et d'une nature a ne pouvoir point être dirigés par un Entrepreneur Général.

4º. Les Etats du Roi et ses Alliés, les Princes neutres et les Provinces ennemies fournissent à present le Charriage ensuit d'un Arrangement pris entre eux et le Commissariat. C'est une grande charge pour tous ces pays là, mais on s'y prête, puis qu'on a de la Difference pour les Demandes du Commissariat et qu'on se fie a ses Dispositions; il en serait bien autrement d'un Entrepreneur; jamais les princes alliés et princes neutres ne souffriraient qu'on abandonna à la merci d'un Entrepreneur leur Charriage, le bien et quasi la vie de leur sujets, dont l'Inconvenient se manifesterait d'abord d'une manière qui deviendrait irréparable.

5°. Il n'y a pas moyen de garder le secret des Operations si je suis obligé de le confier a un Entrepreneur. C'est un point qui mérite la plus grande attention, car si l'Ennemie est informe des Dispositions de mes Magazins et de mes Depots qui sont fait et qui serait à faire encore pendant la Campagne, il peut toujours deviner mes desseins. Et est-il croyable que je puisse compter sur le fidélité et sur la Discretion d'un Entrepreneur de ses Commis?

HI

COMMISSION OF THE COMMISSARY OF ACCOUNTS, CHARLES MASON ESQR. COMMISSARY OF ACCOUNTS TO THE FORCES SERVING ON THE CONTINENT

George R.

George the Third by the Grace of God King of Great Britain, France and Ireland, Defender of the Faith, etc. To Our Trusty and well beloved Charles Mason, Esquire, Greeting:—We do by these presents constitute and appoint you to be Commissary of Accounts to our Forces serving on the Continent, now under the Command of Our most dearly beloved Son, His Royal Highness General Frederick, Duke of York. You are therefore carefully and diligently to discharge the duty of Commissary of Accompts by doing and performing all and all manner of things thereunto belonging; and you are to observe and follow such

Entered with the orders and directions from time to time as you shall receive from
Secretary at War Us, Our said most dearly beloved Son or other your superior
(Sd.) M. Lewis Officer according to the Rules and Discipline of War; in
pursuance of the Trust we hereby repose in you. Given at Our Court of St James's the Twenty first day of June, 1793, in the Thirty third year of Our Reign.

By His Majesty's Command
(signed) Henry Dundas

2

WARRANT OF THE COMMISSARY OF ACCOUNTS

Charles Mason Esquire, Commissary of Accounts to the Army serving on the Continent.

George R.

George the third by the Grace of God of Great Britain, France and Ireland King, Defender of the Faith and so forth. To all to whom these presents shall come Greeting. Know ye that we confiding in the Prudence, Skill and Integrity of our Trusty and Well beloved Charles Mason, Esquire, Have named, ordained and appointed and by these presents Do name, ordain and appoint him to be Commissary of Accounts of our Army now serving or to serve on the Continent of Europe and more particularly to examine, audit and certify all Accounts whatsoever of Money and for Forage, Provisions, Necessaries and Extraordinaries of Our said Army.—

To hold and execute the said Office unto him, the said Charles Mason, during our Pleasure according to such Orders Rules and Directions and subject and liable to such Limitations, Restrictions and Controls, as shall from time to time be given unto him and be appointed by us or by or from the Commissioners of Our Treasury for the Time being, to whom we do hereby strictly charge and command the said Charles Mason to be Obedient in all things concerning the said office and the Executions thereof. And for the Encouragement of the said Charles Mason well duly and diligently to attend, execute and perform the said Office and the Trust hereby reposed in him and in Reward for his Labor Pains and Care therein We do give, grant and allow unto him the sum of Two pounds by the day to commence and be paid from the Day of the Date hereof for and during the Time of his executing the said Office as aforesaid, or until Directions to the Contrary shall be given by Us or the Commissioners of our Treasury for the time being. Given at our Court of St James's, this Twenty first Day of June in the Thirty third Year of Our Reign.

By his Majesty's Command

(signed) $\begin{cases} \text{W. Pitt} \\ \text{Bayham} \\ \text{J. H. Townshend} \end{cases}$

3
INSTRUCTIONS TO THE COMMISSARY OF ACCOUNTS

Instructions to Charles Mason Esqr, Commissary of Accounts of the Army now serving on the Continent of Europe.

Whereas His Majesty has been pleased by Warrant under His Royal Sign Manual bearing date the Twenty first day of June 1793, to appoint you to be Commissary of Accounts to the Army now serving on the Continent of Europe and more particularly to examine audit and certify all Accounts whatsoever of Money due for Forage, Provisions, Necessaries and Extraordinaries of the said Army according to such Orders, Rules and Directions and subject and liable to such Limitations, Restrictions and Controls, as should from time to time be given unto you and be appointed by His Majesty or by or from the Commissioners of the Treasury for the time being:

You are to examine the Accounts for the Expenditure for the Extraordinaries of the Army on the Continent, to attend, whether every Expence is authorized or approved by the Commander in Chief, if such authority or approbation is not produced, to give notice thereof to the Commissary General, but you are nevertheless to examine the Account exhibited to you and from time to time report to the Commissioners of the Treasury the Articles so unauthorized.

You are to attend to the prices charged for each article, the Rate of Exchange and the Current value of every species of Money, all of which ought to be certified, when Circumstances will admit of it, by Two respectable Merchants or Magistrates on the spot to be the market price and rate of exchange at the time. You are then to examine the Computations and Castings and Certify the Amount in Words at Length on each Bill of particulars or Accounts exhibited for your Examination, entering Copies of the whole in your Books, with such observations as may occur to you thereon.

You are to examine, correct and state to the Commissary General all such Public Accounts with the Office of the Commissariat, as may be sent to you for that purpose.

At the end of every Two months you are to call upon the Deputy Paymaster General for an account of all such Payments made by him for the Extraordinaries of the Army during that Period together with the Vouchers for the same, namely the order of the Commissary General for Payment and the Receipts of the Parties, to each of which there must be at least one credible Witness. You are to attend that the Deputy Paymaster General has given Credit for the Stoppages of Provisions if any are ordered, and for all sums which may have come to his hands, as the Produce of old or Damaged Stores or Stores captured from the Enemy and sold within that Period. Having carefully examined this Account you are to certify the same, enter it in your Books and send a Copy of it to the Commissioners of the Treasury for the time being, with such observations as may occur to you thereon.*

You are to obey such further Instructions as you may from time to time receive from Us or from the Commissioners of the Treasury for the time being.

Given under Our Hands at the Treasury Chambers
Whitehall this ninth day of July 1793

(signed)   { W. Pitt
Bayham
J. H. Townshend

* The Writer of this System thinks it his duty to suggest the propriety of adding a clause to the following effect: 'You are to be particularly attentive to the number of Rations of Bread and forage and other contingent allowances drawn by each Regiment, Department or Corps, keeping a distinct account thereof in your Books; and you will from time to time give notice of the amount to the Commissary General, or if need be to the Commander in Chief, and you will send copies of the different statements to the Commissioners of the Treasury for the time being with such observations as may occur to you thereon.'

INDEX

INDEX